PENGUIN BOOKS

MYSTERY TRAIN

'A remarkable study of "the very idea of America:
complicated, dangerous, and extreme", as it is manifested in
the underlying myths of some carefully selected rock and
pre-rock performers . . . The result can be read along with
the most interesting studies of American literature'
– *Washington Post*

'A highly personal view that goes well beyond the scope of
most rock books . . . a refreshing change'
– *New Musical Express*

'Like the best rock 'n' roll music, *Mystery Train* is flashy and
flamboyant; like the best jam session, it sounds both
completely spontaneous and completely controlled'
– *Rolling Stone*

'Provocative and informative' – *Time Out*

'The sheer intelligence with which Marcus approaches
recent American popular music is so evident and so unusual,
and the sheer passion that motivates his love of that music
is so transparent, that his book can be most heartily
recommended to almost anybody. He is a writer of rare
perception and a genuinely innovative thinker'
– *The New York Times*

ABOUT THE AUTHOR

Greil Marcus was born in San Francisco in 1945. He received BA and MA degrees in American political thought from the University of California at Berkeley and taught American Studies there in 1971–2. He was an editor at *Rolling Stone* in 1969–70 and wrote a book column, 'Undercover', for that magazine from 1975 to 1980; from 1983 to 1988 he was a director of the National Book Critics Circle. He has written for the San Francisco *Express-Times*, *RAW*, the *Threepenny Review*, *New Formations*, the *New Yorker*, *Creem*, *City*, *New West/California*, the *Village Voice*, the *New Musical Express* and many other publications. He is the author of one rock 'n' roll song, 'I Can't Get No Nookie', which, as recorded in 1970 by the Masked Marauders, was attacked in a speech by Dean Burch, then head of the Federal Communications Commission in the USA, as an example of 'obscenity on the air'.

Greil Marcus is the author of *Lipstick Traces: A Secret History of the 20th Century* (1989) and *Dead Elvis: A Chronicle of a Cultural Obsession* (Penguin 1992) and the editor of Lester Bangs's *Psychotic Reactions and Carburetor Dung* (1987). He currently writes a music column for *Artforum*. He lives in Berkeley with his wife and two daughters.

GREIL MARCUS

MYSTERY TRAIN

IMAGES OF AMERICA
IN ROCK 'N' ROLL MUSIC

FOURTH EDITION

PENGUIN BOOKS

PENGUIN BOOKS

Published by the Penguin Group
Penguin Books Ltd, 27 Wrights Lane, London W8 5TZ, England
Penguin Books USA Inc., 375 Hudson Street, New York, New York 10014, USA
Penguin Books Australia Ltd, Ringwood, Victoria, Australia
Penguin Books Canada Ltd, 10 Alcorn Avenue, Toronto, Ontario, Canada M4V 3B2
Penguin Books (NZ) Ltd, 182-190 Wairau Road, Auckland 10, New Zealand

Penguin Books Ltd, Registered Offices: Harmondsworth, Middlesex, England

First published in the USA by E. P. Dutton 1975
Second edition 1982
Third edition published by Obelisk/Dutton,
an imprint of Penguin Books USA Inc., 1990
Published simultaneously in Canada by Fitzhenry & Whiteside Ltd
Fourth edition published in Great Britain by Penguin Books 1991

3 5 7 9 10 8 6 4 2

Printed in England by Clays Ltd, St Ives plc

To Emily and Cecily
and in memory of my dear friend and editor,
Bill Whitehead

CONTENTS

AUTHOR'S NOTE   [*ix*]

INTRODUCTION TO THE THIRD EDITION   [*xiii*]

PROLOGUE   [*1*]

ANCESTORS

HARMONICA FRANK, 1951   [*11*]

ROBERT JOHNSON, 1938   [*19*]

INHERITORS

THE BAND: Pilgrims' Progress   [*39*]
Crossing the Border/ Stranger Blues/ This Righteous Land/
Even Stranger Blues/ The Weight

SLY STONE: The Myth of Staggerlee   [65]
Staggerlee/ Sly Stone/ Riot/ Sly Versus Superfly/
A Quiet Rebellion

RANDY NEWMAN: Every Man Is Free   [96]
Pop/ Newman's America, I/ Newman's America, II/
Newman's Failure/ Coda: Newman's Success

ELVIS: Presliad   [120]
Fanfare/ Hillbilly Music/ Raised Up/
The Rockabilly Moment/ Elvis Moves Out/
The Boy Who Stole the Blues/
The Pink Cadillac/ Elvis at Home/ Mystery Train/ Finale

EPILOGUE   [176]

NOTES AND DISCOGRAPHIES   [179]

INDEX   [266]

AUTHOR'S NOTE

Writing these opening notes reminds me of the prefaces to the American history books that were written during World War II, when the authors, looking back for the meaning of the Revolution or the Civil War or whatever, drew modest but determined parallels between their work and the struggle. They were affirming that their work was part of the struggle; that an attempt to understand America took on a special meaning when America was up for grabs. Those writers were also saying—at least, this is what they now say to me—that to do one's most personal work in a time of public crisis is an honest, legitimate, paradoxically democratic act of common faith; that one keeps faith with one's community by offering whatever it is that one has to say. I mean that those writers were exhilarated, thirty years ago, by something we can only call patriotism, and humbled by it too.

Well, I feel some kinship with those writers. I began this book in the fall of 1972, and finished it late in the summer of 1974. Inevitably, it reflects, and I hope contains, the peculiar moods of those times, when the country came face to face with an obscene perversion of itself that could be neither accepted nor destroyed: moods of rage, excitement, loneliness, fatalism, desire.

Like a lot of people who are about thirty years old, I have been listening and living my life to rock 'n' roll for twenty years, and so behind this book lie twenty years of records and twenty years of talk. Probably it began when a kid pushed a radio at me and demanded that I listen to a song called "Rock Around the Clock," which I disliked at the time and still do. I know the music came together for me in high school, thanks to my cruising friend, Barry Franklin. We spent years on the El Camino, driving from Menlo Park to San Francisco to San Jose and back again, listening to Tom Donahue and Tommy Saunders on KYA, trying to figure out the words to "Runaround Sue" and translating "Little Star" into French. Later, we followed the sixties trail to college, Beatle shows, and Dylan concerts.

About a month before the Beatles hit I met my wife Jenny, who confirmed my enthusiasms and who has always kept them alive; it means more to me to say that this book wouldn't have been written without her than to say that it couldn't have been.

The time I have spent talking rock 'n' roll with my friends Bruce Miroff, Langdon Winner, Ralph Gleason, Ed Ward, Michael Goodwin, and many more, has gone into this book; so has talk with my brothers Steve and Bill, with teachers and students, and with my daughter Emily, who picked "Mystery Train" as her favorite song at the age of two. My daughter Cecily is not as yet so discriminating, but I have hopes. As much as anything, rock 'n' roll has been the best means to friendship I know.

I have been writing about the music since 1966—professionally, for publication, since 1968. Before I got up the nerve to see my efforts in print I put together a book of pieces by myself and some friends; one of them, Sandy Darlington, taught me a lot about music and a lot more about writing. After the book was finished I took over Sandy's music-space in the San Francisco *Express-Times*, then edited and inspired by Marvin Garson. Until the events of Peoples' Park sent it reeling into mindlessness, the *Express-Times* was the best underground newspaper in America, and I've always been proud to have been part of it. When it changed I moved across town to *Rolling Stone*, where I wrote and edited for a year. In 1970 I left, and ultimately ended up with *Creem*, a magazine that seemed like a place of freedom and was.

Creem gave me the chance to try out many of the ideas that eventually found their way into this book.

There would be little to those ideas without the study I did in American political thought and American literature with three Berkeley teachers: John Schaar, Michael Rogin, and Norman Jacobson. And there are a few books that mattered a great deal to the ambitions of my own book, and to its content: D. H. Lawrence's *Studies in Classic American Literature*, Leslie Fiedler's *Love and Death in the American Novel*, James Agee's *Let Us Now Praise Famous Men*, Pauline Kael's *I Lost It at the Movies*, Alexis de Tocqueville's *Democracy in America*, and, in a way that is still pretty mysterious to me, Ernest Hemingway's short stories.

Many people helped me in many ways while I was writing: Mary Clemmey, Greg Shaw, Richard Bass, Pat Thomas, Ms. Clawdy, Bill Strachan of Anchor Press, and Wendy Weil. Jenny Marcus, Peter Guralnick, Bruce Miroff, Bob Christgau, and Dave Marsh read every page of the manuscript, and made it far better than it would have been without their help.

Bob and Dave deserve special thanks. They have been part of my work from beginning to end; they encouraged it, at times inspired it, always cared about it. No critic could ask for better colleagues, and no one could ask for better friends.

And I owe as much to my editor, Bill Whitehead. Without his commitment to the book, mine would have faded out a long time ago.

What I have to say in *Mystery Train* grows out of records, novels, political writings; the balance shifts, but in my intentions, there isn't any separation. I am no more capable of mulling over Elvis without thinking of Herman Melville than I am of reading Jonathan Edwards (*not*, I've been asked to point out, the crooner mentioned in the Randy Newman chapter, but the Puritan who made his name with "Sinners In the Hands of An Angry God") without putting on Robert Johnson's records as background music. What I bring to this book, at any rate, is no attempt at synthesis, but a recognition of unities in the American imagination that already exist. They are natural unities, I think, but elusive; I learned, in the last two years, that simply because of those unities, the resonance of the best American images is profoundly deep and impossibly broad. I wrote this book in an attempt to find some of those images, but I know now that to put oneself in touch with them is a life's work.

Berkeley, August 9, 1974

INTRODUCTION
to the Third Edition

When this book was first published in 1975, I imagined that I was telling part of an ongoing story. "The Band, Sly Stone, Randy Newman, and Elvis Presley are still vital performers," I wrote then; not long after, the careers of all but Newman effectively came to an end. Through these and other musicians, I wanted to raise the question of the relationship between rock 'n' roll and American culture as a whole; that, and not a few careers, turned out to be the ongoing story.

Of the two men I chose as "ancestors" of a quartet of "inheritors," black blues singer Robert Johnson had been dead since 1938. Harmonica Frank, a white medicine-show entertainer, continued to play through the late 1970s; he died in 1984. Elvis Presley died in 1977. The previous year, the Band broke up; pianist Richard Manuel committed suicide in 1986. Sly Stone has attempted numerous comebacks since radically challenging popular music with *There's a riot goin' on* in 1971, but each has been little more than a greater step toward oblivion—in Nick Tosches' words, "the place where fame repeats its own name." Only Randy Newman demanded reconsideration, as in 1977 the hero of a cult audience topped the charts with the outrageous "Short People," and thus came face to face with the perils of mass success, and I've tried to explore that dilemma in an addendum to his chapter.

Thus aside from corrections of errors that continue to turn up, and interpolations of new factual discoveries, there are few changes in the body of the book; even the chapter on Elvis Presley remains in the present tense, because Elvis's story, and its continuing presence, seem big enough to hold that tense even though the man himself is dead. (When asked what he would do with his meal ticket in the grave, Col. Tom Parker, Elvis's manager, said, "Why, I'll go right on managing him.")

The long "Notes and Discographies" section of the book has been completely revised, taking in new stories, following old stories around turns no one could have predicted. Whatever rock 'n' roll's future, its past continues to expand at a geometric rate. There has been a flood of blues, country, and rock 'n' roll reissue and archival albums since 1975, and I've taken account of these whenever relevant, along with the concurrent efflorescence of research articles and books (a few of the latter marvelous, most of them bad, but many containing at least one invaluable tall tale or photograph). There is no beginning one can find to any of the stories in this book, and usually no real, as opposed to formal, conclusion: the legend of Stagger Lee continues to generate new versions of itself, as does the legend of "Louie Louie" (for example: in 1988, Richard Berry, the song's composer, finally confirmed there is no comma in the song's title, laying to rest a question that had baffled copyeditors for three decades). Sooner or later, someone will find and release still-unknown recordings by every performer I've mentioned; new books will insist on truths other writers will argue over until everyone now reading this book is dead. For the moment, the chronicles and facts in "Notes and Discographies" are as up to date as deadlines permit.

As for the music that tells the story I've attempted to follow, music now classic or still only implied, it remains as new, as mysterious, as it did, as it must have, when it first appeared, fifteen or fifteen-and-fifty years ago. If *Mystery Train*, this book, remains alive ("Mystery Train," the song, is permanent), that is why, though there is another reason. The comment on my book I value most came from a professor at the University of Alabama, who refused to believe that "a Yankee" could have written it; though I am such, or anyway a Californian, the man who edited and shaped *Mystery Train*, and who remained part of its conversation years after he left its publisher, was not. Bill Whitehead, born in Wilmington, North Carolina, in 1943, who died of AIDS in 1987, made sure that this book, like scores of others he published, would outlive him.

Berkeley, September 1989

PROLOGUE

Our story begins just after midnight, not so long ago. The Dick Cavett Show is in full swing.

Seated on Cavett's left is John Simon, the New York Critic. On Cavett's right, in order of distance from him, are Little Richard, Rock 'n' Roll Singer and Weirdo; Rita Moreno, Actress; and Erich Segal, Yale Professor of Classics and Author of *Love Story*. Miss Moreno and Mr. Segal adored *Love Story*. Mr. Simon did not. Little Richard has not read it.

Cavett is finishing a commercial. Mr. Simon is mentally rehearsing his opening thrust against Mr. Segal, who is very nervous. Miss Moreno seems to be falling asleep. Little Richard is looking for an opening.

Mr. Simon has attacked Mr. Segal. Mr. Segal attempts a reply but he is too nervous to be coherent. Mr. Simon attacks a second time. Little Richard is about to jump out of his seat and jam his face

1

in front of the camera but Mr. Simon beats him out. He attacks Mr. Segal again.

"NEGATIVE! NEGATIVE NEGATIVE NEGATIVE!" screams Mr. Segal. He and Simon are debating a fine point in the history of Greek tragedy, to which Mr. Simon has compared *Love Story* unfavorably.

" 'Neg-a-tive,' " muses Mr. Simon. "Does that mean 'no'?"

Mr. Segal attempts, unsuccessfully, to ignore Mr. Simon's contempt for his odd patois, and claims that the critics were wrong about Aeschylus. He implies that Simon would have walked out on the *Oresteia*. Backed by the audience, which sounds like a Philadelphia baseball crowd that has somehow mistaken Mr. Simon for Richie Allen, Segal presses his advantage. Little Richard sits back in his chair, momentarily intimidated.

"MILLIONS OF PEOPLE were DEEPLY MOVED by my book," cries Segal, forgetting to sit up straight and slumping in his chair until his body is near parallel with the floor. "AND IF ALL THOSE PEOPLE LIKED IT—" (Segal's voice has now achieved a curious tremolo) "*I MUST BE DOING SOMETHING RIGHT!*"

The effort has exhausted Segal, and as he takes a deep breath Little Richard begins to rise from his seat. Again, Simon is too fast for him. Simon attempts to make Segal understand that he is amazed that anyone, especially Segal, takes this trash to be anything more than, well, trash.

"I have read it and reread it many times," counters Segal with great honesty. "I am always moved."

"Mr. Segal," says Simon, having confused the bull with his cape and now moving in for the kill, "you had the choice of acting the knave or the fool. You have chosen the latter."

Segal is stunned. Cavett is stunned. He calls for a commercial. Little Richard considers the situation.

The battle resumes. Segal has now slumped even lower in his chair, if that is possible, and seems to be arguing with the ceiling. "*You're* only a critic," he says as if to Simon. "What have *you* ever written? What do you know about art? Never in the history of art . . ."

"WHY, NEVER IN THE HISTORY!"

The time has come. Little Richard makes his move. Leaping from his seat, he takes the floor, arms waving, hair coming undone, eyes wild, mouth working. He advances on Segal, Cavett, and Simon, who cringe as one man. The camera cuts to a close-up of Segal, who looks miserable, then to Simon, who is attempting to compose the sort of bemused expression he would have if, say, someone were to defecate on the floor. Little Richard is audible off-camera, and then his face quickly fills the screen.

"WHY, YES, IN THE WHOLE HISTORY OF AAAART! THAT'S RIGHT! SHUT UP! SHUT UP! WHAT DO YOU KNOW, MR. CRITIC? WHY, WHEN THE CREEDENCE CLEARWATER PUT OUT WITH THEIR 'TRAVELIN' BAND' EVERYBODY SAY WHEEE-OOO BUT I KNOW IT CAUSE THEY ONLY DOING 'LONG TALL SALLY' JUST LIKE THE BEATLES ANDTHESTONESANDTOMJONESANDELVIS—I AM ALL OF IT, LITTLE RICHARD HIMSELF, VERY TRULY THE GREATEST, THE HANDSOMEST, AND NOW TO YOU (to Segal, who now appears to be *on* the floor) AND TO YOU (to Simon, who looks to Cavett as if to say, really old man, this *has* been fun, but this, ah, *fellow* is becoming a bit much, perhaps a commercial is in order?), I HAVE WRITTEN A BOOK, MYSELF, I AM A WRITER, I HAVE WRITTEN A BOOK AND IT'S CALLED—

" 'HE GOT WHAT HE WANTED BUT HE LOST WHAT HE HAD'! THAT'S IT! SHUT UP! SHUT UP! SHUT UP! HE GOT WHAT HE WANTED BUT HE LOST WHAT HE HAD! THE STORY OF MY LIFE. CAN YOU DIG IT? THAT'S MY BOY LITTLE RICHARD, SURE IS. OO MAH SOUL!"

Little Richard flies back to his chair and slams down into it. "WHEEEEE-OO! OOO MAH SOUL! OO mah soul . . ."

Little Richard sits with the arbiters of taste, oblivious to their bitter stares, savoring his moment. He is Little Richard. Who are they? Who will remember Erich Segal, John Simon, Dick Cavett? Who will care? Ah, but Little Richard, Little Richard *himself!* There is a man who matters. He knows how to rock.

A phrase that Little Richard snatched off Erich Segal stays in my mind: "Never in the history—*in the whole history of art. . . .*" And that was it. Little Richard was the only artist on the set that night, the only one who disrupted an era, the only one with a claim to immortality. The one who broke rules, created a form; the one who gave shape to a vitality that wailed silently in each of us until he found a voice for it.

He is the rock, the jive bomber, the savant. "Tutti Frutti" was his first hit, breaking off the radio in 1955 to shuffle the bland expectations of white youth; fifteen years later the Weirdo on the Cavett Show reached back for whatever he had left and busted up an argument about the meaning of art with a spirit that recalled the absurd promise of his glory days. "I HAVE WRITTEN A BOOK, MYSELF, AND IT'S CALLED . . ."

Listening now to Little Richard, to Elvis, to Jerry Lee Lewis, the Monotones, the Drifters, Chuck Berry, and dozens of others, I feel a sense of awe at how fine their music was. I can only marvel at their arrogance, their humor, their delight. They were so sure of themselves. They sang as if they knew they were destined to survive not only a few weeks on the charts but to make history; to displace the dreary events of the fifties in the memories of those who heard their records; and to anchor a music that twenty years later would be struggling to keep the promises they made. Naturally, they sound as if they could care less, so long as their little black 45's hit number one and made them rich and famous. But they delivered a new version of America with their music, and more people than anyone can count are still trying to figure out how to live in it.

Well, then, this is a book about rock 'n' roll—some of it—and America. It is not a history, or a purely musical analysis, or a set of personality profiles. It is an attempt to broaden the context in which the music is heard; to deal with rock 'n' roll not as youth culture, or counterculture, but simply as American culture.

The performers that I have written about appeal to me partly because they are more ambitious and because they take more risks than most. They risk artistic disaster (in rock terms, pretentiousness), or the alienation of an audience that can be soothed far more easily than it can be provoked; their ambitions have a good deal to do with Robbie Robertson's statement of his ambitions for the Band: "Music should never be harmless."

What attracts me even more to the Band, Sly Stone, Randy Newman, and Elvis, is that I think these men tend to see themselves as symbolic Americans; I think their music is an attempt to live up to that role. Their records—the Band's *Big Pink*, Sly's *There's a riot goin' on*, a few of Randy Newman's tunes, Elvis Presley's very first Tennessee singles—dramatize a sense of what it is to be an American; what it means, what it's worth, what the stakes of life in America might be. This book, then, is an exploration of a few artists, all of whom seem to me to have found their own voices; it is rooted in the idea that these artists can illuminate those American questions and that the questions can add resonance to their work.

The two men whose tales begin the book—white country hokum singer Harmonica Frank and black Mississippi blues singer Robert Johnson—came and went before the words "rock 'n' roll" had any cultural meaning at all. Both men represent traditions crucial to rock 'n' roll, and both are unique. They worked at the frontiers of the music, and they can give us an idea of what the country has to give the music to work with—a sense of how far the music can go. Harmonica Frank sang with a simple joy and a fool's pride; he caught a spirit the earliest rock 'n' roll mastered effortlessly, a mood the music is always losing and trying to win back. Robert Johnson was very different. He was a brooding man who did his work on the darker side of American life; his songs deal with terrors and fears that few American artists have ever expressed so directly. In this book, Frank and Johnson figure as metaphors more than musical influences. Their chapters are meant to form a backdrop against which the later chapters can take shape, a framework for the images the other artists have made.

The Band, Sly Stone, Randy Newman, and Elvis Presley share unique musical and public personalities, enough ambition to make even their failures interesting, and a lack of critical commentary extensive or committed enough to do their work justice. In their music and in their careers, they share a range and a depth that seem to crystalize naturally in visions and versions of America: its possibilities, limits, openings, traps. Their stories are hardly the whole story, but they can tell us how much the story matters. That is what this book is about.

. . . to be an American (unlike being English or French or whatever) is precisely to *imagine* a destiny rather than to inherit one; since we have always been, insofar as we are Americans at all, inhabitants of myth rather than history. . . .

LESLIE FIEDLER, "Cross
the Border, Close the Gap"

It's easy to forget how young this country is; how little distance really separates us from the beginnings of the myths, like that of Lincoln, that still haunt the national imagination. It's easy to forget how much remains to be settled. Since roots are sought out and seized as well as simply accepted, cultural history is never a straight line; along with the artists we care about we fill in the gaps ourselves. When we do, we reclaim, rework, or invent America, or a piece of it, all over again. We make choices (or are caught by the choices others have made) about what is worth keeping and what isn't, trying to create a world where we feel alive, risky, ambitious, and free (or merely safe), dispensing with the rest of the American reality if we can. We make the oldest stories new when we succeed, and we are trapped by the old stories when we fail.

That is as close as I can come to a simple description of what I think the performers in this book have done—but of course what they have done is more complex than that.

In the work of each performer there is an attempt to create oneself, to make a new man out of what is inherited and what is imagined; each individual attempt implies an ideal community, never easy to define, where the new man would be at home, where his work could communicate easily and deeply, where the members of that ideal community would speak as clearly to the artist as he does to them.

The audiences that gather around rock 'n' rollers are as close to that ideal community as anyone gets. The real drama of a performer's career comes when the ideal that one can hear in the music and the audience that the artist really attracts begin to affect each other. No artist can predict, let alone control, what an audience will make of his images; yet no rock 'n' roller can exist without a relationship with an audience, whether it is the imaginary audience one begins with, or the all-too-real confusion of the audience one wins.

The best popular artists create immediate links between people who might have nothing in common but a response to their work, but the best popular artists never stop trying to understand the impact of their work on their audiences. That means their ideal images must change as their understanding grows. One may find horror where one expected only pleasure; one may find that the truth one told has become a lie. If the audience demands only more of what it has already accepted, the artist has a choice. He can move on, and perhaps cut himself off from his audience; if he does, his work will lose all the vitality and strength it had when he knew it mattered to other people. Or the artist can accept the audience's image of himself, pretend that his audience is his shadowy ideal, and lose himself in his audience. Then he will only be able to confirm; he will never be able to create.

The most interesting rock 'n' rollers sometimes go to these extremes; most don't, because these are contradictions they struggle with more than resolve. The tension between community and self-reliance; between distance from one's audience and affection for it; between the shared experience of popular culture and the special talents of artists who both draw on that shared experience and change it—these things are what make rock 'n' roll at its best a democratic art, at least in the American meaning of the word democracy. I think that is true because our democracy is nothing if not a contradiction: the creed of every man and woman for themselves, and thus the loneliness of separation, and thus the yearning for harmony, and for community.

The performers in this book, in their different ways, all trace that line.

If they are in touch with their audiences and with the images of community their songs hint at, rock 'n' rollers get to see their myths and parables in action, and ultimately they may even find out what they are worth. When the story is a long one—a career—they find the story coming back to them in pieces, which of course is how it was received.

Here is where a critic might count. Putting the pieces together, trying to understand what is novel and adventurous, what is enervated and complacent, can give us an idea of how much room there is in this musical culture, and in American culture—an idea of what a singer and a band can do with a set of songs mixed into the uncertainty that is the pop audience. Looking back into the corners, we might discover whose America we are living in at any moment, and where it came from. With luck, we might even touch that spirit of place Americans have always sought, and in the seeking have created.

Ancestors

HARMONICA FRANK
1951

In 1951 Sam Phillips was the owner of a shoestring operation that cut records by young black blues singers in Memphis, Tennessee. A few years later he would shape the careers of such founding rockers as Elvis Presley, Carl Perkins, Roy Orbison, and Jerry Lee Lewis; today, he counts his money. But at least one writer has stepped forward to call him "America's Real Uncle Sam," a title he might like.

Phillips was raised on a plantation in Alabama; when he was a little boy an old black man named Uncle Silas Payne would take him aside and sing him the blues, playing Jim to Sam's Huck. In the fifties, bored by the music business and itching for something new, it would be quite natural for Phillips to look for someone to complete a role that was sketched out in his own past. "If I could find a white man who had the Negro sound and the Negro feel," he was saying in those days (as Huck Finn met the Riverboat Gambler), "I could make a billion dollars." Harmonica Frank Floyd, a white man in his early

11

forties, who held a harmonica in one side of his mouth and sang out of the other, was Sam Phillips' first try.

Harmonica Frank was never famous. Born in 1908 in Toccopola, Mississippi, a short ways from Elvis Presley's birthplace in Tupelo, he was a drifter, who left home at the age of fourteen and bummed his way around the country for the next forty years, a man who came up with his own idea of the country's music, black and white.

In 1973, an old man, Frank wrote: "Just one thang I would love to say the first time I played a rock and roll tune on my oath I had never heard no one else do that type therefore I am almost sure I am the originator of rock and roll regardless of what you may have heard at the time I could not read or write music but now I can I am truly a hillbilly from the state of miss but have traveled all over played in old time vaudeville shows medicine shows on the streets barber shops court house lawns auctions sales woodman halls radios television you name it I've played it comedy fire eaters with carnivals tricks or magic so at least I'm an old showman picked cotton picked fruit dug mussel shells in Ark pan some gold in calif one time on KELW in Hollywood with Bustie steel and log cabin wranglers. . . .

". . . You see I played rock and roll before I ever heard of elvis presley I saw him in memphis before he ever made a record with sam phillips on north main in memphis tennessee. . . ."*

Frank cut many sides in 1951 for Phillips, who leased a few to Chess, the Chicago blues label. They didn't sell. Phillips recorded two more tunes and put them out as a single on his own Sun label in 1954, just before Elvis Presley's first record was released, but the disc went nowhere.

Harmonica Frank's music was a joke, mostly, because there was a little more money for a street-singer who could make people laugh. Yet there was an edge to Frank's music, a fool's resistance to the only role he knew; and that, along with the vitality and invention of the sounds Frank made, was a key to the inarticulate desires shared by Sam Phillips and the impatient new audience whose presence he sensed. "Old Sam Phillips only had one thing to tell me," Harmonica Frank says today. "Said it over and over. 'Gimme something different. Gimme something unique.'"

In his own way Harmonica Frank was as much a maniac as Little Richard. He sounded like a drunken clown who's seen it all, remembers about half of that, and makes the rest up. He put together a style

---

*From a letter Frank wrote to Greg Shaw.

of country rock that did not really find an audience until years later, when Bob Dylan caught the same spirit and much of the sound with "Mixed-Up Confusion," his first single, a lot of the *Freewheelin'* album, and his "I Shall Be Free" songs. In a broader sense Frank can be heard every time a rocker's secret smile breaks open: when Randy Newman sings from the bottom of a bottle, or when Levon Helm gurgles "Hee, hee!" in the middle of "Up on Cripple Creek," the Band's sexiest song.

Harmonica Frank was perhaps the first of the rock 'n' roll vocal contortionists—like Buddy Holly, Clarence "Frogman" Henry, and Bob Dylan—whose mission in life seemed to be the willful destruction of the mainstream tradition of popular singing and the smooth and self-assured way of life it was made to represent. Frank screeched, he bellowed, croaked, cackled, and moaned, carrying his songs and never mind about the tune. He was a noisemaker.

What matters about Frank is the sense of freedom he brought to his music: a good-natured contempt for conventional patterns of life combined with a genius for transforming all that was smug and polite into absurdity. The result was a music of staggering weirdness, dimly anchored by the fatalism of the blues and powered by the pure delight of what was soon to be called rock 'n' roll. Frank wasn't sexy, like the rockabilly singers who were to make Sam Phillips' fortune; he was more like a dirty old man. He was ribald, and he had a flair. "I am," he growled in one of his numbers, "a howling tomcat."

His only Sun single was his best—"The Great Medical Menagerist," a wonderful talking blues, backed by "Rockin' Chair Daddy," a first-rate piece of nonsense that really does set the stage for rock 'n' roll. Here he reaches for falsettos, talks to himself, corrects himself, roaring into town

> *Rock to Memphis, dance on Main*
> *Up stepped a lady and asked my name*
> *Rockin' chair daddy dont have to work*
> *I told her my name was on the tail of my shirt!*

and pounding away to the finish: "Never been to college, never been to school, if you want some rockin' I'm a rockin' fool!"

"The Great Medical Menagerist" is simply a triumph. Probably a miniature autobiography, it is a catalogue of all the prim and decent people Frank made asses of, and of the jobs his fun cost him. The first lines have the perfection of myth:

*Ladies and gentlemens, cough white dodgers and
little rabbit twisters, step right around closely,
tell ya all about a wonderful medicine show I
useta work with. . . .*

"We have Doctor Donicker here with us," he drawls, too sly to
believe, "the Great Medical Menagerist . . . *of the world.*" That little
pause charges the performance with wit and even menace; Frank sings
with a squeak. Frank barely lets on that the menagerie is none other
than Doctor Donicker's audience, which is to say, his.

His most compelling record was "Goin' Away Walkin'," one of
the sides on Chess. It is a classic country blues, and a kind of final
statement. If the form is blues, though, the spirit and the sound come
from the high, lonely whine of the white mountain music that goes
back to the Revolution. The notes seem to hang in the air like ghosts;
the song is bitter, unrepentant, and free. "I ain't gonna get married,"
Frank Floyd sings. "I ain't gonna settle down. I'm gonna walk this
highway, till my whiskers drags the ground."

That was his promise, and he kept it. Of all the characters who
populate this book, only Harmonica Frank did more than keep the
legend of Huckleberry Finn alive—he lived it out. He showed up,
made his records, and lit out for the territory, banging his guitar and
blowing his harp, dodging Greyhounds and working the fields, setting
himself free from an oppression he never bothered to define.

His humor, his cutting edge, came like Twain's from that part
of the American imagination that has always sneered at the limits
imposed by manners; the strain that produced both obscenity and the
tall tale, two forms of a secret revolt against the Puritans who founded
the country and against the authority of their ghosts. It is a revolt
against the hopeful morality of Twain's aunts and the tiresomeness
of Ben Franklin doing good and being right; a revolt against pom-
posity, and arrogance.

And this revolt is powerful stuff, after all. How long would Ahab
have lasted if he'd been up against a howling weirdo like Harmonica
Frank instead of a dumb Christian like Starbuck?

A DIGRESSION THAT MAY PROVE
WORTHWHILE TO THOSE READERS
WHO DO NOT SKIP IT

Our latest Ahab almost had it both ways, because there was a
lot of Harmonica Frank in Lyndon B. Johnson, once President of All

the People; one of America's secrets is that the dreams of Huck and Ahab are not always very far apart. Both of them embody an impulse to freedom, an escape from restraints and authority that sometimes seems like the only really American story there is. That one figure is passive and benign, the other aggressive and in the end malignant; the one full of humor and regret, and the other cold and determined never to look back; the one as unsure of his own authority as he is of anyone else's, the other fleeing authority only to replace it with his own—all this hides the common bond between the two characters, and suggests how strong would be a figure who could put the two together. For all that is different about Ahab and Huck Finn, they are two American heroes who say, yes, they will go to hell if they have to.

The obsessiveness and the wish for peace of mind that most easily set Ahab and Huck off from each other—on the surface, anyway—are cornerstones of how rock 'n' roll works and what it is for, but we will find the two spirits together more often than not.

LBJ had his year on the road, quitting college and hoboing his way out to California, digging ditches and washing dishes, finally coming home after having gone far enough to say, years later, that any member of his generation that hadn't been a communist or a dropout wasn't worth a damn. Deeply contemptuous of Eastern gentility (and attracted by it too), Johnson coupled a devastating talent for obscenity that no Easterner could match with an image of himself as a latter-day Pecos Bill; the American, Johnson might have been telling us, is alive only as long as he is uncivilized. Thus Johnson carefully received his guests on the toilet—the "donicker"—because it threw them off guard. Bob Dylan was pouting that even the President of the Yew-Nited States had to stand naked, but LBJ was way ahead of him: he forced heads of state to strip for a swim and got the upper hand. He showed his scar and the *New York Review of Books* never forgave him. He told them his name was on the tail of his shirt.

But Johnson's best defense was his verbal obscenity, that side of Huck that Twain left out of the book and kept for himself.

Norman Mailer was the only one of Johnson's adversaries who understood this side of the man, and so he took LBJ on with *Why Are We in Vietnam?* It was the most gloriously obscene book Mailer could write, a book whose hero was in fact a Texas Huck on his way to becoming a Texas Ahab, changing fast from a reckless kid into a killer. The job, Mailer knew, was to find the sources of Johnson's power—not merely his political power, but his personal strength. That meant

Mailer had to understand the language LBJ really spoke, and then beat him at his own game. And so the obscenity of Mailer's book, at first so funny, so full of honest rebellion, becomes more and more cruel, until finally it is part and parcel with brutality, and murder.

But Mailer didn't win the fight with Lyndon Johnson. The richest, riskiest passages of his book cannot compare with the off-hand remark Johnson made when he was asked why he had not told the people more about Vietnam: "If you have a mother-in-law with only one eye, and that eye is in the middle of her forehead, you don't keep her in the living room."*

If anything could redeem the arrogant obsessions of the man who introduced us to the obscenity of the burnt baby, it was a style of personal obscenity. This allowed Johnson to transcend, for a time, the self-righteousness (and righteousness pure and simple) of those who vilified him with every obscenity at *their* command. After all, compared to the crowds who hounded him with their mechanical chants, Lyndon Johnson was a poet.

Perhaps, if the political language of America was as free as its secret language, LBJ could have made King Shit a title to be reckoned with. Perhaps, in the presidential election of our dreams, he could have beaten even Lenny Bruce.

And maybe he would have kept Harmonica Frank on retainer, down there on the LBJ ranch.

Harmonica Frank's music, like LBJ's language, has a spirit that occasionally emerges to redeem those impulses in American life that are cold, bitter, and corrupt—just as that book about a river and a raft was meant to displace Mark Twain's dread of what, hard into the Gilded Age, the country seemed eager to believe it was all about. The idea that the two Americas are separable, I suppose, is the heart of our romanticism.

A good part of the impact of rock 'n' roll had to do with its anachronistic essence, the way it seemed to come out of nowhere—the big surprise that trivialized the events that governed daily life. Rock 'n' roll gave the kids who had seen no alternative but to submit to those events a little room to move. Any musicologist, neatly tracing the development of the music, can tell us that rock 'n' roll did not come out of nowhere. But it sounded as if it did. It was one of those great twists of history that no one anticipated—no one, that is, except

*Cited in David Halberstam, *The Best and the Brightest* (New York: Random House, 1972).

a few men like Sam Phillips, who were looking for it, looking for something to break the boredom they felt when they turned on the radio.

Harmonica Frank was part of Phillips' quest for the weird, and weird it had to be if it was to crack the ice that was seeping into Memphis in 1951. When Phillips looked at his town he must have seen the thousands of good country people, the people who worked hard and prayed harder, who had migrated to Memphis after World War II. They wanted a home that was safe, orderly, and respectable, and as far as the old wide-open riverboat town was concerned, they were perfectly satisfied to visit it in a museum. There was a sense that life was set in a pattern; winding down.

"It seemed to me that Negroes were the only ones that had any freshness left in their music," Phillips has said of those days when he was looking for a white man. Maybe it was a white man who sounded like a cross between a barnyard and a minstrel show—Harmonica Frank, say; maybe a cocky kid, child of those new Memphians, who sang a new kind of blues. Certainly it had to be someone who toyed with race, the deepest source of limits in the South.

The alternative for Phillips, as a record producer, was the white country music of the Carter Family, Jimmie Rodgers, Hank Williams, Patsy Cline. But leaving aside the fact that Phillips was not likely to make a billion dollars on it, there was a problem with that music. It so perfectly expressed the acceptance and fatalism of its audience of poor and striving whites, blending in with their way of life and endlessly reinforcing it, that the music brought all it had to say to the surface, told no secrets, and had no use for novelty. It was conservative in an almost tragic sense, because it carried no hope of change, only respite. By the early fifties this music was all limits. Country music was entertainment that made people feel better, as all true American folk music is before it is anything else, but at its deepest country music was a way of holding on to the values that were jeopardized by a changing postwar America. Country music lacked the confidence to break things open because it was not even sure it could find space to breathe. Hank Williams was eloquent, but his eloquence could not set him free from the life he sang about; he died proving it, overdosing in the back of a car, on his way to one more show.

Phillips had not even worked out the sound he wanted; it was music toward which he was only groping, and most important, ready to accept. Frank Floyd, a white man with some life in him, whose music wasn't exactly blues but was too strange to peddle as anything else, couldn't have sounded less like Hank Williams (though he might have picked up some of his twinkle from Jimmie Rodgers, whom he met on the road years before). Maybe Frank's music was something that would make people take notice if they heard him on the radio, which they rarely did; whatever it was, it was music to turn things around a bit—a clue to what Phillips was looking for, to what made rock 'n' roll happen and to what keeps it alive.

What Phillips was looking for was something that didn't fit, that didn't make sense out of or reflect American life as everyone seemed to understand it, but which made it beside the point, confused things, and affirmed something else. What? The fact that there *was* something else.

What finally arrived was a music of racial confusion, Huck and Jim giving America's aunt the slip, no dead-end "white Negroes" but something new, men like Harmonica Frank and Elvis Presley, whose styles revealed possibilities of American life that were hardly visible anywhere else with an intensity and delight that had no parallel at all.

The music unleashed by Elvis, Little Richard, and the rest of the early rockers was a thrill, and it was also unnerving. I recall hearing Little Richard's "Rip It Up" for the first time, loving the sound but catching the line, "Fool about mah money dont try to save," and thinking, well, that *is* foolish. Had Harmonica Frank's "Rockin' Chair Daddy" been on my radio, I would have been appalled that anyone could skip college *and be proud of it*.

I know that when Elvis was drafted I felt a great relief, because he made demands on me. It was close to what I felt when the politics of the sixties faded—an ambivalent feeling of cowardice and safety. I loved his records—"Hound Dog" was the first I ever owned; "All Shook Up" the first I bought; and "(You're So Square) Baby I Don't Care" (the title may sum up this dilemma) my first private treasure, a record I loved that no one else seemed to like.

But I didn't like—that is, didn't understand—what the Big E did to the girls I went to school with or the way he looked on the cover of his first album, demented, tongue hanging down his chest, lost in some ecstasy completely foreign to me. What was this? Harmonica Frank wasn't the source of this confused delight, not in terms of musicology anyway, because almost no one ever heard him. But he was in on it: he helped Sam Phillips open the doors the King walked through. More than that, he was a harbinger of a certain American spirit that never disappears no matter how smooth things get.

ROBERT JOHNSON
1938

When the train
Left the station
It had two lights on behind
When the train left the station
It had two lights on behind
Well, the blue light was my blues
And the red light was my mind.
All my love's
In vain.

ROBERT JOHNSON, "Love in Vain"

You know how it feels—you understand
What it is to be a stranger, in this unfriendly land.

BOBBY "BLUE" BLAND, "Lead Me On"*

It may be that the most interesting American struggle is the struggle to set oneself free from the limits one is born to, and then to learn

*Lyrics as used in the composition, "Lead Me On," by D. Malone. Copyright © 1960 by Lion Publishing Co., Inc., 8255 Beverley Boulevard, Los Angeles, California, 90048. Used by permission only. All rights reserved.

something of the value of those limits. But on the surface, America takes its energy from the pursuit of happiness; from "a love of physical gratification, the notion of bettering one's condition, the excitement of competition, the charm of anticipated success" (Tocqueville's words); from a memory of open spaces and a belief in open possibilities; from the conviction that you *can* always get what you want, and that even if you can't, you deserve it anyway.

Most of the big shore places were closed now and there were hardly any lights except the shadowy, moving glow of a ferryboat across the Sound. And as the moon rose higher the inessential houses began to melt away until gradually I became aware of the old island here that had flowered once for Dutch sailors' eyes—a fresh, green breast of the new world. Its vanished trees, the trees that had made way for Gatsby's house, had once pandered to the last and greatest of human dreams; for a transitory enchanted moment man must have held his breath in the presence of this continent, compelled into an aesthetic contemplation he neither understood nor desired, face to face for the last time in history with something commensurate to his capacity for wonder.

No one ever captured the promise of American life more beautifully than Fitzgerald did in that passage. That sense of America is expressed so completely—by billboards, by our movies, by Chuck Berry's refusal to put the slightest irony into "Back in the U.S.A.," by the way we try to live our lives—that we hardly know how to talk about the resentment and fear that lie beneath the promise. To be an American is to feel the promise as a birthright, and to feel alone and haunted when the promise fails. No failure in America, whether of love or money, is ever simple; it is always a kind of betrayal, of a mass of shadowy, shared hopes.

Within that failure is a very different America; it is an America of desolation, desolate because it is felt to be out of place, and it is here that Robert Johnson looked for his images and found them.

Robert Johnson was a Mississippi country blues singer and guitarist, born in 1911; he was murdered, by a jealous husband, in 1938. He died in a haze: if some remember that he was stabbed, others say he was poisoned; that he died on his hands and knees, barking like a dog; that his death "had something to do with the black arts."

Nearly forty years after his death, Johnson remains the most emotionally committed of all blues singers; for all the distance of his time and place, Johnson's music draws a natural response from many who outwardly could not be more different from him. He sang about the price he had to pay for promises he tried, and failed, to keep; I think the power of his music comes in part from Johnson's ability to shape the loneliness and chaos of his betrayal, or ours. Listening to Johnson's songs, one almost feels at home in that desolate America; one feels able to take some strength from it, right along with the promises we could not give up if we wanted to.

Like Charley Patton, Tommy Johnson, Son House, or Skip James—the men who worked out the country blues form in the late teens and twenties—Robert Johnson sang an intense, dramatic music, accompanied only by his guitar. He put down twenty-nine of his songs for the old Vocalion label in 1936 and 1937; his songs lasted, in the work of other bluesmen, long after Johnson was dead, and in the early sixties Johnson's original versions began to appear on albums. Today Johnson's presence can be felt behind many of the best modern guitar players; in a more subtle and vital way, his presence can be felt behind many of our best singers. And a good musical case can be made for Johnson as the first rock 'n' roller of all. His music had a vibrancy and a rhythmic excitement that was new to the country blues. On some tunes—"Walking Blues," "Crossroads Blues," "If I Had Possession Over Judgment Day"—Johnson sounds like a complete rock 'n' roll band, as full as Elvis's first combo or the group Bob Dylan put together for the *John Wesley Harding* sessions, and tougher than either. Johnson's way of looking at things, though, is just beginning to emerge.

I have no stylistic arguments to make about Johnson's influence on the other performers in this book, but I do have a symbolic argument. It seems to me that just as they all have a bit of Harmonica Frank in their souls, the artistic ambitions of the Band, Sly Stone, and Randy Newman can at times be seen as attempts to go part of the way into the America Robert Johnson made his own; that since his journey into that America knew few limits, his music can help us understand the limits of other artists and the risks they take when they try to break through them.

And as for Elvis Presley—well, his first music might be seen as a proud attempt to escape Johnson's America altogether.

Johnson's vision was of a world without salvation, redemption, or rest; it was a vision he resisted, laughed at, to which he gave himself over, but most of all it was a vision he pursued. He walked his road like a failed, orphaned Puritan, looking for women and a good night, but never convinced, whether he found such things or not, that they were really what he wanted, and so framing his tales with old echoes of sin and damnation. There were demons in his songs—blues that walked like a man, the devil, or the two in league with each other— and Johnson was often on good terms with them; his greatest fear seems to have been that his desires were so extreme that he could satisfy them only by becoming a kind of demon himself. When he sings, so slowly, in "Me and the Devil Blues,"

> *Early this morning*
> *When you knocked upon my door*
> *Early this morning*
> *When you knocked upon my door*
> *I said, Hello, Satan,*
> *I believe it's time to go*

the only memory in American art that speaks with the same eerie resignation is that moment when Ahab goes over to the devil-worshiping Parsees he kept stowed away in the hold of the *Pequod*. That is a remarkable image, but Johnson's images were simply part of daily life.

> *Me and the devil, was walking side by side*
> *Oooo, me and the devil, was walking side by side*
> *I'm going to beat my woman, until I get satisfied*

It may seem strange that in the black country South of the twenties and thirties, where the leap to grace of gospel music was at the heart of the community, the blues singers, in a twisted way, were the real Puritans. These men, who had to renounce the blues to be sanctified, who often sneered at the preachers in their songs, were the ones who really believed in the devil; they feared the devil most because they knew him best. They understood, far better than the preachers, why sex was man's original sin, and they sang about little else.

This side of the blues did not come from Africa, but from the Puritan revival of the Great Awakening, the revival that spread across the American colonies more than two hundred years ago. It was an explosion of dread and piety that Southern whites passed onto their slaves and that blacks ultimately refashioned into their own religion. The blues singers accepted the dread but refused the piety; they sang as if their understanding of the devil was strong enough to force a belief in God out of their lives. They lived man's fear of life, and they became artists of the fear.

Or perhaps that is not the truth; perhaps Robert Johnson was very different from other blues singers. For all his clear stylistic ties to Son House, Skip James, and others, there are ways in which he stands apart. Part of this is musical—it has to do with the quality of his imagery, his impulse to drama, the immediacy of his singing and guitar playing—but mostly it is Johnson's determination to go farther into the blues than anyone else, and his ability, as an artist, to get there. Anyone from Muddy Waters to Mick Jagger to Michael Jackson could put across the inspired pornography of Johnson's "Terraplane [a good, rough car of the thirties] Blues"—

> *I'm gonna get deep down in this connection*
> *Keep on tangling with your wires*
> *I'm gonna get deep down in this connection*
> *Keep on tangling with your wires*
> *And when I mash down on your little starter—*
> *Then your spark gonna give me fire*

—but as for "Stones in My Passway," which was the other side of sex, few have been fool enough to try.

Few men could brag like Robert Johnson: "Stuff I got'll bust your brains out, baby," he sang in "Stop Breaking Down Blues," "it'll make you lose your mind." Women crowded around him at the back country juke joints to find out if it was true, and no doubt it often was. But such tunes gave way to songs like "Phonograph Blues," where Johnson sings, with far too much emotion it seems, about his broken record player. "What evil have I done . . . what evil has the poor girl heard." That one line shows us how far he is trying to go.

The poor girl is the phonograph, softly personified; she refuses to play Johnson's wicked records and breaks down. With a blazing insistence, Johnson intensifies his personification, unveils his metaphors. At once, you see him struggling with his machine, and in bed with his girl. The records are his sins; the phonograph his penis. The song ends as a confession that the sins his records embody have made him impotent.

What Johnson found on his road was mostly this: ". . . the sense that life is essentially a cheat and its conditions are those of defeat, and that the redeeming satisfactions are not 'happiness and pleasure'

but the deeper satisfactions that come out of struggle." So wrote
Fitzgerald to his daughter, about what he had found in Lincoln and
Shakespeare and "all great careers." His words make good company
for Stanley Booth's: "The dedication [the blues] demands lies beyond
technique; it makes being a blues player something like being a priest.
Virtuosity in playing blues licks is like virtuosity in celebrating the
Mass, it is empty, it means nothing. Skill is a necessity, but a true
blues player's virtue lies in his acceptance of his life, a life for which
he is only partly responsible. When Bukka White sings a song he
wrote during his years on Parchman Prison Farm, 'I wonder how
long, till I can change my clothes,' he is celebrating, honestly and
humbly, his life."

When acceptance and celebration mean the same thing, or when
the two words must fill the same space in the mind at once, we can
begin to grasp the tension and the passion of Robert Johnson's music—
because when one accepts one's life by celebrating it, one also asks
for something more. In Johnson's blues the singer's acceptance is
profound, because he knows, and makes us see, that his celebration
is also a revolt, and that the revolt will fail, because his images cannot
deny the struggles they are meant to master.

It is obvious that man dwells in a splendid universe, a magnificent
expanse of earth and sky and heavens, which manifestly is built upon a
majestic structure, maintains some mighty design, though man himself cannot grasp it. Yet for him it is not a pleasant or satisfying world. In his few
moments of respite from labor or from his enemies, he dreams that this very
universe might indeed be perfect, its laws operating just as now they seem
to do, and yet he and it somehow be in full accord. The very ease with
which he can frame this image to himself makes the reality all the more
mocking. . . . It is only too clear that man is not at home in this universe,
and yet he is not good enough to deserve a better.

                    PERRY MILLER, on the Puritan view of the world*

When Robert Johnson traveled through the Deep South, over to
Texas and back to Memphis, into the Midwest and up to Chicago,
across the border to Canada and back to Detroit to sing spirituals on
the radio, to New York City (the sight of this primitive blues singer
gazing up at the lights of Times Square is not only banal, it is bizarre),
to the South again, he was tracing not only the miles on the road but
the strength of its image. It was the ultimate American image of flight

*From *The New England Mind: The Seventeenth Century* (Boston: Beacon Press, 1968).

from homelessness, and he always looked back: the women he left, or who left him, chased him through the gloomy reveries of his songs, just as one of them eventually caught up. Like a good American, Johnson lived for the moment and died for the past.

Sometimes the road was just the best place to be, free and friendly, a good way to put in the time. In "Four Until Late" there is even a girl waiting at the other end.

> *When I leave this town,*
> *I'm gonna bid you fair, farewell*
> *When I leave this town,*
> *I'm gonna bid you fair, farewell*
> *And when I return again,*
> *You'll have a great long story to tell.*

There is the grace and bitterness of "Rambling on My Mind" (which Johnson played with his walking bass figure that was to define Chicago blues, making the song sound just like a man pushing himself down the highway, half against his will); the slow sexual menace of "Traveling Riverside Blues"; the nightmare of "Crossroads," where Johnson is sure to be caught by whites after dark and does not know which way to run; there is always one more "strange man's town," one more girl, one more drink; there is the last word of "Hellhound on My Trail."

> *I got to keep moving, I got to keep moving*
> *Blues falling down like hail, blues falling*
> *down like hail*
> *Blues falling down like hail, blues falling down*
> *like hail*
> *And the days keep on 'minding me*
> *There's a hellhound on my trail*
> *Hellhound on my trail, hellhound on my trail*

It wasn't the open road, to say the least; more like Ishmael falling in behind funeral processions, because they made him feel more alive, and on good terms with death. You could imagine what the two travelers would have to say to each other: *This is no way for a young man to act!*

That spirit gives us what might be Johnson's most American image, these lines from "Me and the Devil Blues"—most American because, as a good, defiant laugh at fate, they are vital not only beneath the surface of American life, but on it. They are often called in as proof of Johnson's despair, and they are part of it, but also his most satisfied lines, a proud epitaph:

You may bury my body, down by the highway side
Babe, I don't care where you bury my body when
I'm dead and gone
You may bury my body, ooooo, down by the
highway side
So my old evil spirit
Can get a Greyhound bus, and ride.

Robert Johnson had a beautiful high voice, a tragic voice when he meant it to be. In "Walking Blues" he wakes up to find that his woman has left him without even his shoes. He is plainly in awe of this woman ("Well!" he sings to himself, "she's got Elgin movements, from her head down to her toes . . . From her head down to her toes!"); when he says the worried blues are the worst he ever had, he's still too full of admiration for that woman to make you believe him.

So he will sing, with a distracted, comic determination:

Lord I—feel like blowin' my, old lonesome home
Got up this morning, my little bunny ears was gone
Now, up this light, ooooo, my lonesome home

and then with utter grace his voice rises, almost fades away, and there is a soft moan that could echo in your heart for a long time, a melancholy too strong to step around:

Well, I got up this morning . . . all I had, was gone.

Johnson was in his mid-twenties when he sang these songs (Don Law, the great recording engineer who handled the sessions, thought of him as a teenager). Johnson didn't have the worldly dignity of Son House or Skip James. Neither House nor James ever sounds confused; they sing as men who live deeply, but within limits. In Johnson's voice, there is sometimes an element of shock—less a matter of lost innocence than of innocence willfully given up and remembered anyway.

Johnson seemed to take more pure pleasure out of making music than any other Delta singer; there is rock 'n' roll fun in his guitar playing you can hear anytime you like. He was, I think, working out a whole new aesthetic that rock 'n' roll eventually completed: a loud, piercing music driven by massive rhythms and a beat so strong that involvement was effortless and automatic. Yet Johnson also had more to say than other singers. His music was half seduction, half assault, meant to drive his words home with enormous force. His technique was not only more advanced, it was deeper, because it had to be.

Only his weakest songs move on an even keel; the greatest shudder and break and explode, or twist slowly around quietly shaking strings into a kind of suspension, until Johnson has created a mood so delicate and bleak one feels he cannot possibly get out of his song alive. Johnson's most distinctive performances have the tension that comes when almost everything is implied, when the worst secrets are hiding in plain talk. With "Come on in My Kitchen" Johnson plays out the sound of a cold wind on his guitar, and his voice rides it; there is a stillness in the music. The loneliness is overpowering and the feeling of desolation is absolute. The most prosaic lines take on the shape of pure terror.

> *When a woman gets in trouble*
> *Everybody throws her down*
> *Looking for her good friend*
> *None can be found.*
> *You better come on, in my kitchen*
> *There's going to be rain in our door.*

It was songs like this one—the combination of voice, guitar, words, and the mythical authority that comes when an artist confirms his work with his life—that made Eric Clapton see Johnson's ghost, and his own, in Jimi Hendrix's death. "Eric wanted to do a Robert Johnson," one of Clapton's friends said when Hendrix died. "A few good years, and go."

Johnson's music is so strong that in certain moods it can make you feel that he is giving you more than you could have bargained for—that there is a place for you in these lines of his: "She's got a mortgage on my body, a lien on my soul." It is no exaggeration to say that Johnson changed the lives of people as distant from each other as Muddy Waters, who began his career as a devoted imitator; Dion, who made his way through the terrors of his heroin habit with Johnson's songs for company; and myself. After hearing Johnson's music for the first time—listening to that blasted and somehow friendly voice, the shivery guitar, hearing a score of lines that fit as easily and memorably into each day as Dylan's had—I could listen to nothing else for months. Johnson's music changed the way the world looked to me. Over the years, what had been a fascination with a bundle of ideas and dreams from old American novels and texts—a fascination with the foreboding and gentleness that is linked in the most interesting Americans—seemed to find a voice in Johnson's songs. It was the intensity of his music that changed fascination into commitment and a bundle of ideas into what must serve as a point of view.

But commitment is a tricky, Faustian word. When he first appeared Robert couldn't play guitar to save his life, Son House told Pete Welding; Johnson hung out with the older bluesmen, pestering them for a chance to try his hand, and after a time he went away. It was months later, on a Saturday night, when they saw him again, still looking to be heard. They tried to put him off, but he persisted; finally, they let him play for a lull and left him alone with the tables and chairs.

Outside, taking the air, House and the others heard a loud, devastating music of a brilliance and purity beyond anything in the memory of the Mississippi Delta. Johnson had nothing more to learn from *them*.

"He sold his soul to the devil to get to play like that," House told Welding.

Well, they tell a lot of stories about Robert Johnson. You could call that one superstition, or you could call it sour grapes. Thinking of voodoo and gypsy women in the back country, or of the black man who used to walk the streets of Harlem with a briefcase full of contracts and a wallet full of cash, buying up souls at $100 a throw, you could even take it literally.

If there were nothing else, the magic of Johnson's guitar would be enough to make that last crazy interpretation credible. But in a way that cannot be denied, selling his soul and trying to win it back are what Johnson's bravest songs are all about, and anyone who wants to come to grips with his music probably ought to entertain Son House's possibility. I have the feeling, at times, that the reason Johnson has remained so elusive is that no one has been willing to take him at his word.

Let us say that Johnson sought out one of the Mississippi Delta devil-men, or one of the devil-women, and tried to sell his soul in exchange for the music he heard but could not make. Let us say he did this because he wanted to attract women; because he wanted to be treated with the kind of awe that is in Son House's voice when he speaks of Robert Johnson and the devil; because music brought him a fierce joy, made him feel alive like nothing else in the world. Or let us say that the idea of the devil gave Johnson a way of understanding the fears that overshadowed him; that even if no deal was made, no promises passing from one to another, Johnson believed that his desires and his crimes were simple proof of a consummation quite beyond his power to control; that the image of the devil appealed to Johnson when he recognized (singing, "I mistreated my baby, but I can't see no reason why") that his soul was not his own, and, looking at the disasters of his life and the evil of the world, drew the one conclusion as to whom it did belong.

Blues grew out of the need to live in the brutal world that stood ready in ambush the moment one walked out of the church. Unlike gospel, blues was not a music of transcendence; its equivalent to God's Grace was sex and love. Blues made the terrors of the world easier to endure, but blues also made those terrors more real. For a man like Johnson, the promises of the church faded; they could be remembered—as one sang church songs; perhaps even when one prayed, when one was too scared not to—but those promises could not be lived. Once past some unmarked border, one could not go back. The weight of Johnson's blues was strong enough to make salvation a joke; the best he could do was cry for its beautiful lie. "You run without moving from a terror in which you cannot believe," William Faulkner wrote in one of his books about the landscape he shared with Robert Johnson, just about the time Johnson was making his first records, "toward a safety in which you have no faith."

We comfort ourselves that we do not believe in the devil, but we run anyway; we run from and straight into the satanic images that press against the surface of American life. I think of Robert Mitchum, the mad preacher in *Night of the Hunter*, with LOVE tattooed between the knuckles of his right hand, HATE tattooed between the knuckles of his left—and he seems, again, like the legacy of the men who began the American experience as a struggle between God and the devil, the legacy of a Puritan weirdness, something that those who came after have been left to live out.

The dreams and fears of the Puritans, those gloomy old men, are at the source of our attempts to make sense out of the contradictions between the American idea of paradise and the doomed facts of our history; they emerge when "solving problems" is not good enough or even the point, when the hardest task is not to denounce evil, but to see it.

Unlike Fitzgerald's Dutch sailors, the Puritans did not take their dreams from the land; they brought them along. They meant to build a community of piety and harmony, what their leader, John Winthrop, called "a city on a hill"—an idea, in its many forms, that we have never gotten over, nothing less than America as the light of the world. They had a driving need to go to extremes, as if they could master God and the devil if only they could think hard enough; that, and a profound inability to make peace with the world as they found it. They failed their dreams, and their community shattered. "This land," Winthrop wrote before he died, "grows weary of her inhabitants."

The Puritans came here with a utopian vision they could not maintain; their idea was to do God's work, and they knew that if they failed, it would mean that their work had been the devil's. As they panicked at their failures, the devil was all they saw. Their witch trials were a decadent version of their America—shlock, as it were, but their biggest hit.

Their initial attempts to shape America, and their failures, set the devil loose in the land—as a symbol of uncontrollable malevolence, of betrayal, of disaster, of punishment. Just as the Puritans' failures and compromises anticipated our own, there is something in us that responds, not always quite consciously, to the original image of American failure—to the terror that image can speak for.

If the presence of that image has been felt from the Puritans' day to ours, it is, perhaps, because that image is a way of getting to the idea of an American curse. The image of the devil is a way of comprehending the distance between Fitzgerald's shining image of American possibility and his verdict on its result; it is a way of touching the sense (there in Fitzgerald's beautiful image of America as "an aesthetic contemplation [man] neither understood nor desired") that America is a trap: that its promises and dreams, all mixed up as love and politics and landscape, are too much to live up to and too much to escape. It is as if to be an American means to ask for too much—not even knowing one is asking for too much—and to trade away one's life to get it, whatever it is; as if this is what makes America special, vital, murderous, and noble.

The Puritan devil endures as a face on the betrayal of the promises we mean to keep; the Puritan commitment to extremes, the willingness to live in a world where the claims of God and the devil are truly at odds, has lasted as a means to comprehend the depths of the promise and the failure alike.

This world may have survived most completely in the tension between the blues and the black church. Robert Johnson inherited this world, and, as a black blues singer, he made a new kind of music out of it. The image of the devil was played out within the matrix of Johnson's struggle with women, and with himself. It was a drama of sex, shot through with acts of violence and tenderness; with desires that no one could satisfy; with crimes that could not be explained; with punishments that could not be escaped.

The most acute Americans, in the steps of the old Puritans, have been suspicious, probing people, looking for signs of evil and grace, of salvation and damnation, behind every natural fact. Robert Johnson lived with this kind of intensity, and he asked old questions: What is our place in the world? Why are we cursed with the power to want more than we can have? What separates men and women from each other? Why must we suffer guilt not only for our sins, but for the failure of our best hopes?

This is a state of mind that gives no rest at all. Even if you have sold your soul to the devil, you cannot rest with him; you have to keep looking, because there is never any end to the price you have to pay, nor any certainty as to the form that price will take. Every event thus becomes charged with meaning, but the meaning is never complete. The moments of perfect pleasure in Johnson's songs, and the beauty of those songs, remind one that it is not the simple presence of evil that is unbearable; what is unbearable is the impossibility of reconciling the facts of evil with the beauty of the world.

This shadow America comes to a verge with "Stones in My Passway." It is the most terrifying of Johnson's songs, perhaps because his desolation can no longer be contained in the old, inherited image of the devil—those lines from "Me and the Devil Blues" seem suddenly almost safe, comfortable, the claims of a man who thinks he knows where he stands. In "Stones in My Passway" terror is too ubiquitous to have a face: it is formless, elusive, overpowering.

A few months before he recorded "Stones in My Passway," Johnson sang these astonishing lines:

If I had possession, over Judgment Day
If I had possession, over Judgment Day
Then the woman I'm lovin', wouldn't have no right to pray

No right to pray—that is a staggering demand to make on life; it is to ask for the same power the devil has over one who has sold his soul. "Stones in My Passway" is the song of a man who once asked for power over other souls, but who now testifies that he has lost power over his own body, and who might well see that disaster as a fitting symbol of the loss of *his* soul. There is no way to "know"; there are no Gothic images in this song. The idea simply takes shape as the song draws in all the echoes of hellhounds, devils, the weirdness of blues walking like a man, draws in those images and goes past them. If those images were a means to expression, they are no longer necessary—they are no longer good enough.

Because not even his body is his own, Johnson cannot satisfy his woman. Because that matters more than anything else in his life, that fact, as a symbol, expands to create more facts, more symbols. Finally, with stones in every passway and no way clear, there is a way in which the singer's life is resolved: he has seen all around his life, for as long as he can hold onto the image. Because the stakes of the song are so high, every word and every note is fashioned to carry the weight of what Johnson wants to say. The four knife-stroke notes that open the song are like a warning; the song is stark. It communicates so directly any distance between the singer and the listener is smashed.

> I got stones in my passway
> And my road seems dark as night
> I got stones in my passway
> And my road seems dark as night
> I got pains in my heart—
> They have taken my appetite.

The tune darts forward on a high, almost martial rhythm; one shattering note freezes the music and the image just before the last line of each verse. "Shock technique," a friend called it.

> My enemies have betrayed me
> Have overtaken poor Bob at last
> My enemies have betrayed me
> Have overtaken poor Bob at last
> And there's one thing certain—
> They have stones all in my passway.

If the passway is in his body, immediately it must stand for every invisible trap on the road; if the stones are at first the most direct, physical description of the sexual collapse that has made Johnson afraid to look his lover in the face, those stones must be made to stand for the men who will soon block the way to his lover's door.

> *I'm crying please*—please, *let us be friends*
> *And when you hear me howlin' in my passway, rider*
> PLEASE *open your door and let me in.*

The song is enormous. I cannot put it any other way. The image of the words is subsumed into Johnson's singing, his guitar, into the eerie, inevitable loudness of the song. The music has its claims to make: no matter how low you set the volume, the music creeps up louder, demanding, and the only way to quiet this music is to shut it off.

> *I got three legs to truck on*
> *Boys, please don't block my road*
> *I got three legs to truck on*
> *Boys, please don't block my road*
> *But I been 'shamed by my rider—*
> *I'm booked and I got to go.*

"Stones in My Passway," like a few others of Johnson's songs— "Love in Vain," "Come on in My Kitchen," "Me and the Devil Blues"—is a two-minute image of doom that has the power to make doom a fact. One hardly knows if it is the clarity of the world Johnson revealed in his music, or Johnson's resilience as he made his way through that world that is most exhilarating; but that so many people—people who have never left the American mainstream that Johnson was never part of—respond to his music is perhaps not such a mystery. Because of our faith in promises, the true terror of doom is in the American's natural inability to believe doom is real, even when he knows it has taken over his life. When there is no way to speak of terror and no one to listen if there were, Johnson's songs matter.

What Robert Johnson had to do with other bluesmen of his time is interesting to me, but not nearly so interesting as what Johnson has to do with those discovering him now, without warning and on their own. The original context of Johnson's story is important, and it is where his story is usually placed; but a critic's job is not only to define the context of an artist's work but to expand that context, and it seems more important to me that Johnson's music is vital enough to enter other contexts and create all over again. Off in the Netherlands to teach college, my friend Langdon Winner wrote back:

> . . . the truth of the matter is that in my first months here I found out a lot more about America than I did about Holland. Hundreds of things which are second nature to us just do not play a part here. Dissatisfaction, for example. Dutch musicians know the techniques pioneered by America's black masters. But they are not interested in extremes of rage, ecstasy, dissipation, or religious enlightenment. And this sums up the place: While jazz has long been popular in the Netherlands, *the blues has never arrived*. How can you understand Aeschylus, Augustine, Shakespeare, and Nietzsche if you can't listen to Robert Johnson in your own time?

Which is to say that if Robert Johnson is an ancestor, or even a ghost, he is really a contemporary.

It is the inescapable pull of Johnson's music that gives us Mick Jagger singing "Love in Vain" in the middle of a rock 'n' roll show— and a rock 'n' roll show is a celebration that is rooted in Little Richard's kind of revolt, or in Harmonica Frank's, far more than it is in Robert Johnson's. Robert Johnson is a presence these days, as rock 'n' roll fans find the world less of a home than it used to be, and yet accept more and more their inability to do anything about their displacement; Johnson is a sort of invisible pop star. He has caught up with us.

The music that is animated by Robert Johnson today is not really found in new rock 'n' roll versions of his songs; Johnson's spirit is not so easy to capture. All of Eric Clapton's love for Johnson's music came to bear not when Clapton sang Johnson's songs, but when, once Johnson's music became part of who Clapton was, Clapton came closest to himself: in the passion of "Layla" and "Any Day." Finally, after years of practice and imitation, Johnson's sound was Clapton's sound: there was no way to separate the two men, nor any need to. And perhaps to keep the story straight, there is, in "Layla," one lost echo buried under Clapton's screams and who knows how many guitars: "Please don't say/You'll never find a way/And tell me, all my love's in vain."

This music sounds like real Delta blues to me, forty years after: Duane Allman's solos on Boz Scaggs' "Loan Me a Dime"; Sly Stone's "Thank you for talkin' to me Africa"; Randy Newman's "God's Song"; much of the Rolling Stones' music from *Let It Bleed* to *Exile on Main Street*; Bob Dylan's "All Along the Watchtower"; Eric Clapton's

"Layla." If someone were to ask me where Johnson's spirit had found a home, I would play these songs.

All the beauty of the world and all the terror of losing it is there in Eric Clapton's rock 'n' roll; Robert Johnson's music is proof that beauty can be wrung from the terror itself. When Johnson sang his darkest songs, terror was a fact, beauty only a glimmer; but that glimmer, and its dying away, lie beneath everything else, beneath all the images that hit home and make a home. Our culture finds its tension and its life within the borders of the glimmer and the dying away, in attempts to come to terms with the betrayal without giving up on the promise. And so at the borders of Elvis Presley's delight, of his fine young hold on freedom, there is, in his "Peace in the Valley," a touch of fear, of that old weirdness:

> *And I'll be changed*
> *Changed from this creature*
> *That I am**

And at another frontier there is Robert Johnson, pausing for a moment in "Hellhound on My Trail," frightened, running down his road, but glancing over his shoulder with a smile:

> *If today was Christmas Eve, if today was Christmas Eve*
> *And tomorrow was Christmas Day*
> *If today was Christmas Eve*
> *And tomorrow was Christmas Day*
> *Aw, wouldn't we have a time, baby?*

Inheritors

THE BAND
Pilgrims' Progress

The Band—four Canadian rockers held together by an Arkansas drummer—staked their claim to an American story from the beginning. The story had its veils, but the fact of the story was plain. "This is *it*," my editor Marvin Garson said in the spring of 1969, as he sent me off to cover the Band's national debut in San Francisco. "This is when we find out if there are still open spaces out there."

Marvin was a New Yorker; living in California sometimes made him talk like Natty Bumppo, but his words were accurate. By out there he meant right here, and he was talking about the Band because it was obvious they were committed to the very idea of America: complicated, dangerous, and alive.

Their music gave us a sure sense that the country was richer than we had guessed; that it had possibilities we were only beginning to perceive. In the unique blend of instruments and good rhythms, in the shared and yet completely individual vocals, in the half-lost phrases and buried lyrics, there was an ambiguity that opened up the world with real force. The songs captured the yearning for home and the fact of displacement that ruled our lives; we thought that the Band's music was the most natural parallel to our hopes, ambitions, and doubts, and we were right to think so. Flowing through their music were spirits of acceptance and desire, rebellion and awe, raw excitement, good sex, open humor, a magic feel for history—a determination to find plurality and drama in an America we had met too often as a monolith.

The Band's music made us feel part of their adventure; we knew that we would win if they succeeded and lose if they failed. That was what Marvin Garson meant. It was a good feeling.

CROSSING THE BORDER

When the Band surfaced in 1968 with *Music from Big Pink*, they had been playing rock 'n' roll music for more than half as long as there had been such a thing. What mattered most, though, was that they had put in their years together, as a group. A rock 'n' roll group is a banding together of individuals for the purpose of achieving something that none of them can get on their own: money, fame, the right sound, something less easy to put into words. But what begins as a marriage of convenience sometimes takes on its own value. An identity comes into being that transcends individual personalities, but does not obscure them—in fact, it is the group, sometimes only the group, that makes individuals visible. The Beatles, after all, were the most satisfying and complex testament to the limits of self-reliance most of us have ever known; they were also proof of the limits of a common bond. Groups are images of community. That the Band had created itself through the years, and had come to our attention bent on demonstrating just what their years together had been worth, was perhaps the most potent image of all.

Like John Lennon and Paul McCartney, Booker T. & the MG's, Bob Dylan, and a few thousand others, drummer Levon Helm, guitarist Robbie Robertson, piano man Richard Manuel, bass Rick Danko, and organist Garth Hudson started out in the high school bands that appeared overnight in the flash of the first great rock explosion.* Still in their teens in the early sixties, they came together in Toronto as the Hawks, back-up band for Ronnie Hawkins, a small-time Arkansas rockabilly singer who had brought Levon north with him around 1958.

Hawkins, though he brushed the charts twice in 1959—with a Chuck Berry remake and an R&B cover—was too little and too late to pass for the next Elvis Presley; his task was to keep himself alive. In the U.S.A. he was one of too many; in Canada, where authentic American rockers were a solid commercial rarity, Hawkins could bill himself "The King of Rockabilly" and get away with it. Sometimes he liked to call himself "Mr. Dynamo." It was, as so many have testified, better than working.

Ronnie Hawkins was a windjammer in the grand style. He claimed to have picked cotton right alongside Bo Diddley; to have made the first rock 'n' roll record of all, back in 1952 (no one, so far as I know, has ever found it, but Hawkins, keeping his story straight, says it was the first version of "Bo Diddley"); to have passed up a chance for stardom when he graciously offered the sure-hit "It's Only Make Believe" to his old pal Conway Twitty; to know more back roads, back rooms, and backsides than any man from Newark to Mexicali. His singing was only fair, though in one sense it was quite distinctive: Hawkins is the only man I have ever heard who can make a nice sexy song like "My Gal Is Red Hot" sound sordid. "None of us rock 'n' rollers could understand all that fuss about Jerry Lee Lewis marrying a thirteen-year-old girl," he is reputed to have said. "All us Southern cats knew she was only twelve."

Hawkins was no fool; he needed a band to carry him, and when the razorbacks he had imported began to scatter, he and Levon re-cruited the Canadian kids one by one. As characters in the classic bildungsroman that tells of the wise old philosopher who initiates innocent young boys into the mysteries of life, Hawkins and his Hawks played their way through the collected works of Gene Vincent, Chuck Berry, Larry Williams, Fats Domino, and the rest, filling out their shows with tunes about the whores they met.

Robbie wrote his first song, "Hey Boba Lu," which Hawkins

---

*The names of those bands are too good to leave out: the Robots, the Consuls, Thumper and the Trombones (Robbie); Paul London and the Capers, later changed to "Kapers" (Hudson); the Rockin' Revols (Manuel); and the Jungle Bush Beaters. The last was Levon's original Marvel, Arkansas, outfit—and as the soubriquet of a bunch of Southern white boys chasing the blues across the tracks, it's rock 'n' roll poetry if anything is.

recorded; on stage, Manuel and Levon handled most of the singing. "When Ronnie sang," Robbie remembers fondly, "we had to count out the beat for him. It was, 'Oh, Carol—one, two, three, *four*—Don't let him steal. . . .' "

The Hawks were looking for their music. When Robbie was fifteen Levon took him into the South, with hopes of putting the Bush Beaters back together. That came to nothing, but the trip changed something in Robertson; just what it was is elusive even to him, but listening to the man retrace his steps, one gets the sense that an enormous creative ambition was set free when he discovered that the place that had put magic into his life was real. There had been the music, of course—rock 'n' roll from Memphis, rock 'n' roll from New Orleans—and Robbie already had the beginnings of his idea that the land makes the music. But there were also the family histories and local legends Levon had told him; the inexplicably exciting foreign names, suddenly right there on billboards and coming over the drifting Southern radio dial in between the fiddles and sermons, names like "Dr. Pepper" and "Ko-Ko bars"; there was the fact of seeing people, black and white, living out the sounds he had heard on his records. The reality only made the magic that much more fierce. Here was a different world, with more on its surface than Canada had in its abyss; you could chase that world, listen to it, learn from it. Perhaps you could even join it.

Before too long, Howlin' Wolf, Junior Parker, Bobby Bland, and other bluesmen were climbing the Hawks' charts, and Hawkins' repertoire no longer seemed so romantic. Robbie had tried to get Jimmy Ray Paulman, Hawkins' original guitarist, to teach him how to play—Paulman, with a good eye for the competition, told the kid to get lost—but now Robbie was in a position to feel the competition himself. For a white boy, that meant James Burton, star of "Suzie Q" and hero of Ricky Nelson's hits; Roy Buchanan, the lonesome master of the blues; Lonnie Mack, who sang from the church and played straight from the alley. To live up to all that Levon had shown him, and to satisfy his own brash self, Robbie had to be better than any of them.

He was listening hard to Wolf's guitarists: Willie Johnson on "How Many More Years" and Hubert Sumlin on "Wang-Dang-Doodle." Johnson and Sumlin had created a guitar style so chaotic and fast it demanded a rhythm section as quick as it was hard just to keep a performance from flying to pieces. There was none of the polite formality of a band setting up a solo, taking turns; there was no showcasing. Wolf's best records came on like three-minute race riots.

The drums, bass, piano, and harp converged on the beat, hammering, shoving; for a moment they let the beat take the song, let you think you had the sides sorted out and the picture clear, and then the guitarist leaped in, heaved himself through the crowd like a tornado, and the crowd paid no attention and went right on fighting. This was the sound the Hawks were after, and on an unbelievably demonic recording of Bo Diddley's "Who Do You Love," they got it. Hawkins' vocal (his only real claim to greatness, but it will do) was one ghastly scream; Robbie fought back with a crazed, jagged solo that to this day has never been matched. It is still possibly the most menacing piece of rock 'n' roll ever made.

The Hawks, however, did not need their front man—fooling around in the studio after the dry sessions for Hawkins' *Mojo Man* LP, Levon took over the mike for Bobby Bland's hard-rocking "Farther Up the Road" and Muddy Waters' slow and sexy "She's 19," and the group left behind the most exciting white blues recordings since the early days of Elvis Presley. "White blues" doesn't really describe the music—though they were white, and the songs were blues—Levon's singing and Robbie's guitar playing fell into no genre. This wasn't like the early Paul Butterfield Band, or John Hammond, Jr., to be judged on how precisely the white music matched the sound of the black idols. The Hawks were a long way past questions of technique; the problem was to find out what they could do with that technique.

Unfortunately, they were making music in a vacuum; in America, those great sides were never released, not that they would have fit the commercial demands of the radio anyway. Like most of the best bands forming at the time, the Hawks were a walking jukebox that played only other people's hits, and the jukebox was a few years out of date to boot. Over in Hamburg, the Beatles too were jamming out five sets a night, as John Lennon shouted "Dizzy Miss Lizzy" with a toilet seat around his neck; Van Morrison and the Monarchs were peddling their Ray Charles imitations to homesick GIs in Germany; the Rolling Stones were up all night trying to figure out how Sonny Boy made his harp sound like that; Elvis was having fun in Acapulco; and Creedence Clearwater, calling themselves the Blue Velvets, were scuffling up and down the road from Sacramento to San Jose, fighting a battle of the bands with Peter Wheat and the Breadmen while John Fogerty scribbled the bayou fantasies that would lift him out of a world he hated. In the early sixties, rock 'n' roll was a waiting game.

After a year or two apprenticed to Hawkins, Levon led the Band out on their own as Levon and the Hawks, sometimes as the Crackers, sometimes as the Canadian Squires. They traveled Hawkins' circuit of honky-tonks and dives—a tough, loud band that played, as Garth Hudson once put it, "for pimps, whores, rounders, and flakeouts." "We had one thing on our minds," Robbie says. "Stomp."

They cut occasional 45's, whenever they found someone to let them into a studio: "Go Go Liza Jane," the old folk song; a good hard punch-out of a record called "Leave Me Alone"; an odd, churchy paean to "this righteous land" with the even odder title of "The Stones I Throw (Will Free All Men)"—crude stuff, but hopeful. "Down in L.A., you know they got everything," Levon sang on "Uh-Uh-Uh." "Think I'll move out there, become the new Southern King."

This was not earthshaking. By 1965 the Beatles and the Stones were running the scene, and from their name to their nightclubs, the Hawks were an anachronism. Still, they built up a vague word-of-mouth reputation on the East Coast; eager to take on the world with a new sound and perhaps feeling a bit anachronistic himself, Bob Dylan got in touch. The combination clicked: suddenly Dylan was singing like a demon, and the Hawks—never introduced, always anonymous—twisted around him with a noise that not even they could have been prepared for. The Hawks backed Dylan through the rough, mean tours of 1965 and 1966, and the Stones sat in the audience. The Hawks left the stage as the best band in the world.

Levon, a pro when Bob Dylan was still hard at work scaring his high school principal, did not go along; the Hawks, after all, had been *his* band. But when the Canadians followed Dylan to Woodstock once the tours were over, Levon joined up again, and the Band made a second founding.

Out of all this they fashioned a music that sounded not at all like what had preceded it; they seemed to draw less on their old music than on the friendship they had discovered making it. Calling themselves "The Band" was proof of their arrogance, but there was a depth of experience in their music that could not be denied, and the fans they won had no wish to deny it. It was, in fact, precisely what a lot of people were looking for.

In 1968 rock 'n' roll was coming out of its San Francisco period—psychedelic music, rebel energy, Father-Yes-Son-I-Want-To-Kill-You, drum solos, drug visions, bright and happy dancing crowds—a fabulous euphoria in the middle of a war, innocence and optimism running straight into the election of Richard Nixon. It had been a fine time, with many chances taken and many chances blown, but it was over, it was soft underneath the flash and it had exhausted itself.

There was a peculiar emptiness in the air, and in the music; *Sgt. Pepper*, generally enshrined a year earlier as the greatest achievement in the history of popular music—by some, in the history of Art—now seemed very hollow, a triumph of effects. The Yippies showed up to take over the politics of the decade, and defrauded them. There were heroes and heroines of the era just past who had only a year or two to live; some of the political heroes had already been murdered. We had gone too far, really, without getting anywhere.

With Bob Dylan, the Band had seen much of this world from the inside, seen it as it was born, even helped bring it into being; but they came through on the other side, in a place very much of their own making. They stepped out, very consciously, as an alternative.

The pictures inside *Big Pink*—of the Band, their friends and relatives, and their ugly but much-loved big pink house—caught some of what they had to say. Against a cult of youth they felt for a continuity of generations; against the instant America of the sixties they looked for the traditions that made new things not only possible, but valuable; against a flight from roots they set a sense of place. Against the pop scene, all flux and novelty, they set themselves: a band with years behind it, and meant to last.

Many young Americans had spent the best part of the decade teaching themselves to feel like exiles in their own country; the Band, particularly songwriters Robbie Robertson and Richard Manuel, understood this, and were sure it was a mistake. They had come here by choice, after all. They had fallen in love with the music, first as they sought it out on the radio and on records, later as they learned to play it, and, wonder of wonders, define it. Coming out of Canada into the land that had kicked up the blues, jazz, church music, country and western, and a score of authentic rock 'n' roll heroes, playing their way up and down the spine of the continent, they fell in love with the place itself.

They felt more alive in America. They came to be on good terms with its violence and its warmth; they were attracted by the neon grab for pleasure on the face of the American night, and by the inscrutable spookiness behind that face. American contradictions demanded a fine energy, because no one could miss them; the stakes were higher, but the rewards seemed limitless. The Band's first songs were a subtle, seductive attempt to get this sense of life across. Their music was fashioned as a way back into America, and it worked.

STRANGER BLUES

With *Music from Big Pink*, the Band presented a rough moral drama. It had none of the mythic clarity of, say, John Ford's movies; it came through a modern haze, something like Robert Altman's *McCabe and Mrs. Miller*, obscure in its plots, dialogue hard to catch, communicating with a blind humor and a cryptic intensity nothing in rock 'n' roll has ever remotely touched.

They began with "Tears of Rage," an eerie invocation of Independence Day, dragging the organ and their secretive horns across a funeral beat, changing the Fourth of July into an image of betrayal, and of loneliness: America betrayed by those who would no longer be part of it. The Band made a claim to an identity others no longer wanted, and the album opened up from there. In its stories, its feel for place and language, its music, and most of all in its quest, this was an American mystery.

The liveliest songs (half Robertson's, half Manuel's, and all of a piece) shared an oddly familiar actor: the voice of "Lonesome Suzie," "Caledonia Mission," "To Kingdom Come," "We Can Talk About It Now," "Chest Fever," "The Weight," and "Long Black Veil."* His part is taken by Levon (gutty, carnal, bewildered, always hanging onto the end of his rope), Rick Danko (quivering, melancholy, hesitant), Manuel (the Band's great sentimentalist, devastated and bursting with joy by turns), Robbie (anxious, yelping), or the four of them at once; but as I hear them now, years after I thought I knew this record, the vocals, like the writing, complete a single story.

The hero of this story (such as I find him, and I ought to note that I am setting the story down—or, if you like, making it up—simply as I hear it, without much regard for song sequence, cross-checked lyrics, or other formalities) has *Big Pink* pretty much to himself. He almost disappears on the next album, *The Band*, returns with *Stage Fright*, loses his voice on *Cahoots*, and perhaps hits the end of his road with Richard Manuel's singing on a handful of the rock 'n'

---

*This last, a modern country tune in the guise of an old Kentucky murder ballad, was not the Band's song, but it fits in perfectly with the rest. "This Wheel's on Fire" and "I Shall Be Released" (the former by Dylan and Danko and the latter by Dylan) don't fit in, not because the lyrics are out of place but because as performances the songs are not emotionally convincing, and the quality of emotion is what makes *Big Pink* a great album, not merely an interesting one. The music and the singing sound strained, contrived, probably because the Band felt obligated to replace the original arrangements they had worked out with Dylan when the songs were first put down on the famous Basement Tape. "Tears of Rage" is another Basement composition, but it works, perhaps because it was so necessary to what the Band was after; but the other two sound like filler on a record that needs nothing of the sort.

roll classics that make up *Moondog Matinee*. To follow his trail is to leave out a good bit of what the Band has done—wonderful tunes like "Get Up Jake" and "Strawberry Wine," and their work with Bob Dylan. But there is a storyteller in their music, and in one form or another, his tale is the one I'm after, because it seems to be the one the Band tells best: the story of the worried man.

"Delivered Under the Similitude of a Dream, Wherein Is Discovered the Manner of His Setting Out, His Dangerous Journey, and Safe Arrival at the Desired Country," as John Bunyan put it. That, really, is only the beginning of his adventure.

He first appears on *Big Pink* as a wanderer, a quester, hoping to brazen his way through a strange land and learn something. He lives by his wits, moving across the territory explored by Robert Johnson and Harmonica Frank, taking his spirit from the best of both men.

To use a dark old word the worried man would recognize, these two men are his familiars. Like Johnson, he is obsessed by choices he never asked for, because he sees too clearly to avoid the guilt and fear that worm out of the Bible he carries in his carpetbag; like Harmonica Frank, he is saved by his sense of humor, and he refuses to take his fears too seriously.

The combination gives us a resurrection shuffle: prophecy, cut with jive. "Been sittin' in here for so darn long, waitin' for the end to come along," he complains in "To Kingdom Come"—Judgment Day is supposed to deliver the answers he wants, but unlike some people he will meet in *Big Pink*, he can't hang around forever. He moves on, but before he is even out of the song a stranger appears to suggest that it might be wiser for him to turn back. " 'Tarred and feathered, thistles and thorns—One or the other,' he kindly warned." Well, that's not much of a choice—what else can you show me? The seeker knows the stakes are high, but he can't believe the game is fixed. He keeps looking, scared to death and full of optimism—careful to watch out for himself, once he's fallen into a trap. The devil might be anywhere—though, thanks to the touch of Harmonica Frank in the story, the devil comes on like the Headless Horseman—so the quester only wants to do the right thing; given the clutch of all-too-human doomsters that fly through the album, he'd better. "Time will tell you well," he offers hopefully, "if you truly, truly fell."

And so he dives headlong into a Gothic world of tricksters, fortune tellers, mummers, lunatics, witch doctors, cops, and lovers, struggling to find a home at the heart of that world. The music, like the character it shapes, is full of chance, uncertainty, and humor; the sound of *Big Pink* is one version of the quester's struggle, and of the world that makes his struggle interesting.

That sound is an uncanny blend of ancient folk songs, New Orleans jazz, postwar blues, white gospel groups, the Monotones, and Motown; and these sources are only a few of the obvious, picked almost at random. Al Kooper, reviewing *Big Pink* in 1968, heard the Beach Boys, the Association, the Swan Silvertones (*black* gospel), Hank Williams, the Beatles, Bob Dylan, and the Coasters. He's right, of course: *Big Pink* music is as dense as it is elusive. All those people are in it, and anyone's listening will turn up dozens more. The richness of *Big Pink* is in the Band's ability to contain endless combinations of American popular music without imitating any of them; the Band don't refer to their sources any more than we refer to George Washington when we vote, but the connection is there. The Band's music on *Big Pink* is personal, their own invention, but not merely personal; it is an unpredictable resolution of a common inheritance, something we shared in pieces. This was a new sound, but you could recognize yourself in that sound. *That* connection is what gives this music its natural authority, and makes it so exhilarating.

There are times when Richard Manuel sounds like the ghost of Johnny Ace (that sweet-voiced fifties R&B singer who died in a game of Russian roulette)—Johnny Ace condemned to haunt a gloomy radio, from which "Pledging My Love," the first posthumous rock 'n' roll hit, issues every time you spin the dial. There are times when the tone is desperate, close to the panicky feeling Marvin Gaye got on "I Heard It Through the Grapevine." But more often than not, the music is simply ominous.

This has to do, I think, with Robbie's hide-and-seek guitar, Garth Hudson's slithery organ, and the Band's collective sense of timing—which is really a sense of freedom. In most blues or rock bands, each musician has to give something up in order to make a performance work; the men in the Band played and sang with second sight, and they made no concessions at all. The beat is tough, but open; fast little riffs shoot out from behind vocals without warning; vocals twist around seemingly random chords. The parts combine to pull the listener into a labyrinth, with no idea of what might be lurking around the next turn.

When the music is most exciting—when the guitar is fighting for space in the clatter while voices yelp and wail as one man finishes another's line or spins it off in a new direction—the lyrics are blind baggage, and they emerge only in snatches. This is the finest rock 'n' roll tradition ("I learned the words to Little Richard's songs the best I could and what I couldn't figure out didn't matter," Robbie said once), but on *Big Pink* such a style also seems to link up with an older tradition: the instinct of the American artist to put his story in disguise, to tell his tale from the shadows, probably because that is where he usually finds it. Those who mean to seduce do not announce their intentions through megaphones.

On the other hand, those who are too subtle wind up plying their seductions in the mirror. If *Big Pink* wasn't good to hear from a distance, no one, certainly myself included, would ever bother to get close to it. The first virtue of the album is that the danger, promise, and craziness of the quester's adventure come across directly in the music; not only can't you understand the words, you don't have to. Garth Hudson's satanic organ playing (straight out of *Sunset Boulevard*, with Erich von Stroheim at the pipes) is the key to "Chest Fever"— the words couldn't be, no one has ever deciphered them anyway. You don't need to analyze the lyrics of "The Weight" to understand the burden Miss Fanny has dropped on the man who sings the song; as Jon Carroll has written, Levon Helm is the only drummer who can make you cry, and drums are all he needs to get across the weary, fated sense of a situation that simply cannot be escaped. We never find out who Miss Fanny is, let alone what the singer is supposed to do for her; but the music, not to mention the singing, is so full of emotion and complexity it makes "the weight"—some combination of love, debt, fear, and guilt—a perfect image of anyone's entanglement.

So the story is revealed, and concealed, in flashes, dreams, pieces of unresolved incident, rumbles of doubt exiting through a joke. Yet if the music is part of the story, it is also the landscape against which the story takes place. Blurred at the edges and unsure of its center, this America is still a wilderness—the moral, social wilderness that is left even when the natural wilderness is gone. Excited and intrigued by the place for just that reason, the worried man has to get on without maps.

He has, however, brought along a lot of time-honored, prudent advice; unfortunately, it's never equal to the imprudent dilemmas life persists in forcing upon him. "Be careful what you do, it all comes back on you," he says, poking his head out of the mad confusion of "To Kingdom Come" (recalling, perhaps, a Sunday School lesson); but a few songs later, stuck in "The Weight" and surrounded by the suddenly comic riddles first set out in Robert Johnson's "Me and the Devil Blues," this is not quite good enough. Miss Fanny has given him his job, packed him off "with her regards for everyone," and since that phrase is as mysterious to him as it is to us, all he can do is stick out his hand and hope that whoever grabs it will eventually let go.

> *I picked up my bag, I went looking for a place to hide*
> *Then I saw Carmen and the devil, walking side by side*
> *I said, Hey, Carmen, come on, let's go downtown*
> *She said, I gotta go, but my friend can stick around.**

The sound of the quester's voice tells us that his first desire is simply to be left alone—left alone by friends, enemies, neighbors, women, relatives, dogs, good and evil—but he was born with his eyes and ears wide open, and he misses nothing. He can't stop asking questions (which is not to say that there aren't times when he wouldn't mind stopping—the golden calf that chases him through "To Kingdom Come" is not his idea of a good time); with nothing but the best intentions, he stumbles into everything in his way. And because he is fascinated by everything the rest of us take for granted, he finds himself caught up with his fellow men and women, and inevitably, their troubles become his own.

Looking for salvation, he ends up trying to save others: the woman of "Caledonia Mission" (she lives hidden behind a wall, and the city has a lock on her gate), "Chest Fever" ("She drinks from the bitter cup," he declares; "I'm trying to get her to give it up"), the daughter in "Tears of Rage," and many more. Whether he succeeds is never made clear, but what is clear is that his salvation is tied to theirs.

There is Lonesome Suzie, for one; an outcast, or maybe an aging spinster, in the timeless and mythical American town in which *Big Pink* seems to be set. She dearly needs a friend, and though the quester isn't willing, he thinks, in Manuel's wonderful phrase, that maybe he can loan her one. But that, he knows, only makes him one of the confidence men his search has bound him to unmask, and so he gives in: "I guess just watching you/Has made me lonesome too."

The whole of *Big Pink*, and perhaps the best of what the Band has had to say over the years, seems to dovetail into those modest lines. The man who lives them feels like part of the crowd, and he is only too happy to fade into it; but he recognizes himself in everyone he meets, and so he is drawn out of himself and into the world. He takes his vitality from that paradox. To survive it, he can't afford to be anyone's fool; to make it worth his considerable trouble, he needs a talent for friendship that is as deep as it is broad. "Save your neck, or save your brother," he shouts a couple of years later in "The Shape I'm In," just out of jail and searching for his woman. "Looks like it's one or the other." But it's one more false choice, one more denial of the fraternity he feels in spite of himself, and he can't rest with it. Maybe that's why he sounds so desperate; even running for his life, his mind is on the people he leaves behind.

Now, taken all at once, this is a remarkable figure: the Band's recreation of an American original, the democratic man—trapped, against his better judgment, in a hilarious and scarified recreation of a very old American idea: this is a joint-stock world. A joint-stock world is open to devils and angels alike; all barriers are betrayals, and the man who sees only himself sees nothing at all.

This is the possibility the Band pursue through the tangles of the country itself. The extraordinary diversity of the place, and the claim of every man and woman to do just as they please, make a joint-stock America both necessary and hard to find; the man who looks for it has a right to be worried.

America has a lot of mottoes—common slogans, because they sum up how individuals act among themselves. "We Must All Hang Together, Or We Shall All Hang Separately" is a sentimental favorite, but the edge goes to "Don't Tread On Me"—which is to say that the man who wants to hang together had best take care not to give the good people he meets an excuse to string him up. America, as the quester finds it in his songs, is not a very friendly place. It is suspicious of itself. Most people no longer even know that they have brothers to save, and if they do, "brother" means men, but not women; the young, but not the old; blues singers, but not country singers; Northerners, but not Southerners; whites, but not blacks; or a general vice versa. The man who tells this story becomes who he is, the one who reaches out, because he responds so deeply to the yearning for unity and affection that these facts hide. Perhaps because he comes from outside, he can see the country whole, just as those who have always lived there see it only in pieces. His job, as in "The Weight," no longer a matter of isolated predicament but of vocation, is to drag that affection out into the open, even if it comes hard, as his did.

The song for that is "We Can Talk About It Now," a wonderful

Richard Manuel tune that sounds like the best merry-go-round in the world. Full of exultation, exhortation, smiles, and complaints, it is the song of a man who has gone far enough to have become a part of what he sings about. "It's safe now," he says, "to take a backward glance."

> *It seems to me, we've been holding something*
> *Underneath our tongues*
> *I'm afraid if you ever got a pat on the back*
> *It would likely burst your lungs*
> *Whoa—stop me, if I should sound*
> *Kinda down in the mouth*
> *But I'd rather be burned in Canada*
> *Than to freeze here in the south!**

If his quest has taught him anything, it is that if he wants to find a home in this country he will have to make it himself, and that means breaking through to the warmth others hide, just as Lonesome Suzie broke through to him. The pure joy of the music unveils the depth of emotion that's his to win; and that must have been the treasure he was after from the beginning, whether he knew it or not. He had to learn, in John Barth's line, that the key to the treasure is the treasure—that to be free is not to get what you want or to settle for what you've got, but to begin to know what you want and to feel strong enough to go after it. So now, out of the claustrophobia of *Big Pink*, he has a glimpse of what he wants. For a moment, to say yes is to say everything.

> *We can talk about it now*
> *It's the same old riddle, always starts from the middle*
> *I'd fix it but I don't know how*
> *Well, we could try to reason*
> *But you might think it's treason*
> *One voice for all*
> *Echoing around the hall,* ECHOING, *echoing around the hall!**

The song is loose and rangy, and the song has plenty of room in it: room for doubt, and room for doubt to turn into love without any explanation at all; room for arguments interrupted by a bottle, room for friends and strangers, room for escape and room for homecoming.

For its moment, the song—a free and friendly conversation between the men in the Band and anyone who might care to listen—is that one voice.

The song creates, out of words and music, a big, open, undeniable image of what the country could sound like at its best, of what it could feel like. One good burst of rock 'n' roll blows the trail clean, and the people our man has seen and the places he has been look brand-new.

"Dontcha see," he shouts, in an extraordinary flash of vision, that seems to reveal the secret America holds, even as it hints at deeper secrets, "there's no need to slave."

"The whip," he sings, "is in the grave."

THIS RIGHTEOUS LAND

Those lines, I think, deserve a pause—there is no bottom to them. Nothing I know captures with such mystery and clarity the circle traced by American optimism, and by the dread that optimism leaves behind and inevitably meets again. You couldn't ask for a more perfect statement of the conviction that America is blessed, or of the lingering suspicion that it is cursed. When the two ideas come together—in a story, a voice, or a group—all things seem possible. The lines touch both sides of the country's soul at once; the tension they create can push out the limits of what an artist can accomplish, for just so long as the spirit of the lines can support their contradictions. By contradictions I mean that a paradise is made out of a line that turns on the image of a whip; by spirit I mean the joy one feels when Richard Manuel shoots the line across Levon's drums—and the way Levon sounds like a man calling a town meeting to order with a gavel in each hand.

When the spirit fades, those lines will contract, and trap the man who sings them. But until then, what they bring is freedom, and the space to use it. The result is *The Band*.

That second album—arriving in 1969, soon after the group went out on the road on their own for the first time since Levon and the Hawks broke up—is the map *Big Pink*'s quester was missing. The new songs roll right over the surface of American life, proof of how magnificent that surface can be.

Turn the sound up, and the music rocks like "Blue Suede Shoes";

keep it quiet, and it sounds as folksy as an old Charlie Poole 78. The good eye of the last record is still working, but instead of probing the dark for phantoms, there is a loving feel for detail, for nuance. With its warm, happy vocals, and an irresistible snapping rhythm square in the middle of almost every tune, *The Band* is the testament of a man who has come up from a netherworld for a breath of air, a man who can now afford to have himself a good, long look around.

The worried man is a settler now, here to stay, complete with wife and kids, and the album opens with his wife holding a gun on him. As he pleads and jokes with her, trying to explain himself (No matter what you think, honey, I didn't do it), he is drawn back to the days when all he wanted was a place to come home to. He remembers his hard times, his fears, how close he came to giving up the ghost; he thinks he just may have to hit the road again if she doesn't put that gun away. By the time his reverie is finished the fight is over—still, he wouldn't mind knowing where she hid the pistol. . . .

The song is called "Across the Great Divide," an appropriate beginning for an album Robbie once said the Band could have called *America*—might as well kick it off right there where the water runs both ways. But there is more to it than that.

The Band gives author's credit to the land because while we usually read our own meanings into the landscape—when we don't miss it altogether—they know that at our best we live and speak according to the metaphors of the land. The land—the image of a place like "The Great Divide," the simple fact that there is such a phenomenon—attracts the Band. The symbol seems full of meaning— the Great Divide is where the two sides of the country separate, but it is also where the two sides meet. If we look into this double metaphor, we can understand the ambitions of *The Band* clearly. That first song and those that follow are meant to cross the great divide between men and women; between the past and the present; between the country and the city; between the North and the South; between the Band and their new audience. The worried man steps back, once he has shown up to play the theme song: he wants to celebrate the country he has discovered, and he celebrates by letting the country speak for itself, in as many voices as can be crammed onto a twelve-inch disc. At home here now, the man from *Big Pink* can sit back and listen with the rest of us.

The songs, mostly by Robbie, are classics now; "Up on Cripple Creek," "Rag Mama Rag," "The Night They Drove Old Dixie Down," "King Harvest (Has Surely Come)" made up the heart of the Band's stage show for years. What they say was clear the moment they were released, and I have nothing to add to that. Their power, though, is too great to take for granted.

The songs were made to bring to life the fragments of experience, legend, and artifact every American has inherited as the legacy of a mythical past. The songs have little to do with chronology; most describe events that could be taking place right now, but most of those events had taken on their color before any of us was born. There is a conviction here that every way of life practiced in America from the time of the Revolution on down still matters—not as nostalgia, but as the necessity of someone's daily life—and the music, though it never bends to any era, never tries for any quaint support of a theme, seems as if it would sound as right to a gang of beaver trappers as it does to us. There is no feeling of being dragged back into the past for a history lesson; if anything, the past catches up with us. Robbie put his stories on the surface, but they hit home because they draw the traces of that legacy out of each of us, bringing them to the surface of our own lives.

"The Night They Drove Old Dixie Down," for one—written for Levon, who sings it—is not so much a song about the Civil War as it is about the way each American carries a version of that event within himself. In this case it is a man named Virgil Kane, who makes no claim to speak for anyone else; but something in his tone demands that everyone listen.

In a few short verses, we learn a lot about him. He is a poor white farmer from the Confederate side of Tennessee, probably not more than twenty years old, a survivor of the attacks made by General Stoneman's cavalry on the Danville train he defended. With the war over, a glimpse of Robert E. Lee is worth as much to him as the memory of his brother, who died fighting for the sense of place Virgil Kane's war was all about. He wants us to understand that the war has cost him almost everything he has.

It is hard for me to comprehend how any Northerner, raised on a very different war than Virgil Kane's, could listen to this song without finding himself changed. You can't get out from under the singer's truth—not the whole truth, simply *his* truth—and the little autobiography closes the gap between us. The performance leaves behind a feeling that for all our oppositions, every American still shares this old event; because to this day none of us has escaped its impact, what we share is an ability to respond to a story like this one.

The scope of the album, words and music, is astonishing. In "King Harvest," probably Robbie's greatest song, we meet a man who might be Virgil Kane's grandson—or our contemporary, you can't tell. He works that same farm, but it fails and sends him into the bitter mills of the New South; when times are slow the mills shut down, and he runs into the arms of a union, hoping for one last chance. Yet wherever he is driven, he carries his roots with him like a conscience. He cannot escape the feel of the land any more than we can escape its myth.

"King Harvest" is the last number on the album; like "Dixie" or the desolate "Whispering Pines" (one of Richard Manuel's two contributions), the song is optimistic only because it is so full of desire. It goes against the usual playful, rocking grain of *The Band*, giving the music the tension it must have if it is to work as a version of our own roots, of our own conscience.

The distance between those songs of struggle is marked by a set of easy, honest affirmations that can be summed up in a dozen lines, but perhaps best by this one: "Life has been so good to us all." Jawbone, the Band's unregenerate thief, would say yes to that; certainly the trucker and his semipro girlfriend down in Lake Charles would, along with the little boy and his grandfather in "When You Awake" and the tired sailors of "Rockin' Chair." Even the people scrambling into the storm cellar in "Look Out Cleveland" and the lover stuck with a woman who only wants to dance would show up to sign that pledge. The man who sings "King Harvest" is alone, and he probably could not agree.

With that last reservation ahead of us we ride down the Mississippi, out to California, through the Midwest to Virginia, back again to Canada. We listen to fiddles, what sounds like an amplified jew's-harp, a rock 'n' roll band, laughing horns, good guitar, yodels, sniggers, snorts, and moans; along with the people we meet we take satisfaction in whiskey, in the grinning joys of miscegenation, in Garth Hudson's mad piano, trickling through the fast steps of "Rag Mama Rag." From song to song paradise means good times—and good times are where you find them.

Up on Cripple Creek she sends me
If I spring a leak, she mends me

I don't have to speak, she defends me
A drunkard's dream if I ever did see one!*

Again and again, the music creates that moment of shared recognition first confirmed in "Dixie"—the songs catch it in sex, in work, in failure, in the weather, in the choice of an instrument, in names lifted from half-forgotten Westerns, in the emotion of a vocal, in a memory of family life. The shifts between the songs finally let us understand that the man who sings "King Harvest" wants nothing more from his life than to sing a song like "Rag Mama Rag"; we understand that the voice of "Rag Mama Rag" is real because it has been shaped by the terrors of "King Harvest," and knows a chance to dance them away for what it's worth.

The album tells no lies. It touches the size and the age of the country, takes in its fabulous multiplicity, but that repeated moment links us to each part of the story even as it knits the songs into one.

For as long as that moment lasts, the story seems complete. Every character, every place, every event in the music looms up at once. Crossing the great divide, the Band left community in their wake.

EVEN STRANGER BLUES

The problem with community, as the Band was to discover when they finally followed their records into the country, is that you have to live in it. They had, in fact, made those first two albums from a distance—isolated in the musicians' haven of Bearsville/Woodstock and walled off from the crowd by their manager, Albert Grossman. *Big Pink* had been out for almost a year and *The Band* was in the can when the group arrived in San Francisco to meet their audience for the first time—people had gathered from all over the West to celebrate *them*.

No matter how many rave record reviews the Band might have read, until they stepped onto a stage there was no way they could have understood how fierce and intense the expectations of their audience would be. Their music had cut even more deeply than they could have hoped—to many, *Big Pink* was one of the memorable events of their lives, and the stakes of that first night were as high as they could be.

After hours of delays, excuses, promises, and interminable tuning up, the Band came on with Robbie dazed and sick, dragging along a hypnotist to cure him. The hypnotist stood on the stage conjuring up spells while the Band fell apart before the crowd's very eyes. They struggled through a handful of weak, ragged tunes, and then they turned and ran. The crowd's hopeful energy had been suspended between disappointment and desire, and it collapsed into fury. The Band's first concert ended with an outpouring of anger and rage unlike anything I have ever seen at a rock 'n' roll show.

Perhaps the crowd's reaction was vicious, but it was certainly real—a good measure of how much the Band had to live up to. They had it all the next night, playing on and on with a wild, raucous delight that finally climaxed with Little Richard's "Slippin' and Slidin'," a number that the five had likely been playing—in afterschool pick-up bands, as the Hawks, up in Woodstock—since it came out in 1956. But we had loved the song as long as the Band had, and as Richard Manuel tossed off the unmistakable first notes of the tune the crowd began to dance and cheer. This was a common celebration now: as we made the old song new, what seemed most remarkable was the recognition that our links to the Band had been forged so long ago, and that our time together was just beginning.

Still, I think something of that initial disaster stayed with the Band. They made a number of cross-country tours after that, but if they never played as badly as they did that first night, they never played with the freedom of the show that followed either. Performing involved all the psychic risks they had faced and dodged in the adventures of *Big Pink*; performing also demanded new links, no matter how tenuous, to the America their audience lived in, which was very different from their own—a scary place, violent with blocked hopes and bad dreams, a place where roots were not enough, where a good concert by the Band was like shelter in the storm, a means to strength and pleasure. And they had aimed for more than that.

Sometimes, though, there was less. The Band began to hedge their bets. They called their next album *Stage Fright*, and both the new songs and the concerts of the time proved they meant it. *Stage Fright* was an album of doubt, guilt, disenchantment, and false optimism. The past no longer served them—the songs seemed trapped in the present, a jumble of desperation that was at once personal and social. The music at its best was still special, but in every sense, the kind of unity that had given force to those first two albums, and to the idea of the Band itself, was missing. Now, instead of hearing music that could not really be broken down, one picked at parts for satisfaction—Robbie's guitar and Garth's organ on "The Shape I'm In," Rick Danko's bass and fiddle on "Daniel and the Sacred Harp." Robbie had completely taken over the songwriting; the surprises of four voices wrestling for a lyric were abandoned for solo vocals. There was an edge of separation in the music: the worried man was back, drawing the shade on his window as the police wailed by in one tune, picked up for vagrancy himself in another, spinning a hilarious but ultimately unsettling tale of sin and damnation in a third. He still reaches out to others—*he* needs shelter now—but no one is there.

Facing an audience, the Band hid in their arrangements. The arrangements were tight, disciplined, precise; the open spirit of their music contracted. They were known to spend more time on testing the sound system than they did playing, but often they didn't play loud enough to come across. They presented perfect replicas of their records—to the point where Rick Danko would back off from the mike at the end of "When You Awake," imitating the studio fade— the surest way to please an audience without really moving it.

From the days when they had first paid out their money to hear Howlin' Wolf, there had been a side to the Band that was anarchic, risky, virtually out of control, and when they caught that spirit, they could take it farther than anyone else. Sometimes Robbie made his guitar sound like a musical equivalent of Jim Brown's big scene in *The Dirty Dozen*—that moment when he takes off on a broken-field run around a Nazi chateau, dropping a hand grenade down an air shaft every ten yards and grinning madly as explosions leap up behind him in sequence—but to bring such qualities into your music you have to touch such emotions in yourself. The Band saw chaos in the crowd, in the country, in the commercial pressures that were driving the five of them apart, driving at least one of them into dope and alcohol, and they stepped back.

Almost always, the numbers they had never recorded—Rick Danko's lovely country version of the Four Tops' "Loving You Is Sweeter Than Ever," or their hard rock assault on Marvin Gaye's "Baby Don't You Do It (Don't Break My Heart)"—were most vital, because you could hear them reaching for the songs and grabbing hold. But most of all they were looking for safety—they rarely cut loose, tried hard not to take chances. Their shows began to lose excitement, their music began to lose its drama, and the Band began to lose their audience.

Cahoots came out in 1971, but only the earlier songs gave any weight to the title—and the title was the best thing on the album. The songs were stiff and the music was constricted; all the humor and drive had gone. On *The Band* Robbie had breathed life into his characters in a line, and the singers made you care about them; here there were only abstractions and stereotypes, and the singers sounded as if they had no real connection to the words they were given.

The music no longer had any life of its own; it took its cues from the lyrics, and when the result wasn't flat, it was cute. "When I Paint My Masterpiece" was about an expatriate artist in Europe, so the tune featured a little Michel Legrand accordion; the utterly pointless "Shootout in Chinatown" came complete with Fu Manchu guitar, a touch so tasteless it verged on racism. The Band's ability to create a sense of place was reduced to a humorless presentation of fixed images. The failure of language made even the good ideas of the lyrics unsatisfying—made the truth sound false.

That sense of struggle and reward that bled through *Big Pink*, *The Band*, and *Stage Fright*, the balance always changing, had collapsed into a nostalgic pastoralism in which few who had felt the strength of their best songs could believe. The last cut on *Cahoots*, a tribute to the white gospel communities of the South, was as sentimental in its performance as it was honest in its intent; hearing it after the strained failures of the rest of the album, I couldn't help but think of the studio happy ending that was tacked onto Fritz Lang's *You Only Live Once*, wherein Henry Fonda, having died tragically in the last shot, suddenly ascends to heaven with a bewildered smile on his face. *Cahoots* was a commercial disaster; the Band retreated even further, playing only an occasional concert, making no tours at all.

In the last week of 1971 they arranged a special set of shows in New York, and with a horn section unlike anything ever heard in rock 'n' roll to force their music past itself, the Band broke through and said their piece once more. Out of those nights came a magnificent live album, *Rock of Ages*—a claim that their music was meant to last, and certainly the best of it will. But as I listened to the live records when they were released in 1972—so full of playfulness and bite, blazing with soul and love—I was struck by how long it had been since the Band had put out a single new song that mattered.

The Band's vision of the country had darkened as they moved farther apart. If they were to keep the group they had made, they could not ask too much of it. The music seemed to say that they had lost their trust in the country, in themselves, and in each other—that they had to fight harder than they were able to touch the spirit that had made their work worth doing in the first place. Like most good American artists, and like their worried man, they had been romantics, but not fools; when the romance began to go, their talent for asking the right questions went with it. They still looked for community, but like many who cannot find it, they fell back into an even deeper privacy than they started out with. Because their dreams were too real and too beautiful to give up, they felt a sense of guilt; their withdrawal—a separation from the country, from their audience, and from each other—was a betrayal of those dreams.

They had closed out *Stage Fright* with a queer song that had all the warmth of "The Man Who Corrupted Hadleyburg," which it resembled: "The Rumor." The old quester who sings it is afraid now, and his voice is muted—no one else speaks at all. He sings to a crowd he has long since joined, but the bonds between them—of loyalty, affection, fascination—have faded away. When the singer first came to the country, he found it poisoned by suspicion and shame; he meant to change it, but instead, the country changed him.

Someone in the crowd has been harmed: "His name abused, his privacy refused." Why he has been harmed is not spelled out, probably no one really knows, and the mystery deepens the malevolence of the scene. "Feel the good," the seeker calls out, "hang down your heads/ Until the fog rolls away—Let it roll away." He means it, but the words no longer mean what they might have, because the community can never be what it was. "He can forgive—and you can regret—but he can never, never forget." Not even the victim is known—the victim might be anyone, as might be the villain.

When the worried man looks into the crowd, as he must, for he has nowhere else to go, the people he sees will seem different to him, as he will to them. The whip will hang over them all.

Perhaps. The last song on *Rock of Ages* was the old Chuck Willis/ Jerry Lee Lewis hit, "(I Don't Want To) Hang Up My Rock and Roll Shoes," and it capped a New Year's Eve night when the Band and their fans had put themselves back in touch with each other. But as the Band left the stage, Robbie says, they felt a common sense of depression—no, they didn't wanna, and they weren't gonna, but the song, like so many, was complex in its context. The Band knew that when Chuck Willis's version was on the radio, he was in the grave; that while Jerry Lee kept his rock 'n' roll shoes, he lost his rock 'n' roll audience. The song was not a curse, but it wasn't the simple affirmation they had bargained for either. It simply raised questions they could not answer, about the cheers that had ridden them off the stage; reaching for the past had forced them to think about what they had left to do.

Many months later, in the fall of 1973, an article appeared in *Playboy*, measuring Richard Manuel for a straight-jacket; at the same time, the Band released *Moondog Matinee*, a collection of some favorite oldies. Manuel had been in bad shape for a long time; he had not finished a song of his own for years, but this was his album.

He sang about giving up the bottle in "Saved," deepened his hopes with "A Change Is Gonna Come," and slowly pulled down his mask with "The Great Pretender." If that last had been more than a little overblown when the Platters first sang it in 1955, one would have thought that after nearly twenty years there would be nothing left of the song but nostalgia. Manuel transformed it into the truest kind of soul music; his singing made the Band's more predictable rockers sound tame by comparison.

The best of the album took the Band's tale back to its beginnings, and eased their special voice into its parts. "Third Man Theme," their little instrumental, had a quiet affection in its modesty and humor—the music asked for good times, perhaps for less than before, perhaps not. The finest cut of all, Manuel's gentle, utterly despairing version of Bobby Bland's "Share Your Love," was as lonesome a song as any can be. As he sang, surrounded again by the old simpatico of the Band, it seemed like the last word of that worried man. Share your love with me, share your love with me—what had he ever said but that, what else had anyone ever said to him?

THE WEIGHT

"It was a rowdy life," Robbie once recalled, thinking back over the years before *Big Pink*. "The places we played had tough audiences. They would throw things at you; they were rednecks. Fighting plays a big part in their life, you know—fighting and woman-stealing. And you fall in, you just do what the custom is. If they take off their shoes, you take off your shoes.

"We were all so young—we were sixteen, seventeen years old at the time. We played in joints. That's what they were. Some of it was great and some of it was scary and some of it was horrible, and some of it was very valuable to us, to this day.

"You see—instead of throwing a knapsack over your back and getting out on the highway, to learn about life, we were able to do it together. We were protected by one another. We were secured by one another."

Those are fine words. They tell us that the Band sought in America what they found among themselves: that their music and their stories were not only a version of America, but a reflection of their own unity. All those years on the road had given them their values; in a sense, community was only a projection of comradeship.

The group was its own joint-stock world, but it could not survive the honest demands of the greater joint-stock world that was the country itself. Every song on the first two albums had been written before the Band had played a single show in public; once they began to tour, the group, as men who contributed what was special about themselves to something bigger than any of them, began to fall apart. Richard Manuel never wrote another song; the singers stopped calling out to one another across the verses; the uncanny sense of timing that had made the Band's early music move disappeared altogether. As the Band stepped back from their audience, you could feel the friendship go out of their sound.

In order to save the group, Robbie took it over. He took it over as lyricist, manager, strategist, savant, visionary, and spokesman. No one else in the Band ever gave an interview; after a time, the rock press began to celebrate Robbie as a genius and the Band as his foil, and the other members were not asked to talk. And yet, because the group was no longer truly whole, Robbie could not really draw on it; since his links to the country and to his audience were no longer strong, he could no longer see the country or his audience clearly. *Moondog Matinee*, for all of its satisfactions, had the melancholy tinge of a reunion—a feeling that became all the more unsettling when one realized the five men saw each other all the time.

Friendship, in the end, is not community, though it was the Band's sense of friendship that let them embody community—in their stories, in their music, in their ambitions. Friendship can be the means to community. But if one does not live in the world, then one will feed off the small world of friendship until there is nothing left.

When I went up to Woodstock to talk to Robbie late in 1972, he was ready to leave. The Band had been hiding out there for years, their houses squirreled off in the Catskills; I had never seen that part of the country before, and I understood how one could read its signs as a promise of peace of mind. Woodstock itself looked like the usual American idea of community—quaint, tasteful, small, homogeneous—but in fact it was more like a private club, inhabited by musicians, dope dealers, artists, hangers-on. The town made me nervous; it seemed like a closed, smug, selfish place.

I asked Robbie about his favorite cities. Montreal and New Orleans, he said, and he began to talk about the cultural confusion that he thought gave those cities their spirit—the mix of languages, customs, religions, music, food, architecture, politics. You could spend your whole life in one of those cities and be surprised every day. He had a house in Montreal—that was his wife Dominique's hometown—and they were going back. What that would mean for the future of the Band I didn't ask; the pastoral traps of Woodstock had already taken too much of the soul out of the group. That they had protected each other years ago was only half of their best music—the other half came from what they had protected themselves against: those rowdy audiences, scattered all over the country in dance halls and bars. "They take off their shoes, you take off your shoes"—in those days, the Band could not afford to keep their distance. They learned to lean on each other and to listen to the crowd; that, in a queer way, brought their commitment to friendship and their feel for community together.

Before I left Woodstock I sat and talked for a long time with Dominique Robertson. She told me about the struggles of the Quebec Separatist movement and what that fight meant to her, that she had tried to find someone to talk to when Trudeau imposed a terror on the people after Separatists kidnapped a government official, that no one in Woodstock had any idea there really was a world different from their own. There's nothing here but dope, music, and beauty, she said; if you're a woman, and you don't use dope and you don't make music, there's nothing here at all.

The Band did leave; they moved to Los Angeles, and early in 1974 they set out on a grand tour with Bob Dylan. With Dylan, they were once again the best rock 'n' roll band in the world; their own sets had all the old limits, and not a song was less than four years old. Still, there was a joy in their faces as they played that I had not seen since that great night in San Francisco.

America is a dangerous place, and to find community demands as much as any of us can give. But if America is dangerous, its little utopias, asking nothing, promising safety, are usually worse. "Look at this," Dominique said, taking in her house, the trees, the mountains. "It's beautiful. It's everything people ought to want, and I hate it." Then she grinned. " 'This country life is killin' me,' " she sang, turning a song we had both heard too many times on its head. "I gotta find my way back to the city, and get some corruption in my lungs."

SLY STONE
The Myth of Staggerlee

I named my son Malik Nkrumah Staggerlee Seale. Right on, huh? Beautiful name, right? He's named after his brother on the block, like all his brothers and sisters off the block. Stagger*lee*.

Staggerlee is Malcom X before he became politically conscious. *Livin' in the hoodlum world*.

You'll find out. Huey had a lot of Staggerlee qualities. I guess I lived a little bit of Staggerlee's life too, here and there. That's where it's at. You move yourself up from a lower level to a higher level. And at one time brother Eldridge was on the block. He was Staggerlee.

"Staggerlee shot Billy . . ." Billy the *Lion*. "Staggerlee had a sawed-off shotgun and a Model A Ford and he owed money on that as well; his woman kicked him out in the cold 'cause she said his love was growin' old. Staggerlee took a walk down *Ramparts Street*, down where all them baaad son-of-a-guns meet. By the Bucket o' *Bluuuuuud*." You know, the main drag? That's from Louisiana, Ramparts Street? Yeah, this is where Staggerlee's history is. Staggerlee is all the shootouts that went on between gamblers, and cats fightin' over women—the black community.

Staggerlee shot Billy, you know? "Shot that poor boy dead." Two black brothers fightin' each other. Billy the Lion was bad too. "Staggerlee walked into a bar and ordered . . . just to get a bite to eat. And he wound up with a glass of muddy water and a piece of rotten meat. He asked the bartender, did he know who he was? And the bartender says, 'I heard o' you across the way,' he says, 'but I serve *bad* son-of-a-guns *three* times a day.' " *Everybody's* bad, you see?

Something else, huh? That's *life*. And all the little Staggerlees, a *lot of 'em*! Millions of 'em, know what I mean?

And so I named that brother, my little boy, Staggerlee, because . . . that's what his *name* is.

> **BOBBY SEALE**, from a jailhouse
> interview with Francisco Newman, 1970.

STAGGERLEE

Somewhere, sometime, a murder took place: a man called Stack-a-lee—or Stacker Lee, Stagolee, or Staggerlee—shot a man called Billy Lyons—or Billy the Lion, or Billy the Liar. It is a story that black America has never tired of hearing and never stopped living out, like whites with their Westerns. Locked in the images of a thousand versions of the tale is an archetype that speaks to fantasies of casual violence and violent sex, lust and hatred, ease and mastery, a fantasy of style and steppin' high. At a deeper level it is a fantasy of no-limits for a people who live within a labyrinth of limits every day of their lives, and who can transgress them only among themselves. It is both a portrait of that tough and vital character that everyone would like to be, and just another pointless, tawdry dance of death.

Billy died for a five-dollar Stetson hat; because he beat Staggerlee in a card game, or a crap game; because Stack was cheating and Billy was fool enough to call him on it. It happened in Memphis around the turn of the century, in New Orleans in the twenties, in St. Louis in the 1880s. The style of the killing matters, though: Staggerlee shot Billy, in the words of a Johnny Cash song, just to watch him die.

Sometimes it was a cautionary tale, as in Mississippi John Hurt's version, recorded in 1929.

> *Po-lice officer, how can it be*
> *You can 'rest everybody, but cru-el Stagolee*
> *That bad man, Oh, cru-el Stagolee*

Billy the Lion tol' Stagolee
Please don't take my life
I got two little babes, and a darlin' lovely wife
That bad man, Oh, cruel Stagolee

What I care about your two little babes
Your darlin' lovely wife
You done stole my Stetson hat
I'm bound to take your life
That bad man, Oh, cruel Stagolee

Boom-boom, boom-boom, went a .44
Well, when I spied ol' Billy the Lion
He was lyin' on the floor
That bad man, Oh, cruel Stagolee

Gentlemens of the jury, what you think of that
Stagolee shot Billy the Lion 'bout a five-dollar Stetson hat
That bad man, Oh, cruel Stagolee

If that was something like the original idea of the story, it didn't hold up very long. Usually, no white sheriff had the nerve to take Stack on, and he got away. When he didn't—when he was caught and hung—it was only for a chance to beat the devil. The song carried Staggerlee down to hell, where he took over the place and made it into a black man's paradise.

Innocent Billy was no longer seen as a helpless victim, but as a hapless mark. Staggerlee's secret admirers came out of the woodwork; the women (all dressed in red) flocked to his funeral (it was the best money could buy). Stagolee was a winner. "GO!" shouted Lloyd Price, caught up in the legend. "GO! GO! Stagger Lee!"

Nobody's fool, nobody's man, tougher than the devil and out of God's reach—to those who followed his story and thus became a part of it, Stack-o-Lee was ultimately a stone-tough image of a free man.

In the blues, Stack changed names, but little else. He was the Crawling Kingsnake; Tommy Johnson pouring Sterno down his throat, singing, "Canned heat, canned heat is killing me"; Muddy Waters' cool and elemental Rollin' Stone; Chuck Berry's Brown-Eyed Handsome Man; Bo Diddley with a tombstone hand and a graveyard mind; Wilson Pickett's Midnight Mover; Mick Jagger's Midnight Rambler.

Stack rode free as the Back Door Man in the deadly electric blues of Howlin' Wolf (" 'Cuse me for murder/First degree/Judge's wife cried, Let the man go free!/*I am* . . ."), and gave up the ghost, proud never to rest easy, in "Going Down Slow." Stagolee was a secret, buried deep in the heart as well as ruling the streets: in Bobby Marchan's "There Is Something on Your Mind," Stackerlee crawled out of a man who only wanted love and pulled the trigger that turned love into death. When the civil rights movement got tough, he took over. And Staggerlee would come roaring back on the screen in the seventies, as Slaughter, Sweet Sweetback, Superfly.

"Stagger Lee shot Billy. . . ." The line echoes from Lloyd Price's rock 'n' roll hit through fifty years of black culture, passing, on its way back to its hidden source, thousands and thousands of Staggerlees and Billys. There is an echo for Jimi Hendrix, a star at twenty-four and dead at twenty-seven; for Sly Stone, "not," as was said of Bob Dylan once, "burning his candle at both ends, but using a blow torch on the middle"; for young men dead in alleys or cold in the city morgue; for a million busted liquor stores and a million angry rapes. Stack and Billy merge into a figure innocent on one level and guilty on another: into Robert Johnson, living from town to town and woman to woman, driven and searching for sin and peace of mind; into junkies twisted from their last OD's; into a young George Jackson, drunk and out for easy money, or his brother Jonathan, rising years later with a gun in his hand. Look and you will see King Curtis, stretched out dead in front of his house; Muhammad Ali; Rap Brown, so bad that Congress passed a law against him. Farther on are pimps like Big Red Little, Jack Johnson in a car full of white women, Sportin' Life steppin' out. It is an echo all the way back to the bullet that went through Billy and broke the bartender's glass, a timeless image of style and death.

SLY STONE

Born Sylvester Stewart in 1944, in Dallas, Sly Stone grew up in Vallejo, California, a tough and grimy polyglot city on the north end of San Francisco Bay. He picked up guitar and drums as a kid, led his own gang into the streets, and played his part in the high school race riots that were endemic in the town. He made it into a few semipro bands in the early sixties; by the time he was nineteen, in 1964, he was producing small hits by local white club bands for Autumn Records, the label owned by the baron of San Francisco Top 40, Big Daddy Tom Donahue. This put Sly right in the mainstream of Bay Area rock 'n' roll; up until 1965, the local music scene pretty much came down to Donahue's kind of radio and the big package shows he and his partner, Bobby Mitchell, booked into the Cow Palace.

There was no big money; in fact, a lot of what there was never seemed to find its way from the distributors back to the company. The music that was going to put San Francisco on the rock 'n' roll map was taking shape; it would wipe out the tight, commercial sounds Donahue and Sly were after—that is, it would make them uncool.

Sly went to radio school and got a job on KSOL, the number two black station in the area. Fast on the air, he was a hit. A brilliant, kinetic DJ, he found the straight soul format a fraud on his taste, and salted it with Bob Dylan and the Beatles. At the same time, he was pulling a band together. There were whites as well as blacks, women— who played real instruments—as well as men: "The Family."

By early 1967 the hippie bands of the Haight had the ear of the nation, and San Francisco geared up for the crunch of the Summer of Love. The first hip FM rock station, led by Larry Miller and a reformed Tom Donahue ("Should I change my name?" he once asked his new listeners. "Send in your suggestions."), was breaking the Top 40 monopoly. *Sgt. Pepper* was on the way, as was the Monterey Pop Festival. It was a genuinely exciting time.

And it was a very white scene. If the Jefferson Airplane had little to say to blacks, the fact that they and bands like them brought a white audience into the Fillmore ghetto every weekend seemed un-important, even if racial tensions were beginning to emerge in the Haight. No one knew what to say about that, so no one said anything, except that they sure dug spades.

Black music, led by Aretha Franklin, Wilson Pickett, and Sam and Dave, had hit a commercial peak and was approaching an artistic impasse, as inspiration turned into formula. Otis Redding became the white hope of the new rock 'n' roll fans, and at Monterey they would cover him with glory because he said they were all right. But six months later he was dead. A musical vacuum was opening up, and the racial contradictions of the counterculture were coming to the surface. There was no music to work out the contradictions, and no music to fill the vacuum.

It was at this point that Sly and the Family Stone emerged from the unhip white bars of Hayward and Redwood City—middle-class suburb towns—with a music they brashly called "a whole new thing," leaving behind (and picking up again on the radio) an audience of small-time boosters, bikers, college students, and the sons and daughters of transplanted Okies.

Sly had mastered the recording studio and a dozen instruments. He was tough and wily, already burned in the record business and determined never to let it happen again; a man out to build something worth the trouble it would take. He was bursting with ambition and ideas, the wildest dresser rock 'n' roll had ever seen—which is saying something—an outrageous showman whose style was a combination of Fillmore district pimp gone stone crazy and Fillmore Auditorium optimism with a point to it. A cultural politician of the first order, Sly was less interested in crossing racial and musical lines than in tearing them up.

In the manner of the very greatest rock 'n' roll, Sly and the Family Stone made music no one had ever heard before.

In moments you could catch echoes of Sam Cooke, the Beatles, a lot of jazz, and even a little surf music. Not just the singers but the whole band seemed to find much of their inspiration in a few classic rock 'n' roll songs, building off the furious vocal lines of the Silhouettes' "Get a Job," the mad desire of Maurice Williams' "Stay," and the chaos of Stevie Wonder's preteen apocalypse, "Fingertips." The band dismissed the simple, direct sound of the black music of the day, from Stax to James Brown, but took advantage of its rhythmic inventions; the Family Stone had much of the exhilaration of the white San Francisco sound, along with the open spirit that sound was already beginning to lose. And there was a keen ear for the hook lines and commercial punch crucial to the charts of any rock era.

The whole was something other than its parts, perhaps because what came across was not simply a new musical style, though there was that, but a shared attitude, a point of view: not just a brand-new talk, but the brand-new walk of young men and women on the move.

There was an enormous freedom to the band's sound. It was complex, because freedom is complex; wild and anarchic, like the wish for freedom; sympathetic, affectionate, and coherent, like the reality of freedom. And it was all celebration, all affirmation, a music of endless humor and delight, like a fantasy of freedom.

They had hits: "Dance to the Music," "Stand!," "Everyday People," "Hot Fun in the Summertime," "Thank you falettinme be mice elf Agin." A smash with black kids and white, these records had all the good feeling of the March on Washington, and the street cachet that march never had.

Sly's real triumph was that he had it both ways. Every nuance of his style, from the razzle-dazzle of his threads to the originality of his music to the explosiveness of his live performance, made it clear he was his own man. If the essence of his music was freedom, no one was more aggressively, creatively free than he. Yet there was room for everyone in the America of a band made up of blacks and whites, men and women, who sang out "different strokes for different folks" and were there on stage to show an audience just what such an idea of independence meant. Vocals were demystified: everybody sang (even Cynthia Robinson, who screeched). When the band growled out "Don't Call Me Nigger, Whitey (Don't Call Me Whitey, Nigger)," they gave pleasure by using the insults for all they were worth, and at the same time showed how deeply those insults cut.

Sly was a winner. It seemed he had not only won the race, he had made up his own rules. Driving the finest cars, sporting the most sensational clothes, making the biggest deals and the best music, he was shaping the style and ambition of black teenagers all over the country—expanding the old Staggerlee role of the biggest, baddest man on the block. Sly was Staggerlee, and the power of the role was his, but he didn't have to kill anyone to get it.

RIOT

Motown raced to absorb Sly's new music, to catch up. They tightened his aesthetic and roared back up the charts with a revamped version of the Temptations and the new Jackson 5. Sly kept up the pace, breaking the color line at Woodstock and emerging as the festival's biggest hit. In early 1970 the band cut a new single, called "Everybody Is a Star," and it was their best—a lovely, awesomely moving statement of what the band was about and what it was for. A new album was on the way, Sly told an interviewer, "the most optimistic of all."

But something went wrong. Sly began to show up late for concerts, or not at all. That caused riots, including a very bad one in Chicago. Performances, when they came off, were often erratic, angry, or uncommitted. There was no new album; there was trouble with promoters; lawsuits; rumors of the band breaking up; rumors of bad dope, gangsters, extortion, death threats. Sly's manager said his client had a split personality.

Finally, in late 1971, the new record hit the stores. There was an American flag on the cover (flowers instead of stars) and happy pictures all over the rest of it (with odd, somber shots of Lincoln and the Gettysburg Address here and there). The album was called *There's a riot goin' on*, and the title cut was blank.

The record was no fun. It was slow, hard to hear, and it didn't celebrate anything. It was not groovy. In fact, it was distinctly unpleasant, unnerving. Many people didn't like it, wrote it off as a junkie bummer. If Robert Johnson were alive today there would be someone around to yell "Boogie!" at him.

There's a riot goin' on was an exploration of and a pronouncement on the state of the nation, Sly's career, his audience, black music, black politics, and a white world. Emerging out of a pervasive sense, at once public and personal, that the good ideas of the sixties had gone to their limits, turned back upon themselves, and produced evil where only good was expected, the album began where "Everybody Is a Star" left off, and it asked: So what?

The album contained, in a matrix of parody and vicious self-criticism, virtually all the images and slogans Sly had given to his audience. The new music called all the old music and the reasons for claiming it into question. Like *Bonnie and Clyde*, which angered critics in much the same way, *Riot* was, and is, a rough, disturbing work that can be ignored, dismissed, but never smoothed over.

Riot joined other pop reversals that confused and divided audiences and created new ones, pop acts that risked the destruction of the artist's audience. It was Sly's equivalent of Van Morrison's *Blowin' Your Mind*, his first solo album, where Van reached for the grotesque because it seemed the only rational description of everyday life; of Dylan's *John Wesley Harding*, in that Sly was escaping his own pop past and denying its value; of John Lennon's screaming break with the Beatles, though Sly worked with much greater sophistication and intelligence. Instead of merely orchestrating his confessions, Sly transformed them into a devastating work of art that deeply challenged anyone who ever claimed to be a part of his audience, a piece of music that challenges most of the assumptions of rock 'n' roll itself.

In an age when politics succeeds by confusing and obscuring matters of life and death, the strongest artists must claim those things as their own and act them out. Not many will ever have the nerve or the vision to do it, but at least for as long as it took to make *Riot*, Sly did.

Riot begins with a slow, stuttering beat, a chanting parody of "Stand!" As Sly comes in, wailing and groaning, half-satisfied, half-desperate, the question that comes through is whether it is worth standing up at all, or possible even if it is worth it. In another world, the man who sings this song did not merely "control the decisions that affected his life," to use a phrase from the decade this album left behind, he made them; now the words "control" and "decision" have lost their meaning. Tense, nervous, creepy, the song careens to an end, and it sets the tone. What follows is an expertly crafted and brilliantly performed review of folly, failure, betrayal, and disintegration—the confession of a man, speaking for more than himself, who has been trapped by limits whose existence he once would not even admit to, let alone respect: trapped by dope; by the weakness behind a world based on style; by the repression that sent black men and women into hiding, into exile, into the morgue; by the flimsiness of the rewards a white society has offered him. A testament to oppression, the music is, on first listening, itself oppressive.

The songs seem to wander, to show up and disappear, ghostly, with no highs or lows. At their kindest, they are simply ironic. Some, like "Africa Talks to You 'The Asphalt Jungle,' " are morbid: chased into hiding by the band, Sly shouts back, "Timmmmmmberrr!" and the guitar mocks him into silence. "Brave and Strong" pleads for survival, but hints that only dope will get it.

Two tracks were released as singles—"Family Affair" and "Runnin' Away"—both were hits, and both had a deceptively easy movement. But the first was about finding your way back to mother and a marriage falling to pieces, and the second used a saucy female chorus to drive nails into a fool.

The album found its end with "Thank you for talkin' to me Africa," a reversal of "Thank you falettinme be mice elf Agin." There is no vocal music in rock 'n' roll to match it; the voices creep in and out of the instruments, cutting out in the middle of a line, messages from limbo, golem-talk. "I'm a-dyin, I'm a-dyin," you can hear Sly wailing, and the only way to disbelieve is to stop listening. The song gathers up all the devastation of the rest of the album and slowly drives it home, grinds it in, and fades out.

This music defines the world of the Staggerlee who does not get away, and who finds hell as advertised. There is an enormous reality to the music: a slow, level sense of getting by. It is Muzak with its finger on the trigger; the essence of the rhythms James Brown has explored without the compensations of Brown's showmanship or his badass lyrics. It is a reality of day-to-day sameness and an absence of variety—like prison—that requires, if one is to endure it, either a deadening of all the senses, or a preternatural sharpening of them, so that the smallest change of mood or event can be seized on as representing something novel or meaningful.

In this sense, and only at the farthest margin, the music is part of the way out of the disaster it affirms. If you listen, you get sharper, and you begin to hear what the band is hearing; every bass line or vocal nuance eventually takes on great force. The disaster gains an emotional complexity, and you enter it. Finally, *Riot* bears the same relationship to most music as George Jackson's *Soledad Brother* does to *Confidential*. The second is easier to get into, but nothing is there.

Stand!, the brilliant album that preceded *Riot* (and literally turned black music inside out with its flash and innovation), had all the drive and machinery of a big semi-truck; listening to it put you in the driver's seat, made you feel like you owned the road. *Riot* is about getting off the truck. The mood is one of standing still; of performing every act with the care of one who is not sure his mind and his body will quite connect; of falling apart; of running, looking back, realizing you can be caught.

> *Lookin' at the devil,*
> *Grinnin' at his gun.*
> *Fingers start shakin',*
> *I begin to run.*
>
> *Bullets start chasin',*
> *I begin to stop.*
> *We begin to wrestle,*
> *I was on the top.*

"Thank you for talkin' to me Africa"

When the song was released a year earlier as "Thank you falettinme be mice elf Agin," it had a snappy rhythm. It was a winner's song, and neither the music nor the vocals left any doubt as to who was going to stay on top. On *Riot* the song comes slowly, emphasizing the thud of the bass guitar. The words are buried in a slurred half-chant; when Sly sings, "Thank you falettinme be mice elf Agin," the contempt in his voice is inescapable.

Notice how the song reads. The words Sly wrote for *Riot* are some of the most imaginative and forceful in all of rock 'n' roll. The images are perfectly developed; the songs achieve a tense and eerie balance, as each element of the music seems to pull more than its own weight. Not one image, not one note, is wasted. Nothing is gratuitous.

One song, "Poet," was called pretentious, because it said such things as, "I'm a songwriter, oh yeh a poet." The number is intentionally crude, but in the end such a song is pretentious only if it is false. And although for rock 'n' roll the terms themselves are probably false, the words of the songs on this album are better "poetry" than anything the "rock poets" have written. The rock poets are all of them white, of course, because the rock 'n' roll audience—and rock critics—often think in neat racial categories, and "black" does not fit into the "poetry" category. When Bob Dylan quipped that Smokey Robinson was America's greatest poet, most people thought that was some kind of joke.

Of all the nonsense that has been written about the poetry of Neil Young, Paul Simon, or even Bob Dylan, no one has ever said anything about Jimi Hendrix's "Little Wing." The poetry question, especially when we are dealing with a song, has to do with how a writer uses language—and his music will be part of his language—to make words do things they ordinarily do not do, with how he tests the limits of language and alters and extends the conventional impact of images, or rescues resources of language that we have lost or destroyed. The music on *Riot* mostly flattens out what Sly wrote, hiding it, telling the truth, but not quite out loud. The words peek out, and only occasionally do they hit you in the face.

> *Lookin' at the devil,*
> *Grinnin' at his gun.*
> *Fingers start shakin',*
> *I begin to run.*
>
> *Bullets start chasin',*
> *I begin to stop.*

The poetry of those lines is the use of the words "start" and "begin," which slow the usual pace of the violent images Sly is presenting. The eye is working here, taking in the scene from the edge of action; the description is minimal and the economy is absolute. The eye turns and the listener, or the reader, is given only a vague sense of physical motion, a whole body aware of itself with the precision of the eye in the first three lines. You feel the slowing down, the endless, instantaneous decisions and hesitations involved in turning to face the gun again. It all moves in pieces, and you are in the song, in the riot, breathing its risk.

Sly saw a band as the means by which each member finds his or her own voice; while he is the source of vision, the emotion of every singer, his included, has been authentic because that vision is shared. I think this is so because Sly's vision, whether one of affirmation, as it was in the sixties, or negation, as it is on *Riot*, is always an attempt at liberation.

It is Sly's musical authority that gives his singers freedom, that builds a home where freedom seems worth acting out. The singing on the Family's records—complex, personal, and unpredictable—really was something new. As opposed to the Temptations or the Jackson 5, whose records were not inspired by Sly's sound so much as they formalized it (just as earlier Motown imposed order on the risky spontaneity of gospel music), what you hear in Sly's music are a number of individuals who have banded together because that is the way they can best express themselves *as* individuals. It's the freedom of the street, not the church.

This was made explicit in "Everybody Is a Star." That meant not that everyone lives in the spotlight, but that every man and woman finds moments of visibility appropriate to what he or she has to give. On *Riot* Sly took this aesthetic—of the group that sings like a band plays—away from the context of celebration, which had seemed not only appropriate but necessary, and made it the means to a dramatization of events and moods that are bitter, mocking, and scary. Voices stretch words until they are drained of their ordinary meanings, just as the guitars, drums, bass, horns, and organ reduce the sensational clichés of the earlier music to bone. The superstar clothes are removed, piece by piece, and what is left, in a weird and modern way, is the blues.

The equality is still there: no one is a star.

With "Family Affair," so direct in its musical impact and so elusive in its meanings, Sly comes close to a conventional lead vocal, but here he needs the isolation of the spotlight because he is singing about the need to lean on other people.

> *Both kids are good to mom*
> *You see, it's in the blood*
> *Blood's thicker than the mud*

He sings from a distance, preaching, trying to explain something that matters. Some people give up on you; some don't, no matter what you do. Sometimes it's important to find out who's who. Sly presented this to the Top 40 audience like a philosophy lesson, holding out knowledge he had paid for.

> *You*
> *It's a family affair don't*
> *know*
> *wbo*
> *turned*
> *you*
> *in.*

With *Riot* Sly gave his audience—particularly his white audience—exactly what it didn't want. What it wanted was an upper, not a portrait of what lay behind the big freaky black superstar grin that decorated the cover of the album. One gets the feeling, listening, that the disastrous concerts that preceded and followed this record were not so much a matter of Sly insulting his audience as they were of Sly attacking that audience because of what the demands of the audience had forced him to produce. The concerts were an attack on himself as well, for having gone along with those demands and for having believed in them. All through *Riot* Sly turned on himself: "Must be a rush for me/ To see a lazy/ A brain he meant to be/ Cop out?" He removed the question mark in the next verse, and ultimately covered the question with poison: "Dyin' young is hard to take/ Sellin' out is harder."

Those last words were shoved under the graveyard chorus, "Thank you, falettinme be mice elf agin," and it is not hard to see why this record was so hard to listen to, which is to say, hard to take.

The bonds of a peculiar aesthetic democracy held, one last time, to reveal a world of terror and falsehood, that moment when Staggerlee runs into the limits his role was meant to smash, the same limits that turned Selma into Attica and "Satisfaction" into "You Can't Always Get What You Want." The endless fantasies piled onto the Staggerlee myth over the years were simple proof of the force of those limits, of the need to transcend them, but the fantasy, remade again and again, had its own force: it created new Staggerlees.

Staggerlee is a free man, because he takes chances and scoffs at the consequences. Others, especially whites, gather to fawn over him, until he shatters in a grimy celebration of needles, juice, and noise. Finally he is alone in a slow bacchanal, where his buddies, in a parody of friendship, devote themselves to a study of the precise moment of betrayal. Out of this disaster the man who lives it sometimes emerges whole: Malcolm did. Sometimes he dies young; sometimes he cops out.

On the way to this silent riot Sly shouldered the racial and sexual fantasies of a huge audience and staggered under them, as if he were Staggerlee himself back from the dead to live up to his myth. The images of mastery, style, and triumph set forth earlier in Sly's career reversed themselves; his old politics had turned into death, his exuberance into dope, and his old music into a soundtrack for a world that didn't exist. As an artist, Sly used those facts to reverse the great myth itself.

The role is all too real. It was forced on Chuck Berry, who never wanted it, and he paid for it in prison; Hendrix resisted, but in the public mind, the role enclosed him anyway. *Riot* is the secret contained in the whole blazing tradition. Something more than a definition of the risks involved in getting your hands on Staggerlee's kind of freedom, more than an illustration of the neat duality of any cultural archetype, *Riot* claims the story.

When new roles break down and there is nothing with which to replace them, old roles, ghosts, come rushing in to fill up the vacuum. Whether or not he thought in these terms, Sly lived out one side of Staggerlee's life until the other side caught up, and took over. Once the first role broke down in the face of social and personal limits it could not countenance and still survive, the rage of Staggerlee intensified as his mastery was defrauded. Instead of breaking the bartender's glass Stack found himself aiming at the mirror behind the bar, and thus discovered that his target was himself.

SLY VERSUS SUPERFLY

The best pop music does not reflect events so much as it absorbs them. If the spirit of Sly's early music combined the promises of Martin Luther King's speeches and the fire of a big city riot, *Riot* represented the end of those events and the attempt to create a new music appropriate to new realities. It was music that had as much to do with the Marin shootout and the death of George Jackson as the earlier sound had to do with the pride of the riot the title track of this album said was no longer going on.

"Frightened faces to the wall," Sly moans. "Can't you hear your mama call? The Brave and Strong—Survive! Survive!"

I think those faces up against the wall belonged to Black Panthers, forced to strip naked on the night streets of Philadelphia so Frank Rizzo and his cops could gawk and laugh and make jokes about big limp cocks while Panther women, lined up with the men, were psychologically raped.

A picture was widely published. Many have forgotten it; Sly probably had not. This again is why *Riot* was hard to take. If its spirit is that of the death of George Jackson it is not a celebration of Jackson, but music that traps what you feel when you are shoved back into the corners of loneliness where you really have to think about dead flesh and cannot play around with the satisfactions of myth.

The pessimism of *Riot* is not the romantic sort we usually get in rock 'n' roll. Optimistic almost by definition, pop culture is always pointing toward the next thing and sure it is worth going after; rock 'n' roll is linked to a youthful sense of time and a youthful disbelief in death. Pop culture pessimism is almost always self-indulgent; not without the power to move an audience, but always leaving the audience (and the artist) a way out. In retrospect, records made in this spirit often seem like reverse images of narcissism. *Riot* is the real thing: scary and immobile. It wears down other records, turning them into unintentional self-parodies. The negative of *Riot* is tough enough to make solutions seem trivial and alternatives false, in personal life, politics, or music.

Rock 'n' roll may matter because it is fun, unpredictable, anarchic, a neatly packaged and amazingly intense plurality of good times and good ideas, but none save the very youngest musicians and fans can still take their innocence for granted. Most have simply seen and done too much; as the Rolling Stones have been proving for ten years, you have to *work* for innocence. You have to win it, or you end up with nothing more than a strained naïveté.

Because this is so pop needs an anchor, a reality principle, especially when the old ideas—the joy of the Beatles, the simple toughness of the Stones—have run their course and the music has begun to repeat its messages without repeating their impact. Rock 'n' roll may escape conventional reality on a day-to-day level (or remake it, minute-to-minute), but it has to have an intuitive sense of the reality it means to escape; the audience and the artists have to be up against the wall before they can climb over it. When the Stones made "Gimme Shelter," they had power because their toughness had taken on complexity: they admitted they had doubts about finding even something as simple as shelter, and fought for it anyway. But because the band connected with its audience when they got that across, and because the music that did it was the best they ever made, the song brought more than shelter; it brought life, provided a metaphor that allowed the Stones to thrive when Altamont proved toughness was not the point, and gave them the freedom to go on to sing about other things— soul survivors, suffocation, a trip down a moonlight mile.

Riot matters because it doesn't just define the wall; it makes the wall real. Its sensibility is hard enough to frame the mass of pop music, shuffle its impact, jar the listener, and put an edge on the easy way out that has not really been won. It is not casual music and its demands are not casual; it tended to force black musicians to reject it or live up to it. Some months after *Riot* was released—from the middle of 1972 through early 1973—the impulses of its music emerged on other records, and they took over the radio.

I don't know if I will be able to convey the impact of punching buttons day after day and night after night to be met by records as clear and strong as Curtis Mayfield's "Superfly" and "Freddie's Dead," the Staple Singers' "Respect Yourself" and the utopian "I'll Take You There," the O'Jays' "Back Stabbers," War's astonishing "Slipping into Darkness" and "The World Is a Ghetto," the Temptations' "Papa Was a Rolling Stone," Johnny Nash's "I Can See Clearly Now," Stevie Wonder's "Superstition," for that matter the Stones' *Exile on Main Street* (the white *Riot*)—records that were surrounded, in memory and still on the air as recent hits, by Marvin Gaye's deadly "Inner City Blues," by the Undisputed Truth's "Smiling Faces Sometimes (Tell Lies)," by the Chi-Lites' falsetto melancholy, by *Riot* itself. Only a year before such discs would have been curiosities; now, they were all of a piece: one enormous answer record. Each song added something to the others, and as in a pop explosion, the country found itself listening to a new voice.

To me, the Temptations took the prize. Imagine—or simply remember—the chill of driving easily through the night, and then hearing, casually at first, then with interest, and then with compulsion, the three bass patterns, repeated endlessly, somewhere between the sound of the heart and a judge's gavel, that open "Papa Was a Rolling Stone." The toughest blues guitar you have heard in years cracks through the building music like a curse; the singer starts in.

More than one person I knew pulled off the road and sat waiting, shivering, as the song crept out of the box and filled up the night.

Four children have gathered around their mother to ask for the truth about their father, who has been buried that very day. They don't know him; he was just another street-corner Stagolee. So they ask. Was he one of those two-faced preachers, mama—"Stealing in the name of the Lord?"* A drunk? A hustler? A pimp? With another wife, more kids? They slam the questions into their mother, and all she can give them is one of the most withering epitaphs ever written, for them, as well as for him: "When he died, all he left us was alone."

Some thought "Back Stabbers" hit even harder. It moved with a new urgency, heading into its chorus with an unforgettable thump; it was like hearing the Drifters again, but the Drifters robbed of the pop optimism that let them find romance even in the hard luck of "On Broadway." The O'Jays sounded scared when they climaxed the song with an image that was even stronger than the music: "I wish somebody'd take/ Some a' these *knives* outta my back!"

Stevie Wonder reached number one with "Superstition"—his first time on top in ten years. It was the most ominous hard rock in a long while, a warning against a belief in myths that no one understood; Wonder made the old chicka-chicka-boom beat so potent it sounded like a syncopated version of Judgment Day.

All these records were nervous, trusting little if anything, taking *Riot*'s spirit of black self-criticism as a new aesthetic, driven (unlike *Riot*) by great physical energy, determined to get across the idea of a world—downtown or uptown, it didn't matter—where nothing was as it seemed. These black musicians and singers were cutting loose from the white man's world to attend to their own business—and to do that, they had to tell the truth. And so they made music of worry and confinement that, in their very different way, the Chi-Lites took to even greater extremes.

The Chi-Lites—like all the artists discussed here—had been around for many years, but they broke into the Top 40 in the seventies, with a dark chant called "(For God's Sake) Give More Power to the People." Stylistically, this was an old kind of record, but it was a new kind of politics; instead of a demand, or an affirmation, it was a plea, and a desperate one at that. The Chi-Lites' persona was open and vulnerable, the antithesis of machismo (something they explicitly dismissed with the great "Oh Girl"). Other hits—"A Lonely Man," "Have You Seen Her," and "The Coldest Day of My Life"—undercut

---

*A reference to Paul Kelly's single of the same name, which, along with Jerry Butler's "Only the Strong Survive," had opened up the new territory the Tempts were exploring.

the high-stepping burst of mastery on which Wilson Pickett and so many other black artists of the sixties had based their careers; the Chi-Lites made Pickett's old bragging music sound fake. Pickett had told his audience that ninety-nine-and-a-half won't do and made them believe it, but the Chi-Lites seemed ready to settle for a lot less—or to beg for something else altogether. The key to any black singer is in that old catch phrase about the way you talk and the way you walk; the Chi-Lites spoke softly and moved with great care.

This new music was a step back for a new look at black America; it was a finger pointed at Staggerlee and an attempt to freeze his spirit out of black culture. On many levels—direct, symbolic, commercial, personal—this music was a vital, conservative reaction to the radical costs Sly had shown that Staggerlee must ultimately exact. And since Stack was roaming virtually unchallenged in the new black cinema, this musical stance amounted to a small-scale cultural war.

All the new black movies—from *Hit Man* to *Trouble Man* to *Detroit 9000* to *Cleopatra Jones*—were cued by the reality behind one very carefully thrown-away line from *The Godfather* (a movie, it is worth remembering, that attracted millions of black Americans, even though it had no black characters, let alone any black heroes).

"They're animals anyway," says an off-camera voice, as the Dons make the crucial decision to dump all their heroin into the ghettos. "Let them lose their souls."

The Mafia may have missed the contradiction in that line, but Francis Coppola certainly did not; neither did the black men and women in the theaters. They suffered it; in *Lady Sings the Blues*, Diana Ross was stalking screens all over the country showing just what it meant. That audience had a right to revenge.

And so the fantasy went to work again. If that line had opened up the abyss, the old black hero shot up from the bottom and pushed in the white man instead. Stack slipped through the hands of the white sheriff, won his fight, got his girl, and got away.

Superfly summed up the genre; perhaps its first scene did, more than it was meant to. The hero, cocaine dealer Priest (played by Ron O'Neal, who looked uncomfortably like a not-very-black Sean Connery) stirs in the bed of his rich white mistress. Some black fool has made off with his stash. Priest chases him through the alleys, up the side of a building, and traps him in a tiny apartment. There, in full view of the man's family, Priest beats him half to death. This was John Hurt's Billy, but Lloyd Price's Stagger Lee.

Still, Priest is nervous. Hustling's all the Man has left us, he tells his partner, who thinks that's just fine; Priest wants out of the Life, but the invisible whites who run the show want him in—or dead. He bets everything on one last big deal. He turns on the pressure; one of his runners, Freddie, can't take it, and he panics and gets himself killed. Another man, a sort of father figure (who started Priest out peddling reefers when just a lad) is talked into the game, and he too loses his life to Priest's bid for freedom. Priest's partner weighs the odds and sells him out.

Moving fast, Priest penetrates the white coke hierarchy, takes out a first-class Mafia contract on Mr. Big to cover his bet, unmasks Mr. Big as a queer, and, with his money and his strong black woman, gets away clean. He turned up one movie later as a crusader for social justice in Africa, where life was simpler.

It was a fairy tale; but like most of the Staggerlee movies, *Superfly* had a soundtrack by an established soul singer, and in this case Curtis Mayfield's songs were not background, but criticism. (Mayfield had appeared in the picture singing in a dealers' bar, grinding out an attempted parody of his audience—but they thought it was a celebration.) His music worked against the fantasy, because to him one incident in the movie counted for more than all its triumphs: Freddie's dead. "Pushin' dope for *the Man!*" he sang, incredulous and disgusted. The movie hadn't even slowed to give Freddie an epitaph, but Mayfield clearly aimed his song at the hero as well.*

Superfly had a black director, Gordon Parks, Jr.; there was a surface ghetto realism, and there were touches of ambiguity, but the movie had Hollywood in its heart, and that was enough to smother everything else. Most of the pictures that followed simply shuffled *Superfly* clichés, but they kept coming.

Young black men began to imitate the movies, and real life put on its own endings. In the tiny black town of Brooklyn, Illinois, the mayor deputized a hustler named Bollinger to run a militant out of town (Priest had only contempt for black politics—not violent enough, he said, he'd deal with the Man his own way). With the competition out of business, Bollinger took over; he ran the town the way Capone ran Cairo, until another black man named Skinner—lacking the hustler's long coat and broad-brimmed hat—faced him down. Anyone doubting they had been to the movies can read the dialogue.

---

*Interestingly, these lyrics were not in the movie, even though the backing track was. Mayfield held off until the film was in the theaters, then wrote the words, released the record, and so took on the picture on his own turf: the radio. You could say he chickened out, and you could also say he was very smart.

" 'I guess you're lookin' for me,' said Bollinger calmly.

" 'That's right,' replied Skinner. 'I'm lookin' for you, man. I know you've heard I'm the police chief now.'

" 'I'm not giving up a goddamn thing,' said Bollinger."

Skinner shot Bollinger dead; then the hustler's girl stood over him. She said: "He lived like a man. He died like one too."*

The story out of Detroit was worse. A group of three young men—determined, like the heroes of so many new black movies, to clean the smack out of their neighborhood—began to lean hard on dealers and junkies. They were armed and violent. A run-in with STRESS (Stop Robberies Enjoy Safe Streets), the killer squad of the Detroit police, which the three men suspected had ties with the heroin trade, seemed inevitable. When it was over two cops were dead and the vigilantes were on the run. The youngest was caught in Detroit, and survived; his two comrades were tailed to Atlanta, set up, and executed. And all the while, in uptown movie houses across the country, Staggerlee killed and fucked and killed and fucked and the white sheriff near died of envy and Billy died to let Stack kill and fuck another day.

One movie was different, but it never found its audience, not among blacks, or whites either. *Across 110th Street* (directed by Barry Shear, who earlier made *Wild in the Streets*, the most paradoxical youth exploitation picture; written by Luther Davis) looked enough like all the others to make it easy for nearly all critics to dismiss it. The film was almost unbelievably violent, which gave reviewers license to attack it. It began with the same clichés everyone else used, but intensified them mercilessly. It pumped so much pressure into the world of the new black movies that it blew that world apart.

Three black men—Jamaica, Superflake, and Dry Clean—murder a pack of black and white Mafia bankers and make off with the week's take for all of Harlem. They don't steal because they hate the mob; they steal because they want the money. A Mafia lieutenant—played by Tony Franciosa—is sent out to bring back the money and execute the thieves, knowing full well he can forget his future if he fails. Anthony Quinn plays a bought cop caught in the middle. He has to take the case straight to make his pension, and a new black cop is keeping an eye on him, but he has to do it without losing his payoff—or his life—to the Mafia hirelings who control his district: a black man who runs a taxi company and looks like Fats Domino risen from

*Dialogue quoted from "High Noon after Nightfall," *Time*, December 17, 1973.

the swamp of evil, and his bodyguard, a Staggerlee who watches over the entire film with the cold eyes of someone who sold his soul to the devil the day he was old enough to know he had one.

You paid for every bit of violence, perhaps because the film refused its audience the pleasures of telling the good guys from the bad guys, and because the violence was so ugly it exploded the violence of the genre. It wasn't gratuitous, but it wasn't "poetic" either. Every character seemed alive, with motives worth reaching for, no matter how twisted they might turn out to be; every character (save for Taxi Man and his gunman) fled through the story scared half out of his wits, desperate for space, for a little more time, for one more chance.

The thieves speed away from the litter of corpses, divide up the money, and go into hiding. Superflake is too proud of himself to stay holed up; good times are what it was all for, right? His best hustler's clothes—tasteless Sly Stone, but gaudy—have been hanging for this moment. Down at the best whorehouse in Harlem Superflake has a dozen women and he's bragging.

Franciosa picks up the scent, and with Taxi Man's Staggerlee at his side, his eyes glazing over with a sadism that masks his own terror, he rips Superflake out of the whorehouse bar. When Quinn finds Superflake crucified, castrated, and skinned alive, you realize that along with no heroes, this movie may offer no way out. It was made to take your sleep.

Jamaica and Dry Clean pass the word and panic; they know that Superflake had to finger them. Dry Clean shoves his money into a clothes bag from his shop and hails a cab for Jersey. The driver spots the markings on the bag, radios back to Taxi Man, and delivers Dry Clean straight to Franciosa at 110th Street—the border of Harlem and the one line the movie never crosses. Dry Clean breaks away; Franciosa traps him on a roof, ties a rope to his leg, and hangs him over a beam, dangling him into space. Staggerlee holds the rope; his eyes show nothing as he watches the white man torture the black. If Dry Clean talks, they say, they won't kill him; he is so scared he believes them. He talks, and the rope shoots over the side.

Jamaica and his girl meet in his wretched apartment (there is a little torn-out picture of Martin Luther King taped to the wall, a gray reminder of some other time) to plan an escape, or a better hideout. And in one of the most extraordinary scenes in any American movie, a death's-head reversal of every warm close-up you have ever seen, Jamaica begins to talk—about green hills and a blue sky; about quiet, rest, peace of mind; about going home. He has only killed nine men to get there. His face is scarred by smallpox; his eyes try hard to explain. Jamaica goes on; you don't hear him; the camera stays in tight. Every few seconds his whole face shudders, seems almost to shred, as a ghastly, obscenely complex twitch climbs from his jaw to his temple, breaks, and starts up again.

It is the visual equivalent of that last song on *Riot*, "Thank you for talkin' to me Africa," another reach for a home that isn't there. Like Sly's music, the scene is unbearably long, it makes you want to run, but each frame like each note deepens the impact, until everything else in the world has been excluded and only one artistic fact remains. Jamaica's twitch traces the fear of every character in the movie; it is a map of the ambiguities the other movies so easily shot away; and in this film, it is most of all the other side of Staggerlee's face, which never moves.

Finally, Franciosa, Quinn, and their troops converge on the abandoned tenement where Jamaica and his girl are hiding. Taxi Man gets word of the showdown. "Wanna watch," says Staggerlee. "No," says Taxi Man. "I know how it's gonna turn out."

A bullet cuts through the girl's forehead and pins her to the wall behind Jamaica. She stays on camera, standing up dead, a blank ugliness on her face. When Jamaica turns to see her you can feel the life go out of him, but he keeps shooting. Franciosa is killed; the cops take over. Jamaica flees to the roof with his gun and his bag of money, still firing. He kills more. Staggerlee, sent to cover for Taxi Man, watches from another rooftop. Jamaica falls, and in the only false moment in the picture, flings his money down to children in a playground. Staggerlee sets up a rifle, takes aim on Quinn, who has proved himself too weak to be worth the mob's time, and kills him.

In one way, then, this movie was like all the others: Staggerlee wins. But this time, the audience was not given the benefit of any masks; they had to take him as he came, and they were not about to pay money to see that.

Almost always, there is a retreat once something like the truth is out. Audiences respond to that moment of clarity, but they only want so much of it; scared of their own vision or not trusting their audiences, artists grow timid and hedge their bets. Follow hard rock with a ballad, follow a threat with reassurance. The O'Jays and their producers, Kenny Gamble and Leon Huff, put as much distance between themselves and "Back Stabbers" as they could with "Love Train" (the tough "992 Arguments" had died); the Temptations, as usual, copied themselves, with the horrendous "Ghetto" ("Hmmm, life sure is tough here in the ghetto"), and turned art into shlock in record time. The perfectly named Brighter Side of Darkness got a hit with "Love Jones," and made dope romantic. The restraint of the Chi-Lites became so stylized they went off the deep end with "We Need Order." The music seemed to lose its edge; it went bland, as if to prove that the only alternative to Stagolee was an imitation of white middle-class respectability.

At the core of the attempt to make artistic and commercial sense out of the world *Riot* revealed—and in terms of black music, almost invented—was a new triumph of black capitalism and controlled craftsmanship, a kind of poetic efficiency. Most of the records discussed here were created by producers, not groups, and while the producers would take virtually any risk to break onto the charts, their real ambition seemed to be to stay on the charts without taking any risks at all.

The team of Gamble and Huff, working out of Philadelphia, epitomized the style. Their records featured beautifully intricate hooks, a sophisticated blend of R&B force and mainstream strings, and irresistible internal riffs that stood up under hundreds of listenings, which meant that when the records got on the radio they stayed there. The Spinners' "I'll Be Around" (produced by Gamble-Huff disciple Thom Bell) featured an up-and-down guitar line that could have carried a French lesson without losing any of its commercial force. But cultural force was something else again.

The new black hit factories—Willie Mitchell in Memphis with Al Green (who found his voice in the gap between Pickett's arrogance and the Chi-Lites' weakness), Lambert and Potter in Los Angeles with the Four Tops (whose "Keeper of the Castle" affirmed the family over hustling—or politics), and Gamble-Huff—spoke of consistency and stability as the crucial values. After that one burst of unity and vitality (which, if we call it a fad, will tell us how good fads can be), black music drifted back into something like a parallel of the most conventional black reality (save for Stevie Wonder and Marvin Gaye, who produced their own records with their own money, and kept moving). This was a limit not only on violence and excess, but on real cultural ambition: a black version of "benign neglect." Daniel Moynihan thought if you removed the promise you would remove the threat;

here, the threat submerged, but so did the promise, because the paradox that gives *Riot* its tension is that Sly knows that Staggerlee holds the key to vitality as well as disaster.

What makes *Riot* truly bleak, after all, is not that Sly ever resists the role Staggerlee has carved out, not that he shrinks from its momentum, but that he cannot survive it. And it was this truth that made *Riot* so different from all the other records, no matter how good they were. The producers' singers moved easily from music that could have made history to music that merely reflected it; many even lost the energy that in popular music can usually be substituted for vision. They drifted, like all cultural reflections, into accommodation, into music for a new normalcy.

"An insufferable deadness had invaded our lives," Frank Kermode has written of the thirties, though his words do well enough for our own time. "We needed . . . to be violently stirred into life . . . intolerable social constraints grew daily upon us."

Nixon's rule made those lines seem quite familiar; their meaning has seeped down into our bones, like a secret second nature. It is a debilitating secret to which those who keep it can barely admit, because, in spite of all the clichés about how nothing can ever imprison an idea or a dream, dreams can be imprisoned inside those who once held to them.

Those dreams are worn down and dissolved as the world mocks them by its versions of reality; they are dissolved because the one who once felt alive because of them must live in that world. He or she does not conform to it, necessarily, but adjusts to it in a hundred ways every day: with every thought he turns away from, with every word she does not speak, with every fantasy of violence, liberation, or death that fades into the nightly dreams one does not understand and does not much want to.

Too much war and too much public crime has poisoned the country to be easily put to rest by any kind of reform or vengeance. There is simply too much to forget. Our politics have robbed the good words of ethics of their meaning; an impenetrable official venality has robbed the good ideas of the last few years of theirs. What, in the sixties, looked like a chance to find new forms of political life, has been replaced by a flight to privacy and cynicism; the shared culture that grew out of a love affair with the Beatles has collapsed (not without their help) into nostalgia and crackpot religion. The revisionists have already gone to work on the last decade—which was, no matter how smug, self-righteous, or naïve, a time of greater cultural and political freedom than most of us will likely know again. Those who, in Leslie Fiedler's words, "lived the mythic life of their generation," those who made it and were remade by it, can now hardly remember it.

Throughout the years of Nixon's ascendancy the *New Yorker* opened most issues with a page of unsigned commentary that tried to see through each week's dose of lies—the obvious lies told by those in power, and the more subtle, pathetic lies told by those who twisted to escape the first. It was something better than comforting to read that commentary every week, and something worse. There was satisfaction in knowing that someone had the will and the talent to work to find the truth no matter how pointless the effort seemed; there was a queasy disgust in knowing that someone else had to do that work for me. Whether my own talents were not up to the job, or my will too weak, didn't much matter. It was too easy to lose touch with rage, with a sense of what is good and evil, to lose touch with the idea that it is worth something to make, and try to live out, such a distinction.

These are politics of the freeze-out. They turn into a culture of seamless melancholy with the willful avoidance of anything—a book, some photographs, a record, a movie, even a newspaper—that one suspects might produce really deep feeling. Raw emotions must be avoided when one knows they will take no shape but that of chaos.

Within such a culture there are many choices: cynicism, which is a smug, fraudulent kind of pessimism; the sort of camp sensibility that puts all feeling at a distance; or culture that reassures, counterfeits excitement and adventure, and is safe. A music as broad as rock 'n' roll will always come up with some of each, and probably that's just as it should be.

Sometimes, though, you want something more: work so intense and compelling you will risk chaos to get close to it, music that smashes through a world that for all of its desolation may be taking on too many of the comforts of familiarity. Sly created a moment of lucidity in the midst of all the obvious negatives and the false, faked hopes; he made his despair mean something in the midst of a despair it is all too easy to think may mean nothing at all. He was clearing away the cultural and political debris that seemed piled up in mounds on the streets, in the papers, in the record stores; for all of the darkness of what he had to say and how he said it, his music had the kind of strength and the naked honesty that could make you want to start over.

A QUIET REBELLION

Sly clearly could not push *Riot* much farther, not without releasing a whole album of silence; and not, perhaps, without losing the audience he had worked to win. *Fresh*, the album that did follow, in 1973, showed Sly clicking his heels for Richard Avedon's camera, and the songs did their best to keep up with the title and the cover. "There's a mickie in the tastin' of disaster," was the first line of *Fresh*—Sly's instinctive paraphrase of Nietzsche's belief that he who gazes into the abyss will find the abyss looking back; that he who looks too long at monsters may well become one.

The music was good, but it lacked the fire of *Riot*, the tiny explosions of a bass riff or a horn part stuttering along vocal lines, ambushing words and transforming emotions. Save for "Que Sera, Sera," which Sly and Rosie Stone turned into a blues (this following months of bizarre rumors of a romance between Sly and Doris Day— "*Riot* or no *Riot*," said a friend, "he hasn't lost his sense of humor"), the music and the singing lacked risk. Most critics applauded Sly's step toward "a more positive" stance, but there was little on *Fresh* to prove that it was more than a stance.

Worse, the complexity of Sly's music, from "Everyday People" to *Riot*—the tension between the individual and the group, the tension of politics orchestrated in personal terms—was overtaken by a straightforward presentation of Sly's role, and the group now seemed little more than his servant. The album's hit, "If You Want Me to Stay," was a conventional comment on the ambiguities of stardom, and there were too many references to Sly's coke habit (switched to pep, he said), the time lag between LP's, and the like. Such subjects may have been meant to work outside the limited context of Sly's personal dilemma, but they did not connect. Still, there was "Que Sera"—and the album could be seen as an attempt to figure out how it would feel to live with honesty and energy in a country that had forced the recognitions of *Riot*, but that had more to show those who knew how to look.

A tour followed the release of *Fresh*—the first Sly and the Family Stone had made in two years (two original members had quit and been replaced)—and the show I saw in Berkeley in the summer of 1973 was both interesting and a fraud. It was Sly's homecoming concert, and he presented it as such; his last in the Bay Area had been a post-*Riot* shambles, with Sly walking off the stage after a few bitter minutes, shouting something about how the audience couldn't handle what he had to give them. He had played the Cow Palace then, which holds 16,000; the Berkeley Community Theatre was nearly full, but it seats only about 3,000.

Sly celebrated trumpet player Cynthia Robinson's birthday by bringing her mother out on stage; he talked quietly about his parents, smiling broadly, trying to get across how appropriate it seemed to him that his mother had given him the ideas for some of his best songs. That was interesting, and moving. It was the music that was a fraud.

The playing was mostly mechanical; as Dave Marsh, who walked out on a similar show in Long Island, put it, the songs were "a rehash of older, more frivolous material . . . also a rehash of the part of [the past] which is most insidious, bypassing the strength of songs like 'Everybody Is a Star' and 'Everyday People' for the relatively empty 'Stand!' and 'M'Lady.' " There was not a single tune from *Riot*; the only performance that had conviction was a stunning "Que Sera," which for a moment almost saved the show; and the concert ended, as all Sly's concerts ended back in the Woodstock days, with "I Want to Take You Higher," which was always facile and is now a stupid lie. It wasn't even an effective one; the audience probably wanted to go farther more than they wanted to be taken higher, and the old piece of frenzy fizzled out in three or four minutes, as if neither the audience nor the band had much heart for the deception.

"It's one thing to change on record, in private," Dave Marsh said to me when we compared notes on the tour. "It's something else to look all those people in the face and tell them the good old days are gone." Maybe so. Perhaps, if Sly had woven a new show out of *Riot* and *Fresh*, the next tour would have had him playing to empty seats. Neither record includes much of an obvious crowd pleaser, and something had already brought Sly down from the big arena to the theater.

Most of all, though, Sly seemed eager to say that *Riot* had been a bad dream best forgotten. But if the weakness and failure of nerve of the concert I saw is what really grows out of *Riot*, that only means that the world Sly discovered and made real on that record is as debilitating as he said it was.

Whether the retreat is one of vision, as I think it is in Sly's case, or of craftsmanship and accounting, as with many black record producers, Sly's truest work has its own momentum ("Never trust the artist, trust the tale," D. H. Lawrence wrote, noting that American artists, because they cannot escape their audiences, are always desperate to cover up whatever they reveal); Sly's work penetrates into black politics just as it changed black music and haunts black movies. The turnaround of the Black Panther party—from the politics of violent rhetoric and armed self-defense to the politics of elections and alliance with the black church—parallels the retreat of the black producers and of *Fresh*. The Panther retreat may produce the same kind of guarded success; it may also tell us how necessary such retreats are. But it is worth remembering that Eldridge Cleaver and Huey Newton fought a war over this change in politics—a very strange war.

After a murderous shootout provoked by the Oakland police in 1968, Cleaver was to be returned to prison as a parole violator. He was willing to stand trial, but he was convinced he would be killed in jail; he would not go back. And there was more to it. He told Gene Marine:

When I went back to prison before, it didn't matter, you know? Nobody cared about me anyway, I was in the same prison, you know? The prison of being alone. Out or in, it didn't matter. But this time—this time I've found something, since I've been in the movement and working with all these cats. I've found people who really dig me, people I really dig. People care about me, people *like* me. I've never had that before, never at all. I can't go back in there now and leave that out here. I've got friends—I've got friends for the first time in my life, and man, I just don't think I can do without that anymore.*

Pushed into a corner, Cleaver jumped bail, escaped to Cuba, and eventually set up headquarters in Algeria. There, if the Panther newspaper is accurate, he terrorized his wife, took a new mistress, murdered a rival, and tumbled into fantasies of sweeping across America at the head of a guerilla gang. He denounced Newton, tried to seize the party from exile, and ordered his followers on the East Coast and in Los Angeles to put his vision into practice. The war for the party commenced; bodies began to turn up.

Newton and Seale had founded the Black Panthers (drawing up their statement of aims and demands while playing Dylan's "Ballad of a Thin Man" over and over) as a local self-defense organization, but the idea was irresistible and soon there were Panther chapters all

*From Gene Marine, *The Black Panthers* (New York: Signet, 1969).

over the country. As Bobby Seale says so well, Staggerlee was crucial to these new politics. A killer, a thief, setting himself up against his own people, plundering them to get what he wanted—they began there. They seized the fact of criminal violence, and tried to turn that fact into a political threat. Since no one doubted the fact was real, the threat was taken seriously.

Newton's idea came down to a new kind of power, growing out of the barrel of a gun that was good only as long as it didn't have to be fired, because once it was fired, the other side was going to win. The Panthers walked that fine edge, threatened by their own rhetoric, which called for actions they could not afford to take; their rhetoric won them some of the space necessary for action, but the police also forced them to live up to it. Police raids on chapter after chapter decimated the party; many of those who were left were junkies, hoods, and spies. Both Newton and Seale had been off the street while murder raps, ultimately tossed out, were hung over their heads; the party had lost its center. Either it changed drastically or it died, and once Newton got out of jail he moved to quiet it down and clean it out.

Cleaver, a confessed rapist who had spent nine years in California prisons, had been valuable to the Panthers not only because he was a superb recruiter and a good theorist, but because their politics were rooted in the streets. Newton's genius had been to bring Staggerlee into politics and there transform him; that also meant Newton had to risk him. Newton's careful arrogance and perfect nerve under the guns of San Francisco cops had inspired Cleaver to join the party, but Newton is a man of tremendous self-discipline; the demands his politics made on all party members were in some ways too much of a reflection of his own unquestionable ability to live up to them. Staggerlee was a mask Newton could put on at will; Cleaver was not always under control, and the myth held more traps for him. But he could take it farther, even as politics: he really was Staggerlee, and the explosive threat of his performance was vital to his role in the party.

Cleaver's worth lay in his ability to balance that role between his exploitation of it and it of him. In Algeria, cut off from the people who had changed his life, that balance shattered absolutely, and his old nemesis roared back with a vengeance. He had been a political man whose politics were rooted in a vitality and rage that had once come out in crime, but he emerged a criminal once again, out for blood.

There were no politics. The balance broke down because the political space necessary to it had been taken away, and what was left was murder, not for a five-dollar Stetson hat, but the old story all the same. Cleaver fell back to Staggerlee; he went all the way into his hands, and it may be that the only way he will ever get out will be with the epitaph John Hurt gave to his Stag-o-lee, the cruelest epitaph of all:

> *Standing at the gallows*
> *Head way up high*
> *At twelve o'clock they killed him*
> *They was all glad to see him die.*

And that is the context of *Riot*.*

These events and Sly's understanding of his own career came together, as most likely they never will again, to form a music of extraordinary depth and power. Sly questioned his earlier music and our love for it; he implied that whatever the beauty of "Everybody Is a Star," that may have been only another way of saying that everybody is a mark. Sly's work was deeply personal and inescapably political; innovative and tough in its music; literate and direct in its words; a parody of the past and an unflinching statement about the present that its present has hardly contained.

Sly returned to the pop arena at a time when black music had remade itself on terms he had defined; he damned those terms and invented new ones. He recognized the expectations of his audience, and moved to subvert them.

---

*It was, I still believe, the context—but events have proved my comments on Newton and Cleaver more than a little naïve.

After a bizarre incident in which he "arrested" fellow-fugitive Timothy Leary in Algiers, Cleaver fled to Paris, where he renounced politics for haberdashery—to wit, "Cleavers," pants cut with an "appurtenance" for genital display. Unable to interest a distrubutor in the latest in rapists' fashions, Cleaver negotiated with prosecutors back in Oakland, proclaimed himself a born-again Christian, returned to the U.S., and copped a plea to reduced charges stemming from the 1968 shootout—which, Cleaver now said, he had provoked. Free at last, he became a shill for the far right, ran unsuccessfully for office as a Republican, and in 1988 was convicted on charges of burglary and cocaine possession.

Newton's story is worse. After the disintegration of the Black Panther Party in the early '70s, Newton received a Ph.D. from the University of California at Santa Cruz, and attempted to set up small-scale protection rackets in Oakland. Over the next years he was charged with many crimes, including the murder of a prostitute (he later admitted to friends that he had killed her, for no real reason, and also that he had ordered the murder of a Panther bookkeeper). He fled to Cuba; when he returned to face trial, an attempt was made to kill a witness; finally the charges were dismissed. Numerous further arrests followed—for drunk driving, weapons possession, and embezzlement—and Newton was briefly imprisoned for parole violations. He had become an alcoholic and a cocaine addict. On August 22, 1989, when for the first time in more than twenty years Newton was legally clean, he was shot to death by a crack dealer on a sidewalk in Oakland. He was 47.

If after a time he allowed his audience to subvert his work, or simply played on and followed where his music led, *There's a riot goin' on* stands as a quiet, bitter, open act of rebellion. It is a rebellion the resolution of which depends as much on the audience as it does on Sly Stone, and a rebellion which as music or politics is not likely to work itself out for a long time. And if that musical insurrection can be captured in a line, it is probably a remark Josef von Sternberg once made: "Obviously, it is easier to kill than to create."

RANDY NEWMAN
Every Man Is Free

I believe . . . that to be very poor and very beautiful is most probably a moral failure much more than an artistic success. Shakespeare would have done well in any generation because he would have refused to die in a corner; he would have taken the false gods and made them over; he would have taken the current formulae and forced them into something lesser men thought them incapable of. Alive today he would undoubtedly have written and directed motion pictures, plays, and God knows what. Instead of saying, "This medium is not good," he would have used it and made it good. If some people called some of his work cheap (which some of it is), he wouldn't have cared a rap, because he would know that without some vulgarity there is no complete man. He would have hated refinement, as such, because it is always a withdrawal, and he was much too tough to shrink from anything.

RAYMOND CHANDLER, 1949,
from *Raymond Chandler Speaking*

POP

Chandler's statement, written in the midst of his failed attempts to do good work as a Hollywood screenwriter, tells us how completely he understood what it means to be an American artist. The momentum of democracy (of equality) (of conformity) that powers American life does not, as Tocqueville thought it might, bleed all the life out of culture; it has created a wholly new kind, with all sorts of new risks and possibilities. At its worst it can do just what Tocqueville expected, and there is always a good example around: *The Sound of Music* ("The audience," Pauline Kael wrote bitterly, "becomes the lowest common denominator of feeling—a sponge"); *Love Story*; the pop group "America" (Tocqueville smiling in his grave at the elegance of their conceit). There is, though, Chandler also wrote, "a vast difference between writing down to the public (something which always flops in the end) and doing what you want to do in a form that the public has learned to accept."

There have been great American artists who have worked beyond the public's ability to understand them easily, but none who have condescended to the public—none who have not hoped, no matter how secretly, that their work would lift America to heaven, or drive a stake through its heart. This is a democratic desire (not completely unrelated to the all-time number one democratic desire for endless wealth and fame), and at its best it is an impulse to wholeness, an attempt not to deny diversity, or to hide from it, but to discover what it is that diverse people can authentically share. It is a desire of the artist to remake America on his or her own terms.

This impulse powers the strongest popular artists as it powers pop culture itself. It is an urge to novelty and necessity; it exhausts most talents with terrific speed and goes on to something else.

The inability of the vital American artist to be satisfied with a cult audience, no matter how attentive, goes right back to the instinctive perception that whatever else America might be, it is basically *big*; that unless you are doing something big, you are not doing anything at all. The Beatles ("those imaginary Americans," Leslie Fiedler called them), madly in love with American popular culture and living out their own American dream, increased their ambitions as they got closer to their goals: first they wanted to be Eddie Cochran, then they decided they could be Elvis, and then they were on their own. They understood, finally, that they could affect the lives of kids all over the world. The fact that they succeeded tells us how much big pop ambitions are worth; everyone who might conceivably read this book has been changed for the better because of what the Beatles did.

When it is alive to its greatest possibilities—to disturb, provoke, and divide an entire society, thus exciting and changing a big part of society—pop says that the game of a limited audience is not really worth playing. It is as contradictory and as American as a politician who can't stand dissent, who gets and keeps his power by dividing the country and turning the country against itself, and then wants everyone to love him.

This is not simply a matter of the depth of the artist's idea, any more than the contours of American history really turn on how well Andrew Jackson understood macroeconomics. What matters is the depth and breadth of response an artist can evoke in an audience, and whether or not that artist is really challenging the audience and not simply playing off its fears and weaknesses. In the case of someone extraordinary like Elvis Presley, or the Beatles, this process becomes its own idea—and a pretty deep one. But who knows if "Eight days a week is not enough to show I love you" is a deep idea, or a trivial one, or any kind of idea at all? And who cares? The joy of pop is that it can deliver you from such questions by its immediacy and provoke them by its impact.

Rock 'n' roll is a combination of good ideas dried up by fads, terrible junk, hideous failings in taste and judgment, gullibility and manipulation, moments of unbelievable clarity and invention, pleasure, fun, vulgarity, excess, novelty and utter enervation, all summed up nowhere so well as on Top 40 radio, that ultimate rock 'n' roll version of America. As one writer put it, describing a classic radio segue of a pimple commercial directly into Bob Dylan's "George Jackson": "Right on."

We fight our way through the massed and leveled collective safe taste of Top 40, just looking for a little something we can call our own. But when we find it and jam the radio to hear it again it isn't just ours—it is a link to thousands of others who are sharing it with us. As a matter of a single song this might mean very little; as culture, as a way of life, you can't beat it.

And what about Randy Newman, who is, unfortunately, somewhere else entirely (that is, buried on an occasional FM radio or in the back of someone's record collection)? "All combined," Newman is fond of saying, "my records have sold as many copies as James Taylor's last album sold in Des Moines. But I'm fantastically wealthy, so nothing matters." Spoken like a pop master: only money counts.

But obviously if his public failure didn't bother him Newman wouldn't complain about it. To the degree that he knows his work is good he will want it to affect everyone in sight. And more than that, a singer whose songs contain an astonishing affection for every American from a middle-class couple wasting away in Florida to a rapist preying on their daughter cannot be satisfied with the attention of an elite, of critics and a few more, because a cult contradicts the best impulses of his work.

NEWMAN'S AMERICA, I

He is, all in all, one of the strangest performers to emerge in rock 'n' roll since the heady days of *Sgt. Pepper*. Born in 1943, raised in New Orleans and then in Southern California, Newman was heir to both a family movie music dynasty (the most famous member was his Oscar-winning Uncle Alfred, whose credits are ubiquitous on late night TV), and along with everyone else his age, to rock 'n' roll. Fats Domino was his man.

Newman took up the piano, was classically trained at UCLA, and got a job with a music publishing company, hacking out songs for money. He made a lot, as he says, but since he didn't much like the way other people did his stuff, he began recording it himself.

Since the release of his first album, in 1968, Newman's singing has shifted from a style that could be called Jewish to one that can only be called black. He has become, as his producer Lenny Waronker likes to call him, "The King of the Suburban Blues Singers."

What Newman has taken from black singers is not what most rock 'n' roll singers have taken: assertiveness, aggression, melancholy, sexual power. His somnambulant personality determined his choice of a lazy, blurred sound, where words slide into each other, where syllables are not bitten off, but just wear out and dissolve. The blues practice of dropping a key word off the end of a line, to hint at ominous sexual mastery or knowledge too strong to put into words, becomes with Newman a wonderful throwaway, a surface lack of seriousness that at first hides, and after a few listenings intensifies, a sense of Newman's commitment to his material. It is as if Randy's real blues hero wasn't Howlin' Wolf, but Stepin Fetchit—and as if Randy had a pretty good idea of what secrets were hidden in the shuffle.

The movie music side of Newman's songs grows out of a tradition so well absorbed by generations of film fans that by now it seems completely American, regardless of its classy European antecedents. Listening to Newman, irrespective of the lyric of any particular song, you might see John Wayne in Monument Valley, Charles Boyer in a final clinch. Chances are it won't be anything so specific; you will hear a hundred movies whose titles you just cannot recall.

Newman's music is stronger than any to be found in those movies; his music is from a movie no one ever made, the score that was never quite written. It is everything that movie music aspired to, richer on his records because he is making records, not movies.

He uses the familiarity of the music to set us in the moods and situations the music automatically calls up; we respond in predictable ways to the music, and as we do, Newman's words and his singing pull us in other directions, or shift the story just enough to make it new. The music defines for us the way we want it to be, the way the movies have told us it is, and then Newman tells us how it looks to him. The tension that comes is almost never facile, because the movie dreams the music evokes are real to him too, and because he loves the music itself. It's not merely a device, but at the heart of the matter; not just half of his strategy, but half of his aesthetic.

When I saw Newman perform one night, I was startled by how many of his songs mattered to me. I was a casual fan, but after each number another came into my head that I had to hear. I hadn't been part of a rock 'n' roll audience that laughed so well since Dylan's tours in the mid-sixties (we forget how funny crowds found "Desolation Row," and how right they were).

Newman could put on the chill, too. He told an old man he ought to give it up and die; he made you feel, with "God's Song," that life is indeed a joke, and that all the laughs belong to its Author. Newman did his Southern California beach song—which must derive, somehow, from "Surf City"—about a girl who has fled from her graduation dance to offer herself to the gears of the beach-cleaning machine, which scoops her up along with the beer cans, candy wrappers, and condoms, like a California teenager hungry after a swim. He sang some of his easy-target tunes, like "Burn On," about the firetrap Cuyahoga River. Best of all was "Davy the Fat Boy," sung in the voice of "Davy's only friend," who has made a deathbed promise to the fat boy's parents to take care of the freak and keeps it by putting him into a sideshow. It reminded me of that unbearable climactic scene in von Sternberg's *Blue Angel*, where Emil Jannings—the fallen professor forced to stand before his ex-students imitating a chicken—holds his body like one enormous clubfoot, his face in a frozen mask of terror and madness, and produces a squawk that can shrivel the soul. As Davy's friend orders him to begin "his famous fat boy dance," Newman leaned back from his piano for a little ballet music, letting the audience see the scene as he did; and as the song ended, one of its lines echoed with a gruesome kind of love: *"You've got to let this fat boy in your life!"*

Newman had asked for requests, and I had yelled out for "Davy" because I had vaguely remembered being moved by it some years before. If I had remembered it better I probably would have kept my mouth shut.

Except in its weaker moments, this was not satire. It was a whole world, irresistibly funny and extremely uncomfortable, like W. C. Fields with the Hollywood varnish rubbed off. But the laughter was not smug, and the scariness of the songs was not smug on Newman's part, but simply presented as what he did for a living, what he did better than anyone else. When he sang his "Suzanne," the tale of a rapist picking a woman's number off a phone booth wall, you were caught up in the woman's terror and the rapist's crime. Both were real, both mattered.

The song was in the great rock 'n' roll tradition of answer records: in this case, an answer to Leonard Cohen's "Suzanne," the tender ballad of a river nymph, as erotic as a $500 book of pornographic etchings. Cohen's song screamed Poetry and Art; it virtually raped the listener with its mastery of the Higher Shlock. "This is not Leonard Cohen's 'Suzanne,'" Newman said. "It's on a somewhat lower moral plane, actually."

He said that with such modesty, fading his comment as if he were throwing away one of his best lines, that you had to think that sometimes, late at night when he couldn't make a song work, he might even believe it.

Newman is afraid of his sensibility, to the degree that he has to get it over to an audience. On one album he sang a version of that old Cotton Club favorite, "Underneath the Harlem Moon," all about the colored singing and dancing, summed up in the classic line: "That's why darkies were born." He sang it straight—beautifully, in fact—and you just couldn't tell. Where was he? Or more to the point, where did he put you? Here he was, a struggling singer whose only possible audience would be urbane, liberal rock 'n' roll fans, and he was unveiling . . . the charms of racism. He would not perform the song in front of an audience. "I was afraid someone might beat me up," he said. The night I saw him he sang his own "Yellow Man"; apparently no one had told him he was singing in a Chinese movie theater in the middle of the biggest Chinese community in the U.S.A. Or maybe he thought his height would save him. His distance from his material is always a bit uncertain.

If Newman's songs are the result of New Orleans R&B and an after-the-ball cul-de-sac of Hollywood movie music, they also grow out of a cul-de-sac pure and simple: Los Angeles, the Edge of America, the City of the Future. As an Angeleno, Randy Newman is something like Nathanael West on the verge of having a good time in spite of himself.

West thought Southern California was where America came to make its last stand, to reach for the last chance; inevitably betraying those hopes, Los Angeles became, to West and to Chandler and others, the place where those now resentful Americans would turn to fantasies of revenge, violence, and death. Looking for rebirth, dreamers found only that they felt older than they had seemed at home. These discrepancies—presented over and over again, in Chandler's *The Big Sleep* and *Farewell, My Lovely*, in *Sunset Boulevard*, from a Holy Roller church in downtown L.A. to the Kirke Order of Dog Blood roaming the desert—created, against the backdrop of an industry based on the inexhaustibility of banal fantasy, a curious sort of moral ambivalence, a state of mind equally capable of producing commonplace boredom and uncommon crime. This ambivalence, I think, grows out of an attempt to come to terms with that sense of discrepancy: an aggressive and in many ways positive denial of the need for roots, a perception that everything that is old must be covered in neon and sandstone before anyone can be really free.

Once this is accomplished, of course, there is little left on which to base an idea of what that freedom could be for. People improvise; nothing seems completely out of the question. Some can endure, and use, this kind of freedom. Some can't; they lust after authority, and there are always too many to provide it: pimps, the Children of God, organized crime, weird figures of extraordinary charisma walking the street devouring souls.

Such a story is familiar enough. The same scared and lustful Americans who changed their names and killed for new lives in Chandler's books crawl through Ross MacDonald's; the rubber horse clumped at the bottom of a swimming pool in *Day of the Locust* was dumped into a bed in *The Godfather*. But because such a vision of Los Angeles pushed West and Chandler into a queer sort of Puritanism, they never noticed something else that matters about Southern California: its incredible exuberance, the talent of Southern Californians for enjoying themselves. It's a little too easy to look at the movement of the place and call it hysterical, too easy to quote Thoreau and pronounce that "the mass of men lead lives of quiet desperation," and think that you have told the whole truth. Put the Beach Boys of the early sixties up against West, and *he* sounds hysterical; there isn't a hint of their warmth and friendliness in his "definitive" book, but no one can tell me that "Fun, Fun, Fun" is a lie. The Beach Boys don't wipe out Chandler's world, but they enlarge it; and if finally the Beach Boys held hands with Charles Manson as the sixties ended, that only meant that they were as vulnerable to the L.A. of West and Chandler as they might have been to the Beach Boys'. You can say that the energy and pride the Beach Boys found cruising the strip in "I Get Around" was never meant to last, that it hardened and cracked like cheap Santa Monica stucco when they found out it was not enough and embraced the authority of the dread Maharishi. You can write their delight off to sun and money, but its value is still strong, still full of life. They felt free to enjoy themselves in every way imaginable, and that freedom from tradition, the freedom to invent, cuts deeply and all across the board. There's no way to separate the Beach Boys' smiling freedom from Manson's knife. Because this new world is a rich one, Randy Newman, as an artist, can work in it—he can laugh well and realize his fantasies of violence and death. "Suzanne" really is the other side of "Surf City"—or part of it.

Nathanael West was an Easterner; in spite of the fact that "West" was a name he chose, he was never at home in California—he was unable to imagine that anyone could be. But many Southern Californias, were they to be told that murder was the price of a way of life based on fun and fantasy, might still pay it. Newman accepts the deal because L.A. provides the indolence that suits his personality, and the risk that suits his art.

As an American artist, Newman represents some kind of opening up of the classic archetype of the keeper of the American imagination; and this too has a lot to do with the peculiar freedoms of Los Angeles. Most American critics—Nathaniel Hawthorne, say—throw up all sorts of horror and pretend they do so only to condemn it. If West, through his transplanted Easterner hero Tod Hackett, admitted complicity in the L.A. nightmare, he had to satisfy the guilt such a confession produced by destroying the city in a private apocalypse. Since Newman takes the moral shapelessness of his hometown as a given, such fantasies would be ridiculously melodramatic for him (they're more than a little ridiculous in West, too). Like the Beach Boys,

Newman builds freedom out of what he's got; his humor is his version
of the Beach Boys' open naïveté. Newman laughs all around his world,
never at it. He is too at home in the place to feel guilty about it, and
anyway, he is a rock 'n' roll singer, and such attitudes are not in the
rock 'n' roll style. As with almost any popular art, the moment rock
'n' roll tries to criticize something, it becomes hopelessly self-righteous
and stupid. It effectively criticizes by rendering a situation with such
immediacy, or by affirming it to the point of such absurdity, that you
can no longer take it straight. That is why there is no tougher antidrug
song than the Velvet Underground's "Heroin," which also risks creating new addicts.

Perhaps because of the ambivalence of Southern California, Newman can sing with the same insulated force. He always writes, and
what is harder, sings, in the voices of his characters (except when they
are women, but he will manage that someday); no matter what gro-
tesquerie is involved, he does not sing about, he sings *as*. He feels
this is dangerous, which it is.

The imagination has fallen upon sorry days in post-Beatle rock
'n' roll. Audiences are no longer used to the idea that someone might
make something up, create a persona and effectively act it out, the
way Chuck Berry and Bob Dylan used to do. Audiences take everything literally, partly because sensitive personal confession, "honesty,"
and one-to-one communication between the singer and whoever is
listening is so attractive and reassuring in times when pop culture and
politics have lost their grander mythic dimensions, when there are no
artists and no politics to create community, and every fan is thrown
back on himself. Let me quote from a typical ad for a troubled trou-
bador, supposedly appropriate to such times, presumably addressed
to a troubled audience:

A few rare performers immediately become your friend the first time you
listen to them. Jonathan Edwards is about to become your friend.

His songs are sensitive and warm, containing feelings and recollections which
are sure to remind you of things in your life as well.

Jonathan Edwards. A new friend.

Courtesy Atlantic Records and Tapes, a Division of Warner Communications, the friendly giant conglomerate.

Note the style of the ad. The cadence is wonderfully smooth, caressing. The grammar is perfect, proper. The voice is fatherly. The whole thing is absolutely unbearable.

But it's always fun to fill in the blanks. Let's say:

A few rare performers immediately become your friend the first time you listen to them. Mick Jagger is about to become your friend.

His songs are loud, brutal, and mean, containing feelings you like to pretend you do not have, recollections you would like to forget, and temptations that up until now you have wisely avoided.

Mick Jagger. A new friend.

Courtesy Rolling Stones Records and Tapes, distributed by Atlantic Records and Tapes, a Division of Warner Communications . . . rock 'n' roll may have no center, but it is nothing if not pluralistic. Newman records for the same company, naturally.

Rock 'n' roll is suffering from that old progressive school fallacy that says if what you write is about your own feelings, no one can criticize it. Truth telling is beginning to settle into a slough where it is nothing more than a pedestrian autobiography set to placid music framed by a sad smile on the album cover. This is about as liberating as thinking typecast movie stars are "really like" the roles they play. In many cases, though, this *has* come to be true in rock 'n' roll: singers have dispensed with imagination and songs are just pages out of a diary, with nothing in them that could give them a life of their own. A good part of the audience has lost its taste for songs that are about something out there in the world that the singer is trying to make real—usually by convincingly assuming the burden of that reality; replacing such songs are tunes that desperately deny the world by affirming the joys of solipsism. The success of this genre, represented by no one so well as James Taylor (along with the Rowan Brothers, Shawn Phillips, "America," and many others who will no doubt be forgotten by the time this book is published), only reminds me of an old philosophy student joke: "Solipsism is great, everyone should try it." That was, actually, the cornerstone of Nixon's Second Inaugural: "What can I do for myself?"

As the members of an audience grow older, they lead less public lives. Their deepest affections shift from a multiplicity of friends—from the idea of friendship itself—to husbands, wives, children; they exchange the noisy heterogeneity of school for the quiet homogeneity of a job. They travel less freely, act less impulsively. If politics once meant the fellowship of the street or the political community of a campus for those who were lucky enough to have known such things, more and more politics comes to mean voting—the most solitary political act there is—or, at best, talk with a few friends. A life that was fluid with possibility can solidify into loneliness. One looks harder for the comforts of similarity, and shies from the risks of diversity. It becomes easy to think that nothing is new under the sun, or that if there is, that one can no longer be a part of what is new. Too much is settled.

If at its best rock 'n' roll *is* a kind of public life (" 'School's Out' is my favorite song and I've been out of school for ten years!" my friend Simon Frith wrote. "What does that mean?"), the cults that have fragmented an audience potentially as big and broad as America itself speak for a less open life, as do the names of some successful post-Beatle record companies: Island, Shelter, Haven, Chrysalis, Asylum. Newman works against the limits of privacy, domesticity, and solipsism with his fantasies and the role playing of his songs, and yet he lacks the obsessive pop ambition to do more than that. Against the ideal community of music he feels the emotional and imaginative poverty of an America where men and women live estranged. But to drive the aesthetic of his fantasies into our heads would require him to value his music more than anything else, to be on the road constantly, to risk the collapse of his own family life, the shelter of his own privacy, and even—after the rock 'n' roll deaths of the last years I don't feel very romantic saying this—his sanity and his life.

"If I couldn't perform I'd give up," said Rod Stewart. "It's not a question of the money side of it. I don't have to work for the rest of my life. I don't want to. But not having that ninety minutes up there anymore. Phew. I don't like to think about it. It frightens me." And he went on: "I'm not willing to get married, because I think there are some people who just shouldn't get married. Elvis Presley should never have been married." He's not talking about the fall-off in a movie star's mail when he takes the sacred vows, but about the freedom to act in the midst of an audience. To be the kind of rock 'n' roll star Stewart is is to be like a politician who campaigns every moment of his life.

"In America," Newman sings, "every man is free/ To take care of his home, and his family." But no more than that, is the bitter, unsung line. And that may not be enough, even if it is all most of us see.

The constriction of vision produced by that kind of life points to why Newman is right when he feels it is risky to get up on stage and sing from inside the soul of a rapist. It's not just a matter of what people will think of Newman; what if someone heard the song and went looking for a woman to rape? Oh, ridiculous, we might say. That's like pretending someone could listen to the Beatles sing a good old rock 'n' roll fuck song like "Helter Skelter" and take it as a sign to go out and murder seven people.

Good art is always dangerous, always open-ended. Once you put it out in the world you lose control of it; people will fit it into their lives in all sorts of different ways. If so much of the rock 'n' roll of the post-Beatle era is closed off and one-dimensional, like the politics it serenades and reinforces, if the aesthetic of solipsism is freezing the imagination and our ability to respond openly, it is Newman's risk taking that makes him so valuable. As a rather lazy Southern Californian who just wants a good life with his wife and his kids, his sense of risk makes him shrink from his audience; but as an artist, that sense makes him reach for bigger risks.

NEWMAN'S AMERICA, II

To introduce his greatest song, Randy will tell a little story about a movie he almost made, with all the big stars: " 'Van,' that's Van Morrison, Elton, you know Elton. . . ." The joke of this small-time rock 'n' roller up there with the big guns is more than obvious, but still funny. It would be even better if Newman made the whole thing up; it would somehow add to the charm of a song he will do later, "Lonely at the Top." It was written for Frank Sinatra, who, most likely thinking it was a slur on his need for a toupee, turned it down.

Up on stage Newman is still entranced by his tale of the silver screen stardom he might have had. Each singer will be given fifteen minutes to prepare and perform any kind of scenario he wants—do it all. And Newman has a wonderful idea. He will dress himself in a pure white planter's suit, white shoes, white hat—perhaps a red string tie, for color. As the camera zooms in for its opening shot, Newman is poised on the quarterdeck of a great clipper ship, testing his profile against the wind. What's he doing there? He's a recruiter for the slave trade.

His profile suitably established, Newman steps ashore. He is met by a hushed crowd of Africans, who hang on his every word. (Finally, Newman is a star.) He begins to sing, in a voice that combines the lazy drawl of the black man (something his audience will invent in their new land) with the gentle assurance of the holiest rabbi. The music, as Newman ultimately recorded it, comes in on the soundtrack (in the theater, Newman begins the song on his piano), and it is beautiful. And the slaver sings:

> *In America*
> *You'll get food to eat*
> *Won't have to run through the jungle*
> *And scuff up your feet*
> *You'll just sing about Jesus and drink wine all day*
> *It's great to be an American*

We are back in Harmonica Frank's medicine show, and it is the softest sell of all. "By the second verse," Randy confides, "they're already running for the boat."

> *Climb aboard little wog*
> *Sail away with me*

And if they are caught up in Newman's vision, the pure feel of it, so am I. "Sail away," he sings, "Sail away," and the grace of his singing conquers the last resistance. It is majestic. You can see the glassy waters, the birds hovering over the ship as the last glimpse of Africa drops over the horizon.

> *We will cross the mighty ocean into Charleston Bay**

You can dredge through all the antebellum fantasies kicked up to defend the peculiar institution and you will never find an image of slavery as lovely as this one.

This peaceful, quiet song is more outrageous than anything the Rolling Stones have ever done—or would be, if the nation heard Newman do it on the radio every day. Scary, astonishing, Newman has presented an American temptation—tempting not only the Africans, who became Negroes, and went on to create the music that finally tossed up Elvis Presley, rock 'n' roll, Newman, and his audi-

---

ence, but tempting America to believe that this image of itself just might be true.

"Sail Away" moves on one of the most seductive melodies ever to grace a popular song. It is just out of reach, with a fabulous edge of déjà vu, calling up the classic Ray Charles records of the early sixties—"Born to Lose," "You Don't Know Me," "That Lucky Old Sun"—calling up a thousand songs and a thousand happy endings.

The power of the song is in the simple, perfectly accomplished idea that something so horrible and charged with guilt as slavery could take on such real beauty. The focus is not on those who are to be enslaved, but on the singer, the confidence man. Of course he is lying. He has seen babies thrown into the sea, smelled the death and excrement in the hold, watched the brand burn into the flesh. He has looked without flinching into the bewildered eyes that are perhaps the most terrible of all. But for the moment, he believes himself. A secret ambivalence of four hundred years of American life finds a voice in this song. It is not particularly liberating; too strange for that, it is like a vision of heaven superimposed on hell.

Y'all gonna be an American

Rock 'n' roll has always specialized in racial paradoxes, but none as queer as this. It has virtually nothing to do with "rock 'n' roll" as a musical form (save that Newman's singing owes so much to the blues) and everything to do with the rock 'n' roll audience. Newman offers it a vision its members have spent years driving from their minds, bringing them back to a home that was never there.

The song transcends its irony. It is, in the end, what America would like to believe about itself, and what ten years of a war across the ocean and ten years of bitter black faces will never let it believe, even in secret: that everything America did was for the good. Better than good: that God's work really was our own and meant to be. That we brought something new and precious into the world, a land even the most miserable slaves would recognize as Eden.

For if they did not, how could we believe it?

Sailing across the ocean, the slaver and his slaves are in love.

NEWMAN'S FAILURE

"Every great artist must create for a great audience," Bob Christgau pronounced one night when we were delving into The Great Randy Newman Mystery (Why isn't this genius as big as he deserves to be?). Christgau meant an aggressive, critical audience, with a conscious sense of itself *as* an audience, but he also meant a big, broad audience, one whose complexity and diverse needs can push an artist beyond comfortable limits.

When a single like the O'Jays' "Back Stabbers" rams home the result of years of shifting black consciousness and takes over the charts, it creates a cultural moment shared by a good part of the country, shoving a particular sensibility through all sorts of ordinary barriers that grow up between audiences. The passion and clarity of the song can connect a black pimp, whose life it was virtually meant to define, to a middle-class white kid, who just digs the beat and will find his or her place in the lyrics soon enough. When a movie like *The Godfather* becomes the national pastime, you can feel, as you sit for perhaps the first time in a theater half black and half white, that for better or for worse America's fantasies are at last becoming common property; that artists and audiences have come to a verge, that the stakes of American life have been raised.

If *The Godfather* had succeeded merely as a genre classic, it would have been a very different movie—the response it provokes changes how we see and understand it. Like "Back Stabbers," it matters, has its particular meanings, partly *because* it is a hit. Without massive public response, we would not even get close to two crucial democratic questions, questions worth asking about any interesting work of popular culture: How far can this work take its audience? How far can its audience go with it? Only works that can't be ignored—liking them is hardly the point—raise such questions and bring them to life. In one way or another we are all affected by hits, and are forced to define ourselves in terms of our response to them, just as we are all, for good or ill, affected by the romantic heroism of the Westerns, and not necessarily by, say, the chaotic heroism that is the subject of Orson Welles' movies. Certainly we are caught up in those things that impelled Welles, but his version of them, the shape of his vision, has not inevitably become part of us; we don't have to live in the world as he tried to define it, as we helplessly live out and respond to the nostalgia of John Ford or Howard Hawks. The life of a whole generation is authentically quickened and brightened by the Beatles, but it is not disturbed and sharpened by Randy Newman. The point is not that it would be "good for people" if the radio were playing "Sail Away" all day long, but that such exposure might be the only way to find out how strong the song really is. But Newman is quite different from Orson Welles, who lost a great fight with Hollywood in his attempt to get his movies made, because Newman is barely on the battlefield.

His quandary is not unlike the one the Kinks fell into in the late sixties. After a string of post-Beatle Invasion hits based on a chopped and channeled version of "Louie Louie," the sensibility of Ray Davies, their resident ex-art-student genius (every British band had one in those days), began to take over the group. The Kinks became less of a band, less a bundle of ambition and lust for money, fame, and fun, and more of a means to Davies' fantasies. He became a social critic, or more appropriate for rock 'n' roll, a social complainer. He squeezed a few hits out of this stance, but the last chart success he got in the sixties crystallized his new view of the world and dropped the commercial bottom out of the group. "Sunny Afternoon" (1966) could have been another put-down of the English middle class, but instead the hunter was captured by the game. This was an ode to upper-class boredom. The Kinks became a classy little outfit, neurotic, long on intelligence and short on raunch, and their album sales dropped into the low thousands. They were idolized by the critics and ignored by everybody else.

You couldn't call Davies' world dark, exactly; it was dimmed. Like Newman's, it was completely idiosyncratic, if generally a lot less compelling. An anthem Davies wrote to himself defined it best: a fearsome, ferocious piece of hard rock he slipped onto the flip side of "Sunny Afternoon," and which didn't surface on an American album until seven years later—"I'm Not Like Everybody Else."

Davies opened the song as a sickly kid pushed up against the wall by a gang of thugs (that is, everybody else), and then broke wide open with a rage that negated the whole world he wouldn't serve, that he wouldn't and couldn't change into. By the last fiery choruses he was free, as free to ignore his listeners as they had always been to ignore him. It was a great record.*

Davies commenced to delineate the subtleties of nostalgia, the quirks of inadequacy, the aesthetics of oddball. For a time his insu-

---

*And I swear I hear a hint of the closet Davies later came out of; doesn't he scream, "I won't go to bed like everybody else?"

lation produced appropriate fantasies, and also his best songs (such as "Waterloo Sunset," an unbearably lovely tune about an old man who watches lovers from his window). Artistic privacy also produced terrible self-indulgence and embarrassing cuteness. The critics cheered the good and the bad, as they do with Newman, but finally even they began to weary in their proselytizing. Paul Williams, an original Kinks booster, reviewed their last bomb "for those who love the Kinks," formally ending the great struggle to spread the word.

But not quite. Davies had written *Arthur*, an "opera" about a post-Victorian lost in a twentieth-century world; some of it was brilliant and some of it wasn't, as with all Kinks albums, which shouldn't have made any difference one way or the other. But an extraordinary push by two *Rolling Stone* reviewers (one of whom, I confess, was me), and its release at the same time as the Who's *Tommy* (suddenly nothing was as salable as the concept of Opera, which is to say, Art), made *Arthur* a decent success. The Kinks stumbled back to America for their first tour in years, and eventually got another hit, a big one, with "Lola," the tender tale of a shy country boy meeting up with a big-city transvestite—superb rock 'n' roll and a pop masterpiece.

The Top 40 audience, which had grabbed for the record, not "the Kinks," settled back, but as happens whenever a group gets a hit, the band picked up enough new fans to make them successful, seventies-style. Instead of a little cult, they had a big cult. Davies' insulation was gone, and the sharp edge of his feel for being different collapsed into gross parody of the big bad world. His songs became either hysterically unfunny (the next album was called *Lola v. the Power-Mad Money Men*, or something like that) or merely dull. An uncritical audience—a cult—was even worse for the band than uncritical critics. Davies' outsider stance, which had given his work what strength and vitality it had, was vitiated by the presence of an automatic audience.

And yet the echo of that wonderful statement, "I'm Not Like Everybody Else," is still there—not in Davies' work, but in Newman's: the idea that communication is failure, because if you get what you have to say across to a mass audience, that means what you have to say is not deep enough, or strong enough, to really matter. Newman has said he feels his songs are disturbing; that his lack of success is due to the weight of his material and the discomfort of his version of the truth. He is not surprised by his small audience, just frustrated by it, because if he cannot get his work across he is failing his work. That is, he can't win.

Newman's most accessible songs (as he performs them, which is all that concerns me, and all I think really concerns Newman) are generally his sledge-hammer ironies like "Political Science" (Let's drop the bomb on all our snotty so-called allies) or "Burn On." The genre only parodies the depth of Newman's talent, and it is impossible that he doesn't know it. If his thinnest, weakest work gets the most applause, what's he to think? That his audience isn't good enough for him? That he panders to his audience? This genre may expand anyway, because one part of Newman wants the great audience because he knows his work deserves it. And what often happens to the American popular artist, who feels he must grab the country itself and fails to even scratch it, is that he tries so desperately and honestly to alter his work in order to make it matter (not even compromising to make it palatable, though the line is hard to draw, especially for the artist), that he loses all sense of what impelled him in the first place. Either his career declines, and he is forgotten, or he hits, and decides that he has betrayed himself—and his audience. Someday this may happen to Newman; his music will lose its subtleties, even his humor will fall flat. Then he will be easier to accept, and useless as an artist.

Well, he knows all this, puttering around the house watching *Secret Storm* and vaginal deodorant commercials just like I do when I'm trying to avoid doing some *serious work* like writing this book, but in one sense none of it matters—in *his* case—because the deepest thing keeping Randy Newman from the American audience is his own sensibility.

There is something to Newman's idea that his marginal status in the rock 'n' roll world is a matter of the darkness and perversity of his vision, but I think it has more to do with the ambivalence that underlies that vision. Pop careers are not gifts of the muse, they are won, and Newman, finally, is all doubt as to whether or not the fight is worth it. There is one song he has written that captures his ambivalence so perfectly I can hardly believe he ever cranked himself up to write another one; it's called "My Old Kentucky Home." Imagine one of those automatic L.A. country backing tracks, straw on the studio floor, anything that helps set the scene, and then Randy (not Jewish or black this time, just drunk), warbling a timeless tribute to nothingness, negating the ambition rock 'n' roll demands just as Davies wiped out his audience:

Turpentine and dandelion wine
I've turned the corner and I'm doin' fine

Shooting at the birds on the telephone line
Pickin' em off with this gun a mine

Brother Gene he's big and mean
And he don't have much to say
He had a little woman who he whupped each day
But now she's gone away
He got drunk last night
Kicked mama down the stair
But I'm alright so I don't care

You can't get any farther into ambivalence than that. The connection between Newman's sense of himself, and the way the world
looks to him, could hardly be more exact. He might turn into a
homosexual someday, he told Susan Lydon, get religion, find a God.
Maybe his entire generation would. Maybe the whole world will turn
upside down and Newman will say Yes to all of it. Or something.

He's not particularly ambiguous; his meanings, though they expand if you keep his songs in your head, are clear enough—even if
some singers have willfully deluded themselves into recording "Sail
Away" as if it were a rewrite of "Born Free" (changing that disagree-
able line about "Climb aboard, little wog" to "little child," which I
suppose means they know quite well what the song is about after all).

But if his meanings are clear, their value is something else. We
know what the slavemaster has in mind and what will happen to his
audience as soon as he gets it on the ship, but who knows how to
take it? You can't get out from under, that music just washes over
you and makes you feel clean. When beauty and evil are so perfectly
intertwined, what choices are really possible?

There are no cheap thrills in "Davy the Fat Boy," because Newman's performance is strong enough to force the listener into all its
roles: purveyor, victim, and drooling carny audience. His best songs
implicate the listener. He goes far enough to wonder if everything
might not be worth doing, which means he is far enough gone to
wonder if anything *is* worth doing—such as pursuing an audience. If
God, as Newman likes to see Him, is something worse than ambivalent in His heaven, how could *man* be any better? Since man is
cursed anyway ("I recoil in horror," says Newman's God, "from the
foulness of thee . . . / How we laugh up here in heaven at the prayers
you offer Me/ That's why I love mankind"), wouldn't any act of will
lead straight to that realm of folly and sin that is Newman's garden—
so far limited to his art, not yet taking over his life? Isn't it almost

true by Newman's definition of how the world works that desire and action produce disaster at worst and failure at best? If Newman is necessarily ambivalent about the ambitions of his characters, how could he regard his own ambitions any differently?

The answer is that he could be filled with such rage at the world for being the way it is that nothing could stop him from conniving against it. Herman Melville's view of the world was not so different, and when he finally understood the trap God had set for man (and he was no older than Newman), he had the time of his life trying to write his way out of it. Even though he saw clearly enough to know he would never make it, he was caught up in a vision of what a remarkable fight it would be.

But if such a perception of the nature of things was enough to set an American's teeth on edge more than a hundred years ago, it may not be anymore. America is tired; Newman is not a driven artist like Melville, or for that matter a sixties Bob Dylan (hero of another young America, itself grown weary by the time Newman arrived to stake a claim to it)—perhaps he cannot afford to be. Newman is ambivalent even about his own talent; as a factual matter of daily life, he cannot decide if it is worth writing a song, let alone recording it once it is written. He lacks what Chandler called "the hard core of selfishness necessary to exploit talent to the full"—the aggression and insanity that lie beneath the pop version of the Alger dream. Newman is very distant from that, and close enough to see it for what it is; he is a Bartleby, the man who would prefer not to.

Newman skirts the rock 'n' roll audience, but he and a few others keep the margins of possibility open. Aesthetically a figure of real genius and culturally a born cult hero, his America does not come across quite as readily as that of Chuck Berry, the Rolling Stones, or the Band. In his own peculiar way, Randy Newman is much closer to the Sly Stone of *Riot*.

Newman's rock 'n' roll is short on musical force, vocal exuberance, and the promise of good times no matter what (everything Sly willfully removed from *Riot*); his work lacks the undeniable satisfaction we get from Mick Jagger roaring he can't get none. *That* kind of satisfaction is what we ask from rock 'n' roll; but if Norman Mailer is right when he says that the worst American promise is the promise of an unearned freedom from dread, Randy Newman's songs may give us some of what we need.

Laconic, funny, grim, and solitary, Randy Newman is a typical figure in the American imagination: the man who does not like what he sees but is wildly attracted to it anyway, a man who keeps his sanity by rendering contradictions other people struggle to avoid. For the moment, he carries the weight of one version of America on his shoulders—not that anyone has asked him to, as audiences have asked Bob Dylan, Elvis Presley, and Sly Stone—but his real task is to make his burden ours.

CODA: NEWMAN'S SUCCESS

Newman's cult status was deceptive. Over the years, he had won more and more fans and more and more rave reviews; as a sort of antipop pop star, he had become more and more hip. His work had grown stronger; the more listeners he attracted, it seemed, the more ambitious he became. In 1974, two years after "Sail Away," he brought out *Good Old Boys*: nothing less than a portrait of the South from the 1920s to the present, as seen through the eyes of a redneck. Newman's cult was, sort of, ready to explode into the pop mainstream. *Good Old Boys* was a small hit—for Newman, it was a big hit—and it hung onto the charts for almost half a year. Newman toured seriously for the first time; at a few concerts, he performed with a full orchestra conducted by his Uncle Lionel. Then, three years later, came the shock. Newman had a national smash—and a national scandal.

"Short People," six-foot-plus Randy tried to convince his interviewers, was a joke: a satire on, you know, bigotry. With its unforgettable tag line—"Short people got no reason to live"—the song went to number two on the *Billboard* charts. It was number one on others, and banned from numerous radio stations: program directors claimed the song was "disturbing to little children," but one suspected little disc jockeys were more to the point. *Little Criminals*, the album that contained "Short People," hit the top ten. Suddenly, Newman was, well, not a star, exactly, but something other than he had been. The effect of all this on his music was very odd.

In pop terms, Newman had already been received as a star on the *Good Old Boys* tour. His fans had given him absolution; he could do no wrong. Applauding wildly for every number, the crowds weren't responding to the songs, but cheering Newman himself. He was "a genius"; he knew.

Newman was being celebrated as someone who was more than, other than, an entertainer; this made him want to entertain, to please, to flatter his audience. The number that made this indelibly clear was "A Wedding in Cherokee County," the most affecting cut on *Good Old Boys*: an almost impossible song about a backwoods farmer, his wedding day, and his impotence.

The man has always been laughed at; no one has considered the woman he is marrying worth laughing at. On record, Newman took a listener to the edge of laughter, but never allowed the listener to cross it; singing as the farmer, his touch was never more delicate. "Lord, help me if you will," he pleaded, anticipating failure; you shared a bit of the man's suffering, knowing there was no help.

It may have been that, in a concert hall, there was nothing Newman could have done to keep an audience from laughing at the people in this song. Newman's audience may have been too smug, and Newman at his best too subtle—and performance, after all, requires a certain level of dramatization. But on stage, Newman made it impossible for a crowd not to laugh at the people in his song. Introducing "A Wedding in Cherokee County" as the surviving remnant of a discarded "rock opera about Albania"—thus distancing himself and his audience from the tune to the most extreme extent—Newman did not merely fail to put the song across, he destroyed it. He promised that the song was a joke, that its characters were jokes, and that their predicament was something those smart enough to buy tickets to a Randy Newman concert could take as a freak show staged for their personal amusement. The farmer and his bride truly became "morons," as one reviewer approvingly called them. On *Good Old Boys*, Newman made a listener respect his characters; in concert, he had the crowd in the aisles before the first verse was over. He turned his audience into the people who paid to see Davy do his famous fat-boy dance, and himself into the carny barker who egged them on. Face to face with the Northern, white, liberal, well-educated audience whose preconceptions about the redneck South *Good Old Boys* was meant to change, Newman—himself a childhood Southerner—stepped back from the complexity of his song, and offered instead a postcard of an old Kentucky moonshiner with flies buzzing around his head.

If Newman's trashing of the man and woman in "Cherokee County" indicated a lack of trust in the ability of his audience to catch the subtleties of his music, it also made the rest of *Good Old Boys*—the autobiography of a Birmingham steelworker and, perhaps, of one of his forebears—seem anything but subtle. It made the disc sound like a liberal fantasy about the goodness of the white South, a fantasy generated more by fears that Richard Nixon and Spiro Agnew were right about the "Silent Majority" than by anything else. The statements Newman made about himself in concerts across the country indicated a more serious insecurity—and allowed his audience a deeper smugness.

Sold-out halls notwithstanding, Newman was appearing as a cult figure; his fans were thus defined as those in the know. So on stage, in the midst of his first full-scale national tour, Newman made much of the fact that—with his album rising to the lower reaches of the top of the charts—he was "selling out" to the mass audience. "I want Shea Stadium!" he cried—the ironic point being that the audience was not to take Newman's rising mass popularity all that seriously. Deep down, Newman was assuring the crowd, he would remain theirs, unsullied by the mob. The audience liked this, and they got the joke.

What the fans missed was the truth—Newman did want Shea Stadium. He thought his work deserved it, and, maybe, needed it. But playing cult hero on the verge of success, Newman found it necessary to speak coyly: to pretend he didn't want the mass audience, and that his fans weren't part of it. His use of the Shea Stadium line at every concert he gave in 1974 made it seem as if he were always selling out *tomorrow* night; his talk allowed even arriviste ticket-buyers admission to his cult. The implicit idea was that Newman's cult could grow bigger and bigger, until it really did become something like a mass, national audience—at which point, still maintaining the cult cachet that was its reason for being, it would have to feel superior to itself. But Randy Newman had not sold out to the mass audience; he had only sold out to his cult.

These contradictions were buried at the time, but they surfaced in 1977 with "Short People" and *Little Criminals*. Released concurrently with the stunning debut of Elvis Costello, whose songwriting showed that he had learned much from Newman, the record was bland; Newman's edge was off, as if he were afraid he might lose his new fans if he challenged them. "Short People" was not that far from such earlier headbangers as "Political Science" or "Burn On," but it had a better melody, a better hook, and a catchier idea—and so it became a hit. Newman's burgeoning cult had nothing to do with the song's chart success; in terms of his career, it was clearly a fluke. What counted was the emptiness of *Little Criminals*, a record that did not connect.

Newman had, far more perfectly than anyone could have expected, fallen into the trap of acclaim: the audience he had won with *Good Old Boys* disarmed him. But the fury over "Short People" made him think; he understood that he, like the Monotones with "Book of Love," was likely destined for one ride on the charts, and one only. And so, as he told the reporters who flocked to him in the wake of the protests against "Short People," he went back to work on "a broader insult."

And he got it. Released in 1979, the prescient *Born Again* opened with a ditty called "It's Money that I Love." Digging in with a rumble of New Orleans piano, Newman tossed off a mad inversion of the Moral Majority's new American agenda: he performed as a good liberal, born-again as a saint dedicated to greed. "I used to worry about the black man/ Now I don't worry about the black man," Randy sang. "Used to worry about the starving children of India/ You know what I say now about the starving children of India?"

What did Randy Newman say now?

He said, "Oh, mama."

He was back at the margin, scheming.

ELVIS
Presliad

FANFARE

Elvis Presley is a supreme figure in American life, one whose presence, no matter how banal or predictable, brooks no real comparisons. He is honored equally by long-haired rock critics, middle-aged women, the City of Memphis (they finally found something to name after him: a highway), and even a president.* Beside Elvis, the other heroes of

---

*Richard Nixon had Elvis over to the White House once, and made him an honorary narcotics agent. Nixon got his picture taken with the King. An odd story, though, from rock critic Stu Werbin: "It seems that the good German who arranges the White House concerts for the President and his guests managed to travel the many channels that lead only in rare instances to Col. Tom Parker's phone line. Once connected, he delivered what he considered the most privileged invitation. The President requests Mr. Presley to perform. The Colonel did a little quick figuring and then told the man that Elvis would consider it an honor. For the President, Elvis's fee, beyond traveling expenses and accommodations for his back-up group, would be

this book seem a little small-time. If they define different versions of America, Presley's career almost has the scope to take America in. The cultural range of his music has expanded to the point where it includes not only the hits of the day, but also patriotic recitals, pure country gospel, and really dirty blues; reviews of his concerts, by usually credible writers, sometimes resemble Biblical accounts of heavenly miracles. Elvis has emerged as a great *artist*, a great *rocker*, a great *purveyor of shlock*, a great *heart throb*, a great *bore*, a great *symbol of potency*, a great *ham*, a great *nice person*, and, yes, a great American.

In 1954 Elvis made his first records with Sam Phillips, on the little Sun label in Memphis, Tennessee; then a pact was signed with Col. Tom Parker, shrewd country hustler. Elvis took off for RCA Victor, New York, and Hollywood. America has not been the same since. Elvis disappeared into an oblivion of respectability and security in the sixties, lost in interchangeable movies and dull music; he staged a remarkable comeback as that decade ended, and now performs as the transcendental Sun King that Ralph Waldo Emerson only dreamed about—and as a giant contradiction. His audience expands every year, but Elvis transcends his talent to the point of dispensing with it altogether. Performing a kind of enormous victory rather than winning it, Elvis strides the boards with such glamour, such magnetism, that he allows his audience to transcend their desire for his talent. Action is irrelevant when one can simply delight in the presence of a man who has made history, and who has triumphed over it.

Mark now, the supreme Elvis gesture. He takes the stage with a retinue of bodyguards, servants, singers, a band, an orchestra; he applies himself vaguely to the hits of his past, prostrates himself before songs of awesome ickiness; he acknowledges the applause and the gasps that greet his every movement (applause that comes thundering with such force you might think the audience merely suffers the music as an excuse for its ovations); he closes with an act of show-biz love that still warms the heart; but above all, he throws away the entire performance.

How could he take it seriously? How could anyone create when all one has to do is appear? "He *looks* like Elvis Presley!" cried a friend,

---

$25,000. The good German gasped.

" 'Col. Parker, nobody gets paid for playing for the President!'

" 'Well, I don't know about that, son,' the Colonel responded abruptly, 'but there's one thing I do know. Nobody asks Elvis Presley to play for nothing.'" (*Creem*, March 1972)

when the Big E stormed forth in an explosion of flashbulbs and cheers. "What a burden to live up to!" It is as if there is nothing Elvis could do to overshadow a performance of his myth. And so he performs from a distance, laughing at his myth, throwing it away only to see it roar back and trap him once again.

He will sing, as if suffering to his very soul, a song called "This Time, You [God, that is] Gave Me a Mountain," which sums up his divorce and his separation from his little girl. Having confessed his sins, he will stand aside, head bowed, as the Special Elvis Presley Gospel Group sings "Sweet, Sweet Feeling (In this Place)." Apparently cleansed of his sins, he will rock straight into the rhythm and blues of "Lawdy, Miss Clawdy" and celebrate his new-found freedom with a lazy grin. But this little melodrama of casual triumph will itself be a throwaway. As with the well-planned sets, the first-class musicians, the brilliant costumes, there will be little life behind the orchestration; the whole performance will be flaccid, the timing careless, all emotions finally shallow, the distance from his myth necessitating an even greater distance from the musical power on which that myth is based.

Elvis gives us a massive road-show musical of opulent American mastery; his version of the winner-take-all fantasies that have kept the world lined up outside the theaters that show American movies ever since the movies began. And of course we respond: a self-made man is rather boring, but a self-made king is something else. Dressed in blue, red, white, ultimately gold, with a Superman cape and covered with jewels no one can be sure are fake, Elvis might epitomize the worst of our culture—he is bragging, selfish, narcissistic, condescending, materialistic to the point of insanity. But there is no need to take that seriously, no need to take anything seriously. "Aw, shucks," says the country boy; it is all a joke to him; his distance is in his humor, and he can exit from this America unmarked, unimpressed, and uninteresting.

"From the moment he comes out of the wings," writes Nik Cohn, "all the pop that has followed him is made to seem as nothing, to be blown away like chaff." That is exactly what that first moment feels like, but from that point on, Elvis will go with the rest of it, singing as if there are no dangers or delights in the world grand enough to challenge him. There is great satisfaction in his performance, and great emptiness.

It is an ending. It is a sure sign that a culture has reached a dead end when it is no longer intrigued by its myths (when they lose their

power to excite, amuse, and renew all who are a part of those myths—
when those myths just bore the hell out of everyone); but Elvis has
dissolved into a presentation of his myth, and so has his music. The
emotion of the best music is open, liberating in its commitment and
intangibility; Elvis's presentation is fixed. The glorious oppression of
that presentation parallels the all-but-complete assimilation of a rev-
olutionary musical style into the mainstream of American culture,
where no one is challenged and no one is threatened.

History without myth is surely a wasteland; but myths are compelling only when they are at odds with history. When they replace
the need to make history, they too are a dead end, and merely smug.
Elvis's performance of his myth is so satisfying to his audience that
he is left with no musical identity whatsoever, and thus he has no
way to define himself, or his audience—except to expand himself,
and his audience. Elvis is a man whose task it is to dramatize the fact
of his existence; he does not have to create something new (or try,
and fail), and thus test the worth of his existence, or the worth of his
audience.

Complete assimilation really means complete acceptance. The
immigrant who is completely assimilated into America has lost the
faculty of adding whatever is special about himself to his country; for
any artist, complete assimilation means the adoption of an aesthetic
where no lines are drawn and no choices are made. That quality of
selection, which is what is at stake when an artist comes across with
his or her version of anything, is missing. When an artist gives an all-
encompassing Yes to his audience (and Elvis's Yes implicitly includes
everyone, not just those who say Yes to *him*), there is nothing more
he can tell his audience, nothing he can really do for them, except
maybe throw them a kiss.

Only the man who says No is free, Melville once wrote. We
don't expect such a stance in popular culture, and those who do might
best be advised to take their trade somewhere else. But the refusal
that lurks on the margins of the affirmation of American popular
culture—the margins where Sly Stone and Randy Newman have done
their best work—is what gives the Yes of our culture its vitality and
its kick. Elvis's Yes is the grandest of all, his presentation of mastery
the grandest fantasy of freedom, but it is finally a counterfeit of freedom: it takes place in a world that for all its openness (Everybody
Welcome!) is aesthetically closed, where nothing is left to be mastered,
where there is only more to accept. For all its irresistible excitement
and enthusiasm, this freedom is complacent, and so the music that it

produces is empty of real emotion—there is nothing this freedom could be for, nothing to be won or lost.

At best, when the fans gather around—old men and women who might see their own struggles and failures ennobled in the splendor of one who came from the bottom; middle-aged couples attending to the most glamorous nightclub act there is; those in their twenties and thirties who have grown with Elvis ever since he and they created each other years ago (and who might have a feeling he and they will make their trip through history together, reading their history in each other)—at best, Elvis will confirm all who are there *as* an audience. Such an event, repeated over and over all across the land, implies an America that is as nearly complete as any can be. But what is it worth?

When Elvis sings "American Trilogy" (a combination of "Dixie," "The Battle Hymn of the Republic," and "All My Trials," a slave song), he signifies that his persona, and the culture he has made out of blues, Las Vegas, gospel music, Hollywood, schmaltz, Mississippi, and rock 'n' roll, can contain any America you might want to conjure up. It is rather Lincolnesque; Elvis recognizes that the Civil War has never ended, and so he will perform the Union.

Well, for a moment, staring at that man on the stage, you can almost believe it. For if Elvis were to bring it off—and it is easy to think that only he could—one would leave the hall with a new feeling for the country; whatever that feeling might be, one's sense of place would be broadened, and enriched.

But it is an illusion. A man or woman equal to the song's pretension would have to present each part of the song as if it were the whole story, setting one against each other, proving that one American really could make the South live, the Union hold, and slavery real. But on the surface and beneath it, Elvis transcends any real America by evading it. There is no John Brown in his "Battle Hymn," no romance in his "Dixie," no blood in his slave song. He sings with such a complete absence of musical personality that none of the old songs matter at all, because he has not committed himself to them; it could be anyone singing, or no one. It is in this sense, finally, that an audience is confirmed, that an America comes into being; lacking any real fear or joy, it is a throwaway America where nothing is at stake. The divisions America shares are simply smoothed away.

But there is no chance anyone who wants to join will be excluded. Elvis's fantasy of freedom, the audience's fantasy, takes on such reality that there is nothing left in the real world that can inspire the fantasy, or threaten it. What *is* left is for the fantasy to replace the world; and that, night after night, is what Elvis and his audience make happen. The version of the American dream that is Elvis's performance is blown up again and again, to contain more history, more people, more music, more hopes; the air gets thin but the bubble does not burst, nor will it ever. This is America when it has outstripped itself, in all of its extravagance, and its emptiness is Elvis's ultimate throwaway.

There is a way in which virtually his whole career has been a throwaway, straight from that time when he knew he had it made and that the future was his. You can hear that distance, that refusal to really commit himself, in his best music and his worst; if the throwaway is the source of most of what is pointless about Elvis, it is also at the heart of much of what is exciting and charismatic. It may be that he never took *any* of it seriously, just did his job and did it well, trying to enjoy himself and stay sane—save for those first Tennessee records, and that night, late in 1968, when his comeback was uncertain and he put a searing, desperate kind of life into a few songs that cannot be found in any of his other music.

It was a staggering moment. A Christmas TV special had been decided on; a final dispute between Colonel Parker (he wanted twenty Christmas songs and a tuxedo) and producer Steve Binder (he wanted a tough, fast, sexy show) had been settled; with Elvis's help, Binder won. So there Elvis was, standing in an auditorium, facing television cameras and a live audience for the first time in nearly a decade, finally stepping out from behind the wall of retainers and sycophants he had paid to hide him. And everyone was watching.

In the months preceding Elvis had begun to turn away from the seamless boredom of the movies and the hackneyed music of the soundtrack albums, staking out a style on a few half-successful singles, presenting the new persona of a man whose natural toughness was tempered by experience. The records—"Big Boss Man," "Guitar Man," "U.S. Male"—had been careful, respectable efforts, but now he was putting everything on the line, risking his comforts and his ease for the chance to start over. He had been a bad joke for a long time; if this show died, little more would be heard from Elvis Presley. Did he still have an audience? Did he still have anything to offer them? He had raised the stakes himself, but he probably had no idea.

Sitting on the stage in black leather, surrounded by friends and a rough little combo, the crowd buzzing, he sang and talked and joked, and all the resentments he had hidden over the years began to pour out. He had always said yes, but this time, he was saying no—not without humor, but almost with a wry bit of guilt, as if he had betrayed his talent and himself. "Been a long time, baby." He told the audience about a time back in 1955, when cops in Florida had forced him to sing without moving; the story was hilarious, but there was something in his voice that made very clear how much it had hurt. He jibed at the Beatles, denying that the heroes who had replaced him had produced anything he could not match, and then he proved it. After all this time he wanted more than safety; he and the men around him were nervous, full of adventure.

"I'd like to do my favorite Christmas song," Elvis drawls—squeals of familiarity from the crowd, the girls in the front rows doing their job, imitating themselves or their images of the past, fading into an undertone of giggles as the music begins. Elvis sings "Blue Christmas," a classically styled rhythm and blues, very even, all its tension implied: a good choice. He sings it low and throaty, snapping the strings on his guitar until one of his pals cries, "Play it dirty! Play it dirty!"— on a Christmas song! All right! But this is recreation, the past in the present, an attempt to see if Elvis can go as far as he once did. Within those limits it works, it is beautiful. The song ends with appropriate, and calculated, screams.

"Ah think Ah'll put a strap around this and stand up," Presley says. AHAHAHAHAHAHAHAHAAHAHA! God, what's that? Nervous laughter from a friend. Slow and steady, still looking around for the strap no one has bothered to hook onto the guitar, Elvis rocks into "One Night." In Smiley Lewis's original, it was about an orgy, called "One Night of Sin" (with the great lines, "The things I did and I saw/ Would make the earth stand still"); Elvis cleaned it up into a love story in 1958. But he has forgotten—or remembered. He is singing Lewis's version, as he must have always wanted to. He has slipped his role, and laughing, grinning, something is happening.

> . . . *The things I did and I saw, could make* . . .
> these dreams—*Where's the strap?*

Where's the strap, indeed. He falls in and out of the two songs, and suddenly the band rams hard at the music and Elvis lunges and eats it alive. No one has ever heard him sing like this; not even his best records suggest the depth of passion in this music. One line from Howlin' Wolf tells the tale: "When you see me runnin', you know my life is at stake." That's what it sounds like.

Shouting, crying, growling, lusting, Elvis takes his stand and the crowd takes theirs with him, no longer reaching for the past they had been brought to the studio to reenact, but responding to something completely new. The crowd is cheering for what they had only hoped for: Elvis has gone beyond all their expectations, and his, and they don't believe it. The guitar cuts in high and slams down and Elvis is roaring. Every line is a thunderbolt. *AW, YEAH!*, screams a pal— he has waited years for this moment.

UNNNNNNH! WHEW! When . . . I ain't nevah did no wrong!

And Elvis floats like the master he is back into "One night, with you," even allowing himself a little "Hot dog!", singing softly to himself.

It was the finest music of his life. If ever there was music that bleeds, this was it. Nothing came easy that night. and he gave everything he had—more than anyone knew was there.

Something of that passion spilled over into the first comeback album, *From Elvis in Memphis*; into "Suspicious Minds," the single that put him back on top of the charts; into his first live shows in Las Vegas; and then his nerves steadied, and Elvis brought it all back home again. You can still hear the intensity, the echo of those moments of doubt, in the first notes of most songs Elvis sings on stage—just before he realizes again that the crowd cares only that he is before them, and that anyway, the music would be his if he wanted it, that his talent is so vast it would be demeaning to apply it. So he will revel in his glory, acting the part of the King it has always been said he is; and if that is a throwaway, it is at least thrown at those who want it. A real glow passes back and forth between Elvis and his audience, as he shares a bit of what it means to transcend the world of weakness, failure, worry, age and fear, shows what it means for a boy who sprung from the poor to be godly, and shares that too.

I suppose it is the finality this performance carries with it that draws me back to Elvis's first records, made when there was nothing to take for granted, let alone throw away. Those sides, like "One Night," catch a world of risk, will, passion, and natural nobility; something worth searching out within the America of mastery and easy splendor that may well be Elvis's last word. The first thing Elvis had to learn to transcend, after all, was the failure and obscurity he was born to; he had to find some way to set himself apart, to escape the limits that could well have given his story a very different ending.

The ambition and genius that took him out and brought him back is there in that first music—that, and much more.

HILLBILLY MUSIC

"This is the mystery of democracy," intoned Woodrow Wilson (dedicating the log cabin where Abraham Lincoln was born, in words ponderous enough to suit the mayor of Tupelo, Mississippi, when he dedicated the birthplace of Elvis Presley), "that its richest fruits spring up out of soils which no man has prepared and in circumstances where they are least expected. . . ."

I like those words. The question of history may have been settled on the side of process, not personality, but it is not a settlement I much appreciate. Historical forces might explain the Civil War, but they don't account for Lincoln; they might tell us why rock 'n' roll emerged when it did, but they don't explain Elvis any more than they explain Little Peggy March. What a sense of context does give us, when we are looking for someone in particular, is an idea of what that person had to work with; but for myself, it always seems inexplicable in the end anyway. There are always blank spots, and that is where the myths take over. Elvis's story is so classically American (poor country boy makes good in the city) that his press agents never bothered to improve on it. But it is finally elusive too, just like all the good stories. It surrounds its subject, without quite revealing it. But it resonates; it evokes like crazy.

Now, the critical (and least tangible) point in the biography of

---

ELVIS ECHOES: Introducing a series of interruptions of Presley-Presence that, occurring while this chapter was written, are an essential part of its context, but do not fit anywhere else. ❈ EE #1. Elvis is to perform at the Oakland Coliseum in 1972. Back in the Dark Ages, two San Francisco high school girls win a "Why I Love Elvis" contest and are flown to Hollywood to be kissed. *Their principal expels them:* "We don't need that kind of publicity," he explains. Now, some babies and divorces later (for Elvis, too), the winners return. The word is passed; they are ushered backstage; they are kissed once more. It is a link to the past, but I am willing to bet that most of those in the hall (16,000) are meeting Elvis in the flesh for the first time, as am I. I have a bad seat, and the fortyish woman next to me passes her binoculars. I trade off with her preteen daughter. I notice that the best seats are occupied by couples who look old enough to substitute for El's grandparents. A thought from my friend Mary Clemmey comes to mind: In his present-day audience, Elvis sees the ghost of his mother, and the family life he has had to give up in order to be what he is. Behind me, a hippie pulls furiously on a joint. Is he performing an act of rebellion? Against Elvis? Or affirming that, in a bouffant utopia, he alone keeps the true Presley spirit alive?

any great man or woman is just that place where that person's story begins to detach itself from those of countless others like it. Take Lincoln again; was it that famous hike when he brought the borrowed book back? The moment on the stand facing Douglas when he knew he had him licked and loved it? The day he was born? You can't answer such questions, not computer-style, but you have no claim on the story unless you risk a guess.

They called Elvis the Hillbilly Cat in the beginning; he came out of a stepchild culture (in the South, white trash; to the rest of America, a caricature of Bilbo and moonshine) that for all it shared with the rest of America had its own shape and integrity. As a poor white Southern boy, Elvis created a personal culture out of the hillbilly world that was his as a given. Ultimately, he made that personal culture public in such an explosive way that he transformed not only his own culture, but America's.

It was, as Southern chambers of commerce have never tired of saying, A Land of Contrasts. The fundamental contrast, of course, could not have been more obvious: black and white. Always at the root of Southern fantasy, Southern music, and Southern politics, black Americans were poised in the early fifties for an overdue invasion of American life, in fantasy, music, and politics. As the North scurried to deal with the problem, the South would be pushed farther and farther into the weirdness and madness its best artists had been trying to exorcise from the time of Poe on down. Its politics would dissolve into night-riding and hysteria; its fantasies would be dull for all their gaudy paranoia. Only the music got away clean.

The North, powered by the Protestant ethic, had set men free by making them strangers; the poor man's South that Elvis knew took strength from community.

The community was based on a marginal economy that demanded cooperation, loyalty, and obedience for the achievement of anything resembling a good life; it was organized by religion, morals, and music. Music helped hold the community together, and carried the traditions and shared values that dramatized a sense of place. Music gave pleasure, wisdom, and shelter.

"It's the only place in the country I've ever been where you can actually drive down the highway at night, and if you listen, you hear music," Robbie Robertson once said. "I don't know if it's coming from the people or if it's coming from the air. It lives, and it's rooted there."

Elegant enough, but I prefer another comment Robbie made. "The South," he said, "is the only place we play where everybody can clap on the off-beat."

Music was also an escape from the community, and music revealed its underside. There were always people who could not join, no matter how they might want to: tramps, whores, rounders, idiots, criminals. The most vital were singers: not the neighbors who brought out their fiddles and guitars for country picnics, as Elvis used to do, or those who sang in church, as he did also, but the professionals. They were men who bridged the gap between the community's sentimentalized idea of itself, and the outside world and the forbidden; artists who could take the community beyond itself because they had the talent and the nerve to transcend it. Often doomed, traveling throughout the South enjoying sins and freedoms the community had surrendered out of necessity or never known at all, they were too ambitious, ornery, or simply different to fit in.

The Carter Family, in the twenties, were the first to record the old songs everyone knew, to make the shared musical culture concrete, and their music drew a circle around the community. They celebrated the landscape (especially the Clinch Mountains that ringed their home), found strength in a feel for death because it was the only certainty, laughed a bit, promised to leave the hillbilly home they helped build only on a gospel ship. Jimmie Rodgers, their contemporary, simply hopped a train. He was every boy who ever ran away from home, hanging out in the railroad yards, bumming around with black minstrels, pushing out the limits of his life. *He* celebrated long tall mamas that rubbed his back and licked his neck just to cure the cough that killed him; he bragged about gunplay on Beale Street; he sang real blues, played jazz with Louis Armstrong, and though there was melancholy in his soul, his smile was a good one. He sounded like a man who could make a home for himself anywhere. There's so much *room* in this country, he seemed to be saying, so many things to do—how could an honest man be satisfied to live within the frontiers he was born to?

Outside of the community because of the way they lived, the singers were tied to it as symbols of its secret hopes, of its fantasies of escape and union with the black man, of its fears of transgressing the moral and social limits that promised peace of mind. Singers could present the extremes of emotion, risk, pleasure, sex, and violence that the community was meant to control; they were often alcoholic or worse, lacking a real family, drifters in a world where roots were life.

Sometimes the singer tantalized the community with his outlaw liberty; dying young, he finally justified the community by his inability to survive outside of it. More often than not, the singer's resistance dissolved into sentiment. Reconversion is the central country music comeback strategy, and many have returned to the fold after a brief fling with the devil, singing songs of virtue, fidelity, and God, as if to prove that sin only hid a deeper piety—or that there was no way out.

By the late forties and early fifties, Hank Williams had inherited Jimmie Rodgers' role as the central figure in the music, but he added an enormous reservation: that margin of loneliness in Rodgers' America had grown into a world of utter tragedy. Williams sang for a community to which he could not belong; he sang to a God in whom he could not quite believe; even his many songs of good times and good lovin' seemed to lose their reality. There were plenty of jokes in his repertoire, novelties like "Kaw-Liga" (the tale of unrequited love between two cigar store Indians); he traveled Rodgers' road, but for Williams, that road was a lost highway. Beneath the surface of his forced smiles and his light, easy sound, Hank Williams was kin to Robert Johnson in a way that the new black singers of his day were not. Their music, coming out of New Orleans, out of Sam Phillips' Memphis studio and washing down from Chicago, was loud, fiercely electric, raucous, bleeding with lust and menace and loss. The rhythmic force that was the practical legacy of Robert Johnson had evolved into a music that overwhelmed *his* reservations; the rough spirit of the new blues, city R&B, rolled right over his nihilism. Its message was clear: What life doesn't give me, I'll take.

Hank Williams was a poet of limits, fear, and failure; he went as deeply into one dimension of the country world as anyone could, gave it beauty, gave it dignity. What was missing was that part of the hillbilly soul Rodgers had celebrated, something Williams' music obscured, but which his realism could not express and the community's moralism could not contain: excitement, rage, fantasy, delight—the feeling, summed up in a sentence by W. J. Cash from *The Mind of the South*, that "even the Southern physical world was a kind of cosmic conspiracy against reality in favor of romance"; that even if Elvis's South was filled with Puritans, it was also filled with natural-born hedonists, and the same people were both.

To lie on his back for days and weeks [Cash wrote of the hillbilly], storing power as the air he breathed stores power under the hot sun of August, and then to explode, as that air explodes in a thunderstorm, in a violent outburst of emotion—in such a fashion would he make life not only tolerable, but infinitely sweet.

In the fifties we can hardly find that moment in white music, before Elvis. Hank Williams was not all there was to fifties country, but his style was so pervasive, so effective, carrying so much weight, that it closed off the possibilities of breaking loose just as the new black music helped open them up. Not his gayest tunes, not "Move It on Over," "Honky Tonkin'," or "Hey Good Lookin'," can match this blazing passage from Cash, even if those songs share its subject:

To go into the town on Saturday afternoon and night, to stroll with the throng, to gape at the well-dressed and the big automobiles, to bathe in the holiday cacaphony . . . maybe to have a drink, maybe to get drunk, to laugh with the passing girls, to pick them up if you had a car, or to go swaggering or hesitating into the hotels with the corridors saturated with the smell of bicloride of mercury, or the secret, steamy bawdy houses; maybe to have a fight, maybe against the cops, maybe to end, whooping and goddamning, in the jailhouse. . . .

The momentum is missing; that will to throw yourself all the way after something better with no real worry about how you are going to make it home. And it was this spirit, full-blown and bragging, that was to find its voice in Elvis's new blues and the rockabilly fever he kicked off all over the young white South. Once Elvis broke down the door, dozens more would be fighting their way through. Out of nowhere there would be Carl Perkins, looking modest enough and sounding for all the world as if he was having fun for the first time in his life, chopping his guitar with a new kind of urgency and yelling: "Now Dan got happy and he started ravin'—He jerked out his razor but he wasn't shavin' "—

He bollered R-R-RAVE ON *chillen, I'm with ya!*
RAVE ON CATS *he cried*
It's almost dawn and the cops're gone
Let's allllllll get dixie fried!

Country music (like the blues, which was more damned and more honestly hedonistic than country had ever been) was music for a whole community, cutting across lines of age, if not class. This could have meant an openly expressed sense of diversity for each child, man, and woman, as it did with the blues. But country spoke to a community fearful of anything of the sort, withdrawing into itself, using music as a bond that linked all together for better or for worse, with a sense that what was shared was less important than the crucial fact of sharing. How could parents hope to keep their children if their kids' whole sense of what it meant to live—which is what we get from music when we are closest to it—held promises the parents could never keep?

The songs of country music, and most deeply, its even, narrow sound, had to subject the children to the heartbreak of their parents: the father who couldn't feed his family, the wife who lost her husband to a honky-tonk angel or a bottle, the family that lost everything to a suicide or a farm spinning off into one more bad year, the horror of loneliness in a world that was meant to banish that if nothing else. Behind that uneasy grin, this is Hank Williams' America; the romance is only a night call.

Such a musical community is beautiful, but it is not hard to see how it could be intolerable. All that hedonism was dragged down in country music; a deep sense of fear and resignation confined it, as perhaps it almost had to, in a land overshadowed by fundamentalist religion, where original sin was just another name for the facts of life.

RAISED UP

Now, that Saturday night caught by Cash and Perkins would get you through a lot of weekdays. Cash might close it off—"Emptied of their irritations and repressions, left to return to their daily tasks, stolid, unlonely, and tame again"—and he's right, up to a point. This wasn't any revolution, no matter how many cops got hurt keeping the peace on Saturday night. Regardless of what a passport to that Southern energy (detached from the economics and religion that churned it up) might do for generations of restless Northern and British kids, there is no way that energy can be organized. But the fact that Elvis and the rest could trap its spirit and send it out over a thousand radio transmitters is a central fact of more lives than mine; the beginning of most of the stories in this book, if nothing near the end of them.

For we are treading on the key dividing line that made Elvis "King of Western Bop" (they went through a lot of trouble finding a name for this music) instead of just another country crooner or a footnote in someone's history of the blues: the idea (and it was just barely an "idea") that Saturday night could be the whole show. You had to be young and a bit insulated to pull it off, but why not? Why not trade pain and boredom for kicks and style? Why not make an escape from a way of life—the question trails off the last page of *Huckleberry Finn*—into a way of life?

You might not get revered for all time by everyone from baby to grandma, like the Carter Family, but you'd have more fun. Reality would catch up sooner or later—a pregnant girlfriend and a fast marriage, the farm you had to take over when your daddy died, a dull and pointless job that drained your desires until you could barely remember them—but why deal with reality before you had to? And what if there was a chance, just a chance, that you *didn't* have to deal with it? "When I was a boy," said Elvis not so long ago, "I was the hero in comic books and movies. I grew up believing in a dream. Now I've lived it out. That's all a man can ask for."

Elvis is telling us something quite specific: how special he was; how completely he captured and understood what for most of us is only a tired phrase glossing the surfaces of our own failed hopes. It is one thing, after all, to dream of a new job, and quite another to dream of a new world. The risks are greater. Elvis took chances dreaming his dreams; he gambled against the likelihood that their failure would betray him, and make him wish he had never dreamed at all. There are a hundred songs to tell that story, but perhaps Mott the Hoople, chasing the rock 'n' roll fantasy Elvis made of the American dream, said it best: "I wish I'd never wanted then/ What I want now twice as much."

Always, Elvis felt he was different, if not better, than those around him. He grew his sideburns long, acting out that sense of differentness, and was treated differently: in this case, he got himself kicked off the football team. Hear him recall those days in the midst of a near-hysterical autobiography, delivered at the height of his comeback from the stage at the International Hotel in Las Vegas: ". . . Had

---

*SEE #2. May 1972. I read in *Modern Screen* that top GOP politicos are giving *serious consideration* to placing Elvis's name in nomination for the vice-presidency (a plot to get around that $25,000 fee?). The article is illustrated by fifteen-year-old shots of girls waving ELVIS-FOR-PRESIDENT banners. Elvis, the story says, thinks this is a good idea, and has recently addressed a group of Black Panthers in order to test his forensic skills. He told them, and I quote: "Violence is not where it's at. It's a real turn-off, man." I do not know how to take this, especially as I recall it a year later when a TV trailer announces, "Tonight, immediately following the President's speech on Watergate, see Elvis further the cause of rock 'n' roll in *Roustabout*." I am more disoriented by the idea that Elvis could further the cause of *anything* in a movie like *Roustabout* than I am by the missed chance of his involvement in the Watergate scandal. But then, he would have known how to handle it. To Elvis, Watergate would have been something like a cosmic paternity suit.

pretty long hair for that time and I tell you it got pretty weird. They used to see me comin down the street and they'd say, 'Hot dang, let's get him, he's a squirrel, he's a squirrel, get him, he just come down outta the trees.' "

High school classmates remember his determination to break through as a country singer; with a little luck, they figured, he might even make it.

Out on the road for the first time with small-change country package tours, though, Elvis would plot for something bigger—for everything Hollywood had ever shown him in its movies.

On North Main in Memphis, as Harmonica Frank recalls Elvis, this was nothing to put into words. Talking trash and flicking ash, marking time and trying to hold it off, what did Elvis really have to look forward to? A year or so of Saturday nights, a little local notoriety, then a family he didn't quite decide to have and couldn't support? It would be all over.

Elvis fancied himself a trucker (if there weren't any Memphis boys in the movies, there were plenty on the road), pushing tons of machinery through the endless American night; just his version of the train whistle that called out to Johnny B. Goode and kept Richard Nixon awake as a boy. If it is more than a little odd that what to Elvis served as a symbol of escape and mastery now works—as part of his legend—as a symbol of everything grimy and poor he left behind when he did escape, maybe that only tells us how much his success shuffled the facts of his life—or how much he raised the stakes.

You don't make it in America—Emerson's mousetrap to the contrary—waiting for someone to come along and sign you up. You might be sitting on a corner like a Philly rock 'n' roller and get snatched up for your good looks, but you'll be back a year later and you'll never know what happened. Worst of all, you may not even care. What links the greatest rock 'n' roll careers is a volcanic ambition, a lust for more than anyone has a right to expect; in some cases, a refusal to know when to quit or even rest. It is that bit of Ahab burning beneath the Huck Finn rags of "Freewheelin' " Bob Dylan, the arrogance of a country boy like Elvis sailing into Hollywood, ready for whatever kind of success America had to offer.

So if we treat Elvis's words with as much respect as we can muster—which is how he meant them to be taken—we can see the first point at which his story begins to be his own. He took his dreams far more seriously than most ever dare, and he had the nerve to chase them down.

* * *

Cash's wonderful line—"a cosmic conspiracy against reality in favor of romance"—now might have more resonance. Still, if the kind of spirit that romance could produce seems ephemeral within the context of daily life, you would not expect the music it produced to last very long either. Not even Elvis, as a successful young rocker, could have expected his new music to last; he told interviewers rock 'n' roll was here to stay, but he was taking out plenty of insurance, making movies and singing schmaltz. You couldn't blame him; anyway, he liked schmaltz.

Within the realm of country music, the new spirit dried up just like Saturday fades into Monday, but since rock 'n' roll found its own audience and created its own world, that hardly mattered. Rock 'n' roll caught that romantic conspiracy on records and gave it a form. Instead of a possibility within a music, it became the essence; it became, of all things, a tradition. And when that form itself had to deal with reality—which is to say, when its young audience began to grow up—when the compromise between fantasy and reality that fills most of this book was necessary to preserve the possibility of fantasy, the fantasy had become part of the reality that had to be dealt with; the rules of the game had changed a bit, and it was a better game. "Blue Suede Shoes" had grown directly into something as serious and complex, and yet still offhand, still take-it-or-leave-it-and-pass-the-wine, as the Rolling Stones' "You Can't Always Get What You Want," which asks the musical question, "Why *are you* stepping on my blue suede shoes?"

✳ EE #3. Elvis's 1973 TV special, *Aloha from Elvis in Hawaii*, was beamed by satellite to one-third of the world's population. Or so his publicity men announced. Perhaps it was that if the one-third of the world—principally the heathen part—had TV sets, it could have watched. It doesn't matter; the conceit of the concept is what matters.

You can see him now, Col. Thomas Andrew Parker, ex-carny barker, the great medical menagerist, tossing helplessly on his bed, scheming—after all these years, still peddling Elvis pens at press conferences, hustling glossies in the aisles at concerts, Colonel Parker does not rest—and what keeps him awake is that *even now there are people who do not know about Elvis Presley!* There are worlds to be conquered! There is work to be done!

Finally, he drops off to sleep. Yes, there are poor beggars somewhere in the Amazon jungle who have yet to get the word (perhaps the King would succeed where dozens of casseroled missionaries have failed—make a note of that), but the Colonel will deal with that tomorrow . . . wait for tomorrow.

Parker dreams.

It is perhaps 1990. Elvis is in his middle fifties now, still young, still beautiful. His latest single—"Baby Let Me Bang Your Box," backed with "My Yiddishe Mama"—has topped all charts. Parker has had his third heart transplant. The world has received the long-awaited actual communication from intelligent beings beyond the solar system. Earth's greatest scientists have assembled in Japan to decipher the message, and after years of error they have succeeded. It

Echoing through all of rock 'n' roll is the simple demand for peace of mind and a good time. While the demand is easy to make, nothing is more complex than to try to make it real and live it out. It all sounds plain, obvious; but that one young man like Elvis could break through a world as hard as Hank Williams', and invent a new one to replace it, seems obvious only because we have inherited Elvis's world, and live in it.

Satisfaction is not all there is to it, but it is where it all begins. Finally, the music must provoke as well as delight, disturb as well as comfort, create as well as sustain. If it doesn't, it lies, and there is only so much comfort you can take in a lie before it all falls apart.

The central facts of life in Elvis's South pulled as strongly against the impulses of hedonism and romance as the facts of our own lives do against the fast pleasures of rock 'n' roll. When the poor white was thrown back on himself, as he was in the daytime, when he worked his plot or looked for a job in the city, or at night, when he brooded and Hank Williams' whippoorwill told the truth all too plainly, those facts stood out clearly: powerlessness and vulnerability on all fronts. The humiliation of a class system that gave him his identity and then trivialized it; a community that for all its tradition and warmth was in some indefinable way not enough; economic chaos; the violence of the weather; bad food and maybe not enough of that; diseases that attached themselves to the body like new organs—they all mastered him. And that vulnerability produced—along with that urge to cut loose, along with that lively Southern romance—uncertainty, fatalism, resentment, acceptance, and nostalgia: limits that cut deep as the oldest cotton patch in Dixie.

Vernon Presley was a failed Mississippi sharecropper who moved his family out of the country with the idea of making a go in the city; it's not so far from Tupelo to Memphis, but in some ways, the journey must have been a long one—scores of country songs about boys and girls who lost their souls to the big town attest to that. Listen to Dolly Parton's downtown hooker yearning for her Blue Ridge mountain boy; listen to the loss of an America you may never have known.

They don't make country music better than that anymore, but it's unsatisfying, finally; too classical. This country myth is just one

---

consists of only one word, one question on which the fate of ten billion people may rest:

"ELWIS?"

So Colonel Parker rests easy. Age has mellowed him, and his expectations do not go beyond the Milky Way.

more echo of Jefferson pronouncing that, in America, virtue must be found in the land. I like myths, but this one is too facile, either for the people who still live on the land or for those of us who are merely looking for a way out of our own world, for an Annie Green Springs utopia. The myth is unsatisfying because the truth is richer than the myth.

"King Harvest (Has Surely Come)," the Band's song of blasted country hopes, gives us the South in all of its earthly delight and then snuffs it out. All at once, the song catches the grace and the limbo of the life that must be left behind.

The tune evokes a man's intimacy with the land and the refusal of the land to respond in kind. The music makes real, for the coolest city listener, a sense of place that is not quite a sense of being at home; the land is too full of violence for that. One hears the farmer's fear of separating from the land (and from his own history, which adhering to the land, is not wholly his own); one hears the cold economic necessities that have forced him out. The melody—too beautiful and out of reach for any words I have—spins the chorus into the pastoral with a feel for nature that is *really* hedonistic—

> *Corn in the field*
> *Listen to the rice as the wind blows cross the water*
> KING HARVEST HAS SURELY COME*

—and a desperate, ominous rhythm slams the verses back to the slum streets that harbor the refugees of the pastoral disaster: "Just don't judge me by my shoes!" Garth Hudson's organ traces the circle of the song, over and over again.

The earliest picture of Elvis shows a farmer, his wife, and their baby; the faces of the parents are vacant, they are set, as if they cannot afford an unearned smile. Somehow, their faces say, they will be made to pay even for that.

You don't hear this in Elvis's music; but what he left out of his story is as vital to an understanding of his art as what he kept, and made over. If we have no idea of what he left behind, of how much he escaped, we will have no idea what his success was worth, or how intensely he must have wanted it.

*   *   *

Elvis was thirteen when the family left Tupelo for Memphis in 1948, a pampered only child; ordinary in all respects, they say, except that he liked to sing. True to Chuck Berry's legend of the Southern rocker, Elvis's mother bought him his first guitar, and for the same reason Johnny B. Goode's mama had in mind: keep the boy out of trouble. Elvis sang tearful country ballads, spirituals, community music. On the radio, he listened with his family to the old music of the Carter Family and Jimmie Rodgers, to current stars like Roy Acuff, Ernest Tubb, Bob Wills, Hank Williams, and to white gospel groups like the Blackwood Brothers. Elvis touched the soft center of American music when he heard and imitated Dean Martin and the operatics of Mario Lanza; he picked up Mississippi blues singers like Big Bill Broonzy, Big Boy Crudup, Lonnie Johnson, and the new Memphis music of Rufus Thomas and Johnny Ace, mostly when no one else was around, because that music was naturally frowned upon. His parents called it "sinful music," and they had a point—it was dirty, and there were plenty of blacks who would have agreed with Mr. and Mrs. Presley—but Elvis was really too young to worry. In this he was no different from hundreds of other white country kids who wanted more excitement in their lives than they could get from twangs and laments—wanted a beat, sex, celebration, the stunning nuances of the blues and the roar of horns and electric guitars. Still, Elvis's interest was far more casual than that of Jerry Lee Lewis, a bad boy who was sneaking off to black dives in his spare time, or Carl Perkins, a musician who was consciously working out a synthesis of blues and country.

The Presleys stumbled onto welfare, into public housing. Vernon Presley found a job. It almost led to the family's eviction, because if they still didn't have enough to live on, they were judged to have too much to burden the county with their troubles. Elvis was a loner, but he had an eye for flash. He sold his blood for money, ushered at the movies, drove his famous truck, and divided the proceeds between his mother and his outrageous wardrobe. Looking for space, for a way to set himself apart.

Like many parents with no earthly future, the Presleys, especially Gladys Presley, lived for their son. Her ambition must have been that Elvis would take all that was good in the family and free himself from the life she and her husband endured; she was, Memphian Stanley Booth wrote a few years ago, "the one, perhaps the only one, who had told him throughout his life that even though he came from poor country people, he was just as good as anybody."

On Sundays (Wednesdays too, sometimes) the Presleys went to their Assembly of God to hear the Pentecostal ministers hand down a similar message: the last shall be first. This was democratic religion with a vengeance, lower class and gritty. For all those who have traced Elvis's music and his hipshake to his religion (accurately enough—Elvis was the first to say so), it has escaped his chroniclers that hillbilly Calvinism was also at the root of his self-respect and his pride: the anchor of his ambition.

His church (and the dozens of other Pentecostal sects scattered throughout the South and small-town America) was one part of what was left of the old American religion after the Great Awakening. Calvinism had been a religion of authority in the beginning; in the middle-class North, filtered through the popular culture of Ben Franklin, it became a system of tight money, tight-mindedness, and gentility; in the hillbilly South, powered by traveling preachers and their endless revivals, the old holiness cult produced a faith of grace, apocalypse, and emotion, where people heaved their deepest feelings into a circle and danced around them. Momentum scattered that old authority; all were sinners, all were saints. Self-consciously outcast, the true faith in a land of Philistines and Pharisees, it was shoved into storefronts and tents and even open fields, and no less sure of itself for that.

Church music caught moments of unearthly peace and desire, and the strength of the religion was in its intensity. The preacher rolled fire down the pulpit and chased it into the aisle, signifying; men and women rocked in their seats, sometimes onto the floor, bloodying their fingernails scratching and clawing in a lust for absolute sanctification. No battle against oppression, this was a leap right through it, with tongues babbling toward real visions, negating stale red earth, warped privvies, men and women staring from their sway-backed porches into nothingness. It was a faith meant to transcend the grimy world that called it up. Like Saturday night, the impulse to dream, the need to escape, the romance and the contradictions of the land, this was a source of energy, tension, and power.

Elvis inherited these tensions, but more than that, gave them his own shape. It is often said that if Elvis had not come along to set off the changes in American music and American life that followed his triumph, someone very much like him would have done the job as well. But there is no reason to think this is true, either in strictly musical terms, or in any broader cultural sense. It is vital to remember that Elvis was the first young Southern white to sing rock 'n' roll, something he copied from no one but made up on the spot; and to know that even though other singers would have come up with a white version of the new black music acceptable to teenage America, of all who did emerge in Elvis's wake, none sang as powerfully, or with more than a touch of his magic.

Even more important is the fact that no singer emerged with anything like Elvis's combination of great talent and conscious ambition, and there is no way a new American hero could have gotten out of the South and to the top—creating a whole new sense of how big the top was, as Elvis did—without that combination. The others—Perkins, Lewis, Charlie Rich—were bewildered by even a taste of fame and unable to handle a success much more limited than Presley's.

If Elvis had the imagination to come up with the dreams that kept him going, he had the music to bring them to life and make them real to huge numbers of other people. It was the genius of his singing, an ease and an intensity that has no parallel in American music, that along with his dreams separated him from his context; and for the rest of this chapter, we can try to discover what that singing was all about.

THE ROCKABILLY MOMENT

There are four of them in the little studio: Bill Black, the bass player; Scotty Moore, the guitarist; in the back, Sam Phillips, the producer; and the sexy young kid thumping his guitar as he sings, Elvis Presley, just nineteen. 1954.

Sam Phillips is doing all right for himself. He has been among the first to record men who will be giants in the world of postwar blues: B. B. King, Junior Parker, and the Howlin' Wolf himself. The names on Phillips' roster show his willingness to try anything: wonderful names like Big Memphis Ma Rainey, the Ripley Cotton Choppers, Dr. Ross, Hardrock Gunter, Rufus "Bear Cat" Thomas, Billy "The Kid" Emerson, the Prisonaires (a vocal group from the state pen), the immortal Hot Shot Love. There are plenty more knocking on the door, and with no more than this, Phillips' place in the history of American music would be assured—not that a place in history is quite what he is looking for.

In the records Phillips makes you can discern something more than taste, something like vision. He has cooked up a sound all his own: hot, fierce, overbearing, full of energy and desire, a sound to jump right out of the jukebox. But Phillips wants money, a lot of it, and he wants something new. Deep down in a place not even he sees clearly, he wants to set the world on its ear.

The kid with the guitar is . . . unusual; but they've been trying to put something on the tape Sam keeps running back—a ballad, a hillbilly song, anything—and so far, well, it just doesn't get it.

The four men cool it for a moment, frustrated. They share a feeling they could pull something off if they hit it right, but it's been a while, and that feeling is slipping away, as it always does. They talk music, blues, Crudup, ever hear that, who you kiddin' man, dig this. The kid pulls his guitar up, clowns a bit. He throws himself at a song. *That's all right, mama, that's all right* . . . eat shit. He doesn't say that, naturally, but that's what he's found in the tune; his voice slides over the lines as the two musicians come in behind him, Scotty picking up the melody and the bassman slapping away at his axe. Phillips hears it, likes it, and makes up his mind.

All right, you got something. Do it again, I'll get it down. Just like that, don't mess with it. Keep it simple.

They cut the song fast, put down their instruments, vaguely embarrassed at how far they went into the music. Sam plays back the tape. Man, they'll run us outta town when they hear it, Scotty says; Elvis sings along with himself, joshing his performance. They all wonder, but not too much.

Get on home, now, Sam says. I gotta figure what to do with this.

They leave, but Sam Phillips is perplexed. Who is gonna play this crazy record? White jocks won't touch it 'cause it's nigger music and colored will pass 'cause it's hillbilly. It sounds good, it sounds sweet, but maybe it's just . . . too weird? The hell with it.

Sam Phillips released the record; what followed was the heyday of Sun Records and rockabilly music, a moment when boys were men and men were boys, when full-blown legends emerged that still walk the land and the lesser folk simply went along for the ride.

Rockabilly was a fast, aggressive music: simple, snappy drumming, sharp guitar licks, wild country boogie piano, the music of kids who came from all over the South to make records for Sam Phillips and his imitators. Rockabilly came and it went; there was never that much of it, and even including Elvis's first Sun singles, all the rock-abilly hits put together sold less than Fats Domino's. But rockabilly fixed the crucial image of rock 'n' roll: the sexy, half-crazed fool standing on stage singing his guts out.

Most important, the image was white. Rockabilly was the only style of early rock 'n' roll that proved white boys could do it all—that they could be as strange, as exciting, as scary, and as free as the black men who were suddenly walking America's airwaves as if they owned them. There were two kinds of white counterattack on the black invasion of white popular culture that was rock 'n' roll: the attempt to soften black music or freeze it out, and the rockabilly lust to beat the black man at his own game.

Sam Phillips had the imagination to take in a country folksinger like Johnny Cash and a Stan Kenton fan like Charlie Rich; he was commercial enough to get rock 'n' roll out of both of them. Phillips gave a funny-looking kid named Roy Orbison the chance to growl that no girl had the style to match him, and the music to prove it. Sun tossed up Warren Smith, who claimed he had a girl who looked like a frog; Sonny Burgess, who dyed his hair red to match his red suit and his red Cadillac and told anyone who would listen he wanted to boogie with a red-headed woman; Sun offered us Billy Lee Riley, who blithely argued that rock 'n' roll was so strange it had to come from Mars. The little green men taught him how to do the bop, was the way he put it.

Carl Perkins found greatness here, and nowhere else; Jerry Lee Lewis simply took greatness as his due. ("*I* played on 'em," Jerry Lee told an interviewer who had asked the names of the musicians who had played on his records, "what else do you need to know?") Jerry Lee stormed his way through the whorehouse rock of "Deep Elem Blues" like Elmer Gantry moonlighting from the revival tent (celebrating the Dallas red light district that crawled with sin and blues piano); he tumbled into "Big Legged Woman," leering at an imaginary audience with the arrogance that would bring him down.

> *Let me tell ya, tell ya, tell ya something*
> WHAT I'M TALKIN' ABOUT
> *I bet my bottom dollar there ain't a cherry in this house**

While it lasted, Sun was a space of freedom, a place to take chances. The music Sun produced was ominous, funny, kicking up

---

*Copyright © P. Donald White. Used by permission.

rhythm and bursting with exuberance, determination, and urgency, full of self-conscious novelty and experiment. Most of the first rock 'n' roll styles were variations on black forms that had taken shape before the white audience moved in and forced those forms to turn its way; rockabilly was almost self-contained, a world of its own, and as authentically new as any music can be.

Back in those days I knew some country kids who captured the spirit of the music as well as any 45: farm boys, long, lean, tough, and good-humored. They flashed me my first picture of Little Richard, kicked raccoons to death with their bare feet, rustled sheep, chased Indian girls into the bushes, and made it into town on Saturday night to watch the razor fights. They were easy to idolize; one night they got drunk, drove their car to the railroad tracks, and got themselves blown to pieces.

Rockabilly was squeaky Charlie Feathers, a country singer of no special talent or even much drive, trekking up to Cincinnati, after failures at Sun, for the chance to yell, "Aw, turn it *loose!*" and then disappear. He reached once, and he missed, but these lines have stayed with me ever since a scratchy tape of his one great song arrived in the mail:

> *Well, I'm a tip-top daddy an' I'm gonna have my way*
> *Dontcha worry 'bout me baby, dont worry what they say*
> *I got one hand, baby, let it swing by my side*
> *Just gimme one hand loose, and I'll be satisfied*
> *Satisfied!**

"Maybe someday your name will be in lights," Chuck Berry promised the young rockers, and most of them never got past the "maybe." There was a price for all that unexpected vitality and flash. Carl Perkins, still billing himself "The King of Rock 'n' Roll" on the thin line of one hit and a score of failures, sunk into alcohol; Johnny Cash nearly killed himself on pills; Gene Vincent found himself exiled to England, where some still remembered, and died of a bleeding ulcer before he was forty. Johnny Burnette, Eddie Cochran, Buddy Holly, chasing after Elvis's pot of gold, died in accidents, in fast cars and chartered planes. Most simply vanished and were forgotten—if they were lucky enough to have been known at all. They fell back into the predictability of country music or the day-to-day sameness

---

*Copyright © 1956 by Fort Knox Music Company.

they had meant to escape. All they left behind was rock 'n' roll, and an audience that twenty years later was still acting out their fantasies and seeking novelty and amusement in their ghosts.

It was an explosion, and standing over it all was Elvis. In the single year he recorded for Sam Phillips—July 1954 through July 1955—ten sides were released (four more were used by RCA to fill up Elvis's first album); about half derived from country songs, the rest took off from blues. His music stands to the rest of rockabilly as genius does to talent.

The blues especially have not dated at all. Not a note is false; their excitement comes through the years intact, unburdened by cuteness, mannerism, or posturing.* Nothing is stylized. The music is clean, straight, open, and free.

That's what these sides are about: finding space in the crunch of the worn-out and overfamiliar; finding a way to feel free in that space and finding the voice to put that feeling across.

The best evidence of Sam Phillips' spirit is in the sound of the records. Each song is clear, direct, uncluttered, and blended into something coherent. There is that famous echo, slapping back at the listener, and a bubbling tension that is never quite resolved; no comforts of vocal accompaniment, but the risk of one young man on his own. The sound is all presence, as if Black and Moore each took a step straight off the record and Elvis was somehow squeezed right into the mike. "I went into the studio," Sam Phillips recalled years later, "to draw out a person's innate, possibly unknown talents, present them to the public, and let the public be the judge. I had to be a psychologist and know how to handle each artist and how to enable him to be at his best. I went with the idea that an artist should have something not just good, but totally unique. When I found someone like that, I did everything in my power to bring it out."†

The sides Phillips cut with Elvis might have worked in the twen-

---

*For most of us, the songs are unburdened by any sort of nostalgia as well. In their time, they were little heard outside of the South, and most turned up on albums only when Elvis was off in the Army and RCA had to scrape its vaults for something to release. None ever made the national pop charts. Today they are rarely played on the radio (though spinning the dial on Elvis's thirty-eighth birthday, I picked up "That's All Right"—on a country station). Until 1976, Colonel Parker, or Elvis himself, deemed it vital that the King be protected from his past, so the songs were not, as with most classic rock, reissued in a package that might attract an audience. Given the publicity that has come with Elvis, these sides remained almost invisible, the result of a prepop moment; but *their* result is as public as rock 'n' roll. From one point of view they are the basis of the whole show. So there is a lot of power packed into these records, and not all of it is musical.

†From an interview with John Pugh, *Country Music*, November 1973.

ties, and they might do for the eighties; not simply as listenable music—there is no doubt about that—but as music that still sounds new, that still breaks things open.*

Elvis can tell us what was new and distinctive about his time without being trapped by it, and without trapping us. He can do it because to a great degree ELVIS PRESLEY was the distinctive item. For all the writers who have found a neat logic to the development of the music Elvis made, and have lost his genius in a process, that is not what I hear; I hear a whole world of music that by no means had to crystallize as it did. "I heard the news," Elvis would sing in "Good Rockin' Tonight"—but he was the news.

Elvis's Memphis records—"Milkcow Blues Boogie," "You're a Heartbreaker," "Good Rockin' Tonight," "Baby Let's Play House"— might be his best; a choice between the Sun sides and "Hound Dog," "Don't Be Cruel," "All Shook Up," "Reconsider Baby," "Suspicious Minds" and "Long Black Limousine" is not one I ever want to make. Elvis's first music deserves a close and loving attention not simply because it represents all that Elvis and those he has sung for have lost—youthful exuberance, innocence, haven't we tired of that story?—but because this is unquestionably great music, fun to think about, and because this music foreshadows, and contains, the entire aesthetic Elvis has worked out over the twenty years of his career. This is emotionally complex music that can return something new each time you listen to it. What I hear, most of the time, is the affection

---

*Even the lyrics evade any possibility of camp—unlike so much of fifties rock 'n' roll, including Elvis's RCA material, which was made with a trendy commercial ear. The blues and country motifs of the Sun sides are as lively today as they were old in 1954; if it takes little effort to trace "That's All Right" and "Milkcow Blues Boogie" back to Son House's epic "My Black Mama," cut in 1930, it takes even less to follow the trail forward to the Rolling Stones or the Allman Brothers.

Not surprisingly, on the album that today features House's masterpiece (*Really! The Country Blues*), there is an ancient, quiet statement of the theme Elvis brought home with such force. Made in 1928, it comes deadpan, spoken over a pretty little guitar line by one William Moore— an old, old mood, there too in Harmonica Frank or the Allmans' "Pony Boy," but to modern ears, *about* what Elvis *was*. This is "Old Country Rock": "Come on, Bill, let's take them for an old country rock. Let's go back down the Rappahanock, down Tappahanock way. Look at Bill while everybody rocks. Get that old rock, Bill. Everybody rock. Old folks rock. Young folks rock. Boys rock. Girls rock. Trot back, man, and let me rock. Rock me, sis, rock me. Rock me till I sweat. Trot back, folks, let your pappy rock. Pappy knows how. Children rock. Sister Ernestine, show your pappy how you rock. Mighty fine, boys, rock it, rock it till the cows come home. Whip that box, Bill, whip it. Too sad, I mean too sad for the public. Now up the country, back down the country again on that old rock. Rappahanock. Tappahanock. Cross the river, boys, cross the river. Man, it's sporty. Play it, Bill, play it till the sergeant comes." No one could ask for a better summation than that.

and respect Elvis felt for the limits and conventions of his family life, of his community, and ultimately of American life, captured in his country sides; and his refusal of those limits, of any limits, played out in his blues. This is a rhythm of acceptance and rebellion, lust and quietude, triviality and distinction. It can dramatize the rhythm of our own lives well enough.

ELVIS MOVES OUT

Elvis first went into Sam Phillips' studio in early 1954, and though it took him months of work to get to the point where he could make his first record, it is impossible to imagine a more natural sound. There's more here than anyone could have guessed, he seems to be saying: more soul, more guts, and more life.

"That's All Right" was one of three Arthur Crudup tunes Elvis recorded. Crudup had cut many sides for RCA's Bluebird outlet in the forties and early fifties; he wrote good songs, pointed little messages of loss fitted to bright blues melodies, but he was a minimal guitarist and an erratic singer, a bit one-dimensional. Only on numbers that verged on country or pop styles (as with his lovely "So Glad You're Mine," which Elvis recorded in a disinterested manner soon after reaching RCA) does Crudup seem to hit his stride.

Elvis reduces the blueman's original to a footnote. He takes over the music, changing words and tightening verses to suit himself, hanging onto the ends of lines as Scotty Moore chimes in with pretty high-note riffs. Elvis sounds very young, sure of himself, ready to win; he turns Crudup's lament for a lost love into a satisfied declaration of independence, the personal statement of a boy claiming his manhood. His girl may have left him, but nothing she can do can dent the pleasure that radiates from his heart. It's the blues, but free of all worry, all sin; a simple joy with no price to pay.

Phillips put out the record on July 19, 1954, and it soon earned its place on the Memphis R&B charts, along with new hits by Muddy Waters and Johnny Ace. *Cashbox*, oblivious to Presley's color, reviewed the side as a blues; *Billboard*, prophetically, saw potential in all markets. It was an event, to some a scary one, but if "That's All Right" brought home the racial fears of a lot of people, it touched the secret dreams of others; if it was a threat, it was also another ride on the raft. "It was like a giant wedding ceremony," said Marion Keisker, Sam Phillips' working partner, and the one who first heard in Elvis's voice everything Phillips was after. "It was like two feuding clans who had been brought together by marriage."

"That's All Right" was a tremendous hit with teenagers, and in Memphis, where the record broke first, the current greeting among the teenagers is still a rhythmical line from the song: "Ta dee dah dee dee dah."

The Memphis Press-Scimitar, 1954

You can't get that kind of success in *Billboard*; "Sun's Newest Star," as the *Press-Scimitar* called Elvis, wasted no time taking advantage of it. He tried out his material in the local clubs, drew three thousand people to the opening of a shopping center, and busted up a big country review when he sang a song called "Good Rockin' Tonight." Phillips, for his part, wasted no time getting Elvis back into the studio and a new record into the stores.

"That's All Right" was an easy ride. "Good Rockin' " is a cataclysm; it reflects the new confidence of a young man who knows what it means to satisfy an audience, to take them beyond their expectations. The record is charged with an authority that no other country rocker ever approached.

Roy Brown, the most influential blues singer of the forties, wrote the tune, and Wynonie Harris made it a hit in 1948. Harris was a sophisticated uptown R&B vocalist; his "Good Rockin' " is a conventional jump blues, lacking real tension or drama. He seems unable to exploit the stomping promise of the lyrics in rhythm or phrasing; he bumps words into each other and sometimes trips on them. He's too removed from the country revel the song is all about, and too cool.

Elvis opens with a high, wild "WELLLLLLLLL . . ." and pulls fast and hard into the first verse before the echo of his shout has had a chance to fade. His voice is raw, pleading and pushing, full of indescribably sexy asides, the throaty nuances that would flare up into "All Shook Up" and "Burning Love." Elvis slows for a second in the middle of a line, drawling softly, over his shoulder, as if he can't quite bring himself to say out loud how good the party's going to be; and then suddenly he is out of breath, as if he's run for miles to tell his story, but there's good rockin' tonight and everybody *has* to know—how could they live if they miss it? Tonight his girl will get everything *she's* been missing. "We're gonna rock—ALL OUR BLUES AWAY!" He can't tell it fast enough, he can barely keep up with himself. Near to bursting, the song slams home.

*   *   *

"Milkcow Blues Boogie" came out in January 1955, with writer's credit on the label going to Kokomo Arnold, a Georgia-born blues singer who recorded "Milk Cow Blues" in Chicago in 1934. One always reads that Elvis recreated Arnold's song, though apparently no one has bothered to listen to both men—Elvis takes all of one verse from the bluesman. Presley's style might well owe something to Arnold; they share a fast, nervous delivery, full of unpredictable swoops and moans, a flair for crazy-quilt tempo changes of tremendous excitement, and the ability to come down with a great force on a key line. But "Milkcow" was a song held in common long before Elvis was born, recorded by more blues and country singers than anyone has bothered to count. What Elvis did, in fact, was to throw a bit of Arnold—who perhaps Phillips played for him—into Bob Wills' western swing hit, "Brain Cloudy Blues," which was cut in 1946. "Brain Cloudy," highlighted by Wills' fiddle and a tough guitar solo, featured the straight, insulated vocal of Tommy Duncan up against Wills' patented cornball asides, which worked very effectively to bleed the punch out of every line. Elvis started with Wills' second verse, dropping the "brain cloudy" motif; faded to Arnold; and then finished off with Wills' words, changing lyrics when Duncan's crisp, almost effete diction threw him off.

I go into the musicology of this song in some detail because of what it can tell us about how these first records came about. The book on Elvis's early music is that it was "spontaneous," "without any evident forethought," "unselfconscious." In other words, Elvis was the natural (and, the implicit assumption is, likely unthinking) expression of a folk culture. I've tried to present some hints of the culture Elvis came out of as a set of forces that could have held him back and worn him down as easily as they gave him life; to build a context that puts us in touch with will and desire, not just smug sociology. Researching his biography of Elvis, Jerry Hopkins dug back into the world Elvis left behind in Memphis, and he found that nearly every record Elvis made with Sam Phillips was carefully and laboriously constructed out of hits and misses, riffs and bits of phrasing held through dozens of bad takes. The songs grew slowly, over hours and hours, into a music that paradoxically sounded much fresher than all the poor tries that had come before; until Presley, Bill Black, and Scotty Moore had the attack in their blood, and yes, didn't have to think about it. That's not exactly my idea of "spontaneity" or "unselfconsciousness."

Elvis had the nuance of cool down pat—the pink pants-and-shirt outfit he wore to his audition, the carelessness of his swagger, or the sneer around the edges of his smile—because the will to create himself, to matter, was so intense and so clear. He strolled into the studio and didn't leave until every note was perfect. Even later at RCA, still on the way up and wavering between complete self-confidence and a lingering doubt, he would demand thirty takes on "Hound Dog," pleading for one more try long after everyone else was satisfied.

Try to wash the images of success from your mind and picture a twenty-year-old in a tacky studio on perhaps his fifteenth take of a song that is coming together out of fragments of memory, old 78's, and pure instinct. Everything was riding on each new release: whether Elvis could really take his career beyond the commonplace expectations of those around him; whether he could top that last record; whether he could find a sound that would give him room to breathe and yet hold the fans he had won and spread the word. The little success he had achieved was fragile; each new record risked it. He had to take that energy of desire and distance himself from it, throw it into the song so that it would be coherent and powerful *as* a song; so that when he sang, "Tonight she'll know I'm a mighty mighty man," it would sound like an obvious, thrilling statement of the facts. Whatever strain there might have been in his voice or his hopes— that unpleasant hint of the small time that you can hear so plainly in Bill Haley and so many of Elvis's imitators—it had to go. The talent was there, and it was extraordinary, but it was complex, and it needed a form. They were in the studio a long, tiresome time to catch the spirit of a boy who, on record, sounded as if he flew in, stopped long enough to blow the walls back, and exited through the unhinged back door with a grin.

With "Milkcow Blues Boogie" we are back to the image Cash chose as the essence of the soul of the back country South: hot heavy air bursting all over the sky in lightning and rain. No music of any kind captures it better than this record.

❋ EE #4. At a DJ convention early in 1973, I sit drinking with Bobby Vee and Brian Hyland, veterans of the Now-That-Elvis-Is-in-the-Army-We-Can-Cash-in-on-the-Vacuum Era. I am interviewing Bob (he has changed his name back to Veline and is a folksinger now) in order to pen six thousand words of liner notes to a greatest hits package, an essay that will no doubt be the only extended critical discussion of his *oeuvre*. Bob tells me that, yes, for him it all began with Elvis—and suddenly the whole tone of the conversation is different. Professional cool drops away and we are shameless fans, awed by our subject. Vee and Hyland have met Elvis: he got drunk with Hyland (so Brian says) and was surly to Vee (I believe that). Well, they are outcasts in the rock 'n' roll world now, two very ordinary looking men; for all their

Wills and Arnold move right into the song; Elvis lingers over the first lines, and his voice drips an erotic tension that must have melted the mike. "Oh well, Ah woke up . . . this moanin'—An' Ah looked out . . . the doah—." He has you; you're hungering for whatever comes next, but he cuts you off. "Hold it fellas!" he shouts. "That don't *move* me!" Soft and sultry again: "Let's get real . . . *real* gone, for a change." It's too perfect; you think he must be reading lines, as if this is a scene from one of his movies; and it is, I guess, even if at this point the dreams were only in his head.

Elvis charges the song, shooting that boundless *Wellllllllllll* out ahead of himself, and the three of them are off. Elvis spurs the changes with his guitar, flying all over the story he is telling—his woman is gone and he wants her back but she's got about five minutes to make up her mind—singing with the crazy shifts from high to low that with Buddy Holly sounded funny and with Elvis sound frightening. In two and a half minutes he carries his listener through anger, loss, bemusement, melancholy, violence, defiance, fatalism, menace, delight, freedom, and regret. The song is as sure and tough a tale of breaking loose as any there is.

Yodeling, roaring his anger, yelling out to Scotty Moore—"Let's *milk* it!"—he comes off the guitar solo in a new mood, almost reflective now, meditating, this is all moving very fast but his guitar has somehow settled the music, and if his girl is gone, if that milkcow is never coming home, he still has time to step back and bring us into the song with a little blues philosophy:

> Wellll, good evenin'
> Don' that sun look good goin' down
> Wee-eee-ell, good evenin'
> Don' that sun look good goin' down
> Well, dont that old moon look lonesome
> When your bay-ay-ayby's not around?

And then rage pours back over his acceptance. He calls back his woman and faces her down, the song picking up momentum, his voice shimmering and shaking through night air:

> Well I tried everything
> To git along with you

---

triviality as rock singers, they once did their best to live up to Elvis and keep the faith. You can almost feel them gazing at Elvis as he is today, as if in his comeback they still see a glimmer of a future for themselves, just as they did when he started out years ago.

> *Now I'm gonna tell you what I'm gonna do*
> *I'm gonna quit my crying*
> *I'm gonna leave you alone*

and suddenly driving even harder, cursing with two of the most perfect lines in blues:

> *If you dont believe I'm leavin'*
> YOU CAN COUNT THE DAYS I'M GONE

Again, it is his authority that is so astounding. Scores of singers, black and white, have sung those lines, but few if any have ever made them seem so real, so *final*. The fatalism that is written right into the song, in that lovely image of the setting sun and the rising moon, will not do for Elvis, and he sings those last hard lines with an intensity that wipes out everything that has come before. A blues singer would use this verse as balance, to dramatize the rise and fall of his spirit, translating the circle the natural world draws around him into a metaphor for his inability to master his life. For Elvis, young and on his way, feeling his growing power over audiences, the growing space between himself and everything he should have taken for granted, there comes a point where he cannot settle for what others have made of this song, and the balance tips to fury. Our boy will get what he deserves; everyone else can get out of the way.

THE BOY WHO STOLE THE BLUES

> *I slicked myself up,*
> *Till I looked like a guinea!*
> CARL PERKINS, "Put Your Cat Clothes On"

For Carl Perkins and the rest of the rockabilly heroes, the liberation of the new music must have been a bit like a white foray into darktown, a combination of a blackface minstrel show and night riding—romantic as hell, a little dangerous, a little ridiculous. At the start, Elvis sounded black to those who heard him; when they called him the Hillbilly Cat, they meant the white Negro. Or as Elvis put it, years later: ". . . made a record and when the record came out a lot of people liked it and you could hear folks around town saying, 'Is he, is he?' and I'm going, 'Am I, am I?' "

Well, I can't hear that anymore. I hear a young man, white as the whale, who was special because in his best music he was so much his *own* man, one who took the musical and emotional strengths of the blues as a natural and necessary part of the world he was building for himself—one part of that world, no more, but clearly the finest stuff around at the time.

True as it is in an historical or commercial sense, too much has been made of Elvis as "a white man who sang black music credibly," as a singer who made black music acceptable to whites. This and too many whites trying to do the same thing have corrupted any sense of what Elvis did do, of what was at stake in his personal culture. Most white blues singing is singing at the blues; what comes out is either entirely fake, or has behind it the white impulse to become black: to ask for too much without offering anything in return.

Real white blues singers make something new out of the blues, as Jimmie Rodgers, Dock Boggs, Elvis, and Bob Dylan have; or, they sing out of a deep feeling for the blues, but in a musical style that is not blues—not formally, anyway. But we can trace their strength to the blues; what links their music to the blues is an absolute commitment to the material, an expressive force open to some whites because they have been attracted to another man's culture in a way that could not be denied. This is the music of whites not so much singing the blues as living up to them.

Van Morrison's "Listen to the Lion" would have to be my best example, but Rod Stewart and Charlie Rich have done their work here too, singing as if the fate of the whole world rested on their ability to reach deeply enough into their souls to get all the way into ours. I saw Rich do it not so long ago, in a setting so anachronistic he came near to leaving his audience behind him, because they were in a mood to be confirmed, not moved.

It was in August 1973, at a country music affair sponsored by Columbia Records, attended mostly by record industry heavies and hangers-on. Singer after singer took the stage, offering songs that made pain trivial and good times bland; music as sterile as it was predictable as it was (within a tight, well-regulated country market) commercially effective. The producers and song publishers and publicists sat near the stage, waiting for the singers to humble themselves before them, and as each did, I thought the humility might be worth a lot more if it were cynical than if it were real. It was that kind of day; I yearned for some rock 'n' roll arrogance, no matter how fake *that* might be.

Charlie Rich, who has always had too much of the blues in his style to fit easily into the country music market, was riding a number one country single that had, because it was more than country, crossed over into the upper reaches of the pop charts. He closed the show. Forty years old, a big man with white hair and lines deep in his face, he took his seat behind the piano and sang a harmless tune from his current album. After almost twenty years in the music business he had only three hits to show for it; even as "Behind Closed Doors" was climbing, the clerk in the record store marked up my Charlie Rich album under "nostalgia." A song Rich's wife Margaret Ann wrote about him, a haunting ballad of failure called "Life's Little Ups and Downs," tells the truth of Rich's career, but that day at the convention the crowd's truth was that Rich was on top and would stay there. Right as they may have been, I could not believe it was more than a public moment in an invisible career, and that made each song more precious and each missed chance that much more depressing.

Rich sang his hit, and it had grown for him. It meant more now than it had when it was just another throw of the dice, and it was a triumph. Because Rich was the star of the day, the men running the show gave him an encore. Staring into the keys, trying to balance the moment, Rich introduced his song. "I wrote this for Peter Guralnick," he said, "who wrote the book *Feel Like Going Home*." Named for the most terrifyingly lonely of all Muddy Waters' songs, it is probably the most loving book ever written about American music; Charlie Rich is the subject of its finest chapter.

"Today," Rich said, "I would like to dedicate this song to the President of the United States." And so for Nixon, just then slipping over the line to the point where his whole existence would become a national joke, Rich sang,

> *I tried and I failed*
> *And I feel like going home.*

The words stayed in my mind throughout the strange, difficult song; they didn't change the president, or the country, or the world, but they changed how a few of us who were there to listen understood those things. They cut through everything I believe to uncover a compassion that I never, never wanted to feel.

We won't find Elvis here. The idea that the blues is a feeling and not a form can bring us closer to what Rich did that afternoon—but for Elvis, the blues was a style of freedom, something he couldn't get in his own home, full of roles to play and rules to break. In the beginning the blues was more than anything else a fantasy, an epic of struggle and pleasure, that he lived out as he sang. Not a fantasy that went beneath the surface of his life, but one that soared right over it.

Singing in the fifties, before blacks began to guard their culture with the jealousy it deserved, Elvis had no guilty dues to pay. Arthur Crudup complained his songs made a white man famous, and he had a right to complain, but mostly because he never got his royalties. Elvis sang "That's All Right" and "My Baby Left Me" (one of his first sides for RCA, and the only one in the Sun rockabilly style) with more power, verve, and skill than Crudup did; his early records were more than popular with blacks; but still the implication, always there when Crudup or Willie Mae Thornton (who made the first version of "Hound Dog") looked out at the white world that gave them only obscurity in exchange for their music and penned them off from getting anything for themselves, is that Elvis would have been nothing without them, that he climbed to fame on their backs. It is probably time to say that this is nonsense; the mysteries of black and white in American music are just not that simple. Consider the tale of "Hound Dog."

Jerry Leiber and Mike Stoller were Jewish boys from the East Coast who fell in love with black music. Hustling in Los Angeles in the early fifties, they wrote "Hound Dog," and promoted the song to Johnny Otis, a ruling R&B bandleader who was actually a dark-skinned white man from Berkeley who many thought was black. Otis gave the song to Thornton, who made it a number one R&B hit in 1953; Otis also took part of the composer's credit, which Leiber and Stoller had to fight to get back. Elvis heard the record, changed the song completely, from the tempo to the words, and cut Thornton's version to shreds.

Whites wrote it; a white made it a hit. And yet there is no denying that "Hound Dog" is a "black" song, unthinkable outside the impulses of black music, and probably a rewrite of an old piece of juke joint fury that dated back far beyond the birth of any of these people. Can you pull justice out of *that* maze? What *does* Huck owe Jim, especially when Jim is really Huck in blackface and everyone smells loot? All you can say is this was Elvis's music because he made it his own.

Here's a better story. In 1955 the Robins (a black vocal group that had passed through seven labels with no real success) and Richard Berry (a black singer with two duds to his name) were brought together by Leiber and Stoller. Together they made the classic "Riot in Cell Block #9," which helped change the Robins into the Coasters and brought Berry his first notoriety. Leiber and Stoller went on to fame and fortune and the Coasters at least to fame; Berry, after losing out with "The Big Break," an outrageous follow-up to "Riot," made "Louie Louie" in 1956, but though it was his biggest hit, it never made the pop charts.

In 1962 a white Portland group called the Kingsmen unearthed "Louie Louie," and their version hit number two in the country. Paul Revere and the Raiders, another Portland band, rode the tune into a gold mine on the West Coast. As rock records, these discs were virtually definitive: hard rhythm, harder lead guitar, and a vocal that made no sense whatsoever. Within months every high school band in the country was playing "Louie Louie," and every other person you met had a copy of the *real* lyrics, which were reputedly obscene. Some highlights I recall from locker room days: "Gonna make her again," "Gotta rag on," "Fuck that girl across the sea." (Not much, I admit, but those were thin years for rock 'n' roll.) Soon even Congressmen got into the act; they investigated the tune, duly played it (at 45, 33, 78, and 16 rpm), and charmingly pronounced the song "indecipherable at any speed." By this time, everyone but the man who owned the copyright—and likely he too—had forgotten all about Richard Berry, whose original lyrics would have been beside the point anyway.

Ten years later a white New York group called Stories released a single called "Brother Louie," and the record went to number one. "Louie, Louie, Loo-aye," went the chorus—familiar, to say the least. Obviously, the chorus was what caught your attention; it always had been. Since rock 'n' roll had been around long enough for its fans to develop a sense of history, a few people remembered Richard Berry. And what was this new "Louie Louie" about? A black girl and her white boyfriend—Louie—and his mean racist parents. "Ain't no difference if you're black or white," Stories sang. "Brothers, you know what I mean." But this time, the "brother" was white; and finally the old song contained the racial contradictions that had sustained it.

If Elvis drew power from black culture, he was not exactly imitating blacks; when he told Sam Phillips he didn't sing like nobody, he told the truth. No white man had so deeply absorbed black music, and transformed it, since Jimmie Rodgers; instead of following Rodgers' musical style, as so many good white singers had—Lefty Frizzell, Ernest Tubb, Tommy Duncan, and, in his more personal way, Hank Williams, following that style until it simply wore out—Elvis followed Rodgers' musical strategy and began the story all over again.

Elvis didn't have to exile himself from his own community in order to justify and make real his use of an outsider's culture (like the Jewish jazzman Mezz Mezzrow, who would claim that his years on the streets of Harlem had actually darkened his skin and thickened his lips; like Johnny Otis and so many real white Negroes); as a Southerner and white trash to boot, Elvis was already outside. In 1955 he had at least as much in common with Bobby Bland as he did with Perry Como. Which is to say that Elvis was also hellbent on the mainstream, and sure enough of himself to ignore the irony that it would be his version of the backdoor freedoms of black music that would attract the mainstream to him, giving him the chance to exchange his hillbilly strangeness for acceptability.

Elvis's blues were a set of sexual adventures, and as a blues-singing swashbuckler, his style owed as much to Errol Flynn as it did to Arthur Crudup. It made sense to make movies out of it.

THE PINK CADILLAC

By the time "Baby, Let's Play House" came out in April 1955, the rockabilly singers were coming out of the swamps. Phillips was shifting his company from black to white, setting up an outbreak of rock 'n' roll that would follow hard on Presley's already discussed and taken-for-granted move up to a national label. Phillips had Malcolm Yelvington (a Memphis country singer endowed with false teeth and the best rockabilly name outside of Elvis's) cut the first of many country rock versions of Stick McGhee's 1949 R&B classic, "Drinkin' Wine Spo-Dee-O-Dee," and its message summed up the new mood: drinkin' and fightin' are what life is all about, and if anybody argues, give 'em a drink or lay 'em out.

Elvis had finished his early tours, ranging from Texas to Florida; he was set for San Francisco—alien territory, crucial to proving himself outside the South—and he was booked into the Cow Palace, the biggest arena in Northern California. The Colonel had made his initial connections. In Lubbock, Texas, a kid named Charles "Buddy" Holly bowed to the East every night and began getting a band together. There was, to put it mildly, excitement in the air.

Elvis's dive into "Baby, Let's Play House"—a wild crash of hiccups, gulps, and baby-baby-babys—measured perfectly the distance he had traveled since he broke into tears at the sight of his first record. There is a new spirit here, a lightness and a sense of fun, as if his whole little career has suddenly hit him as a wonderful joke. The dreams are coming true; that drive and secret ambition can afford to open up. He knows now that his mother was right, and he is safe. That throwaway superiority for which he has worked so hard can blossom out into arrogance, humor, and pure good times.

What was it his mother told him? That he was just as good as anybody? Or did she whisper, late at night when no one else was there to hear, that her boy could never lose?

Arthur Gunter, a black singer working for the Excello label in Nashville, wrote and recorded "Baby, Let's Play House," and got a hit with the black market in early 1955. He used a tight acoustic band and walked right through, vaguely interested in telling his girl that she might think she's hot stuff, but she'd better come on back and get down to it, or there'd be, you know, trouble. It was all very low-key (that splendid intro was all Elvis); Gunter's lack of concern was his charm. Still, he didn't sound very convincing.

Elvis wailed. He turned the song into a correspondence course in rock 'n' roll, and it was by far the most imitated of his first records. For pure excitement, he may never have matched it.

The rhythm was heavy, the syncopation astonishing—a fast, ominous bass tromping over a cottonmouth guitar—the band drove hard into every chorus and cut out for all the best lines. "Aw, let's play house," Elvis shouted, and Scotty punched out a few riffs; "HIT IT!" Elvis cried, and Moore and Black rammed home music so tough it wasn't touched until Elvis pushed them into the earthquake that was "Hound Dog."

Elvis made one crucial change in the lyrics. The girl he's after in this song is high-class stuff: she might go to college, he sings, she might go to school, but she'll never really get away, never be so sure of herself she can get along without the loving only he can give her. She might even get religion, Gunter had added, which won't help her either; but Elvis threw in a faster, flashier image that was more to his own point: "You may have a pink Cadillac/ But dontcha be nobody's fool!" Elvis had just bought one for himself.

Now, the obvious thing to say here is that the Pink Cadillac and all that it implied proved Elvis's undoing: out there in mass culture America, Elvis would lose his talent in its reward. Dontcha be nobody's fool? The poor boy should have taken his own advice.

Well, we should be careful about this sort of thing. There is a deep need to believe that Elvis (or any exemplar of American culture one cares about) began in a context of purity, unsullied by greed or ambition or vulgarity, somehow outside of and in opposition to American life as most of us know it and live it. Even RCA first presented Elvis as "a folksinger" (claiming, in the notes to his second album, that the simple-country-boy-with-guitar stance pictured on the cover was "most appropriate" for him). A writer as tough and sensitive as Stanley Booth can write (in a piece that seems to miss the point of its own title, "A Hound Dog, to the Manor Born"): "All that was really necessary was that [Elvis] stop doing his thing and start doing theirs. His thing was 'Mystery Train,' 'Milkcow Blues Boogie.' Theirs was 'Love Me Tender,' 'Loving You,' 'Jailhouse Rock,' 'King Creole.' " Charlie Gillett, author of *The Sound of the City*, as definitive a history of rock 'n' roll as we are likely to get, complains that Elvis sold out his true culture when he let RCA put *drums* on his records. It is virtually a critical canon that Elvis's folk purity, and therefore his talent, was ruined by (a) his transmogrification from naïve country boy into corrupt pop star (he sold his soul to Colonel Tom, or Parker just stole it), (b) Hollywood, (c) the Army, (d) money and soft living, (e) all of the above.*

This approach may contain some figures, but not Elvis. "Milkcow Blues" was not "his thing"—it was one of many—so much as it was Sam Phillips'. Phillips loved money and he loved the blues, the basic pop combination; pairing a blues and a country tune on Elvis's first record gave him a successful commercial formula, and he stuck to it on every subsequent Presley release and on most of the records he cut by other rockabilly singers. But when Elvis left Memphis to confront a national audience as mysterious to him as he was to it, he had to define himself fully, and he did so by presenting his authentic multiplicity in music. I am, he announced, a house rocker, a boy steeped in mother-love, a true son of the church, a matinee idol who's only kidding, a man with too many rough edges for anyone ever to smooth away. Something in me yearns for a settling of affairs, he said with his pale music and his tired movies; on the other hand, he answered with his rock 'n' roll and an occasional blues, I may break away at any time. You never know. At RCA, where the commercial

---

*This Faustian scenario is an absolutely vital part of Elvis's legend, especially for all those who took part in Elvis's event and felt bewildered and betrayed by his stagnation and decline. We could hardly believe that a figure of such natural strength could dissolve into such a harmless nonentity; it had to be some kind of trick. Even a decade after the fact, Phil Spector was convinced that Colonel Parker hypnotized Elvis.

horizons were much broader than they were down at Sun, Elvis worked with far more "artistic freedom" than he ever did with Sam Phillips.

Two things did happen that led to the collapse of Elvis's music. His multiplicity opened up the possibility that he could be all things to all people, but his eagerness to prove it, with records like *Something for Everybody*, destroyed his ability to focus his talent. He wound up without a commitment to any musical style; his music lost that dramatic shape Sam Phillips helped give it. And his ambition, the source of so much of the intensity and emotion he put into his early music, plainly outstripped itself. Two years after making his first record he had won more than anyone knew was there; he had achieved a status that trivialized struggle and made will obsolescent. His success turned his life upside down; from this point on, he would have in his hands what he set out to get, but he would have to reach for the energy and desire that had made his triumph possible.

The Pink Cadillac was at the heart of the contradiction that powered Elvis's early music; a perfect symbol of the glamour of his ambition and the resentments that drove it on. When he faced his girl in "Baby, Let's Play House" (like Dylan railing at the heroine of "Like a Rolling Stone," or Jagger surveying the upper-class women who star in "19th Nervous Breakdown," "Play With Fire," and "You Can't Always Get What You Want"), Elvis sang with contempt for a world that had always excluded him; he sang with a wish for its pleasures and status. Most of all he sang with delight at the power that fame and musical force gave him: power to escape the humiliating obscurity of the life he knew, and power to sneer at the classy world that was now ready to flatter him. Not the real upper class, of course; it would be years before socialites set out in pursuit of the Rolling Stones and academics began to fawn over the Beatles. Still, the jump Elvis made from the woods and welfare to simple respectability was far more epic. Girls who had turned up their noses in high school were now waiting in line, just as today men and women who are barely hanging on to the edge of the middle class wait in line to see a man who has achieved an eminence class can never bring.

Elvis sang out his song with a monumental disdain for all those folk who moved easily through a world that had never been easy for him (anyone who had ever shown the Presleys *exactly who they were*); he grinned at the big car he had dreamed about, because finally it was within reach, and he could take it, on his terms.

A bit farther into the image of the Pink Cadillac, something more interesting was going on. If Elvis was looking down on his smart girl's Caddy from the vantage point of his own, he was implicitly presenting his new successful self as a target for his own resentments, and singing with more than enough emotion to hit the bullseye. He was the Star; not asserting, in the conventional Uriah Heep country style, that all his wealth don't buy him happiness (it does, it does), but burlesquing and damning the complacency of the rich and powerful by flaunting *his* power and riches, and getting away with it. Somehow taking both sides, Elvis could show his listeners just how much, and how little, that Pink Cadillac was worth: more and less than anyone would have guessed.*

This is a kind of rock 'n' roll drive—the vitality that endows the artifacts of materialism with life—that is captured perfectly in *The Harder They Come*, a movie about the Jamaican version of the American pop dream, when Jimmy Cliff steals a white Cadillac and spins it over a golf course with an unbeatable smile on his face. He's a refugee from the most terrifying poverty, a reggae-singing people's outlaw with reflexes instead of politics. "You can get it if you really want," he sings. "The harder they come, the harder they fall, one and all." He wants the car and the whole world it stands for; he doesn't want it, he wants to smash it all up. He hasn't made the connections; he hasn't worked it all out any more than a twenty-year-old Elvis did. But he knows that car belongs to him because he can take more pleasure from it than anyone else.

What is most remarkable is that Elvis was able to laugh at the persona he drew from "Baby, Let's Play House" as convincingly as he acted it out—as if a combination of the freedom to realize his desires and a freedom to ignore them was what freedom really meant. He was less into the music than on top if it, feigning toughness, feigning anger, finding it, for the famous lines

> *I'd rather see you dead little girl*
> *Than to be with another man*

and then all fun again, as if the venom he'd put into those words struck him at once as ludicrous, and maybe a little frightening. He

---

*In America, after all, the final proof of grace is *economic* sanctification; which is to say, Elvis can have the piety of the poor along with the ease of the rich and know that since he never lost the first, he deserves the last. Still full of the energy of his comeback in early 1969, Elvis went back to Memphis and sang a song called "Long Black Limousine"—the tale of a hometown girl punished for her sins and her fancy city ways, mourned and damned by the poor country boy who has waited all these years for a better ending than the car crash that did his sweetheart in.

put even more of himself into the song, and still parodied his menace, lowering his voice to a rumble, getting out of the tune with a chuckle that gave it all away: deep down he was just a good boy, out for a real good time.

Put it together and you may have the quintessential performance of Elvis's career: an overwhelming outburst of real emotion and power, combined with a fine refusal to take himself with any seriousness at all. Finding that power within himself, and making it real, was part of the liberation he was working out in this music; standing off from that power, with a broad sense of humor and amusement, was another.

This was the saving grace of Elvis's ambition, and a necessary counter to it. It allowed him to transcend his success and his public image just as his ambition allowed him to achieve and enjoy his success; that casual élan would let him see at least part of the way through the unprecedented adulation he received, just as his ambition would ultimately make it impossible for him to be satisfied with anything less. And if that lack of seriousness today distances Elvis not only from the absurdity of his reward but from his talent too, gives us a throwaway and a man virtually unable to take anything seriously, this side of Elvis has also brought a marvelous warmth to his best music, no matter if it's in the records he made back in Memphis, or the show he's sure to be putting on tonight.

ELVIS AT HOME: THE COUNTRY SIDES

Elvis's blues are music of drama, humor, and risk; the country tunes are very different. At their most vital, they capture the kind of beauty and peace of mind that can be found only within limits, when a lot has been given up, and you know exactly how far you can go.

Elvis gives us respect—for the musical form, for the established country music audience these songs were aimed at, for his mother, who was sure to be listening to *this* music—in place of resentment and personal authority. The music flows with the kind of grace the Allman Brothers found in their incandescent "Blue Sky": a sense of

---

The tension as the song opens is almost unbearable, and Elvis never lets go of the song. He is completely convincing. And yet of course he is the country boy captured by the city if there ever was one; he's that girl, riding in her long black limousine on her way to the graveyard, as surely as he is King Elvis, speeding away from the studio in his own black limousine. When he smashes through the contradictions of his career with such music, we have Elvis at his greatest.

value that seems to come not from a feel for the open possibilities of life, but from a pretty deep understanding of its fragility.

There is a modesty of spirit. In this world you will hope for what you deserve, but not demand it; you may celebrate your life, but not with the kind of liberation that might threaten the life of someone else. The public impulse of the music is not to break things open, but to confirm what is already there, to add to its reality and its value.

This is the kind of freedom D. H. Lawrence had in mind when he wrote about America in an essay called "The Spirit of Place."

Men are free when they are in a living homeland, not when they are straying and breaking away. Men are free when they are obeying some deep, inward voice of religious belief. Obeying from within. Men are free when they belong to a living, organic, *believing* community, active in fulfilling some unfulfilled, perhaps unrealized purpose. Not when they are escaping to some wild west. The most unfree souls go west, and shout of freedom. Men are freest when they are most unconscious of freedom. The shout is a rattling of chains, always was.

Men are not free when they are doing just what they like. The moment you can do just what you like, there is nothing you care about doing.*

So speaks the stern English father to his rowdy American children; it's not a message America has ever had much time for. We much prefer Elvis's shout of freedom, sure that what chains there are in our world must be applied by other men. Something close to Lawrence's idea, though, that sense of staying at home in a place where one belongs, is part of what Elvis has always offered America— on the flipside, as it were.

Elvis's country sides, like his later gospel records for RCA, reveal how deeply he felt a pull at odds with the explosions of his new rock 'n' roll and the frenzy of his first stage shows. They let us in on the secret that his little drama of breaking loose could take on the extremes that gave it power because he knew he had a home to which he could always return; even as he set out to win his independence, he prepared his accommodation. The America that Elvis brings to life in this music grew out of his willingness to accept the limits of a community, and his desire for the pleasures of familiarity. It's a place of gentleness, and restraint.

In the least of this music, though—"I Forgot to Remember to Forget," "I Don't Care If the Sun Don't Shine," "Just Because," "I

*From *Studies in Classic American Literature* (New York: Viking, 1964, originally published 1923).

Love You Because," "I'll Never Let You Go (Little Darlin')"—it is the sound of a young man confined by his community that is most striking. Elvis is faceless, indistinguishable from a hundred others; he sounds less like a man who has been defeated than like one who has never wondered what it might mean to try to win. There's no real warmth in the music, only an imitation of it; if on the blues sides he took on the originals and outclassed them, here he defers. The emotional tone seems contrived, almost secondhand; this is the music of someone doing what he has always been told to do.

"I Don't Care If the Sun Don't Shine" has energy, but not soul; "Just Because" has a little bounce, but no passion. "I Love You Because" (actually the very first song Elvis recorded professionally) is truly painful to hear; he's so polite to the material he can't even sing it. There is certainly nothing that could give that "believing community" any strength.

Here Elvis embodies exactly that world his blues fantasy let him escape. If murder—the face of Charley Starkweather imposed on Elvis's, the edge of sadism in Presley's music that made one producer tag him as just right for *In Cold Blood*—was the dark side of rockabilly flash and the flight from limits, then a death of possibility and a stupefying ordinariness was the dark side of this music, the first version of Elvis's empty Yes.

You can't have a community that grows and renews all who are a part of it without the tension that comes from the need to break away, without the resentment produced by the tendency of any community to grow in on itself and shut out the rest of the world. Tom Sawyer's fooling around won't give us that tension; you need Huck's nerve and his suffering, perhaps an edge of Ahab's obsessions, and, in America, you probably need Nigger Jim too.

Elvis was a rebel in the music that made him famous. But he knew, and has always told anyone willing to listen, how hard it is to break away, and how much you have to give up to make it—more than he has been willing to part with. So Elvis lives out his story by contradicting himself, and we join in when we take sides, or when we respond to the tension that contradiction creates. The liveliness of that tension is as evident in the best of Elvis's country sides as it is in his blues.

When Elvis sings Bill Monroe's "Blue Moon of Kentucky" as if he's going to jump right over it, he isn't, as has always been said, singing the blues on a country song, any more than he was really singing hillbilly on a blues with "That's All Right." What Elvis is doing is both more complex and more coherent.

When I listened to an early take of "Blue Moon of Kentucky" (on a rockabilly bootleg that includes studio dialogue as well as music), I heard Elvis lost in the song, touching each line gently, playfully, bringing every word to life. The singing is rough, even though Elvis is clearly a long way past the first tries; Scotty Moore has trouble following the vocal. He drops back, and then there is just Elvis, drawing out an unbelievably sensual portrait of his Southern landscape.

It sounds so primitive to me; music out of the Mississippi woods, a hundred years gone. Sam Phillips hears something else.

PHILLIPS: Fine, *fine*, man, hell, that's different! That's a *pop song* now, little guy! That's good!
SCOTTY MOORE: Too much vaseline!
Elvis laughs, nervously, proudly.
MOORE: I had it too!
ELVIS: Y'aint just a-*woofin'!*
MOORE (imitating an eye-rolling black falsetto): Please, *please*, please—
ELVIS: What?
MOORE: *Damn*, nigger!

By the time Elvis reached the fast, confident version that appeared on the flip of his first record, most of the primitive feeling had disappeared, but not the vaseline; Elvis was celebrating a classic piece of white country music, but more than that he was celebrating himself. He was keeping the old song alive by bringing something new to it, putting some life back into his community by telling an old story in a way that no one had heard before—and he was reaching beyond his community, with the "pop song" Sam Phillips knew he had to make.

There is a delight in adventure and novelty here that we can't touch with pure musicology: Elvis's affection for a song he's heard for years, combined with the exuberance and satisfaction of a kid who's worked for months to make a record, and who is now actually pulling it off. And there are the new rhythms of "That's All Right," cut a few nights before—not "blues" now, but Elvis's music, Scotty Moore's music—Southern energy that blacks had trapped and put into the air where anyone could get it.

Elvis could not have sung "Blue Moon of Kentucky" as he did without the discoveries of "That's All Right"—but what he discovered was not his ability to imitate a black blues singer, but the nerve to cross the borders he had been raised to respect. Once that was done, musically those borders dissolved as if they had never existed—for Elvis. He moved back and forth in a phrase. But Scotty Moore might well have been speaking for the audience waiting outside the studio when he called Elvis a nigger—for many, it was the *fact* of a white boy singing a black man's song without clothing it in fiddles and steel guitar that they heard, not the strange ambiguities of the music. Perhaps if Phillips had put out the "country" side without the "blues," it would have warmed the community; the combination thrilled some and threatened others. There were country stations that refused to play any Elvis records, no matter how white they seemed to be. He was too complicated, this Presley boy; you couldn't tell what he might be slipping over, could you?

Yet "You're a Heartbreaker," another country side, is a masterpiece of reassurance. It is one of the most affecting records Elvis ever made; it gives us a young man who takes comfort, and pleasure, from a sure sense of all that he has to fall back on when something goes wrong: his self-respect (the rounded edge of the new superiority of the blues-boy); the steady, ongoing patterns of life that never range too far in one direction or the other. If the impulses of community

---

✱ EE #5. I know a woman, black and about sixty, who loves old country blues. The albums I have given her are mostly unheard, though, because she lives with her mother, a devout woman in her eighties, who forbids her to play them. The mother, who is blind, spends much of her time listening to the TV set, and once I found her attending to a kind of blues she apparently considered innocuous enough to tolerate: Elvis's film *G.I. Blues*.

I didn't know what to make of that. It seemed to represent a double dead end of American cross-culture, but there was something I liked about it. Partly, it was the movie itself. Elvis, as usual, plays a good-natured stud who breaks into song about every ten minutes and makes all the women snap their fingers (though curiously, none of them can keep time). The Sergeant Bilko-reject plot has to do with El's attempt to raise a stake for the nightclub he and his two Army accompanists want to open when they get back in mufti. It comes down to rival platoons placing bets on which can field a man to seduce Juliet Prowse, the biggest glacier in Germany. Elvis, naturally . . .

He walks through the flick with the same air of What-Am-I-Doing-Here bemusement he employs in most of his other movies. When he strums his acoustic guitar, an electric solo comes out. When bass and guitar back him, you hear horns and electric piano. When he sings, the soundtrack is at least half a verse out of sync. These films are the throwaways of a man—perhaps I ought to say an industry—who doesn't even need to title his product as long as he can put his name on it, much like Elvis's post-comeback albums (randomly constructed out of leftover recordings, unmixed live tapes, plastered with shoddy composite promo photos and ads for old LP's), all of which seem to be called simply "E L V I S," in fact. The movies are so tacky no one else could possibly get away with them—and still make money.

Someday, French film critics will discover these pictures and hail them as a unique example of *cinéma discrépant*; there will be retrospectives at the *Cinémathèque*, and five years after that Harvard students will cultivate a lopsided grin and Elvis movies will be shown on U.S. public TV, complete with learned commentary deferring to the French discovery and bemoaning America's inability to appreciate its own culture. Elvis will be touring the People's Republic of were at odds with the extremes of Southern life, here Elvis captures the soul of the one just as he acted out the other side. It is a tribute to his range and his honesty that he can do this without making you feel he is offering less than the whole story.

How would you act if you lived in a community that *did* enclose extremes without making life banal and dull? You might act as Elvis sounds on this song, with a delicate grace and a modest affection. Flip the record over to "Milcow Blues Boogie," and the same story— Elvis's girl has left him—is a matter of life and death. And yet, despite the apparent lack of struggle, of intensity, a certain truth is being told here; a balance is being worked out; and the song is satisfying, leaving any listener richer than before.

With "Tryin' to Get to You," the boy who always seemed bent on escape in the blues now has his eyes turned toward home. I got your letter and I came a-runnin' is the plot—"I've been traveling over mountains," Elvis sings, and you believe him. The passion is there (also humility—Elvis remembers to thank the Lord for helping him along), but what is interesting is how controlled the feeling is. This is an elegant record. The arrangement is very professional, very strict; Elvis sings beautifully, but he submits to the music. He never really takes it over. Some emotions, he might be saying, are authentic only when they are restrained—just as some emotions are authentic only when they are utterly free.

"I'm Left, You're Right, She's Gone" is cut from the same mold. It brings together a superb vocal, an unforgettably clean guitar solo,

China and during an audience with Chairman Mao will be drawn into a discussion of the conflicting aesthetics of "Milcow Blues Boogie" and "No Room to Rhumba in a Sportscar." The Chairman, being a staunch advocate of "The Folk," will cite James Agee's famous essay on the corruption of folk art by the nature of reality; Elvis will reply that while he has never read the piece, he once saw some pictures from *Let Us Now Praise Famous Men* in a copy of *Life* he picked up on an airplane, and thought they were all right. "My 'folk' can be summed up very easily," he will tell Mao with a knowing smile. " 'The short and simple annals of the poor.' "

All right, then—where does all this fit in with an old woman hardening her heart against Skip James and passing her time with Elvis? Only in that at its blandest, the American mainstream has no limits at all; even Mao could get his hand caught in this tar-baby. It contains everyone from moment to moment, covering over and melting down and seducing the best along with the worst, until the toughest, wisest pessimist is defeated by his secret yearning for a happy ending and the cheap tears it brings to his eyes. And that mainstream—which could turn "Bartleby" into a musical as easily as it allowed Elvis to turn himself into *Tickle Me*— provides such a perfect antithesis to the realities of American life that inevitable discrepancies come out of the woodwork, come with enormous force—a surprise, again—and with them come the resentment and the humor that keep the soul of the place hanging onto life.

Big words? Heavy stakes? Too much to drop on a vitiated country boy and an old lady who in all probability was just too bored to change the channel? Well, if that's not America, I'll never recognize it.

and a good rhythm—no rave-up, but just over the line into rock 'n' roll. There is a happy ending—Elvis finds a new girl—and maybe that's the real clue to these sides. Everything works out, in the lyrics, in the music (even the guitar parts are neatly resolved, while those in the blues tempt chaos), in the commercial and cultural context the singer can take as close to a given. What is missing is the suspense of a man creating himself, by the pure force of his will and desire, that one can hear in Elvis's blues.

There is an alternate version of "I'm Left," usually called "My Baby Is Gone," that shows how naturally Elvis's flair for this kind of material evolved into his later—and present-day—ballad style. All the mannerisms are there.* The performance is stunning: every line is measured out as if it costs the singer his soul to confess his loss. Elvis drops down so low on the scale he can barely get the words out; he blows up the subtleties of his phrasing into shameless melodrama, and it works. The song tells us what Elvis was after and where he was going as well as anything. The tune was written as a conventional country tear-jerker, but in this version Elvis stepped gently away from his community even as he gave that community something it could accept: a Hollywood movie, a Valentino love scene complete with heavy breathing. "Blue Moon" takes this blending of cultures even farther; it's more like "pre-Elvis" pop music than any of these sides, and queerer, too. "Blue Moon" comes with clippity-clop hoofbeats worthy of Gene Autry, and with a bit of Elvis's acoustic guitar; he sings like a swamp-spirit, making his way through the fog to that lamp post Frank Sinatra used to cart out for all his album covers. Whining and wailing between the lyrics—which, as Elvis sings them, sound quite surreal—he turns this old standard into a combination of a supper club ballad and an Appalachian moan.

This music is good enough, committed enough, to make you almost forget Elvis's Wild West. He played both ends against the middle; in the good moments, he escaped the deadening artistic compromise the middle demands. This seems to have worked because both sides of his character, at this point in his career, were pulling so hard.

Jerry Lee Lewis, second in the hierarchy of white Southern rockers, had talent and drive that stopped just short of Presley's, but he

---

*The mannerisms of his great ballads, like "I Was the One," "Is It So Strange," "Don't," "Fame and Fortune," "Anyway You Want Me," "If I Can Dream," or "Suspicious Minds," and the awful ones, like "Tonight's All Right For Love," "Fool," and a couple of hundred others.

gained only a fraction of Presley's success, perhaps because he lacked the broad scope of Elvis's ambition and Elvis's sure sense of where he meant to go—not to mention Elvis's understanding of how to act once he got there. If Elvis had a bit of grace to him, Jerry Lee seemed possessed; and Jerry Lee, far more than Elvis, came to represent all the mythical strangeness of the redneck South: lynch-mob blood lust, populist frenzies, even incest. When Jerry Lee made it onto national TV, Steve Allen didn't bother squeezing him into white tie or chaining him to the floor: in a vain attempt to parody the excess that made Jerry Lee Lewis great, tables and chairs were thrown across the stage while Jerry Lee pounded out "Whole Lotta Shakin'." Elvis's early music has drama because as he sang he was escaping limits, testing them, working out their value; unlike Jerry Lee, he at least knew the limits were there. With Southern power in his music, Elvis had mainstream savvy in his soul.

The problem was that the shallowness of the poorest of the music that captured Elvis's restraint, and the inoffensiveness of the best of it, opened up the I-Walked-Like-a-Zombie saga that Elvis would act out in the long years before his comeback in 1968—a saga that, in a much more extravagant way, he acts out today.

Elvis was very comfortable with his country music, and with the romantic ballads that were its mainstream equivalent; so were his first teenage fans. This was mother's milk; the responses the music elicited were virtually automatic. Elvis's ability to sing this music and to like

---

✳ EE #6. One night in 1973 we went out to catch El's latest movie; the theater was almost empty. There were a few couples in their late twenties, an elderly pair who left almost immediately, an old black man sitting alone, maybe just looking for a roof in the rain. The film was *Elvis on Tour*, a documentary of his post-comeback apotheosis—with gestures toward History.

There are kinescopes of the first triumph: Elvis rocking out on the Ed Sullivan Show with "Ready Teddy." The performance is astounding, otherworldly, and it is hard to believe anyone now living was really around to see such a sight (though, of course, *we* were). "That's All Right" plays under a shot of a train running on down the line, as Elvis talks about his childhood. "Never saw a git-tar player was worth a damn," he remembers his Daddy telling him. "I was born about ten thousand years ago," Elvis sings in one of his recent songs, and that seems to say it all, to sum up the jumbled sense of time that governs the movie, and us; the beginning of it all seems at least that distant, and brings home just how long Elvis and we have been caught up with each other.

Somewhere near the end of the flick is a wonderful sequence of Elvis-movie kisses, a perfect critical attack on the aggressive meaninglessness of the movie years: like dominoes, one starlet after another falls into Elvis-arms. Ah, Elvis says to us here, this is what I *became*, but this is not the *real me*. Well, what is? That pudgy flyer up on the screen, filmed live in concert after concert, mechanically grinding out the same songs and choreographed karate chops (the seventies equivalent of swiveling hips?) as if his life were a tape loop? The kiss sequence is meant to parody the past, but it only parallels the present.

it—to put it across without lying to himself or to anyone else—would never have brought him fame or burst any limits. But that ability was crucial to his power to hold onto his success, and to keep at least that part of his original audience (and to attract so many more) who didn't grow with the musical culture Elvis founded: those who, all through the sixties, lived in an America that was ignored or damned by the Rolling Stones and the counterculture; those who put the endless movies into the black; who made the soundtrack to *Blue Hawaii* the best-selling Elvis album of all (over 5 million copies at last count); those who bought reassurance tinged with a memory of excitement and independence. When all this proved too dull and predictable even for Elvis—when he came roaring out in the explosion of vitality and commitment that was his comeback (returning, then, as a King of Rock 'n' Roll who was also a definitive Middle American)—there were plenty from every sort of white rock 'n' roll audience who were glad to leave whatever they had made of the sixties behind and join him in his pageant. Elvis's accommodations, all larger than life, and brilliantly orchestrated on stage to preserve the thrills that were once discovered in his blues, make a very glamourous home for our own retreats.

The country sides, the later music that derived from them, the shining acceptance of the great stage show, give us the contradictions that have kept pace with rock 'n' roll from the beginning (contradictions that are, of course, much bigger than the music): the desire of the rebel to conform; the wish for quiet despite allegiance to an ideology of noise; the need for rest after excitement; the retreat that replaces ambition, be that ambition personal, cultural, or political. But this aesthetic—of rest, of quiet, of retreat—so convincing in those first country records, grows easily into a riskless aesthetic of smooth-it-away. This is really the last word of our mainstream; its last, most seductive trap: the illusion that the American dream has fulfilled itself, that utopia is complete in an America that replaces emotion with sentiment and novelty with expectation. Elvis contained this aesthetic within himself—Tocqueville's bad dream, the aesthetics of playing it safe. When he is ready to play it safe, that aesthetic contains him, just as it usually contains most of us. Breaking loose and starting over cost more every time, and in the America that Elvis has come to symbolize so powerfully, in an America that only wants to applaud, to say Yes and mean it, the risks are hard to find.

MYSTERY TRAIN

It was the last record Elvis made at Sun; to me, it tells the best tale of all.

Junior Parker and Sam Phillips wrote "Mystery Train" together in 1953; the original, a slow, dark blues released under the name of Little Junior's Blue Flames, was exquisite. An odd, chopping beat carried the threat of the title; a sax brought out the inevitable train sound with an unusually ominous flair. And Parker sang halfway from the grave, chasing his lover through the gloom, giving just the slightest suggestion that she had been kidnapped by a ghost. There was a feeling of being in the wrong place at the wrong time, a hint of a curse.

This was the blues realism of Robert Johnson: one of those tunes that says, this is the way the world is, and there's nothing you or anyone can do about it.

> *Train I riiide,*
> *Sixteen*
> *Coaches long*
> *Train I riiide,*
> *Sixteen*
> *Coaches long*
> *Well, that long black train*
> *Carry my baby and gone*

They may ride the same train—somehow, it runs away from itself.

To understand the strangeness of those lines, we have to go back to the place where Parker and Phillips found them: back to the Carter Family's "Worried Man Blues" of some twenty years before. It was a folk song, passed back and forth between the races, that in truth was older than anyone's memory.

"Worried Man" is the story of a man who lays down to sleep by a river and wakes up in chains. The Carters don't tell you if the man is black or white; if he killed someone, stole a horse, or did anything at all, and the man doesn't know either. You would have to go a long way to match that as an image of the devil in the dream, or as the plain symbol of a land whose profound optimism insures that disaster must be incomprehensible.

There is no protest in the song, no revolt, only an absolute, almost supernatural loneliness: a bewilderment that is all the more terrifying because it is so self-effacing and matter-of-fact. The emotion is there in the steady roll of the beat, in the resignation of Mother Maybelle's guitar, and in A. P. Carter's squeaky, toneless singing: the sound of a man who has told his story more times than he can remember, and who hopes that one more telling will finally let him rest. He rides a train to nowhere.

> *The train I ride is sixteen coaches long*
> *The train I ride is sixteen coaches long*
> *The girl I love is on that train and gone**

Like the rest of the song, it makes no sense; it simply defines the singer's world, and there is no way out, save for the death the man promises will someday save him from his song.

Even without these details—the mystery behind their train song—and even with a tacked-on happy ending that gives the singer back his girl, Parker and Phillips recreated this mood, or submitted to it. So, when Parker sings that his baby will come home, that the train will surely bring her back, you don't really believe him. He sounds as if he has already lost more than anyone can return.

The Carter Family was completely real to Elvis; the white gospel culture they represented was implicitly *his* in a way that no other culture, be it Hollywood or the blues, could ever quite be. This was his inheritance and his birthright; the blues and the movies were something he made real for himself. On the earlier Sun records, Elvis had left home with the blues and come back on the flipside; "Mystery Train" gave him a blues that was rooted in his own community, and the context was not so open.

There was the purely musical side; most of the material Elvis had used at Sun was weak or undeveloped in its original form, giving him plenty of freedom to exploit possibilities others had missed. With "Mystery Train," both originals were brilliant. They took the train

---

✳ EE #7. I had a dream one night, 4/25/73. In the dream, I am looking into a carny peep-show machine, wherein tiny shots of Elvis, Scotty Moore, and Bill Black, circa 1954, flicker in and out of view. Naked, they are rehearsing their live act, kicking their legs in tandem like the Rockettes. Slowly, the camera moves in on Elvis's penis. It is an accurate dream: I look to see if Elvis is circumcised, and of course he is not. In close-up his member fills the screen. A message has been carved on his penis in block letters. "ELVIS LIVE AT THE INTERNATIONAL HOTEL LAS VEGAS," it reads.

as far as it could go—in one direction—and the hard meaning Junior Parker and the Carter Family gave to the song was also part of Elvis's inheritance. If that meaning was forcefully obscure, that uncertainty was the song's point: the uselessness of action, the helplessness of a man who cannot understand his world, let alone master it. The singer was to enter this world, suffer it, make that world real, and thus redeem it. Elvis had his job cut out for him if he was to make the song his own.

One more time, he found an opening and made it through. His attack on "Mystery Train" is as strong as Sly Stone's transformation of "Que Sera, Sera" from a little hymn to the benevolence of fate into a massive ode to dread. If the two performances go in different directions, maybe that tells us how far we have come; tells us that rock 'n' roll had to begin with an honest refusal of doubt and fatalism, and grow, along with its audience, to the point where it would have to absorb such things to survive.

Inspired by the feeling of going up against the old meaning of the tune, or determined to beat out Junior Parker, the black man, or simply thrilled by the music, Elvis sings this song with shock: he rebels against it. There is so much fire in his singing, so much personality and soul, that he changes the meaning of the song without smoothing it over. There is a tremendous violence to the record: "Train I ride," Elvis sings, but he sounds as if he's going to run it down. "It took my baby," Parker had moaned (riding us back to the days when a black locomotive was the symbol of a force no one could resist, of fate on wheels): "It's gone do it again." "Well," Elvis declares, "it took my baby—BUT IT NEVER WILL AGAIN—no, not again." His rhythm guitar seizes the music, forcing the changes; Scotty Moore, as he always did, lives up to Elvis's passion. Moore gives us one hard solo, which seems to hang the song between what it has always been and what Elvis is making of it, and then Elvis is back, and he turns the train around. As he speeds off into the night with the girl he has stolen off that mystery train, he cuts loose one more time. "Woo, woo—WOOOO!" he shouts, full of delight; he laughs out loud; and he's gone.

Elvis escaped the guilt of the blues—the guilt that is at the heart of the world the blues and country music give us—because he was able to replace the sense that men and women were trapped by fate and by their sins with a complex of emotions that was equally strong and distinctive. As he sang, Elvis changed the personae his songs originally offered his listeners. When the persona was one of anger, or delight, he outdistanced it. He didn't have to tell us that the blues is about displacement, about not being at home, about a brooding fear the music was meant to ease, but not resist. And if at its deepest the blues is hellfire music, worth the trouble of the black preachers who have damned it, that Elvis escaped this truth and still made his music ring true was precisely his genius.

FINALE

These days, Elvis is always singing. In his stage-show documentary, *Elvis on Tour*, we see him singing to himself, in limousines, backstage, running, walking, standing still, as his servant fits his cape to his shoulders, as he waits for his cue. He sings gospel music, mostly; in his private musical world, there is no distance at all from his deepest roots. Just as that personal culture of the Sun records was long ago blown up into something too big for Elvis to keep as his own, so the shared culture of country religion is now his private space within the greater America of which he has become a part.

And on stage? Well, there are those moments when Elvis Presley breaks through the public world he has made for himself, and only a fool or a liar would deny their power. Something entirely his, driven by two decades of history and myth, all live-in-person, is transformed into an energy that is ecstatic—that is, to use the word in its old sense, illuminating. The overstated grandeur is suddenly authentic, and Elvis brings a thrill different from and far beyond anything else in our culture; like an old Phil Spector record, he matches, for an instant, the bigness, the intensity, and the unpredictability of America itself.

It might be that time when he sings "How Great Thou Art" with all the faith of a backwoods Jonathan Edwards; it might be at the very end of the night, when he closes his show with "Can't Help Falling in Love," and his song takes on a glow that might make you feel his capacity for affection is all but superhuman. Whatever it is, it will be music that excludes no one, and still passes on something valuable to everyone who is there. It is as if the America that Elvis throws away for most of his performance can be given life again at will.

At his best Elvis not only embodies but personalizes so much of what is good about this place: a delight in sex that is sometimes simple, sometimes complex, but always open; a love of roots and a respect for the past; a rejection of the past and a demand for novelty; the kind of racial harmony that for Elvis, a white man, means a profound affinity with the most subtle nuances of black culture combined with an equally profound understanding of his own whiteness; a burning desire to get rich, and to have fun; a natural affection for big cars, flashy clothes, for the symbols of status that give pleasure both as symbols, and on their own terms. Elvis has long since become one of those symbols himself.

Elvis has survived the contradictions of his career, perhaps because there is so much room and so much mystery in Herman Melville's most telling comment on this country: "The Declaration of Independence makes a difference." Elvis takes his strength from the liberating arrogance, pride, and the claim to be unique that grow out of a rich and commonplace understanding of what "democracy" and "equality" are all about: No man is better than I am. He takes his strength as well from the humility, the piety, and the open, self-effacing good humor that spring from the same source: I am better than no man. And so Elvis Presley's career defines success in a democracy that can perhaps recognize itself best in its popular culture: no limits, success so grand and complete it is nearly impossible for him to perceive anything more worth striving for. But there is a horror to this utopia—and one might think that the great moments Elvis still finds are his refusal of all that he can have without struggling. Elvis proves then that the myth of supremacy for which his audience will settle cannot contain him; he is, these moments show, far greater than that.

So perhaps that old rhythm of the Sun records does play itself out, even now. Along with Robert Johnson, Elvis is the grandest figure in the story I have tried to tell, because he has gone to the greatest extremes: he has given us an America that is dead, and an unmatched version of an America that is full of life.

All in all, there is only one remaining moment I want to see; one epiphany that would somehow bring his story home. Elvis would take the stage, as he always has; the roar of the audience would surround him, as it always will. After a time, he would begin a song by Bob Dylan. Singing slowly, Elvis would give it everything he has. "I must have been mad," he would cry, "I didn't know what I had—Until I threw it all away."

And then, with love in his heart, he would laugh.

EPILOGUE

ITINERANT SINGER REVEALS NAME ON TAIL OF SHIRT
'Disgusting,' Witnesses Charge

REPORT HUGE STONES BLOCK ALL ROADS

MAN WITH BLACK WHIP SEEN AGAIN IN CEMETERY—
ONLY COMES OUT AT NIGHT
Gravediggers Threaten Walkout

ALTERCATION OVER STETSON HAT ENDS IN DEATH

AFRICANS EAGER TO 'SEE THE USA' ASSERTS TRAVEL AGENT—
'BIG BUCKS IN NEW TOURIST MARKET'

MAN FOUND IN CHAINS HELD, DENIES ALL WRONGDOING
'Only Wanted Nap,' Claims Prisoner

FIANCEE DISAPPEARS ON TRAIN, REPORTS ASTONISHED PASSENGER—
'Old Story,' Says Stationmaster

MAN AND WOMAN ESCAPE TRAIN WRECK UNHARMED
'Line Hasn't Run For Thirty Years,' Maintains Rail Exec

Walt Whitman once wrote that he didn't want an art that could decide presidential elections; he wanted an art to make them irrelevant. He was interested in an artist's ability to determine the feel of American experience; to become a part of the instinctive response of the people to events; to affect the quality and the costs of daily life. Whitman cared less that he would be remembered (though he certainly cared about that) than that his beliefs in the promises of American life would be lived out by other Americans—those of his time, and those far beyond his time. He thought that his work might affect whether or not his country would grow, and die, and start over again; whether his country would, at the margins of change, maintain a soul and a vitality that could be recognized, loved, and feared far more easily than it could be defined.

I think few artists have come closer to these dreams than those whose stories make up this book. Harmonica Frank, known to no one; Elvis, known to all; and the others: each catch an America that has shape within an America that is seamless—and that, most likely, is the best one can really hope for.

But Whitman, like Elvis or the Beatles or any true pop original, wanted it all, a grand battle between art and politics pitched right here. "Did you too," he wrote in *Democratic Vistas*, "suppose democracy was only for elections, for politics, for a party name?" Whitman thought limits were undemocratic. As good democrats, we fight it out within the borders of his ambition.

Notes and
Discographies

This section, organized by chapter, covers the records, books, movies, and essays discussed in the main text, along with others that seem relevant. There are a lot of the latter. In 1975, when this book was first published, there were usually one or at most a half-dozen records available to serenade a narrative; as I write now, after the explosion of rock, blues, and country reissues from the U.S., Great Britain, Japan, and elsewhere, it is no exaggeration (I wish it were) to say that there are a score or a hundred. I haven't attempted to be completist: I've looked for the best, for albums that tell a story or contain a single vital recording that can be found nowhere else. Often only original releases are cited, because so many reissues remain in print for less time than it takes a book to go through the press.

I have included information on year of original release and *Billboard* chart position whenever that seemed to the point. Most of that information comes from Joel Whitburn's invaluable Record Research compilation books, especially *Top Pop Singles 1955–1986*, *Top Pop Albums 1955–1985*, and the heroic *Pop Memories 1890–1954*, a reconstruction from numerous fugitive sources of the true mass popularity of Tin Pan Alley, military, Hawaiian, ragtime, jazz, Broadway, blues, country, and early rock records that, for the first time, makes it possible to judge the impact of American popular music in the pre-chart era. Whitburn almost never makes mistakes; his books are available from Record Research, P.O. Box 200, Menomonee Falls, WI 53501.

There is also a great deal of other material: tall tales, obituaries, discursive notes on legends, myths, and metaphors; an account of rare and officially unreleased music by the Band; the truth about Stagger Lee (such as I have been able to put it together), plus new sightings of the archetype; a long look at the music, memoirs, analyses, fictions, and souvenirs that continue to appear in the wake of Elvis's death (given the mountain of gold and pyrite, it's also a brief look); and, in the Elvis section, the transcript of a furious argument between Sam Phillips and Jerry Lee Lewis, from 1957, over whether rock 'n' roll is or is not music of the devil. Jerry Lee takes a strictly orthodox position; Phillips falls back on Anne Hutchinson's doctrine of the Inner Light, and carries the day.

HARMONICA FRANK

Frank Floyd was born without a given name (after years as "Shank," he chose "Frank" for himself as a teenager); he got his first regular job in the late '20s, with the Cole Brothers Carnival, and for the next two decades trekked through the country, spending most of his time in the South with such legendary outfits as Happy Phillipson's Medicine Show and the Dr. Hood Medicine Show. In 1951, after nearly thirty years of living off his music and his wits, he cut his first records with Sam Phillips; in 1954 they recorded "Rockin' Chair Daddy" and "The Great Medical Menagerist." Of the many numbers put down in 1951, five were released (the rest, including "Christmas Time Again," were erased: tape was expensive). These sides were once very hard to come by, and I thank Greg Shaw for providing the bootlegged tapes that sparked my interest in the first place.

All of the 1951 and '54 sides, plus a dazzling 1958 single, "Rock a Little Baby," that Frank issued on his own F&L label (a forgotten Larry Kennon took the B-side with "Monkey Love"), are included on *The Great Original Recordings of Harmonica Frank* (Puritan 3003).* Along with the album come photos of Frank in 1930 (a ringer for any drawing of Huck Finn), the late '40s (in cowboy regalia), and 1972—one of the latter showing how Frank played two harmonicas simultaneously, one with his mouth, the other with his nose.

Frank's music does not lend itself to classification. He told blues researcher Steve LaVere, who rediscovered him in 1972: "I spent a lot of time

---

*This album, and many of the other rock, blues, folk, country and foreign reissue LPs and CDs mentioned here, plus music books and videos, can be ordered by mail from Down Home Music, 6921 Stockton Ave., El Cerrito, CA 94530 (tel. 415-525-1494, fax 415-525-2904).

listening to the darkies in days gone by singing in the cottonfield down South, and I picked up their songs and speech. That is the reason people think I am a colored man, but I really am white." That seemed to matter. "I never played with no blacks," Frank wrote me in response to a query, "but I was a fan of Blind Lemon Jefferson, Lonnie Johnson, and Fats Domino." And, he might have added, a contemporary of all three.

Frank learned many styles so he could play for many audiences—which by the '70s included college students at folk and blues festivals across the U.S. His music can be heard in the context of early rock on *The Best of Sun Rockabilly, Vol. 1* (Charly 30123, UK), an unmatched collection of Sun rarities. His masterpiece, "Goin' Away Walkin'," can be heard in the context of Memphis blues on *Memphis and the Delta: The 1950s* (Blues Classics 15). Somewhat inappropriately, his music can be heard in the context of country on *The Sun Country Years, 1950–1959* (Sun/Bear Family 5197, W. Germany), a ten-LP boxed set that includes a book-length discography. "Train Whistle Boogie," written by Frank and recorded in 1959 by Charles Dean and the Rondells on the Benton label in Dyersberg, Tennessee, can be found on *Rare Rock-a-billy, Vol. 2* (Collector 1020, Holland), or on *Ten Years—Collector Records* (White Label 8816, Holland); no version of the song by Frank himself is known. The anthology *Step It Up and Go* (Redita 130, Holland) includes three Frank tunes purportedly recorded in the late 1960s; all but the mostly instrumental "Memphis to New Orleans" are available in more accessible versions.

Following his rediscovery, Frank cut a new album, but *Harmonica Frank Floyd* (Adelphi 1023) was a severe disappointment; virtually every cut lacked flair and spirit. In 1975, though, Frank recorded a magnificent LP, *Blues That Made the Roosters Dance* (Barrelhouse 05), that fully equaled his Sun sides. The man was close to seventy; he sounded thirty. Tunes included the Mississippi Shieks' 1930 "Sittin' on Top of the World," a fine tribute to Jimmie Rodgers, "Ring Tail Tom Cat Rag" (featuring several of Frank's many animal imitations), "Shanghai Rooster Breakdown," and "Shampoo (The Whorehouse Special)," a blues that was not merely dirty, but filthy—you've got to hear it to believe it.

Frank Floyd died in 1984. He once asked me to mention that of all those who reissued his music, only Chris Strachwitz, who runs the Blues Classics label, and Down Home Music, ever paid him any money for it.

ROBERT JOHNSON

Before Columbia Records began its release of Johnson's music in 1961, his tunes traveled by rare 78 rpm originals, an occasional foreign blues bootleg, cover versions by Chicago bluesmen, tapes passing from hand to hand. Some of his most important compositions—"If I Had Possession Over Judgment Day," for one—had never been heard on record at all.

The sixteen tracks of *Robert Johnson: King of the Delta Blues Singers* (Columbia 1654) offer virtually all of Johnson's greatest songs: "Crossroads Blues," "Terraplane Blues" (his only real hit: Johnny Otis heard it on the radio in Berkeley in 1936), "Come on in My Kitchen," "Traveling Riverside Blues," "Walking Blues," "Rambling on My Mind," "Me and the Devil Blues," "Hellhound on My Trail," "Stones in My Passway." There has not been a better album in the history of the recording industry.

Sales throughout the 1960s probably did not exceed fifteen thousand copies, but only a handful of albums released in that decade were so influential. Cream's version of "Crossroads" and the Rolling Stones' "Love in Vain" (Johnson's original was still officially unreleased when the Stones' cover appeared in 1969) prompted *King of the Delta Blues Singers, Vol. II* (Columbia 30034). It collected the remainder of Johnson's recorded compositions, and included "Love in Vain," "Stop Breakin' Down Blues," "Phonograph Blues," "I Believe I'll Dust My Broom," "Sweet Home Chicago" (a longtime South Side standard), and others, plus some alternate takes, and was graced by Tom Wilson's remarkably evocative paintings of Johnson's first recording session. *Delta Blues* (Roots 339, Austria), a various-artists anthology, includes eight further alternate takes—"Come on in My Kitchen," "Love in Vain," and an important variant of "Crossroads Blues" among them. These and others can also be found on *Mississippi Blues (1927–1937)* (Document/HK 4001, Austria) and *Mississippi Country Blues—Vol. 1 (1935–1951)* (Document 519, Austria); the latter contains searing 1941 electric performances by Robert Jr. Lockwood, Johnson's stepson, of two tunes attributed to Johnson, "Little Boy Blue" and "Take a Little Walk with Me." No less fiery is Johnny Shines' version of Johnson's unrecorded "Tell Me Mama," on his 1972 *Sitting on Top of the World* (Biograph 12044). The anthology *The Roots of Robert Johnson* (Yazoo 1073) assembles blues that may have directly influenced Johnson's composition of specific songs, connecting Leroy Carr's "When the Sun Goes Down" to "Love in Vain," Skip James' "Devil Got My Woman" to "Hellhound on My Trail," etc. The record is fascinating, but the dogmatic, reductive claims of the liner notes dissolve as soon as you go to your turntable and replace "the roots" with the result. What remains unheard, save for "They're Red Hot" on *King of the Delta Blues Singers, Vol. II*, is the non-blues side of Johnson's repertoire. As a street singer, Johnson no less than Harmonica Frank had to be ready to sing anything, and he did: Jimmie Rodgers blue yodels, Bing Crosby favorites, current hits, show tunes, spirituals, novelties, "the dozens," scatology, children's songs—maybe even commercial jingles. Imagine: "I got stones in my passway/And my road seems dark as night/But you know that Ex-Lax/Makes everything all right . . ."

In 1975 Columbia announced the imminent release of *The Complete Robert Johnson: A Man and His Music*, a three-record set, but legal conflicts put the project on the shelf. The occasion for the new album was the discovery of the facts about Johnson, along with the discovery of the Grail of the blues:

photographs of the man himself. Twelve years would pass before even one saw the light of day.

Working independently, two researchers—Steve LaVere, Harmonica Frank's rediscoverer, and Mack McCormick, a blues writer associated with the Smithsonian Institute—had after years of work made contact with Johnson's surviving sisters in Baltimore. This led to a full reconstruction of Johnson's life, including details of his murder. But both men came up with much of the same material; releases were obtained from Johnson's heirs, but they canceled each other out; a struggle over possible copyrights and invasion of privacy provoked a battle that may never be settled.

Much of the information, however, has surfaced—and though McCormick's own *Biography of a Phantom*, conceived as a detective story, has yet to appear, three works based on his and LaVere's research are available. Robert Palmer's *Deep Blues* (New York: Viking, 1981) includes a good summary; Peter Guralnick's fully realized essay, *Searching for Robert Johnson* (New York: E. P. Dutton, 1989, originally published in *Living Blues* magazine #53, 1982), combines biography with a close musical analysis, focusing on the sense of mystery that has always surrounded Johnson, a mystery that has survived its formal solution; Alan Greenberg's *Love in Vain* (Garden City: Doubleday/Anchor, 1983) is a blazingly readable screenplay for an as yet unproduced film (a lengthy appendix fixes all references and clarifies the departure of the text from known facts) that I recommend without reservation. (It is cruelly ironic that of all the many screenplays inspired by Johnson, the only one that has been filmed is John Fusco's moronic *Crossroads*, a 1986 Walter Hill movie about a smarmy white Juilliard guitarist who thinks the discovery of an unrecorded Johnson tune will make him rich and famous, and who, in a cutting contest with a white blues guitarist standing in for Old Scratch, triumphs by playing classical music; Ry Cooder disgraced himself for the soundtrack.) My "When You Walk in the Room" (*Village Voice*, December 9, 1986, revised as "Possession Over Judgment Day," *Wire*, UK, September 1987) is an extension of the Johnson chapter in this book, centering on the uniqueness of his work.

This is not the place to explore the details of Johnson's life, but a few demand inclusion. Almost every great early bluesman was said to have a shadowy teacher who provided instruction both in musical technique and the black arts, and Johnson, it seems, was no different: after being chased off as an incompetent by the ruling Delta players, Johnson returned to Hazelhurst, the site of his early childhood, and (to quote Palmer) came under the "tutelage of a musician named Ike Zinnerman, who was from Alabama and claimed to have learned to play while visiting graveyards at midnight." Zinnerman never recorded, so one can only guess at the sound he made—but Johnson returned from Hazelhurst as a titan. Startlingly, Johnson attracted international attention in his lifetime: an item from a 1937 issue of *Melody Maker*, the British music weekly, referred to him as "the star" of Hot Springs (while bemoaning the lack of protest material in his songs). Shortly before his death, Johnson reportedly formed a band, drums included; there are even claims he was using an electric pickup on his guitar. These developments by themselves would not have been unknown (Howlin' Wolf may have been playing an electric guitar in Mississippi at about the same time; Son House's driving 1941 small-band recordings can be heard on the anthology *Walking Blues*, Flywright 541, UK). But the rhythmic structures of Johnson's songs suggest that any band of his would have been making music recognizable as rock 'n' roll—full-blown, not protean rock 'n' roll—at least by 1938, the year he was murdered.

Poisoned during a Mississippi juke joint show by a jealous husband (McCormick, having identified the still-living killer, reported him to the local police; they were not interested), Johnson lingered for several days before passing away on a date that now marks the death of Elvis Presley: August 16. Reputedly, Johnson used what strength he had left to set down a final testament: "I pray that my Redeemer will come and take me from the grave." Well, maybe; in the words of "I've Been a Moonshiner," an ancient, authorless Appalachian ballad (best heard in Bob Dylan's 1963 treatment, a demo collected on *the bootleg series, volumes 1–3 [rare & unreleased] 1961–91*, Columbia 47382), "Let me eat when I'm hungry/Let me drink when I'm dry/Give me dollars when I'm hard up/Religion when I die."

And, finally, the pictures. The first to surface appeared in a special issue of *Rolling Stone* (February 13, 1986) celebrating the induction of the first members of the Rock & Roll Hall of Fame; Johnson was honored as a precursor. Originally made in a coin-operated photo booth in the early 1930s, the shot shows Johnson in a white shirt and suspenders, with a cigarette in his mouth and a guitar in his hands. The face is smooth and serious, and you can read any of Johnson's songs into his flat, silent gaze, but it is the fingers that are riveting: long, almost prehensile fingers that snake over the neck of the guitar like hoodoo bone charms. Three years went by before a second photograph appeared, in *78 Quarterly*, vol. I, no. 4, 1989 (the issue also included the first photo, plus a debunking essay by Stephen Calt and Gayle Wardlow—interviews with various knew-him-whens insisting that Johnson was nothing special as either a guitarist or a singer, you should have heard my cousin Ira—and a useful guide to local, archaic, or misleading terms in Johnson's lyrics, by Calt). This photo (like the first, provided by LaVere) was a formal studio portrait, with a grinning, handsome man superbly dressed in fedora, dark pinstripe suit, and shiny black shoes; only the fingers on the neck of the guitar matched the power of the first shot.

Both pictures were used, along with photos of Johnson's mother, stepfather, sister, wife, and contemporaneous blues players, including Ike Zinnerman, for *Robert Johnson: The Complete Recordings* (Columbia 46222, two CDs or three LPs), which in 1990 finally kept, or broke, the promise of *The Complete Robert Johnson*. To my mind, the set, produced by LaVere and Frank Driggs, was a botch from beginning to end. Both photos of Johnson were badly cropped; Johnson's forty-one discovered recordings were programmed with alternate takes following the masters, in the order in which he (apparently) recorded them, resulting in a series that, while academically correct, was not much fun to listen to. LaVere's extensive historical and interpretive essays were an embarrassment: cretinous at best, at times verging on surely unintentional racism. LaVere's comments on his sometimes incomplete transcriptions of Johnson's lyrics boggled the mind: he noted Johnson's "I can study rain" and "I been studyin' the rain" (in "Preaching Blues") as "phonetically correct, correct, although meaningless." Presumably he meant "syntactically" or "grammatically" correct, but it's the second claim that's meaningless. "Studying rain" is symbolism, blues symbolism, carried forward into dozens of Bob Dylan songs, echoing back to Shakespeare: it means to contemplate dread, to absorb fear into the soul.

The most effective critical attack on LaVere's packaging was Gene Santoro's "Robert Johnson," in the *Nation*, October 8, 1990; the most gratifying spawn of the set was Tony Scherman's "The Hellhound's Trail: Following Robert Johnson," in *Musician*, January 1991. Scherman drew out Eric Clapton, Keith Richard, Billy Gibbons, Vernon Reid, Robert Plant, Ry Cooder, Robbie Robertson, and more, on Johnson: as shameless fans and resentful competitors, they talked about genes, madness, Faust, and rhythm, in almost every case adding something new to the music. Dollars, in a way, confirmed the story: *Robert Johnson: The Complete Recordings* made the *Billboard* charts; it went gold; it won a Grammy. Johnson was no longer an invisible pop star; he was merely not present. The Columbia publicity department got used to journalists and disc jockeys calling to inquire whether Mr. Johnson might be available for interviews.

There will be more to say about Bobby Bland in the Band discography, but I should mention that "Lead Me On," recorded in 1959 and quoted at the beginning of the Johnson chapter, comes from Bland's finest album, *Two Steps from the Blues* (Duke 74, reissued as MCA 27036). The cover shows Bobby posed in front of a blue building, which does indeed have two steps. Songs include "I Pity the Fool," "St. James Infirmary," and the ghostly "I'll Take Care of You," which opens with these lines: "I know you've been hurt/By somebody else/I can tell by the way/You carry yourself." Bobby Bland and Robert Johnson would have had a lot to say to each other.

JOHNSON AND ROCK 'N' ROLL

As Johnson's music was recorded by more and more rock 'n' roll groups, someone calling himself "Woody Payne" took to putting his name on Johnson's songs ("Love in Vain" on the Rolling Stones' *Let It Bleed*, for example). "Payne" isn't the first and he won't be the last, but such piracy merely illustrates how wasteful some find it that such valuable material is in the public domain (even if, on *The Complete Recordings*, all of Johnson's compositions were presented as copyrighted). At any rate, I offer a rock 'n' roll top five of Johnson's tunes: the greatest hits of, as he is usually known, P.D.

1. The Rolling Stones, "Stop Breaking Down," from *Exile on Main Street* (Rolling Stones 0996), 1972. This was the fifth straight LP on which the Stones included a country blues, but the first album on which they approached country blues as rock 'n' roll—perhaps because in sound and spirit the rest of the album approached rock 'n' roll as country blues. *Exile* was a nice tour of morgues, courthouses, sinking ships, claustrophobic rooms, deserted highways; the whole album was a breakdown, one long night of fear. Johnson's hottest bragging song gave the Stones a chance to blow the fear away. With Mick squeaking his harp, calling for chorus after chorus, this stands as one of the Stones' best.

2. Taj Mahal, "The Celebrated Walking Blues," from *Taj Mahal* (Columbia 9579), 1967. Still *his* best. Not completely Johnson—Taj recreates the lyric with bits and pieces from Willie Brown's 1930 "Future Blues" ("Minutes seem like hours/Hours seem . . . just like days"), Muddy Waters' variant, and other sources. Taj's first guitar strokes are straight from "Stones in My Passway," but he doesn't take the performance all that seriously; his "Walking Blues," like Johnson's, is one cosmic joke life is playing on him, but no one can say he doesn't get it.

3. Eric Clapton, "Ramblin'," from *John Mayall's Bluesbreakers Featuring Eric Clapton* (London 492), 1965. The liner notes to the first Cream album described Clapton as "formerly a rustic"; this peaceful, convincing performance is what was meant.

4. Cream, "Crossroads," from *Wheels of Fire* (Atco 2-7000), 1968. Though the album title is description enough, this live recording is the only cut that lives up to the title.

5. The Rolling Stones, "Love in Vain," from *Get Yer Ya-Yas Out!* (London 5), 1970. The studio version on *Let It Bleed* is stiff; on stage, Mick Taylor's guitar and Charlie Watts' drums said whatever it might have been that Mick Jagger left out. (Author's credit went to "Traditional"—you remember him—this time around.)

JOHNSON AND POSTWAR BLUES

Johnson's impact as a stylist cut all across the board, but within the Delta-to-Chicago tradition, Muddy Waters, Robert Jr. Lockwood, Elmore James, and Johnny Shines were his most direct inheritors. Waters' first, Mississippi recordings, cut in 1941–42 for the Library of Congress (see *Down on Stovall's Plantation*, Testament 2210), were uncertain imitations; by 1948, with "Feel Like Going Home," and 1950, with the extraordinary "Rollin' Stone" (see Muddy Waters, *The Chess Box*, Chess 6040/50, Japan, or, for "Rollin' Stone," the superb collection *Sail On*, Chess 1539), Waters (1915–83) had taken what he wanted from Johnson and made it his own. The spidery lines of his guitar playing are unparalleled for their tension; his singing is hard, unassuming, and terrifying.

As Peter Guralnick once wrote, Elmore James (1918–63) took Johnson's "Dust My Broom" and made a career out of it. Waters reached for the distant margin of Johnson's music; James went for his sound, his volume, and his flash. A near-contemporary of Johnson, and later the idol of the Rolling Stones, the Yardbirds, the Peter Green–Jeremy Spencer incarnation of Fleetwood Mac, and numerous other British bands, James did not record until 1951, when he "Dust My Broom" as "Elmo James," with Sonny Boy Williamson (Rice Miller) on harp; he soon stepped out with a wild, trebly electric guitar style and a slashing vocal attack that traded subtlety for excitement. My favorite James LP is *The Best of Elmore James* (Sue 918, UK), which collects powerful versions of "Dust My Broom," "Stranger Blues," "The Sky Is Crying," and the stunning "Done Somebody Wrong" (Eric Clapton's first moment of greatness, with the early Yardbirds)—all free of the horns and clumsy rhythm sections that marred much of James' work in the years just before his death. Less shapely, perhaps, but more accessible, are *The Original Meteor & Flair Sides* (Ace 112, UK), early recordings, and *Something Inside of Me* (Fire 6005/7, Japan), a three-record set of cuts from 1959–63.

Johnny Shines often traveled with Johnson in the '30s. Shines moved to Chicago in 1941, but recorded only occasionally until the blues revival of the mid-1960s; with James dead and Muddy Waters committed to the Chicago band style, Shines emerged as the true master of Johnson's legacy. In his best moments, he doesn't simply add to Johnson's story, he tells his own. There is a horror in his 1966 "Tom Green's Farm" (see *The Johnny Shines Band*, Testament 2212) that fully equals anything Johnson ever conjured up, but speaks a different language. Shines finds evil in the white man's rule while Johnson found it in himself no less than in the world, but it is Shines' ambiguous acceptance of the horror—I mean the peculiar strength he assumes when he speaks *for* it—that makes the song so disquieting.

Shines' first recordings, made in 1946, can be found on the anthology *Chicago Blues: The Beginning* (Testament 2207); his scorching "Joliet Blues," cut in 1950, which Chess left unissued for almost twenty years, is on the anthology *Drop Down Mama* (Chess 411); *Johnny Shines and Robert Lockwood: Dust My Broom* (Flywright 563) collects early '50s sessions for the Chicago J.O.B. label, notably "Fishtail," a reworking of "Terraplane Blues"; including "Dynaflow" ("Terraplane" again), Shines' six numbers on *Chicago/The Blues/Today!* (Vanguard 79218), from 1965, amounted to his "rediscovery," but his best work was still to come. Of the numerous LPs Shines put out over the next years, strongest are *Johnny Shines* (Blue Horizon 4607, titled *Last Night's Dream* in Britain, Blue Horizon 7-63212, and worth ordering for the astonishing cover photo of a woman who has awakened to find that her hair has turned into a nest of snakes), and the incomparable *Too Wet to Plow* (Blue Labor 110, Tomato CD 2696362). This set, cut in 1975, is the record Shines was born to make: all acoustic, unutterably controlled and passionate singing, timeless songs, a touch on the guitar strings so light you can feel rain clinging to leaves on the trees. It's hard to find, and worth any search.

A NOTE ON MISSISSIPPI COUNTRY BLUES

The Mississippi blues was worked out from about 1900 in and around Dockery Farms, though whispers of the voice came from all over the Deep South. First recorded in the '20s and '30s, it makes up an aesthetic world that is complete in in itself—but while Sam Charters has written that only a black man, living in the Mississippi Delta in the '30s, could possibly understand what Son House meant when he sang "My black mama's face shines like the sun," to say that the world of country blues is complete is not to say that it is exclusive. There is a uniquely American language in the shared body of riffs and lyrics that change in meaning from singer to singer: an attempt to confront a landscape and a way of life that, as a language, escapes the limits of both. There is something very old about this music, a distance that has little to do with dates, or with such words as "archaic" or "primitive." The music is old in the way that some of Faulkner's characters, black and white, seem to have been old before they were born.

There are far too many good country blues collections to note here. The best introduction is *Really! The Country Blues* (Origin Jazz Library 2), which brings together the supreme performances of Skip James ("Devil Got My Woman"), Garfield Akers ("Cottonfield Blues"), Tommy Johnson ("Maggie Campbell Blues"), and Son House ("My Black Mama"). Other Origin releases, especially *The Mississippi Blues 1927–1940* (OJL 5), *Country Blues Encores* (OJL 8), and *The Mississippi Blues: Transition, 1926–1937* (OJL 17), are hardly less rich. Anthologies on Yazoo generally feature better sound and less acute selection. Absolutely indispensable, as a document and as an experience in time-travel, is *Blues in the Mississippi Night* (Rykodisc RCD 90155). Recorded in 1946 by folklorist Alan Lomax, falling somewhere between New Deal-era interviews with ex-slaves and Theodore Rosengarten's *All God's Dangers: The Life of Nate Shaw* (Ned Cobb) (New York: Knopf, 1974), this is bedrock American history: a long talk between Lomax, Memphis Slim, Big Bill Broonzy, and Sonny Boy Williamson—a talk sometimes played and sung—about peonage, white supremacy, labor, professionalism, violence, death, and the blues tradition. There is a stunning conversation and performance on "Stagger Lee," which is presented as ordinary, everyday life; slavery is not distant here and there is no future. The language spoken summons up an ancient world still promising most of all that it will never change: mentioning a holster, Memphis Slim (Peter Chatman, 1915–88) referred to it as a scabbard. He and his fellow bluesmen were certain they and their families would be killed if their talk were made public, so Lomax held it to himself; when he finally released the session, in the late 1950s, the names of the speakers stayed missing. Now along with the tape there is a complete, word-for-word transcript: a brutal and poetic prehistory of the civil rights movement.

Charlie Patton (1887–1934), a rough, fierce singer who may have had as much influence on Captain Beefheart as he had on Howlin' Wolf, was the originator of the music if anyone was; *Charlie Patton: Founder of the Delta Blues* (Yazoo 1020), augmented with *The Remaining Titles* (Wolf 103, Austria), sums up his work. Skip James (1902–69) was the most individualistic of the Mississippi singers (and guitarists, and pianists); along with Johnson he was most consciously an artist, and some rank him higher. *Skip James: King of the Delta Blues Singers* (Biograph 12029)—too bad James and Johnson can't have a battle of the one-man bands—collects ten of James' performances from the late '20s and early '30s. The records James made after his rediscovery in the '60s, especially the ineffable *Devil Got My Woman* (Vanguard 29237), capture him shortly before his death, and at the height of his powers. Tommy Johnson (c. 1896–1956) made only a few records between 1928 and 1930, but continued playing around Jackson until his death; his songs are among the most delicate in the blues, and his slurred, fading moans are a secret language in and of themselves. *Tommy Johnson (1928–30): Complete Recordings in Chronological Order* (Wolf 104, Austria), plus "Morning Prayer," "Boogaloosa Woman," and "Black Mare Blues," all 1929, on the anthology *Delta Blues—Vol. 1 (1929–1930)* (Document 532, Austria), collect his discovered work.

Paul Oliver's superbly illustrated *The Story of the Blues* (Baltimore: Penguin, 1972) tells the story from Africa to Chuck Berry; Peter Guralnick's *Feel Like Going Home* (New York: Harper & Row, 1989; originally published 1971) combines an excellent short history with wonderful portraits of Skip James, Johnny Shines, Howlin' Wolf, and Muddy Waters; Guralnick's *Nighthawk Blues* (New York: Thunder's Mouth Press, 1988; originally published 1980) is a fine novel about the strange process by which forgotten black men were "rediscovered" in the '60s by white admirers they could hardly have imagined existed; *The Blues Line: A Collection of Lyrics from Leadbelly to Muddy Waters*, compiled by Eric Sackheim and illustrated by Jonathan Shahn (New York: Shirmer/Macmillan, 1975), is a triumph of scholarship and design; Robert Palmer's previously mentioned *Deep Blues* makes the development of the country blues as clear as it will likely ever be. More speculative, and just as essential, are Albert Murray's *The Omni-Americans: New Perspectives on Black Experience and American Culture* (New York: Avon, 1971), and Michael Ventura's essay on hoodoo, "Hear that Long Snake Moan," in his *Shadow Dancing in the USA* (Los Angeles/New York: Tarcher/St. Martin's, 1985). And there is Stanley Booth's "Even the Birds Were Blue," in *The Rolling Stone Rock & Roll Reader*, ed. Ben Fong-Torres (New York: Bantam, 1974), from which I drew in the Johnson chapter; it stands as a moving, depressing account of black bluesmen suffering the good intentions of their white fans, and as the finest example of neo-Raymond Chandler prose I've come across. It's a piece that anyone who cares about the complexities of race and American music ought to read.

THE BAND

Music from Big Pink (Capitol 2955) came out late in the summer of 1968, and while it never rose higher than #30 on the charts, it stayed on the charts for nearly a year, and a lot of people thought it was number one anyway. In a review in *Rolling Stone*, Al Kooper called the Band's debut an event, and in youthful communities around the country it was that and more. The day after the record hit the stores you could hear people on the street singing the chorus to "The Weight"; before long, the music became part of the fabric of daily life. As they had with Dylan songs, people used *Music from Big Pink* as a new way of talking—if not a new way of walking.

The leitmotif of the record, I think, was obligation: a kind of secret theme, at the heart of both words and music. What do men and women owe each other? How do they keep faith? How far can that faith be pushed before it breaks? Those are questions community and friendship share, and they arose naturally from men who were preparing to present their partnership to the public, and who, after all their years together, had to find out what the essence of their particular group identity was.

Certainly "Long Black Veil," the only song on the album written neither by the Band nor Bob Dylan, takes obligation as far as it can go. A murder has been committed; a man is singled out from the crowd as the culprit, but he will not confess his alibi, because he's "been in the arms of his best friend's wife." She keeps silent as well. The singer, the man accused, owes something to justice, something to his lover, and something to his friend; the woman won't injure her husband by revealing the secret, and she keeps faith with her lover as he goes to the gallows—allowing him to die with his friendship intact, and then haunting his grave. The song took the shape of an ancient Southern murder ballad, on the order of "Omie Wise" or "Pretty Polly"; it was written in 1959 by Danny Dill and Marijohn Wilkin, and was a country hit for Lefty Frizzell that same year. It was "an instant folk song," Dill told country music historian Dorothy Horstman—inspired by "The Lady in Black" who appeared annually at the grave of Rudolph Valentino, Red Foley's "God Walks These Hills with Me," and an old news item. "There was a Catholic priest killed in New Jersey many years ago," said Dill, "under a town hall light [a key image in 'Long Black Veil']. There were no less than fifty witnesses. They never found a motive. They never found the man."

Shortly before making *Big Pink*, the Band, having brought Levon back to the fold, signed on for soundtrack work on the hippie film *You Are What You Eat* (a 1968 exploitation number Pauline Kael described as "The kind of movie about youth one might expect Spiro Agnew or George Wallace to make"), backing Tiny Tim on "Be My Baby," "I Got You, Babe" (a duet with Robbie), "Memphis," and "Sonny Boy"; the results, which scale the heights of the ridiculous, can be heard on *Blind Boy Grunt & the Hawks: The Basement Tapes, Volume Two* (Surprise bootleg 1967B). Around the same time, they put down demo versions of several tunes intended for *Big Pink* but left unissued. "I Want to Be a Single Girl Again" (thank you, Levon) and "Little Birdie," the latter a highlight of the Band's early tours that featured Levon on mandolin, have yet to surface; "Ferdinand the Impostor," versions of "You Say You Love Me," and various instrumentals are collected on *Blind Boy Grunt & the Hawks: The Basement Tapes, Volume One* (Surprise bootleg 1967A). "Ruben Remus," the lovely "Katie's Been Gone," "Ain't No More Cane" (a Texas chain gang song that ranks with the Band's best recorded work), "Orange Juice Blues (Blues for Breakfast)," "Bessie Smith," "Don't Ya Tell Henry," "Long Distance Operator" (a Chicago-style blues), and "Yazoo Street Scandal" were officially released in 1975 as part of Bob Dylan and the Band's *The Basement Tapes* (Columbia 33682). "Yazoo" is one of the Band's finest rockers: good-humored menace in the vein of Bo Diddley's (and the Hawks') "Who Do You Love," with Levon shouting out his unique mixture of comic horror and helpless delight. The off-the-wall characters ("The Cotton King," "The Widow," "Breezy," "Sweet William," "Liza"—or is it "Elijah"?) and Biblical imagery that sailed through *Big Pink* spur the tale of a man seduced by the local mystery woman—apparently at the urging of his girlfriend. What's he to make of that? "She rocked me kinda slow, and kinda easy," is all he can tell us.

The Band (Capitol 132), #9 in the fall of 1969, was the group's most popular album, as it deserved to be. The sound was clean and immediate; in every way, the record was easier to hear than *Big Pink*. The single, "Up on Cripple Creek" (in American folklore, Cripple Creek is like the Big Rock Candy Mountain, a place where all fears vanish beyond memory), even got some airplay, though the Band never had much impact on AM radio. The closest they came was via Joan Baez's massacre of "The Night They Drove Old Dixie Down" (#9 in 1971), in which she turned Robert E. Lee, in the Band's version the general, into a boat.

Stage Fright (Capitol 425), out in the summer of 1970, climbed a bit higher on the charts than *The Band*—#5—but it was not truly as popular, probably because as a collection of songs rather than a complete world it depicted so accurately the uncertainty and fragmentation that were its subject. A certain vibrancy was missing; the music was too worked out, too careful. "The Rumor," potentially the most compelling of the tunes, was at once overarranged and unfinished. "*Stage Fright* needs one cut to really shake things up," Dave Marsh wrote; "The Shape I'm In" came close, but it wasn't the one. "Baby Don't You Do It (Don't Break My Heart)," recorded as a studio tryout in Bearsville, planned as a single but left unissued, was.

This was hard rock beyond the reach of any band you'd care to name, including, as far as official releases went, the Band itself. On stage they sometimes risked going out of control to make music that can't be reached any other way; on record, never. Here, with a 1964 Marvin Gaye tune they had worked into their act some time before (along with the Four Tops' "Loving You Is Sweeter Than Ever," which Rick Danko sang—a live version appears on *To Kingdom Come*, a 31-cut retrospective issued in 1989, Capitol double CD 92169, which also includes a live cover of Chuck Berry's "Back to Memphis"), the Band acknowledged their enormous debt to Motown (mostly the Temptations in the vocals, James Jamerson in Danko's bass, and perhaps the essential Motown aesthetic of control and craftsmanship in the music as a whole); on this one song, the Band outdid Motown as well. They made most rock 'n' roll sound fragile.

What the Band did with Gaye's performance was what white groups usually do with black material: they held to the original arrangement, amplified the beat, turned up the volume, and yelled. They delighted in the technology of two or three electric guitars, an electric organ, super-miked drums. They didn't worry about "worrying" a line into an elusive rendering of "soul"; they simply sang as hard as they could.

They hit everything hard. Robertson is all over the music; Levon sounds as if he has four hands. Danko's bass works like fuel injection on a '63 Corvette. Hudson lets loose a mighty screech that stays constant throughout the number, while Manuel hangs on to the edge of the noise, hitting one key on his piano over and over again. "My biggest mistake was loving you too much"—*blam blam*—"and letting you know—"

Gaye's "Baby Don't You Do It" is perfectly adequate. It's thin, careful, much like "Ain't That Peculiar," to which it was the follow-up: genre music, a play on the expectations of an audience that had already proven it would buy a similar sound. Motown's strategy of change was always incremental. The Band's version is every man at extremes. Gaye sings against a polite female chorus, and you get the idea his girl won't really do it—break his heart—because, after all, her sisters are right there pleading alongside of him. The Band enlist their full arsenal of voices, each man coming in at his own pace to declaim, "Oh, baby, don't do it, don't break my heart, *please*, don't do it," marching across the battlefield of broken dreams like an army ready to give it all for love. They wail on until they reach the point where the song ought to end, and suddenly Robbie seizes the music and drives straight out of the song. His pals catch up, cut him off, and slam the tune to a close. There were moments like this in the Band's concerts, but there were never enough of them.

Cahoots (Capitol 651), #21 in late 1971, was literal where the other records were tantalizing, strained where they moved. There was a flatness in the music, good ideas forced through a banal, didactic mesh; the idea of "cahoots" was the soul of the group, but nothing about the LP captured it, except perhaps the original cover photograph. Robbie had chosen an Irving Penn portrait of two Peruvian children (see *Photographing Children*, New York: Time-Life Books, 1971): brother and sister, dressed in work clothes and posing formally. They weren't cute. The way they looked at the camera and held their small bodies told you they would stick to each other forever—told you that as long as their bond held they were ready for whatever life had in store for them. It was a photograph of very strange beauty, and Capitol vetoed it because someone, no doubt remembering the old story of the Peruvian child who gave birth at the age of eight, thought the little girl looked pregnant.

Rock of Ages (Capitol 11042), a two-record set recorded in New York City, mainly on New Year's Eve 1971, and released in the fall of 1972, hit #6, and it remains one of the best live albums of the '70s. The sound was deep and full, the Band was blazing, and the hornmen—New York jazzmen on a busman's holiday with the strong, witty charts of Allen Toussaint, the premier rock 'n' roll producer of New Orleans—added a new dimension to mostly familiar material.

On almost every song, the Band and their horn section outran studio versions. They fought over "Chest Fever"; it took on a strident urgency as the hornmen slapped back at Levon's hammering drums near the end. "Rag Mama Rag" was the knockout: Rick Danko's opening slices on his fiddle just before the song kicked off were inexplicably spooky, and Howard Johnson's unhinged tuba solo ranks with anything King Curtis played with the Coasters.

Toussaint dug deeply into New Orleans traditions for his charts—into Dixieland, blues, '50s and early '60s rock. There had always been a lot of New Orleans in the Band, especially the wild piano and general hilarity of Huey "Piano" Smith, and Toussaint brought it to the surface. The riff he used to open the encore, Chuck Willis's 1958 "(I Don't Want To) Hang Up My Rock and Roll Shoes," which runs, "Dat DAH (boomp boomp)/Dat DAH (boomp boomp)," teases the memory, because it's one of those timeless fragments that can pop up anywhere, like an ancient blues line in a Top 40 hit, for a moment seemingly tying all of American music together. It linked the Band to the first bars of Shirley and Lee's 1956 Crescent City classic, "Let the Good Times Roll"; to the pre-jazz, second line funeral marches of the 1890s; and to a half-forgotten New Orleans blues singer named Richard "Rabbit" Brown, who probably got more feeling out of the notes than anyone else when he used them to open his 1927 "James Alley Blues," which I sometimes think is the greatest record ever made. "I seen better days," Brown sang. "But I'm puttin' up with these." (For "James Alley Blues," see *The Anthology of American Folk Music*,

Volume Three: Songs, compiled by Harry Smith, Folkways 2953; for that and Brown's remaining recordings, the anthology *Country Blues—The First Generation*, Matchbox 201, UK.)

Rock of Ages also documented Garth Hudson's crazy concert piano on "The Weight"; his long organ fantasia, which from the Band's first tours grew out of the fanfare that begins "Chest Fever" (the lead-in here pretentiously titled "The Genetic Method," but nevertheless a walk through 19th-century popular music, from stovepipes to bandboxes to merry-go-rounds, with a pause for "Auld Lang Syne"); a staggering "Don't Do It"; and a tune written years earlier but not released, "Get Up Jake." This last—about a man so lazy the whole town turns out to watch him get out of bed—was in some ways the best of all. "Me and Jake worked out on the river, on a ferry called the *Baltimore*," it began: one of those commonplace evocations of a hazy frontier the Band had made their signature. It's a very modest song, and perfect. Garth never played more prettily.

Moondog Matinee (Capitol 11214) came out late in 1973. The title was a tip of the hat to Alan Freed's founding 1951 Cleveland rock 'n' roll radio show (the "Moondog Rock 'n' Roll Party" on WJW, which featured black R&B exclusively), to which all of the future Band members listened at the time; Edward Kasper's finely detailed sleeve painting pictured the Band haunting a Toronto dive that once knew them as the Hawks. Made up of rock classics they often played in those days, the album sold poorly, topping out at #28, even though it coincided with the Band's 1974 tour with Bob Dylan, up to that time likely the most publicized outing in rock history.

Flop or not, *Moondog Matinee* contained some of the Band's best music, and the instrumental "Third Man Theme" might have been the hit single they never had, though it would have had to cross over from the Easy Listening charts to make it. (The single that was released, a remake of Clarence "Frogman" Henry's 1956 "Ain't Got No Home," held a surprise; on the flipside the *Rock of Ages* live version of "Get Up Jake" was listed, but pressed instead was the original studio take of the song, dating from the sessions for *The Band*—see Capitol 3758, or the *To Kingdom Come* anthology.) "Share Your Love" outclassed Bobby "Blue" Bland's 1964 original; Manuel had more to give the song, and Garth's knack of making his Lowrey organ sound like a complete string section added greath warmth. "Mystery Train" was almost completely retooled by Robertson; he kept the first verse, added two of his own, and made up the chords from scratch. After a ha'nt-ridden false start, the Band crept into the standard and took it over, the music dark and funny; when Robbie's new lyrics emerged, you might have thought they'd been in the song since it was first sung, eighty years or twice as long ago. Levon cried,

Come down to the station meet my baby at the gate
Ask the station master if the train's running late
He said, If you're a-waitin' on that old 44
I hate to tell ya son that train don't stop here anymore

"I tried to get to that old Robert Johnson–Arthur Crudup mood," Robbie said. Well, he did; those were the best lines he'd written since *The Band*.

Northern Lights—Southern Cross (Capitol 11440) appeared in 1975; as the Band's first album of new material since 1971, it proved disappointingly quiet, reaching only #26 on the charts, but it was also a record of deep feeling. The action took place between the lines; if *Moondog Matinee* was Manuel's album, this one, despite the fact that Robbie wrote all the songs, was Garth Hudson's. He played with deceptive anonymity; his music worked as a presence, tapestries hung on back walls. No nuance escaped him—no shade of emotion, no matter how elusive, seemed beyond him. The set's big piece, "Acadian Driftwood," the story of French Canadians forced to emigrate to Louisiana, where they turned into Cajuns, aimed for the level of *The Band*, and missed.

1976 saw the release of *The Best of the Band* (Capitol 11553), which included one previously unissued cut, the inconsequential "Twilight." There was a new single in the fall, a remake of "Georgia on My Mind" (Capitol 4361), nicely sung by Manuel and meant as the Band's endorsement of Jimmy Carter for the presidency. The flip, appropriately enough, was "The Night They Drove Old Dixie Down." The disc missed the charts, but Jimmy was said to be pleased.

Shortly thereafter, on Thanksgiving night, the Band formally ended their years on the road with "The Last Waltz," a long, star-laden concert at Winterland in San Francisco, where they had made their stage debut some seven and a half years before. On hand to perform (with the Band backing them up) were Paul Butterfield, Ronnie Hawkins, Muddy Waters, Dr. John, Bobby Charles (composer of "See You Later, Alligator"), Van Morrison, Joni Mitchell, Neil Diamond, Neil Young, Eric Clapton, and Bob Dylan, plus a *Rock of Ages*-style horn section. Robbie promised the farewell did not mean the Band was breaking up—"The Band will never break up," he said, then echoing Otis Redding's "I've Been Loving You Too Long (To Stop Now)," "it's too late to break up"—but that is what it meant.

It was a year and a half after Thanksgiving 1976 before the film and album of the concert appeared; in between, in 1977, came *Islands* (Capitol 11602), the Band's weakest and weakest-selling album (#64). It was notable for the Band's first certifiable clinker since *Cahoots* (a cover of Sam and Dave's "Ain't That a Lot of Love"), and for two small gems: "Knockin' Lost John," a tune about the Great Depression (vocal by Robertson), and "Livin' in a Dream," a lovely Levon Helm reverie based on "Row Row Row Your Boat."

The Last Waltz, directed by Martin Scorsese, was released in the spring of 1978; available now on video (CBS/Fox 4567), it was an immediate hit, and reviewed almost unanimously (and correctly) as the finest rock 'n' roll concert movie yet made. The strongest moments came with Muddy Water's performance of "Mannish Boy": for seven minutes, the camera kept Waters in tight focus, his face lit by a single ghostly spot, and he held the screen like no singer ever had. The album, a three-record set (*The Last Waltz*, Warner Bros. 3146), was not nearly as popular as the film (though it reached #16), and lacked the rough, passionate clatter of the in-theater soundtrack. Highlights were a ripping "Who Do You Love," sung by Ronnie Hawkins and powered by Garth Hudson; "Mystery Train" (the Junior Parker/Elvis Presley version), featuring a hurricane vocal by Levon Helm and the strongest harp work of Paul Butterfield's career; "The Night They Drove Old Dixie Down," which Levon sang with the anger he'd always meant the song to have; a stunning "Caravan" by Van Morrison; and the two takes of "Baby, Let Me Follow You Down" with which Bob Dylan both opened and closed his set.

The last side of the LP was made up of studio material; most impressive was a new recording of "The Weight," with lead vocals shared by Levon, Danko, and black rhythm 'n' gospel singers Pop Staples and his daughter Mavis Staples. Exactly what Elvis aimed for with "An American Trilogy," the performance quite intentionally took in the whole of the country: blacks and whites, men and women, Northerners and Southerners, old and young. It was also a dirge, dark and pietistically apocalyptic. It seemed to end the Band's story right where it had begun.

Endings are never so simple, or so shapely. After the demise of the group, the various members contributed star turns to albums by various other people, none of the records particularly memorable. In 1977 Rick Danko, whose singing had become impossibly mannered after *Stage Fright*, made a desultory solo LP (*Rick Danko*, Arista 4141, #119), and undertook a few even more desultory tours. Levon Helm became a sometime movie actor, with strong turns as Loretta Lynn's father in *Coal Miner's Daughter* (1980) and Chuck Yeager's sidekick in *The Right Stuff* (1983); he made a flat LP with Paul Butterfield, Dr. John and Booker T. & the MGs (*Levon Helm and the RCO All-Stars*, ABC 1017, #142, 1977), a vaporous one with Muscle Shoals backup (*Levon Helm*, Capitol 12201, 1982), and, in between, with many of the Nashville studio musicians who had worked on Bob Dylan's *Blonde on Blonde*, one worthy of his name (*American Son*, MCA 5102, 1980). Robertson too went into movie work: he coproduced, cowrote, and starred in *Carny* (1981), and scored or produced source music for Scorsese's *Raging Bull* (1980), *The King of Comedy* (1983), and *The Color of Money* (1986—a film where the soundtrack music, or rampant noise, had far more life than anything on the screen).

Absent Robertson, in 1984 and again in 1985 the Band reformed as an oldies act. It was the ultimate indignity, the final rock 'n' roll self-humiliation, the earthly version of the Great Car Wash in the Sky, but they needed the money and, no doubt, the audiences. They hired a new guitarist and went back to where they'd been twenty years before; on March 4, 1986, after a performance at the Cheek to Cheek Lounge in Winter Park, Florida, Richard Manuel went next door to his motel room, wrapped his belt around the shower curtain rod, and hung himself. He was forty-two.

Robertson included a song about Manuel, "Fallen Angel," on *Robbie Robertson* (Geffen 24160), released in 1987. Save for a song here and there on his Scorsese soundtracks, this was his first significant music since *The Last Waltz*: a concept album about the complexities of American identity, with Robertson himself, as "The Half-Breed" (Robertson's mother was Iroquois, his father Jewish), at the center. With small contributions by Hudson and Danko and more prominent offerings from members of U2, Peter Gabriel, Gil Evans, Maria McKee, and the BoDeans, the record was vastly overproduced and labored; it received enormous publicity and celebratory, fawning reviews, but all I heard was grandiosity without detail, stories without wit, ambition without goals. Levon, Danko, and Hudson continue to pop up here and there, with Los Lobos, in occasional solo concerts, with Ringo Starr, wherever you might not be looking. In 1990 the three of them appeared as part of Roger Waters' *The Wall: Live in Berlin* (Mercury 846 611-2), a staging of the Pink Floyd epic at the site of the former Berlin Wall, accompanying Van Morrison and Sinéad O'Connor. They have music left in them, and one day it might get made.

Despite their popularity with critics, not much of real merit has been written about the Band; there are books on Huey Lewis & the News, but none about them. Worth seeking out is Ralph J. Gleason's work, particularly his review of *The Band* (in *The Rolling Stone Record Review*, New York: Pocket Books, 1971); his account of the Band's disastrous/triumphant first nights in San Francisco (in *The Rolling Stone Rock & Roll Reader*, ed. Ben Fong-Torres, New York: Bantam, 1974), and his piece on the 1974 tour with Dylan, "Like a Rolling Stone, Again" (in *Knockin' on Dylan's Door*, ed. Rolling Stone, New York: Pocket Books, 1974). Perhaps the most straightforward and detailed of Robertson's many interviews is the transcript of a talk with Roelof Kiers, recorded for VPRO-TV, Holland, in 1970, and published that year in successive issues of the Dutch music paper *Aloha*; Robertson's "once said" quotes in the Band chapter come from this source. In 1985, Ruth Albert Spencer conceived a remarkable project—she would actually interview *all* the members of the Band—and the results can be found in *Woodstock Times*, March 21, March 28, April 4, and April 11, 1985. My own "Rock-a-Hula, Clarified" (*Creem*, June 1971) includes a long discussion of *Stage Fright*; my "Save 'The Last Waltz' for Me" (*New West*, May 22, 1978) came out of a conversation with Robertson and Scorsese after the film's premiere. And there is Ron Horning's "The Moving Shadow of Richard Manuel" ("Rock & Roll Quarterly,"

Summer 1988, *Village Voice*, July 5, 1988), a two-part meditation on Manuel's death. Horning begins in Manuel's voice, describing in all too naturalistic detail what it meant to go back on a narrow road as "The Band," to be thrown back not just on yourself but on your own past; then Horning shifts, and begins to invent stories about Manuel's suicide, turning it into an accident, various sorts of murder, each tale more scandalous and unacceptable than the last, until finally all that remains is waste.

RONNIE HAWKINS & THE HAWKS

Born in Huntsville, Arkansas, in 1935, Ronnie Hawkins claims to have assembled his first group of Hawks in 1952, while a student at the University of Arkansas; Roy Orbison remembered them opening a show for him where, to upstage him, they played only *his* songs. In 1957 Hawkins auditioned for Sun Records in Memphis, but nothing came of it. Later that year, after six months in the Army, Hawkins joined with former Conway Twitty guitarist Jimmy Ray "Luke" Paulman to form a new band. Not long after, on Twitty's advice, Hawkins was in Canada, working the Golden Rail in Hamilton, Ontario.

As leader of the Ron Hawkins Quartet, Hawkins made his first documented recording in 1958, in a Toronto garage: "Hey Bo Diddley" b/w "Love Me Like You Can," which was issued on the tiny Canadian label Quality (see the reissue single, Ozark 9001, or Hawkins' *rrrracket time*, Oxford/Charly 3221, UK). The Quartet included Paulman, Will "Pop" Jones on piano, and Levon Helm, fifteen, on drums. The disc went nowhere, but someone must have heard it, because in the spring of 1959 it got Hawkins his first break.

Working with the New York Fury label and producer Bobby Robinson, longtime one-man-band Wilbert Harrison redid an old Jerry Leiber–Mike Stoller tune, "K.C. Loving," changing the title to "Kansas City." The record took off like a shot, but Robinson was unable to keep the disc in the stores; the record hung between a gold mine and oblivion as people all over the country tried to find the hit they were hearing on the radio. Quick to take advantage, label after label rushed out cover versions (the best, and most successful, was Little Richard's). One producer on the case was the legendary George Goldner; he put Hawkins into the studio posthaste. Credited to Rockin' Ronald and the Rebels, Hawkins' "Kansas City" (End 1043, reissued on *Rockin' Ronnie Hawkins*, Pye 28238, UK) stands as perhaps the least potent of all attempts to steal Harrison's thunder (when all was said and done, it was he and no one else who took "Kansas City" to the top of the charts). But End was under the umbrella of Roulette, run by Morris Levy, famous for his connections with Alan Freed and other parties; he signed Hawkins to a long-term contract. Still working out of Toronto, Hawkins and the Hawks—now adding James Evans on bass—cut *Ronnie Hawkins* (Roulette 25078) in 1959, and, with Fred Carter, Jr., replacing Paulman, *Mr. Dynamo* (Roulette 25102) the following year.

By this time the Hawks were a rough combination of Clyde McPhatter's Drifters and rockabilly, bent on speed and flash. The endless rehearsals Hawkins demanded put them well beyond most journeyman backup bands of the day; Paulman and Carter sounded like Carl Perkins, Jones like Jerry Lee Lewis, and Levon sounded like himself. He was faster than most rock drummers, and he used a heavier beat: at his best, he dominated the music. The Hawks played brash and dirty; Hawkins sang like a lunatic when he could pull it off, which put him square into the company of the heroic Southern rockers he longed to emulate.

Ronnie Hawkins contained two chart entries: "Mary Lou," a remake of Young Jessie's 1955 R&B ballad (revived again in 1976 by Bob Seger on *Night Moves*), and "Forty Days," a remake of Chuck Berry's 1955 "Thirty Days." They reached #26 and #45, respectively; "Mary Lou" went top ten on the R&B charts. Also memorable was "Odessa," a tribute to the Hawks' favorite whore (who perhaps reappears as "Bessie" in the Band's "Up on Cripple Creek"). *Mr. Dynamo* was highlighted by the spooky "Southern Love," Hawkins' most distinctive number from this period, and by "Hey Boba Lu," Robbie Robertson's first recorded composition—and, I think, his first recording as a guitarist, though he was not credited, having joined Hawkins as a roadie and occasional bass player at this point. He was soon very much more, appearing with Hawkins at Alan Freed's last Brooklyn Paramount shows ("How old are you, kid?" said Freed, then under assault from bluenose district attorneys and federal prosecutors on charges ranging from payola to criminal anarchy. "You want them to get me on a child-labor rap, too?"), scouting songs in New York from the likes of Doc Pomus and Mort Shuman, learning the music business from the inside.

Not long after, Robbie took over as lead guitarist, and Manuel, Danko, and Hudson were recruited in turn out of local acts over the next year or so.* The Hawks began to play blues, and two of the albums they treasured most were by Howlin' Wolf (1910–76). *Moanin' in the Moonlight* (Chess 1434, reissued as *Evil*, Chess 1540, and under its original title, Chess 9183) collected Wolf's early sides, and featured Willie Johnson's fiery guitar on "How Many More Years" (cut by Sam Phillips in Memphis in 1951), along with "Smoke-

---

*Hudson's group, Paul London (Paul Hutchins, from London, Ontario) and the Capers, was formed in Ontario but soon began working bars in Detroit, at times backing up everyone from Bill Haley to Johnny Cash. An ambitious and professional combo, they made two singles: "Rosie Lee" (a cover of the 1957 hit by the Mello-Tones) b/w "Real Gone Lover," recorded in Toronto in about 1960 for the Fascination label, and, as Paul London and the Kapers (another band was claiming the "C"), "Sugar Baby" b/w "Big Bad Twist", cut in Chicago in about 1961 at the Chess studios and released as Checkmate 1006; Hudson arranged and played piano on all four sides, plus saxophone and other instruments here and there. Additional material was recorded in Chicago around the same time for Columbia, but never issued; Hutchins, who remembers the sessions with pride, would still like to hear the results.

stack Lightning," "I Asked for Water" (Wolf's remake of Tommy Johnson's 1928 "Cool Drink of Water Blues"), and other classics. *Howlin' Wolf* (Chess 1469, with the famous rocking chair jacket, reissued in stereo as *Rocking Chair*, Chess 9183e, and in pristine mono under its original title, Chess 838, Japan) was all Chicago, and guitarist Hubert Sumlin's record as much as Wolf's; Sumlin contributed a crazed solo on "Wang-Dang-Doodle" (the model for Robbie's solo on the Hawks' "Who Do You Love"), plus stunning efforts on "Down in the Bottom," "Spoonful" (a Charley Patton standard), "You'll Be Mine," and "Going Down Slow." This music, which was to have such an impact in Britain, was at once rougher and more sophisticated than the rockers and ballads the Hawks played nightly as a living jukebox: it had drive and nuance, stomp and style.

Just as important to the Hawks was an album split between Junior Parker (1927–71) and Bobby "Blue" Bland: *Blues Consolidated* (Duke 72, reissued as MCA 27037), which collected '50s singles by the two men. Both had started out in the late '40s in Memphis, singing with the Beale Streeters, a seminal group that also included Johnny Ace on piano (see the anthology *Blues for Mr Crump*, Polydor 2383 257, UK). Recording in Memphis for Sam Phillips (among others), and later for the Duke label in Houston, the three, as soloists, were to define a whole new form of rhythm and blues, stressing a kind of tragic sentimentality expressed through delicate, carefully arranged ballads. *Blues Consolidated* showcased Bland's first big hit, "Farther Up the Road," and his incredible "It's My Life, Baby." The latter was a much more exciting performance than "Farther Up the Road," which may have been why the Hawks didn't attempt it. They would pass Bland with their version of "Farther," but there was no way on earth they were going to catch him—or his guitarist—on "It's My Life."

At first one of many Roy Brown imitators, Bland found his style and began a string of superb recordings that still continues; kin to Charlie Rich, whose songs he covered (as vice versa), he remains the most sensitive and original blues singer of the last forty years. The deceptively quiet, despairing moods of his most distinctive tunes shaped Richard Manuel's singing in particular, not merely in terms of phrasing, but in terms of sensibility. See, for Bland, *Two Steps from the Blues* (Duke 74, MCA 27036), *The Best of Bobby "Blue" Bland* (Duke 84, MCA 27013), and *Best of, Vol. 2* (Duke 86, MCA 27045); for Junior Parker, the EP *Junior Parker* (Charly 104, UK—Sun material) and *The Best of Junior Parker* (Duke 83, MCA 27046); for Johnny Ace, *Memorial Album* (Duke 40, MCA 27014).

While the Hawks were listening to Bland and Wolf—and to Ray Charles ("I don't sound like Ray Charles," Richard Manuel told Ruth Albert Spencer in 1985. "I imply, I make the same implications, I infer the same kind of things. You know what I mean?"), early Motown, the "5" Royales, a lot of gospel music (especially the Staple Singers), the New Orleans rock of Ernie K-Doe and Irma Thomas, and everything else (Manuel: "Ricky Nelson was probably an influence")—they and Hawkins slogged on together. During the folk boom Hawkins grew so desperate he even recorded "The Ballad of Caryl Chessman" (who knows, maybe he thought it'd get him a spot on "Hootenanny"). He cut two more albums with the Hawks, both in 1963 and neither released in the U.S.: *The Best of Ronnie Hawkins* (Canadian Roulette 252250), which featured "Who Do You Love," and *Mojo Man* (Canadian Roulette 25390), which contained Levon and the Hawks' versions of "Farther Up the Road" and Muddy Waters' "She's 19" (mistitled "Have a Party"). On his own numbers, Hawkins sounded very tired.

A good selection of tracks from Hawkins' first two albums, plus "Who Do You Love" and others less memorable, can be found on *Rockin' Ronnie Hawkins* (Pye 28328, UK). Steaming, little-known versions of "Little Red Rooster" and Fats Domino's "Going to the River" (both featuring Helm, Robertson, Danko, Manuel, and Hudson, and both probably dating from 1963) are on *Transfusion* (Union Pacific 044, UK), an excellent anthology of pre-Beatles rarities. More accessible is *The Best of Ronnie Hawkins and the Hawks* (Rhino R2 70966), which includes Hawkins' hits, plus "Hey Boba Lou" ("Lu" now passing into history).

Hawkins gained new fame after the success of the Band, and went on to make two smooth, expert albums—*Ronnie Hawkins* (Cotillion 9019, 1970) and *The Hawk* (Cotillion 9039, 1971)—and even brushed the charts again with a good cover of the Clovers' 1953 "Down in the Alley," #75 in 1970 (included on the Rhino set). Among many halfhearted, small-label efforts that followed, there was one definitive, drooling mess-around, *Rock and Roll Resurrection* (Monument 31330, 1973), which finally told his story as it was meant to be told: "Willie and the Hand Job," more or less. Now well past fifty, Hawkins still performs in his own club in Toronto, cuts records, cultivates his legend, embroiders his tall tales, hopes for one more hit—and in his own way remains as unregenerate as Jerry Lee Lewis.

On their own from 1963 into 1965, drifting from border to border, the Hawks made three singles: "Leave Me Alone" (a nasty rewrite of Chuck Berry's "Almost Grown") b/w "Uh-Uh-Uh" as the Canadian Squires (Ware 6002), and, as Levon and the Hawks, "Go Go Liza Jane" b/w "He Don't Love You" (Atco 6625) and "The Stones I Throw (Will Free All Men)" b/w "He Don't Love You" (Atco 6383). All of the reach, a bit of the sound, and none of the poetry of *Music from Big Pink* and *The Band* are present in "The Stones I Throw": "Something makes me want to stand up and do what's right . . . and take my brother's hand," Richard Manuel sang. "I will show them by the that I throw." Anything this explicit would have sunk *Big Pink*; that was a drama of morals, not moralism, and the difference is everything.

In 1965, Robbie and Rick Danko worked with John Hammond, Jr., on the sessions that in 1967 came out on Hammond's *I Can Tell* (Atlantic 8152, much of it reissued on *Spoonful*, Edsel 129, UK, which also includes cuts from

Hammond's good *Southern Fried*). Anyone with the stamina to sit through Hammond's ludicrous blackface vocals can hear what Robbie considers some of his best blues playing: all rough edges, jagged bits of metal ripping through the spare rhythm section.

WITH BOB DYLAN

Stories about how the Hawks hooked up with Bob Dylan abound: through John Hammond, Jr.; through Mary Martin, a Canadian working in the music business in New York; through pure serendipity. However it happened, Robbie and Levon, with Harvey Brooks on bass and Al Kooper on organ, backed Dylan at his chaotic 1965 Forest Hills concert—the first to follow the infamous Newport Folk Festival performance at which Dylan, with members of the Paul Butterfield Blues Band, scandalized much of the audience by singing his "poetry" with "commercial" electric accompaniment, thus demonstrating that he'd sold out to the almighty dollar. ("Cocksucker!" shouted one offended fan at Forest Hills. "Aw, it's not that bad," Dylan replied.) As for Levon and Robbie, to whom rock 'n' roll was as commercial as living off peanut butter and nevertheless the staff of life, the response could only have seemed absurd.

Dylan's tours with the Hawks began that fall. Levon left the group, replaced by Bobby Gregg, himself replaced by Mickey Jones, then Trini Lopez's drummer, and later Kenny Rogers'. Boos and catcalls from disillusioned folkies followed the troupe all the way to the West Coast—where, for a change, crowds fidgeted during the first half of the shows, when Dylan appeared alone with acoustic guitar, and welcomed the electric noise with standing ovations. The boos returned with a vengeance in early 1966, when Dylan kept the tour going through Australia, Europe, and the U.K.

In October 1965 Dylan and the Hawks went into the studio in New York to cut singles. The first to be released was "Can *You* Please Crawl Out Your Window?" (Columbia 4-43477, included on Dylan's *Biograph*, Columbia 38830, a five LP-retrospective). It was a wild, carnival version of the song Dylan had earlier recorded (and accidentally released, and then pulled) with the musicians used on *Highway 61 Revisited*. I don't think he and the Hawks ever sounded as if they were having more fun. "You gotta lotta *nerve* to say you are my friend," Dylan croaked, parodying "Positively Fourth Street," a hit some months earlier, "if you won't crawl out your window!"

"Crawl Out" missed the Top 40; next up was "One of Us Must Know (Sooner or Later)" (Columbia 4-4341), which didn't make the charts at all. The record was frenzied, yet stately; Manuel never played with more soul, and Robbie closed out the tune with a few stinging notes worth more than all the solos Dylan's songs had no room for. The tune appeared at greater length on Dylan's *Blonde on Blonde* (Columbia 2 841), released in June 1966 and cut mostly with Nashville sidemen, though Robbie also played guitar on

"Obviously Five Believers." "I Wanna Be Your Lover," a straight rocker with chains of images that go nowhere in particular, also from this session, is on *Biograph*.

The remainder of the work from this date remains officially unreleased, though most of it has been bootlegged, notably on *Zimmerman: Ten of Swords, 1961–1966* (Tarantula 16319, a 10-LP set). "Midnight Train" is just a fragment. "Number One" is the instrumental track to lyrics that were never written; close to "One of Us Must Know" in sound, it stands on its own as a recording, mostly because of the power of Garth Hudson's straining organ. There are two very different versions of "Seems Like a Freeze-Out" (the original title for "Visions of Johanna"), which Dylan and the Hawks were performing on stage at the time, either as a Dylan solo or as a group. One take moves on a loose, startlingly syncopated rhythm; the piece is irresistible, but the beat doesn't give Dylan the groove he needs to find the rhythm in the lyrics. The other take is gorgeous—perhaps too gorgeous for the doomy, fated mood Dylan is trying to build. Garth's organ seems instantly to lift the song about twenty feet off the ground; with Manuel's piano on one side and Robbie's unobtrusive guitar on the other, the music swirls, round and round, until Dylan ends it with a long, low moan. And there is "She's Your Lover Now," also in two versions, both rough: one with Dylan alone on piano, singing tentatively, the other with the Hawks. A guitar chord cutting in here, a piano rumble there, Dylan's bitterest lyrics and an unforgiving vocal make it a terrifying performance. "You just sit around and ask for ashtrays," Dylan sings. "Can't you reach?" This take was included on Dylan's *the bootleg series, volumes 1–3 [rare & unreleased], 1961–91* (Columbia 47382).

Many of the concerts Dylan and the Hawks played in 1965 and '66 were recorded. Officially, only two numbers have ever been released: "I Don't Believe You (She Acts Like We Never Have Met)," an unfocused version taped in Belfast and included on *Biograph*, and "Just Like Tom Thumb's Blues," the flipside of "I Want You" (Columbia 4-43683), taped in Liverpool. On "Tom Thumb," the Hawks outran themselves, if only to keep up with Dylan—this was pure hoodoo. When Dylan sang his lines about Angel, "who just arrived here from the coast/Who looked so fine at first/But left looking just like a ghost," Garth's organ made it clear Angel got off lucky.

"He didn't know anything about *music*," Robbie said of the Hawks' partnership with Dylan. "He was all folk songs, Big Bill, and we were Jerry Lee. So it'd be, 'Down the streets the dogs are barking—WHAM!' A huge noise. And Bob would say, 'Hey, that's great. Do it again that way.' We had no help; everyone who wasn't telling him the combination was wrong for him was telling us it was wrong for us."

What Dylan didn't know about music was how to work with a group. The marriage of his instincts, his hipster savvy, and his unmatched feel for the mysteries of American song to the Hawks' training and flair took them both to places they never could have reached alone. The music they made in 1965 and

'66 was hard, hard rock, surrealistic dandy's blues subsuming moments of extreme gentleness and extreme confrontation. On stage, they moved. Dylan and Robertson charged across the boards, stopping dead to play head to head, so close it seemed their hands would tangle in each other's strings; Rick Danko rocked back and forth on his heels, as if, in Ralph J. Gleason's memorable line on their San Francisco shows, he could swing Coit Tower. They reveled in provocation. In Paris, to face a crowd of French students who understood Bob Dylan as the definitive anti-American ("*Il est un Vietnik*," said a student in Godard's then-current *Masculin-Féminin*), Dylan wangled an enormous Stars and Stripes (from the American embassy, it's said), hung it up behind the amps, and almost caused a riot. They reveled in melodrama. To open a number, Dylan, Robertson, and Danko would turn from the audience toward drummer Mickey Jones, who would raise his sticks high, hold the pose, and then suddenly bring the sticks down with a crash as the three guitarists leaped into the air, kicking off the song as they hit the ground and whirled to face the crowd.

Out of this period came one album and one-and-a-half movies. The album, a bootleg, was *The Royal Albert Hall Concert 1966* (Royal Albert Hall 3, UK, with numerous copies in its wake, and included in its entirety on *Ten of Swords*). Recorded not at the Albert Hall in London (though today thousands of people swear they were there to hear an outraged fan scream "Judas!", as one can on the record), but in Manchester, the set features eight songs—a complete electric half of a Dylan–Hawks concert—beginning with the otherwise unreleased "Tell Me Mama" and ending with the famous verbal battle between Dylan and the crowd ("I don't *believe* you!" Dylan shouts; Robbie says, "C'mon, c'mon" as Mickey Jones picks up the beat) that leads into, and is resolved by, "Like a Rolling Stone." "Tell Me Mama" has some good lines ("Your cemetery hips . . . your graveyard lips"); more to the point, it is one of the most exciting pieces of rock 'n' roll ever made. The musicians' timing—the way Robbie's careening solo falls perfectly into Jones' thump, the way Danko's bass flips into a cymbal smash, a dozen other unparalleled moments—is unlike anything in pop music, unless you count the doo-wop patterns Phil Spector came up with for Curtis Lee's 1961 "Pretty Little Angel Eyes." "If I told you what our music is really about we'd probably all get arrested," Dylan said to an interviewer in Detroit in 1965. Listening to "Ballad of a Thin Man," to the shocking blues chord Robbie uses to open it, to Dylan's fury, or to the otherworldly tentacles of Garth's organ work, that boast still seems credible.

D. A. Pennebaker, who filmed Dylan in London the previous year for the cinéma verité documentary *Don't Look Back*, shot the 1966 tour as well: mostly in the U.K., with some footage from Europe. With Howard Alk, Dylan edited bits and pieces into "Eat the Document," intended for television but turned down by the networks, and screened only occasionally since. It's not much of a movie: there is a lot of travelogue, endless shots of crowds gathering outside the Albert Hall, much hotel-room composing and playing between Dylan and

Robertson, and the fundamental text seems to be a variation on the theme of the betrayed fan ("Rubbish," says one English student after another of Dylan's electric music) and the artist-who-to-himself-must-be-true. The many songs included are only touched on—a verse here, a chorus there.

"Something Is Happening," Pennebaker's own version, is far stronger; he was never permitted to release it, and it remains unfinished. There are a score of unforgettable incidents: Dylan and a very thin, scarred Johnny Cash harmonizing on "I Still Miss Someone," going on and on as Dylan tries to find the melody on the piano, the duet finally succeeding in glorious camaraderie, and then Cash leaving the room while Dylan begins to pick out a ballad on the piano, suddenly changing the mood into midnight and rain as the film runs out and the soundtrack stops cold; Dylan on stage, singing a long and ragged "Like a Rolling Stone," so unyielding it seems like a crime, a kidnapping of all the listener's hopes, Dylan shouting into the microphone through cupped hands; a cut from pushing and shoving on the street into the middle of "Ballad of a Thin Man," the shift coming just as the song's chords change from narrative to threat.

On record and on film, in biographies and in anthologies of reviews and essays, this remains the great undocumented period of Dylan's career: even the Pennebaker version of "Like a Rolling Stone," once leaked to a New York radio station and then circulated all over the country on reel-to-reel tape, has hardly been bootlegged. I said it fifteen years ago, and I will say it again: the concert recordings ought to be released, and Pennebaker's film ought to be seen. Today nobody would believe either one.

In July 1966, just after the release of *Blonde on Blonde*, Dylan's tours with the Hawks came to an end when he was injured in a motorcycle accident near his home in Woodstock. The next year, Dylan, Robertson, Danko, Manuel, and Hudson—the former Hawks now sometimes calling themselves the Crackers, or the Honkies—regrouped in the Catskills, worked on "Eat the Document," and began writing and rehearsing songs. From June to October they made the Basement Tape, so named because it was cut in the basement of the Crackers' house in West Saugerties. Never intended for release (the new tunes were formally publishing demos, and sent off to various artists—the Byrds, Manfred Mann, the Rolling Stones, Peter, Paul & Mary, etc.—who, save for the Rolling Stones, immediately began recording and releasing their versions), but soon bootlegged all over the world, the music the combo made was of greater emotional depth and subtlety than any either Dylan or the Hawks had recorded, and it was also more of a collaboration.

Much of the material was finally issued in 1975 on *The Basement Tapes* (Columbia 2 33682), a two-record set that included sixteen of Dylan's vocals, plus the eight previously noted numbers the Band (with Helm back on drums) cut soon after the sessions with Dylan. Of Dylan's songs, "I Shall Be Released" (unbearable in its '70s incarnation as a pious, "Will the Circle Be Unbroken" mass-concert-closer, but still unearthly as it was first sung—"Aretha Franklin!" said a friend on hearing Dylan on the Basement Tape), "Sign on the Cross" (a Primitive Baptist recital), "Quinn the Eskimo (The Mighty Quinn)," the hilarious "Get Your Rocks Off," and the chilling, lovely, incomprehensible "I'm Not There (I'm Gone)," plus dozens of fragments and alternate takes, remained available only on bootlegs, most comprehensively the two volumes credited to Blind Boy Grunt and the Hawks, though "I Shall Be Released" and the previously unknown "Santa Fe" were included on Dylan's *the bootleg series, volumes 1–3*. The sessions were loose and experimental, with Dylan sometimes offering typescripts of his lyrics to Rick Danko or Richard Manuel for music, thus producing Dylan's first coauthor credits. Danko and Manuel often sang backup to Dylan's leads; with Levon not yet on hand, Robbie sometimes played drums. The sound was quieter, funkier, and funnier than that Dylan and the Hawks had made on stage; just right for songs divided about equally between the confessional and the bawdy house, and which drew their inspiration from the fated ballads of the Blue Ridge and the nonsense of folk standards like "Froggy Went A-Courtin'" ("ZOOLOGIC MISCEGENY ACHIEVED IN MOUSE-FROG NUPTIALS, RELATIVES APPROVE," wrote Harry Smith in his notes to "King Kong Kitchie Kitchie Ki-Me-O," the variant he included on his *Anthology of American Folk Music, Volume One: Ballads*, Folkways 2951; his notes were the inspiration for the headlines in my Epilogue, and I'm happy to acknowledge him). This is not the place to probe music as satisfying and complex as anything on *Blonde on Blonde* or *The Band* (see my liner notes to *The Basement Tapes* for an attempt), but that Dylan went on to *John Wesley Harding* and the Band to *Music from Big Pink* is not hard to understand. I like a line from Paul Nelson's *Rolling Stone* review of *The Basement Tapes*: "If there are tests, they've all been passed, and what you're hearing are the results."

On January 20, 1968, Dylan and the Band showed up for the Woody Guthrie memorial concert in New York; the album made from the show was badly recorded, and most of the performances were maudlin. Dylan and the Band tore out a lean, grimy rockabilly; with "Grand Coulee Dam," they came across (see *A Tribute to Woody Guthrie*, Columbia 31171). Their show at the Isle of Wight Festival late in the summer of 1969 did not fare as well; the recording was atrociously produced, with the Band shoved far into the background and Dylan's muddled, unsure singing forced up front. A planned live LP was killed, but four numbers were spliced into Dylan's 1970 *Self Portrait* (Columbia 2 30050). Most of the Isle of Wight bootlegs that appeared were better, because they caught what the performance sounded like to the audience— occasionally distracted, sometimes tight and mean. On such evidence, the highlight was "Highway 61 Revisited," with Garth leading the way around supercharged twists and turns while Dylan, Levon, Robertson, Manuel, and Danko screamed "OUT ON HIGHWAY SIXTY-ONE!" like PCP junkies hustling tourists into the worst whorehouse in Tijuana.

Late in 1973, gearing up for a joint comeback tour, Dylan and the Band cut *Planet Waves* (Asylum 1003), mostly first takes of songs the Band had not heard before they walked into the studio. They came up with a loose, rangy sound—"stray-cat music," Bob Christgau called it—nothing like the past music they had made together or solo, and nowhere near so good, either. The joys-and-sorrows-of-family-life tunes that dominated the album tended to the slick in concept ("Wedding Song," which Dylan recorded alone, was an exception), but the shows that followed made *Planet Waves* irrelevant.

Before the Flood (Asylum 201), a two-record set recorded almost entirely on February 14, 1974, in Los Angeles, on the last night of the tour, caught the guts of the performance Dylan and the Band offered the country (scores of bootlegs, usually more than one from every city visited, collected the rest of it). It was proof that the best music of both had endured and changed along with those who made it.

Separately, neither Dylan, in his acoustic set, nor the Band, in their own concert segment, did anything extraordinary. The Band's eight numbers on *Before the Flood* ("Après moi, le déluge"? Now, really!) included an old, never before performed number called "Endless Highway" (the song was no more imaginative than its title), but in general their music was a lot more raucous than on *Rock of Ages*; "Up on Cripple Creek" was a party of falling down drunks. Together, Dylan and the Band cut loose with a noise that made the Rolling Stones' concerts of the time seem polite, and yet within the storm was an emotional paradox that often went beyond Dylan's lyrics. Roaring with fury and happiness, riding Levon's enormous beat, fusing all parts into a collective momentum, this was rock 'n' roll at its limits.

With Dylan there to take the heat, that side of the Band that was scared of the crowd, that sought shelter in craftsmanship and careful arrangements, disappeared, replaced by the chaos and intensity of those old Howlin' Wolf records. With the Band around him, Dylan broke through the strictures of false casualness and ease that had weakened his albums after *John Wesley Harding*. He was forced to use most of what he had just to keep up, and so he became that stray cat, howling at the moon.

The music, as I heard it in concert, was hard and angry, payback for the boos of 1965 and '66, with Levon (sometimes Richard Manuel joined him on a second drum set) at the center. On record, the textures in the sound were primary, with Garth Hudson the fulcrum: shifting the rhythms, darting in and out of every song like a phantom horn section, sometimes wrestling the tunes away from the other five and tossing them back like lit firecrackers. The music broke open with a freedom few other records have documented: the earlier, studio versions of "Highway 61 Revisited" and "All Along the Watchtower," both realized recordings, were momentarily blown away as Dylan and the Band charged through the songs as if they had never heard them before, as if they had little idea what route they were traveling, let alone where they were headed, playing with the good-humored, nervy conviction that the journey would return in surprise whatever it cost in doubt.

The music was made in a particularly American spirit: loud, crude, uncivilized. It was an old-fashioned, back-country, big-city attack on all things genteel, on all things genteel in the audience, in Bob Dylan, and in the Band, an up-to-date version of Walt Whitman's YAWP. Given the other endings available, I choose this one.

SLY STONE

Ben Fong-Torres' "Everybody Is a Star: The Travels of Sylvester Stewart" (see *The Rolling Stone Rock & Roll Reader*, ed. Fong-Torres, New York: Bantam, 1974), a history of Sly and the Family Stone through 1970, is one of the finest rock profiles I have ever read, and I relied on it for much biographical information, not to mention inspiration. Thanks, Ben.

Fong-Torres notes that Sly Stone's first record was "On the Battlefield for My Lord," cut in Dallas with his siblings under the name of the Stewart Four. Sly played drums and guitar. He was five.

Thanks to tapes and details provided by collector Steve Propes, Sly's early secular discography can be pieced together. "The Rat" b/w "Ra Ra Roo" (Ensign 3-4032) and "Sleep on the Porch" b/w "Yum Yum Yum" (Keen 8-2113), both made under the name of the Stewart Brothers in Los Angeles in 1959, all four tunes written by Sly, are fully arranged, sophisticated novelty discs complete with horns and complex vocal parts. They follow the path blazed by the Coasters and the Olympics, with "The Rat" the standout: a loud combination of "The Signifying Monkey" and "Purple People Eater." There's a hint, maybe, of racial metaphor: "The rat made the cat scratch his back." The tunes were very much of their time, but for all the rough singing and guitar, what's notable is the care that went into the music: the will to get it right.

"A Long Time Alone" b/w "I'm Just a Fool" (Luke 1008), released in 1961 under the name of Danny (Sly) Stewart (later reserviced as "Long Time Alone" b/w "Help Me with My Broken Heart," under the name of Sylvester Stewart, G&P 901), is a complete shift—to late doo-wop, echoing Little Anthony, Shep and the Limelights, and, with baion rhythm and strings, the Drifters of "This Magic Moment." None were written by Stewart ("Why did we have to part?" asks "A Long Time Alone"), and none are good—but all are all business. And what other seventeen-year-old black teenager had talked nowhere labels into recording him with strings, horns, choruses?

Back in Vallejo, California, with Joey Piazza and the Continentals and the Viscanes, Sly was part of the Viscanes' "Stop What You Are Doing" b/w "I Guess I'll Be" (Tropo 101, 1961—the latter cut bearing one of the more sublimely incomplete titles in the annals of rock), and Viscanes and the

Continental Band's "Yellow Moon" b/w "Uncle Sam Needs You" (VPM 1006, 1961, later reserviced as "Yellow Moon" b/w "Heavenly Angel"), or he wasn't—he's said to be there, but he can't be heard. These three cuts, "Long Time Alone," and "Help Me With My Broken Heart" — plus other pseudo-doo-wop tunes and two weird, minimalist demos that may date from the formation of the Family Stone — turned up in 1991 on Sly and the Family Stone, *Dance to the Music* (Thunderbolt CD TB 1.029, UK).

Three years later, in 1964, Sly was at the heart of what passed for the music business in San Francisco, co-authoring Bobby Freeman's "C'mon and Swim" (a dance popularized by a North Beach topless club) with disc jockey and promoter Tom Donahue. It was a national smash (#5), but Sly's own "I Just Learned How to Swim" b/w "Scat Swim" (Autumn 3, 1964), both awful, barely made local noise. Sly cut other numbers for Donahue's Autumn label, but they flopped or remained in the can. As collected on *Sly Stone—Recorded in San Francisco: 1964–67* (Sculpture 2001), there is one bizarre anomaly in the wash of bad funk, cheap jazz, and stripper blues: a flat, pious reading of T. Texas Tyler's 1948 "Deck of Cards," a country gospel recital. "I was that soldier," Sly says, concluding the uplifting story of a grunt who found God in a front-line poker game—and you almost believe him.

By 1966 Sly had taken over as house producer for Autumn and its spinoff, North Beach; his efforts can be found on *San Francisco Roots* (Vault 119) or *Nuggets, Vol. 7: Early San Francisco* (Rhino 31), where lie the hits and nonhits of the Beau Brummels, the Mojo Men, the Vejtables, the Tikis, and the Great Society (Grace Slick's first band). Legend has it that Sly drove the Great Society through more than two hundred takes of "Free Advice," the dull flipside of the strong, first version of "Somebody to Love."

Sly formed the Stoners, staying out of the city, playing bars in the nether regions of the Bay Area. They turned into Sly and the Family Stone—Sly, guitar, organ, other instruments; Rosie Stone (Stewart), piano; Freddie Stone (Stewart), guitar; Larry Graham, bass; Jerry Martini, sax; Cynthia Robinson, trumpet; Gregg Errico, drums—and released "I Ain't Got Nobody" b/w "I Can't Turn You Loose" in 1966 on a local label (Loadstone 3951, later reissued on Epic, and collected on *Recorded in San Francisco*). Their first album, *A Whole New Thing* (Epic 30333), appeared in 1967. It missed the charts, and while the 1968 *Dance to the Music* (Epic 26371) did little better (#142), the title song—which really was a whole new thing—made the top ten. *Life* (Epic 26397), also 1968, did poorly (#195), but the band broke through with "Everyday People," a number one single in early 1969.

Stand! (Epic 26456) appeared in mid-1969 and changed black popular music. Among white American bands only cross-Bay Creedence Clearwater Revival (from El Cerrito) was left with a shred of credibility: such San Francisco groups as the Jefferson Airplane and Quicksilver Messenger Service were left for dead. *Billboard* ranked the LP no higher than #13, but it sold over two million copies and stayed on the charts for two years. From it came the songs that made the Family name: "Stand!," "I Want to Take You Higher," "Sex Machine," all suffused with determination and delight. Spread across the country from the Woodstock Festival, live versions of "I Want to Take You Higher" and "Dance to the Music" confirmed the band's ability to set any crowd on fire (see *Woodstock*, Cotillion 3-500).

Next up was the mild "Hot Fun in the Summertime," #2 in 1969 (the Beach Boys did summer better), and the straight, pre-*Riot* version of "Thank you falettinme be mice elf Agin," b/w the transcendent "Everybody Is a Star," number one in 1970. Sly announced the next album, *The Incredible and Unpredictable Sly and the Family Stone*; unpredictably, it did not materialize. (For the reasons why not, and for an unmatched portrait of the personal and professional troubles behind *Riot*, see Timothy Crouse's "Sly Stone: The Struggle for His Soul," in *What's That Sound?*, ed. Ben Fong-Torres, Garden City: Doubleday/Anchor, 1976, or in *Reporting: The Rolling Stone Style*, ed. Paul Scanlon, Garden City: Doubleday/Anchor, 1977.) To fill the dry spell between releases, Epic assembled *Greatest Hits* (Epic 30325) in late 1970, and it reached #2, eventually selling over three million copies. A collection of singles and crowd-pleasers, it remains an essential album.

There's a riot goin' on (Epic 30986) reached back to the chorus of the Robins' (later the Coasters) 1955 hit "Riot in Cell Block #9" for its title: "Scarface Jones said, 'It's too late to quit/Pass the dynamite, 'cause, uh, the fuse is lit,'" wrote Jerry Leiber and Mike Stoller—"There's a riot goin' on" (see *The Coasters—The Early Years*, Atco 371). The album shared its time with George Jackson's *Soledad Brother* (New York: Bantam, 1970), a book that, while now almost as discredited as its author, certainly had its effect on my ideas about Sly Stone and Staggerlee. (The great study of Jackson, the break-up of the Black Panther Party, and the collapse of radical left politics in the U.S. is Jo Durden-Smith's *Who Killed George Jackson?*, New York: Knopf, 1976; completely ignored or misconstrued on publication by both leftist and mainstream reviewers, it provides no comfort to anyone—and no excuses.) *Riot* was an immediate number one when it was released in late 1971, as was the first single taken from it, "Family Affair," which was about families breaking up: perhaps more important to *Riot* than the Family Stone's contribution was the guitar playing and arranging of R&B veteran Bobby Womack. Whether Sly's many white listeners were more open to his difficult new music than his white critics, who almost unanimously dismissed it, is a question chart positions will not answer: by this time, the black album-buying public was big enough to put an LP over the top all by itself.

Fresh (Epic 32134), complete with Richard Avedon portrait (the curse of rock—the Band's *Cahoots* had one, too), arrived in 1973, and promptly settled into the top ten (#7); its single, "If You Want Me to Stay," topped out at #12. *Fresh* documented conflicts within the group: Rusty Allen replaced Larry Graham on bass (Graham went on to a successful career as a purveyor of bland funk), and Andy Newmark briefly replaced Gregg Errico on drums. Added were Pat Rizzo on sax and Little Sister (a female vocal trio headed by Sly's sister Vanetta) on backing vocals. Rumors of Doris Day accompanying Sly on "Que Sera, Sera" did not pan out.

In 1974 Sly and Kathy Silva celebrated their marriage (they were later divorced) and the birth of their son with a sold-out wedding at Madison Square Garden—the subject of a *New Yorker* feature. Arriving about the same time was a new album, *Small Talk* (Epic 32930), which documented, by way of further personnel changes and failed music, the disintegration of Sly's "family." The album peaked at #15, a good deal higher than it deserved to go.

From there the road was downhill. In 1975, absent the Family Stone, came *High on You* (Epic 33835), a pointless set that reached #45; *High Energy* (Epic 33462), from the same year, a repackaging of the first two LPs, did not make the charts at all. By 1976 Sly was beholden to Parliament-Funkadelic (a band whose leader, George Clinton, told anyone who would listen he was simply building on the inventions of Sly and James Brown) for a spot as opening act; he had to leave the tour after only a few gigs. There were no bookings; *Jet* magazine reported Sly was broke and in hiding. He did release the optimistically titled *Heard Ya Missed Me, Well I'm Back* (Epic 698), complete with on-the-jacket apologies from writer Al Aronowitz, an endorsement from producer Kenny Gamble, and a happy-face, one-man-band picture of Sly, but the album did not live up to its title—or make the charts. The last cut on the LP was "Family Again"; it convinced no one.

In 1979, as the disco craze was fading, Epic released *Ten Years Too Soon* (Epic 35974), an album of old Sly hits remixed disco-style. (After all, hadn't Sly anticipated the entire movement? But who remembered?) Later that year, Sly "& the Family Stone" (a few original band members returned, for the moment) issued *Back on the Right Track* (Warner Bros. 3303, #152). Though it was a more than decent album, the "Hey, I'm *fine*, don't believe what you've heard, I'm *O.K.!*" titles had begun to drag, and the record had no impact at all. In 1981, Sly collaborated with George Clinton on Funkadelic's excellent *The Electric Spanking of War Babies* (Warner Bros. 3482), and also collaborated with Clinton in getting arrested for drug possession (charges were later dropped); a good two-LP Sly and the Family Stone collection, *Anthology* (Epic 37071), which stopped with "Que Sera, Sera," was released to universal disinterest. In 1982 there was another Sly Fam Stone bid, *Ain't But the One Way* (Warner Bros. 23700-1), which featured the Kinks' "You Really Got Me" and "High Y'All," a rewrite of "I Want to Take You Higher"; a few pathetic, stumbling, abortive shows in small clubs led the record into oblivion. There were more arrests, a stay in a rehab clinic, "performing therapy" with Bobby Womack, then bench warrants issued after failures to appear in court, arrests compounded by arrests. In 1985 A&M proclaimed the *real* comeback, promising that Sly had tracks in the can that would blow Prince, rap, and hip-hop right off the charts, announcing that the label had signed the once-and-future pioneer to a long-term contract—which, as it turned out, guaranteed only one 45:

"Eek-a-Bo-Statik" (A&M 2890, 1986). After the tune appeared on the sound-track of the racist movie *Soulman* (a white college student with bad grades dyes his skin black and gets into Harvard Law under an affirmative action program — see A&M SP 3903), the deal fell apart; the whole sordid story is in Edward Kiersh's "Sly Stone's Heart of Darkness" (*Spin*, December 1985). By 1986, Sly was a fugitive from cocaine charges in Los Angeles; he was arrested in Connecticut in 1989, extradited to California, and finally sentenced to nine to 14 months' incarceration in a drug rehabilitation center. In 1990 he took the lead on "Good Times," a track on Earth, Wind & Fire's *Heritage* (Columbia 45268); in stray moments, he was spidery, elusive, strong, but by the end he was barely audible, buried in the mix, as if he were trying most of all to remember himself.

Sly may still return to surprise everyone, but there is no real reason not to believe his career is over. One fact remains: in the twenty years since *There's a riot goin' on*, only the Sex Pistols' singles have touched it.

STAGGER LEE

"Stack O'Lee" or "Stagolee" was one of several turn-of-the-century ballads about semilegendary characters (they were real, but their legends were more so): figures like Tom Dula (Dooley), John Henry, Casey Jones, Railroad Bill, Frankie and Albert (later Johnnie). Endless variants were popular among both blacks and whites; they were first recorded in the '20s by such songsters as John Hurt, Furry Lewis, and many others (see *Anthology of American Folk Music, Vol. 1, Ballads*, compiled by Harry Smith, Folkways 2951). These tunes form a special genre; characters sometimes jump from song to song. Furry Lewis put Alice Fry (source of the trouble between Frankie and Albert) into his "Kassie Jones"; in country singer Tom T. Hall's modern "More About John Henry," John Henry meets up with Stackerlee, kills him, and throws his body into a river.

Yet while folklorists have tracked down Tom Dula, Railroad Bill, Frankie and Albert, and Casey Jones, and have come close to agreeing on a "real" John Henry, Stagger Lee remains a mystery. Most versions of the song share certain details: Stagolee fights Billy over Stack's Stetson hat (in a version collected by John Lomax, Billy spits in it); Billy begs Stackerlee not to kill him because he has a wife and children to support; Stack-o-Lee invariably kills him anyway. Beyond that, the story, and Stacker Lee's fate, were up to the singer.

John Lomax seems to have been the first to publish the song; it was given to him in 1910 by one Ella Scott Fisher of San Angelo, Texas, as an account of a murder that had taken place in Memphis about ten years earlier. At the time, Memphis was said to have the highest murder rate in the world; the daily carnage among blacks was so great meat wagons were stationed at the end of Beale Street on Saturday night. It seemed odd to me that a single incident, no matter how colorful, would be considered so memorable; that thought, plus the confusion in early versions of the song as to whether Stagger Lee was black or white, made me wonder if a reversal was hidden in the ambiguities of the story. Perhaps, I speculated, a white man—Stacker Lee—killed a black man— Billy Lyons. Stagolee was no doubt never even charged, let alone hung. So blacks might have fought back through myth, first exacting justice in song, and then, wishing for a freedom and mastery they could never possess, identifying with their oppressor, subsuming his image into their culture, taking his name, and sending him out to terrorize the world as one of their own. Inversions of this sort are what myth is all about—Frankie, celebrated in most variants of her ballad for shooting her unfaithful lover, in fact died by his hand—but proof that the original Staggerlee was white would constitute almost as deep a smearing of cultural identity as Freud's claim that Moses was an Egyptian, and I had to find out.

I asked my friend Pat Thomas, a Nashville journalist, to go to Memphis and try to dig out the truth. The truth seems to be that there were two Stagger Lees: one black, and one white.

Samuel Stacker Lee was born on May 5, 1847; he died on April 3, 1890. According to Paul Coppock, a Memphis newspaper writer, Stacker Lee was the brother (others say the son) of James Lee, Sr., who founded the Lee Steamship Line, which ruled the Mississippi from St. Louis to New Orleans after the Civil War. Lee himself was born in 1808 and died in 1889; that makes him an unlikely brother, but not an impossible one.

"Father of the river packet service," James Lee began his career as a river man in 1833, on the Cumberland. He was a friend of Jefferson Davis and Nathan Bedford Forrest, later a Confederate hero and a founder of the Ku Klux Klan; in 1863, at the age of sixteen, Stacker Lee went off to fight at Forrest's side, black manservant in tow. According to Shields McIlwaine's *Memphis Down in Dixie* (New York: E. P. Dutton, 1948), which was researched by William McCaskill, Stacker Lee came out of the war ready for bear: a hell-raiser, gambler, rounder, all-around tough guy and ladies' man, known up and down the Mississippi once James Lee gave him a boat of his own. Lee liked the boy, McCaskill told Pat Thomas; the rest of the Lee family, developing pretensions to gentility, spurned him—perhaps because his women were mulatto as often as they were white. And though Stacker Lee did have at least one legitimate son—Samuel Stacker Lee, Jr., whom Memphians lost track of when he "moved west"—the second Stacker Lee seems to have been Samuel Stacker Lee's son by a mulatto mistress: to put it mildly, his father's son in every way.

That, at least, is what many older black residents of Memphis believed in 1975. Stacker Lee, Thomas was told by Thomas Pinkston ("the last man alive to have played with W. C. Handy," Pinkston said), was a roustabout, a waterfront gambler, a legend in his own time; when someone threw a seven, it was called a "Stagolee roll." An early version of the song places Stagger Lee in "the Bend"—the Tennessee penitentiary—but that was a common ending to ballads of the 1910s and '20s. In *Memphis Down in Dixie*, McIlwaine identifies Stagger Lee as a small, dark man with a bad eye, who worked on the Anchor Steamship Line, but there is no documentation; Pinkston remembers hearing his elders speak of Stack-o-Lee as tall, good-looking, and mean.

1900 seems distinctly too late as a date for Stacker Lee's encounter with "Billy"; the late Furry Lewis, who was singing the song well before he recorded it in 1927, recalled nothing of any specific incident. There are claims the first written version of the Staggerlee story, if not the song, dates to 1865, but no texts. Lawrence W. Levine notes in his *Black Culture and Black Consciousness* (New York: Oxford, 1977) that "Charles Haffer of Coahoma County, Mississippi, remembered first singing of Stagolee's exploits in 1895, while Will Starks, also a resident of the Mississippi Delta, initially heard the Stagolee saga in 1897 from a man who had learned it in the labor camps near St. Louis." No one recalls anything very clearly about a Billy Lyons, or Billy the Lion, or Billy the Liar—though, McCaskill told Thomas, Billy Lyons might be a recasting of Sam de Lyon, a Memphis police officer famous for killing five men in one night. That would turn my imagined reversal on its head: if the Stagger Lee ballad truly incorporated de Lyon, it would mean that in the fantasy of the song a black man, Stagolee, killed a white sheriff. But McCaskill may have confused de Lyon with "Wild Bill" Latura, a notorious white racketeer and craps cheat—who, Kenneth Neill writes in "Beale Street Remembered" (*R.P.M.* magazine, January 1984), "blew away five black patrons at Hammitt Ashford's saloon on the corner of Beale and Fourth" on December 10, 1908. "'I just shot 'em,' shrugged Bill when the police arrived, 'and that's all there is to it.' Despite the statement, the all-white jury before which he was tried in 1910 handed down a verdict of not guilty."

What happened to Staggerlee, Pat Thomas asked Pinkston. "He just disintegrated; old Joe Turner took him up . . . he took 'em all up." By that, Pinkston meant to prison in Nashville; Sheriff Joe Turner was infamous for running black prisoners, or sometimes just blacks rounded up off the streets, from Memphis to Nashville, where the state sold their labor to white planters. "They tell me Joe Turner come to town, brought one thousand links of chain," Leadbelly sang in "Joe Turner." "Gonna have a nigger for every link." But Thomas's search of prison records, birth records, death certificates, and burial records turned up nothing.

In 1902, twelve years after the first, white Stacker Lee was buried (not, for what it's worth, in the Lee family plot), James Lee, Jr., put a boat called the *Stacker Lee* on the river. It was the crack boat of the Lee Line, 223 feet long, built at a cost of $75,000, the most famous boat on the Mississippi, known not only as "Stack O'Lee" but also as "Stack O'Dollars." In 1916 it dragged a landing and went down; the Lee line itself was soon to be put out of business by land transport. James Lee, Jr., was the last river man in the family, and he died in 1905; he left well over a million dollars, and the members of his family fought over the money for thirty years. There was a strange match in southern California almost fifty years after that: "The parents of a college football player who died in 1981 in a jail cell will receive about $1 million in a legal settlement," *The New York Times* reported in 1983; it was Stacker Lee who forced the deal.

Ron Settles, a twenty-one-year-old black man, was arrested for speeding in the private, white community of Signal Hill, and taken to jail; later he was found dead in his cell. His parents sued for $62 million, charging their son had been beaten and then strangled to death by Signal Hill police; the police claimed suicide. There never was a trial. The parents settled out of court, "as a result of a high school composition written by Settles his father provided in a deposition" a few days before the case was closed—so said Stephen Yagman, the Signal Hill attorney. "Yagman called the composition highly damaging, saying it demonstrated that Ron Settles was 'aware of the notion of jailhouse suicide,' had contemplated it and, in fact, 'admired it,'" the *Times* went on. "Yagman said the composition,which Settles purportedly wrote about four years before his death, concerned the legend of Stagger Lee, a black folk hero of the South. According to legend, Stagger Lee enjoyed superhuman powers. In the paper, Yagman said, 'Settles said he admired Stagger Lee because people had shot at him and he didn't die, but particularly that he had hung himself in a jail cell and hung there for 30 minutes and in the end lived to laugh at everybody.'" Latura's revenge—or somebody's.

Still, the fight over Stagger Lee's legacy is a fight over meaning, not money; in 1987 blacks tried to take the legend back with the off-Broadway musical *Staggerlee*, written by Vernel Bagneris, with a score by Allen Toussaint. Set in New Orleans in the late '50s during Mardi Gras, the production starred Ruth Brown, a top '50s R&B singer. Employing a *Rashomon*-style narration ("Stackolee shot Billy Lyons"—"Stag-o-lee fighting with Billy the Lion over a Stetson hat"—"Stagerlee shot Billy Bottom"), the script turned the story around until it swallowed its tale: not only was Bagneris' Staggerlee innocent of any crime, his "dissatisfaction with his lifestyle and the possibility of being thought a criminal" leads him "to seek redemption" and try "to 'straighten up.'"

The play closed quickly; the legend had never sold tickets to heaven. But there were other plays.

In 1977, in Washington, D.C., a man named Mike Malone was fired as arts director of the Western High School for the Performing Arts. Relying on his ties with the virtually all-black student body, he responded with a street play called *The Life and Times of Stagolee* (the play was originally meant to be staged in a nightclub, but shortly before it was to open, the owner was shot to death and the club closed). The *Washington Star* tells the story: "Malone's adaption of the Stagolee ballad is [a] somewhat allegorical view of the problems at Western. . . . To Malone, Stagolee 'represents that part of each of us that strives to be free to live our lives as we wish.' And more than that, said one teacher who worked closely with the production, Stagolee represents Malone himself, who fought unsuccessfully to lift the school for the arts out of the institutional constraints of the school system.

"The symbolism comes out strongest when Stagolee, who has 'shot poor Billy dead' over a gambling argument, is called before the Lord to answer for his sins. The teacher pointed out that the Lord took on the image of Superintendent Vincent E. Reed, who dismissed Malone. The Lord's chief advisor in the play consults a female St. Peter, who was said to represent Superintendent Dorothy L. Johnson, who bumped heads with Malone throughout the Western controversy. In the play, the Lord tells Stagolee: 'You have been disruptive and insubordinate and you ain't got no respect for nothing. So we gone have to get rid of you because if there's one thing we cannot have, it's disorder.' But down on earth, Stagolee's mentor, the Voodoo Woman, complains that the powers that be don't understand Stagolee, because they have 'stopped up their ears and closed their minds,' a charge Malone's supporters have often leveled at school authorities.

"Whether or not the audience understood the allegorical connections, they clearly enjoyed the play, despite the poor acoustics and faulty sound system. The audience was made up mostly of residents and regulars of the 14th and T Street area—children, teenagers on bikes, winos and prostitutes. Some T Street residents had box seats at their bedroom windows and front stoops. Some stood on milk crates or trash cans to watch the action.

"Assistant D.C. Police Chief Tilman O'Bryant, one of the Street Theatre's strongest supporters, said he attends the opening performance every year. 'It takes the kids out of the ghetto, develops their talent, and then brings it back to the ghetto,' he said. 'Who else has nerve enough to bring something into the ghetto? They're all scared to come down here.'"

As usual, Billy got lost in the shuffle—unless, through Chief O'Bryant, he had the last word.

The first recorded version of the Stagolee ballad may have been by Frank Westphal and His Regal Novelty Orchestra, an "instrumental foxtrot" released in the early 1920s; another white dance band, Fred Waring and His Pennsylvanians, got a hit out of "Stack O'Lee Blues" in 1924. The earliest black recording seems to be Ma Rainey's 1925 "Stack O'Lee Blues," a full jazz-band orchestration with Fletcher Henderson on piano and Coleman Hawkins on bass sax (see *Ma Rainey's Black Bottom*, Yazoo 1071). But these were only records.

Frank Hutchinson, who was white, cut "Stackalee" in 1927; remarkably, its details (not merely the inevitable Stetson hat, but the barking bulldog, the fight in the alley) seem to reappear more clearly in Lloyd Price's 1958 pop hit than in any of the countless versions put down in the intervening years. Hutchinson makes a good joke out of the story: "'God bless your children, I'll take care of your wife,'" Stack says after Billy begs for deliverance. "They taken him to the cemetery," Hutchinson sings. "They failed to bring him back." But as the song ends we find Stack in jail—haunted by Billy's shade crawling around his bed (see *Anthology of American Folk Music, Vol. 1, Ballads*).

Mississippi John Hurt's "Stack O'Lee Blues," made in 1929 and featuring an irresistibly pretty guitar intro, is one of the most indelible of his many recordings (see *The Mississippi Blues: Transition, 1926–1937*, Origin Jazz Library 17; the tune is also included on *The Story of the Blues*, Columbia 30008, but with very inferior sound quality); the 1946 performance by Memphis Slim, Big Bill Broonzy, and Sonny Boy Williamson, with their accompanying conversation on the ballad as nothing more than a version of the next day's labor (on *Blues in the Mississippi Night*, Rykodisc RCD 90155), is probably the most chilling. The most influential postwar version, before that of Lloyd Price, was by the New Orleans singer Archibald; his "Stack-A-Lee I & II" was a top ten R&B hit in 1950 (see his *New Orleans Sessions*, Krazy Kat 7409, UK). Archibald offers the complete scenario of Stagger Lee's fight with the devil: here we find not Stack haunted by Billy's ghost, but Stagolee chasing his soul down to hell, where Billy suffers still further tortures. White New Orleans R&B singer Dr. John covered Archibald on his Crescent City tribute, *Gumbo*, in 1972 (Atco 7006, reissued as Alligator 3901), retaining the complex lyrics and adding the classic guitar solo from Guitar Slim's 1954 "The Things That I Used to Do," plus a horn intro that can break your heart. It is said Dr. John can sing "Stagger Lee" for half an hour without repeating a line.

Lloyd Price, also from New Orleans, put the tale on jukeboxes and car radios across the country in 1958. "Stagger Lee" was his first and only number one hit; he had topped the R&B charts in 1952 with his lovely "Lawdy, Miss Clawdy." Judging strictly by lyrics, Price's version takes the prize, if only for his completely original introduction: four lines that, with the perfection of a haiku, set the scene with extraordinary tension and grace.

> *The night was clear*
> *And the moon was yellow*
> *And the leaves . . . came . . . tumbling*
> *Down.*

Price's record was all momentum, driven by a wailing sax, and in retrospect his manic enthusiasm seems to be what many earlier versions lacked. However, an interesting thing happened. As "Stagger Lee" was rising up the charts, Dick Clark booked Price onto "American Bandstand"—and then realized he could not possibly take the responsibility of exposing his millions of young viewers to a song that celebrated gambling and murder. So, true to form, he had Price change the lyrics. Immediately, Price's label pulled the original record, had Price record the "Bandstand" version, and the result was a story wherein Stack and Billy "argue," not gamble, about a woman, not money and a hat. Stagger Lee and Billy go home, suffer remorse for all the mean things they've said to each other, and then apologize. "Stagger Lee and Billy were no more sore," Price concluded. Paradoxically, Price sounded even more impassioned on this version than he had in the first place, and his band outdid itself. Though Price (or Dick Clark) had succeeded in turning the great tradition not just on its head but inside out, the tradition, as might have been expected, won in the end: today, when the radio calls up Price's hit, it is only the once banned version that is played. The reformed Stagger Lee must be sought out on a 45 (ABC-Paramount 9972); you can hear the bullet go through Billy and break the bartender's glass on *Lloyd Price's 16 Greatest Hits* (ABC 763).

Wilbert Harrison's 1970 version, which follows Price's story line, is unique among modern treatments for its cautionary tone: "That'll teach ya 'bout gamblin'," Harrison warns (see his *Let's Work Together*, Sue 8801). The Isley Brothers may have added to the subtradition of Billy's "sickly" wife when in 1963 they cut a raging stomp (withering guitar fire courtesy of a young Jimi Hendrix) that, swears Dave Marsh, has Billy trying to talk Stack out of the inevitable by hinting, "I got four little children and a very *shapely* wife." I confess I don't hear it, but I do like the idea, and it's a great record anyway (see *The Famous Isley Brothers Twisting and Shouting*, United Artists 6313, or *The Isley Brothers—The Complete UA Sessions*, EMI CDP-7-95203-2). Ike and Tina Turner's "Stagger Lee and Billy," from the early 1960s (on *It's Gonna Work Out Fine—The Best of the Sue Years*, EMI America Treasury Series 4xT17212, cassette), tells the story from the perspective of the innocent bystander: Tina hides under a table and puts her hands over her ears, but somehow misses nothing.

Because Jamaican rock began in the 1950s partly in response to R&B broadcasts originating in New Orleans, it's no surprise that Stagger Lee made himself felt in early reggae—but in fact he virtually took it over, ruling the symbolism of the new music at least until the late '60s, when he was ousted by Natty Dread and the Rastafarians (much as Malcolm X finally buried Big Red Little). The years between were spent in a long and frequently hilarious cultural struggle, as Stagolee in the person of the rude boy—the Kingston hooligan who terrorized his own community—claimed his rights, celebrated his prowess, and then fought off the inevitable answer records that called for his rehabilitation (or, failing that, his demise). Of the hundreds of discs that told this story, the most striking were the mid-'60s tunes that made up Prince Buster's "Judge Dread" trilogy ("Judge Dread," "The Appeal," and "Barrister Pardon" or "Judge Dread Dance," all collected on *Judge Dread Featuring Prince Buster—Jamaica's Pride*, Melodisc/Blue Beat 809, UK), which were naturally accompanied by numerous rudie-talks-back 45s. Buster produced a set of three-minute morality comedies: a black judge arrives from Ethiopia to clean up the Kingston slums, sentences various murderous rude boys to hundreds of years in prison ("I am the rude boy now," he crows), jails their attorney when he has the temerity to appeal, and then, having reduced all wrongdoers to tears, sets everyone free and steps down from the bench to dance in the courtroom. The final lines—"I am the judge, but I know how to dance"—pretty much sum up the ethos of post-rude-boy reggae, but Prince Buster was years ahead of his time.

Merging Jamaica's cultural work with the street life of punk-era Great Britain, in 1979 the Clash used the Stagger Lee–rude-boy conflict as the underpinning of their epochal *London Calling* (Epic 36328). Changing names, faces, and races, the old troublemaker appeared in "Jimmy Jazz," "Rudie Can't Fail," "The Guns of Brixton," and, most powerfully, in the shattering "Death or Glory," which was Stackerlee brought down to earth and made domestic. "Every cheap hood strikes a bargain with the world," Joe Strummer sang, piercing the Stagger Lee aura with a realism it had always deflected. "And ends up making payments on a sofa or a girl/Love 'n' hate tattooed across the knuckles of his hands/The hands that slap his kids around cos they don't understand/How death or glory/Becomes just another story." Fittingly, Stack had surfaced under his own name just a cut earlier, in "Wrong 'em Boyo," originally a Jamaican rock-steady hit by the Rulers. The Clash redid the number with a version of the old ballad itself ("Billy said, 'Hey, Stagger!/I'm gonna make my big attack/I'm gonna have to leave my knife/In your back'") before making a conventional plea for good behaviour.

Those seem to me the most memorable Stagolees, though I've omitted many of the more famous recordings. A version very close to that offered by Bobby Seale can be found on *Get Your Ass in the Water and Swim Like Me!—Narrative Poetry from Black Oral Tradition* (Rounder 2014), historian Bruce Jackson's recordings of jailhouse "toasts"—ritualized declamatory insults and stories that in many cases date back to the last century. All of them, not the least "Stackolee," are so obscene they constitute an assault not only on rational discourse but on English itself. It's out of this tradition, far more than from the Stacker Lee story in ballad form, that the reemergence of the archetype in 1980s rap music came: thousands of brags, taunts, celebrations of violence and impulse, from the self-affirmation of Run-D.M.C. to the heedless verbal terrorism of Schoolly D and the dope-king brags of Ice-T. But that is another chapter in another book.

As for the Stagger Lee reflection in blues and rock 'n' roll, the records referred to in the text are "Crawling Kingsnake," by John Lee Hooker, first recorded in 1949 (available in many versions); "Canned Heat Blues," by Tommy Johnson, 1928 (*Tommy Johnson*, Wolf 104, Austria); "Rollin' Stone," by Muddy Waters, 1950 (see *Sail On*, Chess 1539, or *The Chess Box*, Chess 6040/50, Japan); "Brown-Eyed Handsome Man," by Chuck Berry, 1956 (*Chuck Berry's Golden Decade, Vol. 1*, Chess 1514, or *The Great Twenty-eight*, Chess 9190); "Who Do You Love," by Bo Diddley, 1960 (*Got My Own Bag of Tricks*, Chess 60005, or Chess 427.011, France); "Midnight Mover," by Wilson Pickett, 1968 (*The Best of Wilson Pickett, Vol. 2*, Atlantic 8290, or

Greatest Hits, Atlantic 2-503); "Midnight Rambler," by the Rolling Stones, 1969, 1970 (the studio version on *Let It Bleed* is weak; see the definitive, live performance on *Get Yer Ya-Ya's Out!*, London 5); "Back Door Man" and "Going Down Slow," by Howlin' Wolf, 1960 and 1961, respectively (both on *Rocking Chair*, Chess 9183e, or, with better sound, on *Howlin' Wolf*, Chess 838 Japan), and "There Is Something on Your Mind," by Bobby Marchan, 1960 (*Bobby Marchan: Golden Classics*, Collectibles 5113).

RECORDS BEFORE AND AFTER 'RIOT'

The tension between black movies and black records that emerged in the late '60s and early '70s brought a realistic necessity to the pop charts—but explicit social comment has not been particularly common in black American music. One could point to the occasional blues about the Great Depression or Leadbelly's Party-line "Bourgeois Blues," a few tunes about Korea (brought up to date for Vietnam)—not much more. Many of the Coasters' records— "Riot in Cell Block #9," "What About Us" ("He's got a car made of suede . . . If we go out on dates we go in a box on roller skates"), "Framed," "Hongry," and the cryptic "Run Red Run" (a monkey, who may represent the Negro, pulls a gun on his master, who may represent the white man)—are notable partly because in the '50s they were so anomalous. All were strictly white inventions, or white fantasies about black life, written and produced by Jerry Leiber and Mike Stoller.

More typically, black voices have channeled the emotions kicked up by political exclusion and social despair into songs of sexual and romantic tragedy. It took the civil rights movement (and the riots in Watts, Harlem, and Detroit in the mid-'60s, plus the riots that broke out all over the country following the assassination of Martin Luther King in 1968) to make black protest acceptable on the radio, not that protest was always needed: for the 1967 Detroit riots, Martha and the Vandellas' 1964 "Dancing in the Street" served as a readymade anthem. Sly's "Everyday People" was a turning point, along with Jerry Butler's saddening "Only the Strong Survive," #4 in 1969 (see *The Best of Jerry Butler*, Mercury 61281, or Rhino 216) and the Temptations' "Cloud Nine," #6 in 1968. The last was the first black pop record to hit dope head-on—as far as the singer was concerned, with open arms, though the irony of the song was hard to miss (see the Temptations' *Anthology*, Motown 782, a well-organized, three-LP career survey, as are all the Motown, Tamla, or Gordy "Anthologies").

Butler's hard look at the world at large and the Tempts' tour of the streets led Paul Kelly into the church to cast out the money changers; his "Stealing in the Name of the Lord" (Happy Tiger 541), #49 in 1970, #14 on the soul charts, was a sharp attack on shyster preachers preying on the misery of the black community. "Step right up, drop a buck," Kelly chanted over a fast blues guitar. Even more impressive was Swamp Dogg's *Total Destruction to Your Mind*, 1970 (Canyon 7706), which combined a weird selection of protest songs, among them Joe South's "Redneck," with the year's most elegantly executed soul arrangements. Other seminal discs included Edwin Starr's "War," number one in 1970 (Gordy 7101), with its nicely understated chorus: "WAR! What is it good for? ABSOLUTELY NUTHIN'!"—and, all from 1971, the Chi-Lites' brooding "(For God's Sake) Give More Power to the People," #26 (see *The Chi-Lites' Greatest Hits*, Brunswick 754184, reissued as Epic 38627); Marvin Gaye's *What's Going On*, #6 (Tamla 310, Motown 5339), and his historic "Inner City Blues," #9 (see *Anthology*, Motown 9791); Undisputed Truth's "Smiling Faces Sometimes (Tell Lies)," #3 (Gordy 7108), and the Staple Singers' "Respect Yourself," #12 (Stax 0104). The music was even stronger and more inventive than the politics, which only made the politics more convincing.

If the breakthrough came in late 1971 with *There's a riot goin' on*, the takeover came in 1972 with Curtis Mayfield's soundtrack to *Superfly* (Curtom 8014). With the Impressions and later as a soloist, Mayfield had been exploring a somewhat bland progressivism for years, complete with open heart, boundless optimism, tortured lyrics, and brotherhood speeches to nightclub audiences; he sang buoyant numbers like "We're a Winner," sticky ones like "Choice of Colors" ("Which one would you choose, my brother?"). With the blasted truths of "Freddie's Dead," #4 in October, and the sardonic yet sympathetic "Superfly," #8 in December, Mayfield found a new voice, and "new thing" music to go with it. His triumph was complete when the album hit the top of the charts.

Along with *Superfly* came the deluge: the O'Jays' "Back Stabbers," #3 (on *Back Stabbers*, Philadelphia International 31712, which also includes "Love Train" and "992 Arguments"); War's "Slipping into Darkness," #16 (United Artists 50867; on LP, the complete version can be found only on War's *All Day Music*, United Artists 5546); Stevie Wonder's "Superstition," number one (on *Talking Book*, Tamla 319); Johnny Nash's shimmering "I Can See Clearly Now," number one (Epic 10902); the Staple Singers' "I'll Take You There," number one (Stax 0125); and the Temptations' terrifying "Papa Was a Rolling Stone," number one (on *Anthology*)—most of them crammed into the last months of 1972.

Contrasting most sharply with the heroes of the new black inner-city Westerns were the Chi-Lites and Al Green: they were vulnerable, unsure, searching for new ways to define what it meant to be a man. Green's string of hits began in 1970, with "Tired of Being Alone," #11; "Let's Stay Together" was quickly number one in 1971; "Look What You've Done for Me," likely his best, was one of three top ten hits in 1972 (see *Greatest Hits*, Hi 32089, Motown 5283). His superb albums from this period, topped by *Call Me* in 1973 (Hi 32077, Motown 5286), drew on Hank Williams as easily as gospel—but not as deeply. After a scandalous incident in which a woman killed herself after covering Green with scalding grits. Green turned ever more surely toward sanctified music, in 1977 producing one last masterpiece, *The Belle Album* (Hi 6004, Motown 5318); he then began recording for the Myrrh label, a subsidiary of Word, Inc., the giant religious conglomerate that has given us the born-again testimony of, among others, Eldridge Cleaver and Charles Colson. The Chi-Lites' more extreme and at times even more moving music is best heard on their *Greatest Hits* (noted above), which collects "Have You Seen Her," #3 in 1971, "Oh Girl," number one in 1972, plus "A Lonely Man" and "The Coldest Day of My Life."

The chart positions of these post-*Riot* records were, flatly, extraordinary: they represented both the most politicized black music in the history of rock 'n' roll, and the most commercially potent. Never before, and certainly never since, have black voices so dominated American radio. But even as this unique outburst of creativity and success was peaking, a retreat was underway—as if those responsible for the music trusted neither themselves nor their audience.

The Chi-Lites' "We Need Order" (Brunswick 55489), which died at #69 in 1972, was joined in anti-Stagger Lee overcompensation by the Four Tops' "Keeper of the Castle," #10 in 1972 (Dunhill 4330), which linked Superfly street life to politics and damned both: "While you're worryin' about society/ The leaves are witherin' on your family tree." Such rational conservatism was matched in a completely idiotic way by Brighter Side of Darkness' "Love Jones," #16 in 1973 (20th Century 2002), and more subtly by the Gamble-Huff labels. The contingent social vision of the O'Jays' "Back Stabbers" was undercut by the sentimental social vision of "Love Train," a brotherhood anthem (and a wonderful sound); when the O'Jays' next few releases flopped, the group returned with *Ship Ahoy* (Philadelphia International 32408), #11 in late 1973, and almost an answer record to Randy Newman's "Sail Away"—because the ship in question was a slave ship. The album was tied to a single, "For the Love of Money," that rather tiredly pegged all evil to filthy lucre, but the killer was the title tune, a ten-minute Middle Passage epic. It was pretentious, overblown, and powerful.

Most black groups, writers, and producers continued to step back from the work of 1971–72, or trivialized that work with poor self-imitations; their music, like Sly's *Fresh*, though formally well-made, lost much of its feeling. Still scoring in 1973 were Marvin Gaye, who turned to pure sex with "Let's Get It On," number one (see his fine LP of the same name, Tamla 329, Motown 5192, certainly the first Motown album to be emblazoned with a quote from T.S. Eliot), and Stevie Wonder, who continued his mastery of the charts with "Higher Ground" (#4) and the deathly "Living for the City"— wherein the young hero of the film *Sounder* leaves his Southern home for New York, is set up for a bust by a black "brother," and, years later, emerges from prison trying to remember the dream that first brought him to the city streets he now haunts, his search reduced to an endless circle. The top ten version of the tune stopped with a description of the man's ambitions—you have to go to the album for his fate—but it was to Wonder's credit that the song worked either way (see *Innervisions*, Tamla 326).

Four other records deserve mention; they fell into no genre, but played in the gap between the imperatives of the new black movies and the music discussed above. First and most important was Diana Ross's much sneered-at soundtrack to *Lady Sings the Blues*, number one in 1972 (Motown 758), a remarkably personal and vital piece of music that served as a backdrop, and a necessary historical anchor, for the other records of the period. It was also perhaps the first time since the careers of Bessie Smith and Billie Holiday herself ended that the Staggerlee story had been revised and publicly acted out by a woman—if not the first time Ross kept company with Stack. In 1961, as a member of the Primettes, she backed Don Revell on his "Return of Staggerlee" (see *The Soul of Detroit*, LuPine/Relic 8009).

The Credibility Gap's comedy album, *A Great Gift Idea* (Warner Bros. 2154, 1973), featured a trailer for the ultimate blaxploitation flick: "Black Ivory Productions' *King Pin*, the first movie that has dared to be suggested by the life of the late Dr. Martin Luther King, Jr.—a film of great importance not only to the Afro-American community, but to all Negroes." Opening with an uncanny imitation of Curtis Mayfield's *Superfly* soundtrack ("He's a king, he's a pin"), the piece offered the audience "Denver Deveroll, eighth-round draft choice of the New York Jets, who *is* King Pin." "He's got a plan—to stick it to the Man—they call him *'The Doctor'*—and he's got a special treatment—for *whitey!*" Executive producer, "Samuel Hirschorn," of course. Also on the album was an "Evening with Sly Stone" in the form of a public TV show, where one could find Sly discussing the most arcane points of black culture with William F. Buckley, and then begging off because he has to get to bed by ten so as not to be late for the next day's "recital."

Taj Mahal's music for *Sounder* (Columbia 31944), variations on traditional themes played on traditional instruments, was to me the finest black album of 1972. The movie could not have been more different from every other black film on the market: this was a story (based on a white writer's book for children) about sharecropping, family life, oppression, and education. Taj's music and the performances of Cicely Tyson and Paul Winfield spoke for a kind of strength and pride that have everything to do with love between a few people—the mother, father, and children of *Sounder* did not stand simply for their "race," but for themselves. The movie was more painful than the big-city romances that outflanked it; Taj's music had more joy than the records that were hits.

And there was *Hustler's Convention* (Douglas–United Artists 156, 1973), by Lightnin' Rod, a former member of the Last Poets: a two-LP version of a story implicit in all of the blaxploitation films. In first-person monologue, with music in the background, Lightnin' Rod recounted the adventures of Sport, a black street kid who reaches the top of the hustler's heap. About halfway through the opus, Lightnin' Rod moved into a detailed account of Sport's climactic poker game. Sport is way ahead (about $100,000 ahead) when an opponent accuses him of cheating; Sport pulls his gun, grabs the pot, and flees. The losers give chase; Sport shoots two dead, but the rest follow—and duck out when the cops arrive. Sport is shot, caught, sent up, and spends twelve years on Sing Sing's death row. "But I kept on coppin' a stay/Till the death penalty was done away/And after a retrial they let me go." It cost him all that time, Sport says as the record ends, to discover that he lived exactly as the white man wished him to.

No one picked up the movie rights.

RANDY NEWMAN

Randy Newman seems to have taken his first small step toward fame in 1962, when the Fleetwoods recorded his "They Tell Me It's Summer" as the B-side of "Lovers by Night, Strangers by Day" (Dolton 723). Much beloved for such masterpieces of white doo-wop as "Come Softly to Me," "Mr. Blue," and "(He's) The Great Impostor" (like the Band's "Ferdinand the Impostor," inspired by the exploits of Ferdinand Demarest), the Fleetwoods (whose *Greatest Hits* can be found on Dolton 8018, or on *Best of the Fleetwoods*, Rhino CD 70980) vanished from sight almost immediately.

Working from age seventeen as a contract songwriter for Metric Music, a division of Liberty Records, which passed his compositions on to singers on the label and its subsidiaries, Newman (sometimes aided by his father, Irving, a physician who dabbled in songwriting—one of his compositions was recorded by Bing Crosby) turned out formula pop songs, made demos, and released one teen-market disc under his own name: "Golden Gridiron Boy" b/w "Country Boy" (Dot 16411), coproduced by Pat Boone and issued in October 1962. Neither tune was exceptional, though "Golden Gridiron Boy" today has a certain poignancy—since, here, Randy sings in the voice of one who is "too short" to get the girl.

While Randy tried to emulate such Brill Building writers as Carole King and Gerry Goffin, and longed for a chance at a Bobby Vee B-side, Gene McDaniels cut "Somebody's Waiting" as the flipside of "Spanish Lace" (Liberty 55510), also in 1962; Newman considers it his first "big record" ("Spanish Lace" topped out at #32), probably because it brought him his first measurable royalty check. Other singers who recorded his early songs included Irma Thomas ("While the City Sleeps" on her classic *Wish Someone Would Care*, Imperial 9266), Billy Storm ("Baby Don't Look Down," Loma 2001), Frankie Laine ("Take Her," Columbia 42884), Claudine Longet ("Snow," A&M 1384), Little Peggy March ("Leave Me Alone," RCA 8357), the O'Jays ("Friday Night," Imperial 66197), Irma Franklin ("Love Is Blind," Epic 9610), and Harper's Bizarre ("The Debutante's Ball," Warner Bros. 7028). He cowrote "She Don't Understand Him Like I Do" with Jackie DeShannon (it appeared along with Newman's "Did He Call Today, Mama" on her 1965 *You Won't Forget Me*, Imperial 12294; their "Hold Your Head High" came out with Newman's "Take Me Away" in 1968 on DeShannon's *Lonely Girl*, Sunset 5225, collected on *The Best of Jackie DeShannon* (Rhino R2 70738)). Moonlighting at 20th Century-Fox Music, Newman composed background "rock" for the "Peyton Place" TV show ("something for Betty and Rodney to dance to"); in 1965, without Newman's knowledge, but no doubt hoping the public might confuse Randy with his famous film-scoring uncles Alfred and Lionel, the results were assembled into *The Randy Newman Orchestra Plays Original Music from Peyton Place* (Epic 24147). Reports that Newman also wrote theme music for the 1964 Republican Convention, the 1963 Girl Scout Cookie campaign, and a December 7, 1965, meeting of the Los Angeles chapter of the Croatian-American Benevolent Society ("Dead Serb Blues") are spurious.

Newman's first real notoriety came in 1966, with Judy Collins' recording of "I Think It's Going to Rain Today" on her arty *In My Life* album. In 1967 there was Van Dyke's Parks' fey version of the fabulous "Vine Street," a Hollywood "On Broadway" (Newman conducted, but never released the number himself; see Parks' *Song Cycle*, Warner Bros. 1727). 1968 brought Alan Price's *This Price Is Right* (Parrot 71018), which featured five Newman songs, including the perfect sweet-sixteen fantasy, "The Biggest Night of Her Life" (she has "a promise she must keep"—presumably, to sleep with her boyfriend, or else to save herself for "The Biggest Day of Her Life").

Randy Newman Creates Something New Under the Sun (Reprise 6286) also appeared in 1968, decked out with a cover photo that pictured Newman as a throwback to the thrilling days of, say, 1951; Reprise later substituted a picture of Randy with longer hair, but it had no impact on sales. Overproduced, occasionally musically cute, the album lived up to its title anyway. "Love Story," the first cut, was the clincher: here was an American romance, from proposal to the grave, with every warm promise undercut by a darker promise. When the kids are grown. Randy-the-Suitor tells his bride-to-be, "They'll send us away, to a little home"—and that's all part of the dream, or the deal. Also included were "So Long Dad" ("Love Story" sung from the point of view of Dad's grownup son: "Drop by anytime," he assures his father. "Just be sure and call before you do"), "Living Without You" (marvelously covered in 1972 on *Manfred Mann's Earth Band*, Polydor 5015), "Davy the Fat Boy," and "The Beehive State" (later cut by the Doobie Brothers, of all people), a weird little wonder about the forgotten territory between L.A. and New York. At some grand national convention, the delegate from Utah rises. "We gotta tell this country about Utah," he says with all his courage, "because nobody seems to know."

12 Songs (Reprise 6373), released in 1970, was far better; Randy's piano and voice were up front, the orchestration stripped down and muted. If *Something New* was a showbiz fantasia with dim echoes of Charles Ives buried by Broadway kitsch, *12 Songs* leaned on the blues and New Orleans piano rock. Newman's imagination went wild within his tight little structures, producing "Let's Burn Down the Cornfield" ("And I'll make love to you, while it's burning," Newman added), "Suzanne," "Lucinda" (victim of the beach-cleaning machine), "Yellow Moon," "My Old Kentucky Home," his version of the 1932 hit "Underneath the Harlem Moon," and a few other works of genius. Three Dog Night got a number one hit out of a Stepin Fetchity version of "Mama Told Me Not to Come" later in 1970.

Randy Newman Live (Reprise 6459) was Newman's first chart entry, fading away at #191 in 1971. Despite "Lonely at the Top," it's not a good record; originally pressed as a promotional item for disc jockeys, the sound is thin, and little of Newman's stage personality comes across. "Tickle Me" and "Maybe I'm Doing It Wrong," neither much more than one-line jokes, were thankfully left off other albums.

Sail Away (Reprise 2064) was issued in 1972, and rose to #163. It included "Lonely at the Top," "Burn On," "Political Science," and "Memo to My Son," a song about fatherhood that insisted on the locker-room motto "When the Going Gets Tough, the Tough Get Going" as an absolute non sequitur. The album closed—and felt as if it were closing down the world—with "God's Song (That's Why I Love Mankind)."

No doubt because of its melody, "Sail Away" was covered by many singers; Linda Ronstadt accomplished the most uncomprehending version, while Salvation was responsible for altering the "little wog" reference to "little child"—as if such a term, addressed to African men and women, would be less offensive. (Bobby Darin used "little one.") Newman's ironies were compounded geometrically when the tune was cut by veteran black songsters Sonny Terry and Brownie McGhee: they sang "Sail Away" as the lament of two former slaves reminiscing about the good old days before the Yankees came and ruined their happy home, and it was not for the tender-hearted (see *Sonny & Brownie*, A&M 4397, an album that promoted some ironies of its own when it showcased archetypal British bluesman John Mayall on "White Boy Lost in the Blues").

In 1974 Newman unveiled a project he'd been threatening for years: *Good Old Boys* (Reprise 2193), a picture of the American South that spanned half a century. The ethos Newman aimed for was one of fierce pride undercut by terrible guilt, guilt driven off by pride—or, when that failed, whiskey. Included were love songs, work songs, a tune by Huey Long ("Every Man a King," done as the singalong the Kingfish had written it to be—though he probably hadn't imagined a couple of the Eagles in the chorus—and not as the weird piece of soul music Newman singing alone might have made it), and a few strange adventures involving whites disguised as blacks, rural degeneration, exhibitionism, and the like.

The album's moment of triumph was "Louisiana 1927." A beautiful Stephen Foster-like string intro—close to something out of Walt Disney's *The*

Song of the South—kicked it off, and then piano notes from "Sail Away" drifted in, guiding a first line that in its mystery and simplicity—"Art," to quote Kathleen Cleaver, "that conceals art"—is as pure an American language as anyone will ever hear. To begin a song about a flood, Newman sang: "What has happened down here, is the wind have changed," And then, as one of the people that happened to, he tried to tell you what it meant. It was, the song struggled to say, no accident: the country, providence, nature, or God, was taking revenge on the South. The great Mississippi flood of 1927 inspired dozens of songs—Blind Lemon Jefferson's "Rising High Water Blues," Bessie Smith's "Muddy Water (A Mississippi Moan)," Vernon Dalhart's "The Mississippi Flood," and Led Zeppelin's "When the Levee Breaks," originally by Memphis Minnie, among them—but Newman's is the best, because it has the strongest sense of place; in 1989 it made a quiet end to *Blaze*, a film about the 1959 love affair between stripper Blaze Starr and Governor Earl Long, Huey's damned, heroic brother. How Pete Daniel missed mentioning the tune in his *Deep'n As It Come: The 1927 Mississippi Flood* (New York: Oxford, 1977) is beyond me: he missed nothing else.

Good Old Boys fell short of its subject, perhaps because Newman's ambitions were a good deal grander than his will to put them into practice. Many of the songs on this concept album are part of the concept only by fiat, and the orchestration is sometimes out of control, as if to hide the real action, or lack of it. Still, the concept sold the record, which did well for a Newman set, reaching #36 in the U.S., and even winning Randy a gold record—in Holland. "I think they like me there because they think I hate America," Randy said. "How depressing."

In 1977 Newman got his hit: the notorious "Short People," which, climbing to #2 on the *Billboard* chart and to number one on others, pulled the accompanying *Little Criminals* (Warner Bros. 3079) to #9, high enough to achieve all-American gold record status. The single, which remains Randy's sole dent in the top ten, could have been taken as a slap at the irrationality of prejudice; many heard it as a pleasurable indulgence hiding in its own irony. Rock 'n' roller Graham Parker and novelist John Irving, both certified short people, told me how impressed they were that "a short person like Randy Newman had the nerve to write a song like that"; both were notably unhappy to learn of Randy's excessive height. Addressing the controversy ("Short People" was actually "banned in Boston"), Dave Marsh, himself once known as "the teenage dwarf," formulated the doctrine that no one was "short" who was taller than he; he also coined the word "sizist," which was immediately put into use by organizations representing people with the appropriate physical deformity.

Randy Newman Live aside, *Little Criminals* was Newman's poorest LP. With such tunes as "Jolly Coppers on Parade," "In Germany Before the War" (an equation of fascism and sexual perversion no more convincing than Alberto Moravia's in *The Conformist*), and "Sigmund Freud's Impersonation of Albert

Einstein in America" (inspired by E. L. Doctorow's puerile novel *Ragtime*), the music was pallid, and Newman's indirection seemed more than anything a blithe substitute for a commitment to his material. Backing vocals by the Eagles didn't just sound smooth, they were highlights.

Born Again (Warner Bros. 3346), released in 1979, was a rebound—significantly going no higher than #41 on the charts. The sleeve pictured Randy in Kiss-style makeup, with dollar signs painted over his eyes. "It's Money That I Love" was a number Fats Domino would have appreciated, if not sung. "I don't love Jesus, he never done a thing for me," Randy proclaimed. "Short People" had clearly made Randy suspicious of his audience, and of himself—not, perhaps, an ideal position for a popular artist, but the only position Newman can work from. If nothing else on *Born Again* quite matched "Money," at least "The Story of a Rock and Roll Band," "Half a Man" (an unfashionable dramatization of homophobia), and "Pretty Boy" (an unfashionable assault on, depending on how one heard it, John Travolta or Bruce Springsteen), kept up the pace. The disc ended in a tailspin with "Pants," yet another kinky-sex joke, and there were easy-target tunes throughout—but it was, as Newman said, a "nihilistic, no-human-feeling album . . . a comedy record."

Though "It's Money That I Love" might have seemed to set up Newman perfectly for termite work in the Reagan years, it was 1983 before his next album appeared, and it was disappointingly vague. *Trouble in Paradise* (Warner Bros. 23755-1, #64) was loosely based around the concept of the falsity of sun-drenched utopias: there were songs about Capetown, Miami, and Los Angeles, but they didn't hurt. "I Love L.A.," despite its line about the town's attractions including the sight of bums throwing up in the street, was appropriated by happy Angelenos as a new city song; Randy obligingly made a popular video of himself cruising the boulevards in an open convertible. The LP included the then requisite guest spots by pop heavyweights: Linda Ronstadt, Bob Seger, Don Henley, Rickie Lee Jones, Lindsey Buckingham, Christine McVie, on and on down to Paul Simon.

Newman killed time in the 1980s with soundtrack work, scoring and winning an Oscar nomination for *Ragtime* (Elektra 565, #134, 1981; the LP included a Newman vocal omitted from the film, "Change Your Way"), scoring *The Natural* (Warner Bros. 25116, 1984), and writing ditties (sung by Steve Martin, Chevy Chase, and Martin Short) for the instantly forgotten *Three Amigos* (Warner Bros. 2558-1, 1987). Such production—which continued with soundtracks for *Avalon* (Reprise 26437-2, 1990), *Awakenings* (Reprise 26466-2, 1990), and the short-lived 1990 television series *Cop Rock*—made the irreducible substance of *Land of Dreams* (Reprise 1-25773) a shock. Released in October 1988, it featured Randy singing as himself for the first time—if "Dixie Flyer" and "New Orleans Wins the War" were not autobiography, they were presented as such, and as the work of a man who had always sung as a character actor, they threw the listener off, made the listener listen in a new way. In these two songs, there was no level on which Randy Newman was kidding.

He was singing about what it meant to be a Jew in the Deep South, to want to be a gentile; he was singing from memory, no self-pity, only confusion. On a light, easy-swinging piano, "Dixie Flyer" opened up a tricky map, too tricky a child to follow; "New Orleans" inked it in. "Mama used to take me to Audubon Park, show me the ways of the world," Randy sang happily, with no irony at all: "She'd say, 'Here comes a white boy, there goes a black one . . .'" Racism becomes part of the song not as an issue, not even as a subject, merely as a fact the singer couldn't understand, and still can't. Perhaps the best moment comes when Newman's father returns to New Orleans—in 1948—to tell everyone the news of the Allies' victory over the Axis ("Maybe they'd heard it, maybe not," Randy remembers; "Probably they'd heard about it, just forgot"—and the way he sings "maybe not" and "just forgot" is as profound as anything in "Sail Away"). A huge celebration breaks out: "New Orleans had won the war." You can sense what it must have felt like to win a war, to win a war worth winning— but in a way *Land of Dreams* was about a war that hadn't been fought, that would be fought in America by blacks and whites in the decades to come, a war that is worth winning, and hasn't been won. That was Newman's reply to Ronald Reagan, to his parents, to himself. And there was as well the single "It's Money That Matters," at once a first-rate driving song and a tougher, painful version of *Born Again*'s "It's Money That I Love"—though, hitting the air on the eve of George Bush's election to the presidency, it seemed likely the country would turn its no into a yes just as Angelenos did with "I Love L.A." Newman raised his head early in 1991 with "Lines in the Sand," a tune about Bush's triumphalist Gulf War, which was passed on to radio stations (it was not generally released) about the same time various Hollywood stars gathered as Voices that Care for a "We Are the World" reprise that should have been called "We Are the War." Against that apology, by the likes of Kevin Costner, for not supporting the Vietnam crime, Newman offered only a certain out-of-fashion stoicism: an elegy in advance, quiet, cold, and defeatist. I heard it on the radio, once.

Newman's only other recorded vocal work is from the movies: "Gone Dead Train" from the soundtrack to the 1970 *Performance* (Warner Bros. 2554), a near-hysterical rocker about premature ejaculation titled after an old King Solomon Hill blues; a straight cover of Fats Domino's 1956 "I'm in Love Again" on the soundtrack to the 1989 *Shag* (Sire 25800–1), and a slotmouth account of his "I Love to See You Smile" on his soundtrack to the 1989 *Parenthood* (Reprise 9 26001–1, or Reprise cassette single 22798-4). Of post-Metric songs Newman wrote for others but never recorded himself, Dusty Springfield's ethereal "Just One Smile" and her "I Don't Want to Hear It Anymore" (both on her great *Dusty in Memphis*, Atlantic 8214, 1969) are probably the best. Newman played piano on Harry Nilsson's *Nilsson Sings Newman* (RCA 4289, 1970), which contained the otherwise unheard

"Caroline"; he was not present for the off-Broadway cabaret-style Newman-tune revues *Maybe I'm Doing It Wrong*, directed by Joan Micklin Silver in 1982, and *The Middle of Nowhere*, directed by Tracy Friedman in 1988. Newman's remarkable arrangement of Peggy Lee's 1969 version of Jerry Leiber and Mike Stoller's art song "Is That All There Is" (Capitol 2602) was not credited (for that matter, Randy didn't credit Kurt Weill), but it brought Miss Lee back from the dead.

Steve Harvey's "Randy Newman" (*Goldmine*, November 1981) is a good exploration of the dimmer corners of the Newman discography; much of my information on early songwriting credits comes from this source. I thank Susan Lydon for the help she gave me on the Newman chapter proper; I had the benefit of her unpublished conversations with Randy, and I have taken some quotes and much biographical information from her profile "Randy Newman—Out of Cole Porter, Hoagy Carmichael, Bob Dylan, Groucho Marx, Mark Twain, and Randy Newman" (*The New York Times Magazine*, November 3, 1972). We had a good time trading ideas one night at the Palace Theatre in San Francisco, as Randy played God up on stage and the crowd gave him the cheers he deserves.

CAMEOS: RAYMOND CHANDLER, NATHANAEL WEST, THE BEACH BOYS & OTHERS

All of my quotes from Chandler come from *Raymond Chandler Speaking* (New York: Schocken, 1984), an indispensable collection of letters, articles, and fiction fragments. Chandler's mysteries, especially *The Big Sleep* (1939) and *Farewell, My Lovely* (1940), influenced my picture of Los Angeles, and I think Nathanael West's 1939 *Day of the Locust*, though inferior to Chandler's best, belongs to the same "There's nothing wrong with Southern California that a rise in the ocean level wouldn't cure" (Ross MacDonald) genre—the difference is that Chandler would have expected to go under along with everybody else.

The other side of the Southern California story ("There's nothing wrong with surfing conditions a rise in the ocean level wouldn't cure") is best told by Jan & Dean and the Beach Boys. The former's immortal "Surf City," number one in 1963 and cowritten by Beach Boy Brian Wilson, can be found on *Jan & Dean Anthology Album* (United Artists 9961), a crazed two-record set that comes with a concordance that matches the duo's discs with the car and girlfriend each singer had at the time any given 45 was released; Richard Compton's insistently quotidian 1978 TV biopic "Dead Man's Curve" (based on Paul Morantz's "The Road Back from Dead Man's Curve," *Rolling Stone*, September 12, 1974) is remarkable for its portrayal of denizens of California subcultures as real people in a real place. The Beach Boys' wonderful mid-'60s

work is best heard on *The Best of the Beach Boys, Vol. 2* (
includes "409," "Let Him Run Wild," the touching what-if-
last-forever anthem "When I Grow Up to Be a Man," "Californ
the never-topped "I Get Around," or on the reissues *Be True to Yo*
(Capitol 16273) and *Beach Boys/Brian Wilson Rarities* (EMI 26463, Austra
the big hits are most easily found on *Made in U.S.A.* (Capitol 12396), a two-
record set with questionable sound. Worth seeking out are *Beach Boys Party!*
(Capitol 2364, 1965), to which Dean of Jan & was luckily invited, and the
marvelous *Wild Honey* (Capitol 2859, 1967).

The Beach Boys wanted more out of life than cars and surf could give
them; their vision was always a passive one, and like many they went from easy
questions to easy answers. When they recorded "Cease to Exist" (retitled
"Never Learn Not to Love" on "Bluebirds over the Mountain," 1968, and on
20/20, Capitol 133, 1969), a composition by an aspiring Los Angeles singer-
songwriter named Charles Manson—a pal of Beach Boy Dennis Wilson, and a
shaman who combined in equal parts the displaced lumpen proletariat
Nathanael West found crusted beneath the Hollywood sign and the high-rent
Doctor Feelgoods Raymond Chandler hated above all others—the Beach
Boys were truly faced with the challenge of growing up; a challenge they failed
to meet. *The Family* (New York: E. P. Dutton, 1971, revised and updated
edition 1990, NAL/Signet), Ed Sanders' terrifying investigation of Manson
loose in post-surf Los Angeles, lays out the facts of the Southern California
synthesis of sun and horror, just as Newman's songs capture its soul.

Unlike so many L.A. groups that come from somewhere else, the Beach
Boys were not fakes. Empty, tired, desperate, and stupid as they were through
the next decades, for a time they nevertheless performed life as some people
actually lived it. The Beach Boys celebrated California hedonism, looked for
its limits, found them. Their pleasures, as opposed to those offered by such
latter-day inheritors as the Eagles, always radiated affection—because those
pleasures were rooted in friendship, or its memory.

THE KINKS

The Kinks will likely be remembered as one of the oddest rock 'n' roll bands,
and as one of the best. For crude, brutal hard rock, their early singles
sometimes outclassed those of the Beatles and the Rolling Stones, probably
because the resentment and rage such music communicates was exactly what
Kinks leader Ray Davies felt: he truly didn't like it here, wherever that
happened to be. For a long time, at least through the mid-'70s, Davies was
genuinely at home only in his fantasies of a simpler day, when class lines were
clear, when everyone knew everyone else and everyone else's place; when,
presumably, there would have been a place even for Davies. His search for a
phantom paradise took him as deeply into the throes of nostalgia as anyone in

of the Br... ...eprise 6366), released in 1969, and *Lola Versus Powerman
and the Moneyg...* ...(Reprise 6423), from 1970, brought the Kinks new fans
even as Davies' songs grew more heavy-handed. The latter's unforgettable
"Lola" is best heard on *The Kink Kronikles* (Reprise 6454), a collection of '67–
'71 album cuts, nonhits, and unreleased tunes.

Ever campy, struggling, hopefully trendy—with "Superman" and a
sniffling attack on punk—the Kinks rolled on through the years, until their
very "survival" was cause for praise, but save for the occasional surprise like
"Celluloid Heroes" or "20th Century Man" (both of them, now that I think of
it, more than fifteen years old), they rolled downhill. Davies has become a
fixture in pop culture—every once in a while you can spot him in a British
music movie, looking sly and moving well, or on late night American TV,
promoting a new album, looking as if he'd rather be anywhere else.

ELVIS PRESLEY

In 1974 RCA issued *Elvis: A Legendary Performer, Vol. 1* (RCA 0341), a single
album that illustrates, historically and aesthetically, virtually every side of the
man's music. For my concerns it is a perfect outline.

Legendary Performer begins at Sun, with "That's All Right (Mama),"
Elvis's first single, followed by "I Love You Because," the sentimental country
tune with narration that was in fact his very first officially logged professional
recording, though Sam Phillips never released it, and this unedited version was
never previously released by RCA. Then immediately to "Heartbreak Hotel,"
altogether unlike any of the Sun sides (a concession to the "cool jazz" sound
popular in the mid-'50s, if the truth be told), number one on pop, country, and
R&B charts early in 1956. A snatch of interview from that time: a reporter asks
Elvis if his success is due to luck or talent, and Elvis naturally answers luck.
Without a pause we are into "Don't Be Cruel," also a 1956 three-chart number
one, and it gives the lie to Elvis's modesty (if not his guile): no one has ever sung
with such confidence.

We hear "Love Me Tender," the title song from Elvis's first movie; we hear "(There'll Be) Peace in the Valley (For Me)," from 1957—Elvis's first, and perhaps best, gospel record.* Then to "(Now and Then There's) A Fool Such As I," from 1958, where Elvis distances himself from his style with outrageous parody; then to "Tonight's All Right for Love," a ghastly number from the 1960 film *G.I. Blues*, where the parody has become the style.

Scattered through the album are three performances from the 1968 television comeback show, cut with a small combo in front of an audience: a joking "Are You Lonesome To-night?"; a staggering "Love Me," with Elvis wavering between parody and passion until passion wins; and "Tryin' to Get to You," a song Elvis first recorded in 1955. Thirteen years later he sings it as a message to his listeners: his way of telling anyone who cared how hard it was for him to find his way back, and what the trip was worth. His singing makes his early classics seem immature, unfocused, hesitant. They weren't, but this music—all glamour, fury, and drama—is not like anything else in rock 'n' roll.

Legendary Performer ends, as it should, with "Can't Help Falling in Love," from the *Blue Hawaii* soundtrack of 1961—the song that became Elvis's touchstone in the '70s, at least until the end, when it was replaced by "My Way." Here, it sounds like a hymn.

On this album, Elvis's long career makes sense, it has shape. You can hear the artist grow, the god fail, the King return, the man endure and change. As a version of American possibility and American limits, it is fully the equal of Robert Johnson's *King of the Delta Blues Singers*. Given hindsight, a version of "Hellhound on My Trail" is all that is missing.

With *Legendary Performer* as a map, we can turn to Elvis's music in detail.

SUN, 1953–55

Original Sun discs by Elvis, 78s or 45s, now go for impossible sums; RCA Victor reissued all five singles immediately upon signing Elvis in November 1955, and reissues of those 45s are still available (and, because of the drop in sound quality or fade edits in most cases when the Sun sides have been transferred to LP, worth ordering). Save for a dubious track noted below, all of

*A country hit in 1951 for Red Foley, this remarkable song was written by the Rev. Thomas A. Dorsey, a man who might understand the contradictions of Elvis's music: in the 1920s, as bluesman Georgia Tom, he scandalized pious black families throughout the South with his suggestive lyrics. Born in 1899, he became the "father of modern gospel" by combining blues and jazz modes with sanctified themes; drawing on the spiritual "We Shall Walk Through the Valley in Peace," Dorsey composed "Peace in the Valley" while riding on a train in 1939, thinking about the war that had just begun in Europe, measuring his fears against the suddenly comforting valley he found himself passing through. For his blues, see *Georgia Tom Dorsey, 1928–1932: Come on Mama Do That Dance* (Yazoo 1041) and *Georgia Tom and Friends, 1929/31* (Mercury 6332 991, France); for his gospel, *Precious Lord: New Recordings of the Great Gospel Songs of Thomas A. Dorsey* (Columbia 32151) and *Say Amen, Somebody* (D.R.G. 12584), an augmented soundtrack to the 1982 film about Dorsey's life and work that includes performances by him. For an inspired essay on Dorsey, Elvis, and much more, see Tom Smucker's "Precious Lord," in *Stranded*, ed. Greil Marcus (New York: Knopf, 1979).

the Sun studio material that has so far come to light, false starts and alternate takes included, is collected on *The Complete Sun Sessions* (RCA 6414), a 33-track double-LP with notes by Peter Guralnick.

Elvis's earliest recordings were made in June 1953 by the Memphis Recording Service, a cut-your-own-disc operation ("$3 one side, $4 two sides") Sam Phillips had set up to supplement the uncertain income of the prerock Sun label. According to legend, Elvis showed up to make a birthday record for his mother; I once sided with Hans Langbroek, author of a pioneering booklet called *The Hillbilly Cat* (wherein it was first revealed that Col. Tom Parker, Elvis's manager, was not born in West Virginia with carny in his soul, but rather in Breda, Holland, as Andreas Cornelis van Kuijk), who suggested that since Gladys Presley's birthday fell in April, Elvis actually made the record for himself, hoping someone would notice him. With the late Marion Keisker, Phillips' co-manager at Sun, running the machines (Phillips claims *he* was), Elvis put down two songs: "My Happiness," a 1948 hit for both Ella Fitzgerald and the Pied Pipers, though for Elvis the Ink Spots' 1950 version is a more likely source, and "That's When Your Heartaches Begin," a country weeper in its 1951 version by Bob Lamb, but also recorded by the Ink Spots in 1950. Long believed lost, the original acetate surfaced in 1988, in the possession of Edwin S. Leek, a high-school friend of Elvis's; RCA released "My Happiness" in 1990 on *Elvis: The Great Performances* (RCA CD2227-2-R), and the performance seems to validate the legend—devotion bleeds from every note. Elvis's style is already present, indeed shockingly complete; Keisker heard something unusual in the boy's voice, secretly taped some of his singing, took a number where he might be reached, and pushed her boss to give him a formal audition. Phillips demurred, but on January 4, 1954, Elvis was back, this time with Phillips definitely at the controls, to cut "Casual Love Affair," about which nothing is known, and "I'll Never Stand in Your Way," a then recent hit for Joni James; this disc has yet to be found.

Not long after—in the spring of 1954, or in June 1954, depending on which story one chooses to believe—Elvis got his chance. According to Keisker, an acetate demo of a song called "Without You" arrived in the mail at Sun from a music publisher in Nashville (according to Phillips, he had cut the acetate himself in Nashville, recording a singer in the state prison); Phillips liked the song, Keisker said, but was even more taken with the black singer's voice. Phillips tried to locate the man to make a finished record, but the publisher had no idea who he was—just someone hanging around the studio. "Why not try the boy with the sideburns?" Keisker said. ("Why not try the boy with the sideburns?" Phillips thought to himself.)

Elvis was called back to the studio; Phillips played him the demo. The original Nashville recording has never been released or bootlegged; there is only one copy, which Keisker gave some years ago to a Memphis friend, and to listen to the disc today is ghostly—it is to be transported back to the very instant before the beginning of the present age. The unnamed singer's voice is full of pain and full of acceptance, gliding along the stately lines of the song, reaching for solace, falling short, reaching again. It's pure Sisyphus—and, as Camus said of Sisyphus, one must imagine the singer happy.

One can hear the gospel tones of Johnny Bragg and the Prisonaires, Sonny Til of the Orioles, Bill Kenny of the Ink Spots. But most of all, one hears—Elvis. And yet as soon as one identifies what, it seems, Elvis must have taken from the demo, the element vanishes. Then it creeps back. What could Elvis have heard?

All through the afternoon, Elvis tried to sing "Without You." He couldn't do it; take after take ended in shambles. He turned away from the mike and pounded his fists on the wall. "I hate him!" Elvis shouted. "I hate him!"

Supposedly, the session was not a total loss: Elvis is said to have taped a lost version of "Rag Mop," a 1951 novelty tune first recorded by Johnnie Lee Wills and popularized by Lionel Hampton, the Ames Brothers, and Joe Higgins and the Honeydrippers. Phillips was intrigued; he brought Elvis together with guitarist Scotty Moore and bassist Bill Black, and bid them rehearse. They spent months, or days, trying to work out a distinctive sound; on July 5, 1954, they found it. Elvis's Sun singles* followed in this order:

"That's All Right (Mama)" b/w "Blue Moon of Kentucky," released July 19, 1954 (Sun 204, RCA 447-0601). Original version of "That's All Right" by Mississippi blues singer Arthur "Big Boy" Crudup, 1946, as "That's All Right" (see *Arthur Crudup: Father of Rock and Roll*, RCA 573; also included are Crudup's originals of "So Glad You're Mine" and "My Baby Left Me," which Elvis recorded soon after leaving Sun for RCA). Original version of "Blue Moon of Kentucky" by bluegrass singer Bill Monroe, 1946 (see *Bill Monroe's 16 Greatest Hits*, Columbia 1065).

"Good Rockin' Tonight" b/w "I Don't Care If the Sun Don't Shine," released September 25, 1954 (Sun 210, RCA 447-0602). Original versions of "Good Rockin' Tonight" by urban jump blues singers Roy Brown (who wrote it), 1947, and Wynonie Harris (who had the bigger hit), 1948 (for Brown's version, see his *Good Rocking Tonight*, Route 66 #6, UK; for Harris's see his *Good Rockin' Blues*, King 1086). "I Don't Care If the Sun Don't Shine" composed in 1949 for Walt Disney's *Cinderella*, and recorded in 1950 by Patti Page and in 1951 by Georgia Gibbs. Percussion on Elvis's version (hands slapped on cardboard box to simulate bongo drums) by Sun singer Buddy Cunningham.

---

*Elvis's first two singles featured only "Scotty and Bill" (as the labels read), but later Sun recordings often included drums (on the "country" sides more frequently than on the "rhythm" sides, interestingly enough). The drummer was not D. J. Fontana, Elvis's first on-stage drummer, but one Johnny Bernero, leader of a local show band (see Malcolm Yelvington/Johnny Bernero, *Memphis Rockin' Country*, P-Vine 330, Japan, though forget the title for Bernero's side); Bernero soon vanished into oblivion, where he is no doubt trading tales of what might have been with Jimmy Nicol, who replaced an ailing Ringo Starr when the Beatles toured Australia in 1964.

"Milkcow Blues Boogie" b/w "You're a Heartbreaker," released January 8, 1955 (Sun 215, RCA 447-0603). Original versions of "Milkcow" by many singers, most relevantly Georgia country bluesman Kokomo Arnold, 1934 (as "Milk Cow Blues"; see *Kokomo Arnold/Peetie Wheatstraw*, Blues Classics 4), and western swing orchestra Bob Wills and His Texas Playboys, 1946 (as "Brain Cloudy Blues"; see *The Bob Wills Anthology*, Columbia 32416). "You're a Heartbreaker" first recorded by Elvis.

"Baby Let's Play House" b/w "I'm Left, You're Right, She's Gone," released April 1, 1955 (Sun 217, RCA 447-0604). Original version of "Baby, Let's Play House" by R&B singer Arthur Gunter, 1955 (see his *Black & Blues*, Excello 8017). Buddy Holly's clumsy first attempts to turn himself into Elvis can be heard in his version, cut in late 1955 as "I Wanna Play House with You" (see *The Complete Buddy Holly*, MCA 6-80.000). "I'm Left, You're Right, She's Gone" first recorded by Elvis; seven takes of "My Baby Is Gone," the slow, torchy version Phillips sent to DJs, are collected on *The Complete Sun Sessions*. "Baby Let's Play House" was Elvis's first record to make the national charts, reaching #10 on the *Billboard* country list.

"Mystery Train" b/w "I Forgot to Remember to Forget," released August 1955 (Sun 223, RCA 447-6000). Original versions of "Mystery Train" by the Carter Family, 1930 (as "Worried Man Blues"; see *The Famous Carter Family*, Harmony 11332), and by Little Junior's Blue Flames (blues singer Junior Parker), 1953 (see *Sun Records: The Blues Years, 1950–1956*, Sun Box 105, UK, a magnificent nine-LP set, or the EP *Junior Parker*, Charly 104, UK). "I Forgot to Remember," cowritten by Charlie Feathers and first recorded by Elvis, was a number one country hit.

All of Elvis's unreleased Sun production passed to RCA along with Elvis's contract in 1955; five numbers were used to fill out *Elvis Presley*, Elvis's first album, in 1956. "I Love You Because" was recorded by Leon Payne in 1949 and by Eddie Fisher in 1950; "I'll Never Let You Go (Little Darlin')" by Jimmy Wakely in 1943; "Just Because" by Dick Stabile (with Bunny Berigan) in 1937 and by the Shelton Brothers in 1942 (if one has a horror of blandness, these three numbers are the soundtrack to a horror movie); "Blue Moon" by Shirley Ross for the 1934 film *Manhattan Melodrama* (the movie John Dillinger watched just before he was ambushed by FBI agents), in 1935 by Glen Gray and Benny Goodman, in 1949 by Billy Eckstine (a big hit, and likely the proximate source of Elvis's unearthly treatment), and in 1952 by Ivory Joe Hunter; "Tryin' to Get to You" was first recorded in 1954 by the Eagles, a black harmony group from Washington, D.C. (see the Eagles, *Trying to Get to You*, Bear Family 15322, W. Germany).

Other Sun moments, including the "primitive" version of "Blue Moon of Kentucky," bits of studio dialogue, fragments, and completed takes, surfaced more slowly, either chopped or overdubbed on RCA LPs, on bootlegs, or on scattered reissues; *The Complete Sun Sessions* covers them all (except for the "Nigger!" dialogue quoted in the main text; for that one must seek out the bootleg anthology *Good Rockin' Tonight*, Bopcat 100, Holland), or, given the academic programming, subsumes them. "Harbor Lights," first recorded by Rudy Vallee in 1937, featured in John Ford's 1940 film *The Long Voyage Home*, and cut as well by Sammy Kaye, Guy Lombardo, Bing Crosby and Harry James and His Royal Hawaiians, comes from one of Elvis's first sessions; "Tomorrow Night" is a 1948 ballad by blues singer Lonnie Johnson; "When It Rains, It Really Pours," with Carl Perkins on guitar, is a first halting, then messy, then searingly erotic reading of Sun R&B singer Billy "The Kid" Emerson's 1955 original (see "When It Rains It Pours" on *Sun Records: The Blues Years*, or Emerson's *Little Fine Healthy Thing*, Charly 30187, UK). The ten-LP box *The Sun Country Years, 1950–1959* (Sun/Bear Family 5197, W. Germany) claims "How Do You Think I Feel" as the final, extra-*Complete Sun Sessions* Sun track extant, but if you can hear Elvis in the bop-bop-bop of the off-mike singer (or, for that matter, Scotty Moore in the guitar work) you have better ears than I. Over the years, rumor, wish, and conspiracy theories have pushed the number of Sun tracks still unaccounted for into the dozens (the "unreleased" material is all said to be from straight country or blues sources, reflecting nothing of the pan-American sensibility that could combine Roy Brown with *Cinderella*, Rudy Vallee with Junior Parker): most often mentioned are versions of Bill Monroe's "Uncle Pen," Red Foley's "Tennessee Saturday Night," and Roy Acuff's "Night Train to Memphis." My guess is that between six and ten cuts remain in the RCA vaults, to be held for release on the 100th anniversary: of Elvis's birth, his first session, his first number one hit, his induction into the Army, his mustering out, his death . . .

Those seeking more music from this period should look for *Elvis: The Beginning Years* (Louisiana Hayride 3061), which collects nine strong numbers broadcast live on radio in 1954 and '55 (the album includes a forty-page photo booklet): one tune not otherwise recorded by Elvis is a cover of Laverne Baker's 1955 "Tweedle Dee." *Elvis, Scotty and Bill: The First Year* (Sun 1007, UK) includes five songs recorded at Eagles Hall in Houston on March 19, 1955, plus a side of interviews, notably a long reminiscence by Scotty Moore. Elvis is quite audible from the stage, his band less so ("I'd like to shake around here for you all night," Elvis says, "but we're booked into Alcatraz tomorrow—got a long drive ahead of us").

The Sun story ends on December 4, 1956, when Elvis, already a national hero/Antichrist, returned to Sam Phillips' "chicken shack with the Cadillacs out back" and fell into an informal country sing with Carl Perkins and Jerry Lee Lewis. Phillips recorded the session, which became famous as the "Million Dollar Quartet" (Johnny Cash, who was thought to have completed the "quartet," appeared in group photos taken that day, but left before the singing got going), and the release of the music was announced several times following Elvis's death. But it was only after the appearance of a few truncated, indeed rather dull LPs, that the real thing appeared: *The Million Dollar Quartet* (RCA CD 2023-2-R), issued under Elvis's name—forty-one pieces and performances spread over sixty-seven minutes. Suddenly Presley, Perkins, and Lewis were in your living room, throwing sound in your face; you were part of their conversations, you got their jokes. They went on and on, each sound a physical fact, the trio starting songs, failing them, then realizing them or throwing them aside, moving through gospel to Chuck Berry to "Don't Be Cruel" (Elvis recounts seeing Jackie Wilson singing it in Las Vegas, with the Dominos, Wilson utterly outclassing Elvis's hit, Elvis now trying to follow Wilson's version, giving up, going on to "Paralyzed," attempting to match Wilson once again), then Lewis emerging from his piano-man role to challenge the King, taking over, trying to turn the meeting into a cutting contest, except that Elvis won't play. And there is an hilarious, stirring version of Pat Boone's "Don't Forbid Me": "Hey, have you heard Pat Boone's new record?" Elvis says, to laughter all around. "It was written for *me*. It stayed around the house for ages, never did see it—*junk!*" So they wail on.

THE TRIUMPH, 1956–59

Elvis's first record for RCA, "Heartbreak Hotel" b/w "I Was the One," coincided with his first national television appearances (Elvis was rejected in 1955 by "Arthur Godfrey's Talent Scouts," then the country's principal showcase for unknown performers), and the exposure did much to divide the nation into friends and enemies. The U.S.A. initially saw Elvis on Tommy and Jimmy Dorsey's "Stage Show" (six slots in the first three months of 1956); these performances, and extensive selections from the other TV appearances noted in this subsection, can be found on *Elvis—A Golden Celebration* (RCA 5127), an essential six-LP boxed set. Kinescopes are presented in sequence in the expanded 144-minute video version of *This Is Elvis* (Warner 11173), a biopic by Malcolm Leo and Andrew Solt, composed of documentary footage and scenes reconstructed with actors, that was first released theatrically in 1981; much TV footage is also used in Alan and Susan Raymond's 1987 video *Elvis '56*, narrated by Levon Helm (Music Media 470). Highlights from the Dorsey shows include Carl Perkins' 1956 "Blue Suede Shoes," Little Richard's 1955 "Tutti Frutti," Joe Turner's 1955 "Flip, Flop and Fly," and Clyde McPhatter and the Drifters' 1953 "Money Honey"—Elvis's musical personality was suddenly narrowing, and intensifying. In April and June there followed two appearances on "The Milton Berle Show," the second featuring a funny exchange between Elvis and Debra Paget, later his costar in *Love Me Tender*.

It was at about this time that Ed Sullivan, then king of American television, declared that "Elvis will never appear on my show." However, since Elvis turned up on "The Steve Allen Show" on July 1 (the notorious appearance where Allen humiliated Presley by forcing him to dress in tails and sing "Hound Dog" to a dog), opposite Sullivan's presentation of skits based on

John Huston's film *Moby Dick*, and, not unlike Melville's monster, sunk Sullivan in the ratings, "never" meant only a few months—probably about as long as it took to negotiate Elvis's fee. The three appearances Elvis made on "The Ed Sullivan Show" (September 9 and October 28, 1956, and January 6, 1957) put Elvis over the top as a national figure; the first show pulled 82.6 percent of the viewing audience. Songs included "Don't Be Cruel," "Love Me," "Too Much," "Love Me Tender," and an amazing "Ready Teddy" (not up to Little Richard's 1956 original, but it was Richard's greatest performance—see *Little Richard's Grooviest 17 Original Hits!*, Speciality 2113, or the historic 8-LP box *The Specialty Sessions*, Ace/Specialty 1, UK). It was only on the 1957 date that Elvis was televised "from the waist up"; the previous shows displayed him in—as the vaguely pornographic phrase generally used has it—"full body shot."

A single look at *This Is Elvis* or *Elvis '56* makes it plain why Elvis's early TV performances caused so much trouble: Elvis, clearly and consciously perceiving the limits of what Americans had learned to accept as shared culture, set out to shatter them. He turns toward the camera, and suggests a body in freedom, a kind of freedom for which, at the time, there was no acceptable language; then he turns away, and suggests that he is only kidding; then he moves in a manner so outrageous memory cannot hold the image. Were he to appear on TV today, for the first time, with the world somehow still changed as he changed it, the spectacle would be no less shocking. "My God," I said to myself as I watched him move a quarter-century after the fact. "They let that on television?"

Earlier, Elvis had played the New Frontier Hotel in Las Vegas (it seems Judith Campbell Exner wasn't all JFK picked up there), third-billed under the Freddy Martin Orchestra and comedian Shecky Greene as "The Atomic-Powered Singer"; his show from May 6, 1956, was released in 1980 as part of *Elvis Aron Presley* (RCA 3699), an eight-LP boxed set of rarities one mostly wished had stayed rare. The music on the four New Frontier cuts isn't bad (though drummer D. J. Fontana plunges into nightclub shlock with terrifying enthusiasm); Elvis does his best to mock the setting, the audience, his music, and himself.

There are two notable accounts of the new Elvis facing his true audience. The first, live recordings from afternoon and evening shows at the Mississippi-Alabama Fair and Dairy Show, Tupelo, Mississippi, September 26, 1956 (on *Elvis—A Golden Celebration*), combine sometimes distant sound with an excitement and fervor that dissolve all distance.

Elvis had won second prize at the same fair in 1945 for his rendition of "Old Shep"; now the mayor gave him the key to the city, the governor gave him a scroll, and twenty thousand people listened on the verge of riot. At one point Elvis seems genuinely afraid the crowd will go out of control, worrying from the stage over casualties in the audience, introducing "Blue Suede Shoes" as "a song that says you can do anything—but don't. Just don't." Given what he and Scotty Moore had just done with Ray Charles' "I Got a Woman," he had only himself to blame if his fans burned down the fairgrounds in appreciation.

Even stronger, in its way, is Gordon Bowker's "Rock!" (*Seattle*, February 1970; my thanks to Ed Leimbacher), which places several teenagers at Elvis's 1957 Seattle concert, and then catches up with them twelve years later. Bowker's concluding paragraphs sum up the time:

"The rosy glow had gone from the cap of Mount Rainier, and the infield was bright with the best night-baseball lights in the minor leagues. The noise from the 15,000 people was immense. Finally the crowd grew quiet.

"'I alluz like to begin mah concerts with the national anthem,' the King said, into the mike. 'Will y'all please rise?' Boyd Grafmyre and Willie Leopold and Ted Shreffler and Dennis Lunder and Merrilee Gunst [as Merrilee Rush, she would score a top ten hit in 1968 with the shimmering "Angel of the Morning"] and Tom Hullet and Pat O'Day who had driven over from Yakima with his wife to celebrate his second anniversary and the other 15,000 people all stood up. Also on his feet was Jimi Hendrix, then a Seattle schoolboy.

"Elvis picked up his guitar, twitched once more, took a breath, and groaned: 'You ain't nothing but a hound dog . . .'

"The crowd was stunned. Then it erupted into a frenzy that dwarfed the one a few minutes earlier. The grandstands seethed back and forth like a huge sea anemone. Not even Elvis could be heard above the roar."

On TV, on stage, and on his early RCA recordings, Elvis was backed by Scotty Moore, Bill Black, D. J. Fontana, and (usually) the Jordanaires on vocals. In the studio, saxophonist Shorty Long, pianist Floyd Cramer, guitarist Chet Atkins, and others were later brought in. Though Atkins was nominally in charge, in effect Elvis served as his own producer.

His first album, *Elvis Presley* (RCA 1254, reissued in original mono but with erratically faithful digital remastering as RCA 5198), number one in 1956, was, as noted above, made up of Sun leftovers, plus covers of recent rock 'n' roll hits. His second LP, *Elvis* (RCA 1382, reissued as RCA 5199), also number one in 1956, was quite mild (this was the "folksinger" album)—as if Elvis were in retreat from the furor he'd kicked up. But neither album contained the hits of the period, most of which are on *Elvis' Golden Records* (RCA 1707, RCA 5196), #3 in 1958, an interestingly annotated LP that includes "Hound Dog," "Don't Be Cruel," "Jailhouse Rock," "All Shook Up," "Treat Me Nice," and "Anyway You Want Me"; it was one of the founding rock 'n' roll records. (Compact disc configurations of early Presley material meet Roland Barthes' musical standards—"You can actually hear 'the grain of the voice,'" critic Jim Miller said as he punched up "Hound Dog"—but not necessarily those of Alan Freed. The balance between voice and instruments is lost, and so is much of the tension. The CDs are revelatory footnotes; the original recordings remain events.)

Elvis' Christmas Album (RCA 1035), number one in 1957, a foldout LP with a color-picture booklet, has been reissued in its original form (RCA 5486); along with predictable standards, Elvis added "Peace in the Valley," an R&B-styled recasting of Ernest Tubb's 1949 "Blue Christmas," a version of "White Christmas" based on Clyde McPhatter and the Drifters' weird 1954 rendition, plus Jerry Leiber and Mike Stoller's "Santa Claus Is Back in Town," which gave the Big E the chance to leer, "Santa Claus is coming in a big black Cadillac!" It was, in Charles Perry's phrase, like finding a hamburger in a medicine cabinet.

50,000,000 Elvis Fans Can't Be Wrong—Elvis' Gold Records, Vol. 2 (RCA 2075, RCA 5197), with the gold lamé suit on the cover, #31 in 1960, collected chart entries from 1957 through 1959. It was during this period, as Langdon Winner once put it, that Elvis "sold out to girls," by which Winner meant Elvis had stopped threatening and begun pleading. Already, the music was somewhat hackneyed, and even the parodies ("Wear My Ring Around Your Neck") communicated as the real thing. The highlight was a comparatively small hit, the 1958 "One Night," a cleaned-up cover of New Orleans R&B singer Smiley Lewis's sinful 1955 original (see his *I Hear You Knocking*, EMI America 17236); Elvis's rehearsal version, with Lewis's words, can be heard on the posthumous collection *Reconsider Baby* (RCA 5418). As with Lloyd Price's sanitized "Stagger Lee," repression put the edge on; the take RCA first released was far more dangerous than the lyrically more transgressive cut that stayed in the can.

By this time, Elvis was devoting himself almost strictly to the movies; soundtracks of *Loving You* (1957) and *King Creole* (1958) offered dubious rock and ineffectual ballads. Elvis's best movie, the 1957 *Jailhouse Rock*, also contained his best movie music, partly because Leiber and Stoller were writing the songs (see *Jailhouse Rock/Love in Las Vegas*, RCA 9020, UK, for released versions, and *Essential Elvis Presley*, RCA 6738, for alternate takes from *Jailhouse Rock*, *Loving You*, and *Love Me Tender*). "Young and Beautiful" and "(You're So Square) Baby I Don't Care," both from *Jailhouse Rock*, still sound perfect; Elvis left for the Army on top.

THE DECLINE, 1960–67

Elvis returned in 1960 (*Elvis—A Golden Celebration* includes five tunes taped between 1958 and 1960 in Germany, among them a version of the Penguins' 1954 "Earth Angel"), and immediately made *Elvis Is Back* (RCA 2231), #2 in 1960; though the LP is uneven, every minute of it screams release, freedom, relief. And what better way to affirm that rules and regulations were behind him than to cut loose with the blues? The sound Elvis and his band got for this record was nothing like the country blues of the Sun singles, but full-blown Chicago menace, driven by Elvis's super-miked rhythm guitar, brutal playing by Scotty Moore, and demonic sax work from Boots Randolph. Elvis's singing wasn't sexy, it was obscene. "Dirty, Dirty Feeling" and the Drifters' 1954 "Such a Night" were standouts, but the clincher was bluesman Lowell Fulson's 1954 "Reconsider Baby." Fulson had recorded the tune on his knees (see his *Hung Down Head*, Chess 408, Chess 826, Japan); Elvis, pushing his band like a ringmaster cracking his whip, first coolly, then as if nothing but strategy could hold him back, sang the song as a slow, measured dare.

With that burst of passion out of the way, Elvis settled down to work. He made two, sometimes three movies a year, with full soundtracks for each. He was more successful than ever—"It's Now or Never" (1960) sold nine million copies; the *Blue Hawaii* soundtrack sold five million straight off—and counted for less than ever before. As a contract player in his own B-movie factory, he did his job. There were echoes of humor and excitement, even of genius, in his singles, but they were only echoes. *Elvis' Golden Records, Vol. 3* (RCA 2765) collected hits from 1960 through 1963, but there was a soullessness in the music (even "Little Sister," formerly a tough pop blues, is ultimately slick) that he escaped only with the lovely "Fame and Fortune" and a remake of Chuck Willis's 1954 "I Feel So Bad," a frenzied piece that owed more to Boots Randolph's saxophone than to Elvis's fine vocal, and which sounded like nothing so much as a cut left over from the sessions for *Elvis Is Back*.

One must look long and hard through *Elvis for Everyone*, and soundtracks to the likes of *Roustabout*, *Girl Happy*, or *Paradise Hawaiian Style*, for even a glimmer of style and feeling. One such moment comes on *Spinout* (RCA 3702, 1966), with Elvis's version of Bob Dylan's then unreleased "Tomorrow Is a Long Time." ("Are there any particular artists that you like to see do your songs?" Jann Wenner asked Bob Dylan in 1969. "Yeah, Elvis Presley," Dylan said. "He recorded a song of mine. That's the one recording I treasure most.") Invariably, Elvis's best music in this period was gospel. *His Hand in Mine* (RCA 2328), #13 in 1961, was straightforward and convincing; *How Great Thou Art* (RCA 3758), #18 in 1967, which included a profound "Crying in the Chapel," a 1953 hit by the Orioles (Elvis's version was recorded in 1960, but inexplicably left unissued until 1965, when it appeared as a single), was enough to make you convert. But there was little more. When *Elvis' Gold Records, Vol. 4* hit #38 in 1968 (RCA 3921—really, somebody could have decided whether it was "Gold" or "Golden"), the disc contained not a single interesting track.

The one priceless document of this era is an impeccably pressed and packaged bootleg, *Elvis' 'Greatest Shit'!!* (Dog Vomit SUX-005)—which features a picture of Elvis in his coffin on the sleeve, production credit to Albert "Greatest Shit" Goldman, a facsimile of Elvis's last prescription from Dr. George Nichopolous ("Dilaudid—50, Quaalude—150," etc.), a complete lyric sheet, and released and unreleased versions of "Old MacDonald Had a Farm," "Song of the Shrimp," "Yoga Is As Yoga Does," "The Bullfighter Was a Lady," and, among eighteen others, "Can't Help Falling in Love." "What's that doing here—that's not 'shit,'" said a friend. "Aaaaahhhh, *shit!*" Elvis immediately replied, as the take collapsed in confusion. Advertised on the back are a number of other LPs (which, unfortunately, have yet to surface), including *Vocal Duets*, with the famous picture of Elvis and President Nixon on the cover; tunes were to include "How Much Is That Doggie in the Window" and the hard-to-find Elvis single "King of the Whole Wide World."

This was a labor of love—a lot more love than went into Elvis's music of the mid-'60s. But late in 1967, Elvis had begun to stir. In short order he released covers of blues singer Jimmy Reed's 1961 "Big Boss Man," and of country rocker Jerry Reed's 1967 hits "Guitar Man" and "U.S. Male." They weren't big records ("U.S. Male," the most successful, reached only #28, in 1968), or even particularly good; all had a gruff, obviously contrived toughness, but even that was enough to make people wonder if something wasn't about to change.

THE COMEBACK, 1968–69

Thanks to producer Steve Binder, Elvis reappeared on December 3, 1968, before a national TV audience, and saved his career. "Elvis TV Special" opened with "Trouble" and closed with "If I Can Dream," a roughly sung ballad; in between were the pretaped live performances that proved Elvis really was the King.

There were two sorts of live performances: those done with a large studio orchestra ("Jailhouse Rock," with a flute, "Heartbreak Hotel," and others), and those done informally, without rehearsal, with a small audience, as Scotty Moore, D. J. Fontana, a couple of Elvis's pals, and the man himself casually made history. ("Casually" is perhaps not strong enough a word; Fontana kept time banging his sticks on a guitar case.) Except on the first few numbers, Elvis took over on lead electric guitar—the first time he had ever been seen playing the instrument—and he did so with the same violent emotion he put into his singing.

Over the years, these performances—taken from two invitation-only concerts held in a Burbank studio auditorium on June 27, 1968—have cropped up in disparate places: on the *Elvis TV Special* soundtrack LP, on various of the *Legendary Performer* sets (there are four, so far), on throwaway budget albums, on *Elvis Aron Presley* and *A Golden Celebration*; the video *Elvis: One Night with You* (Music Media M647) covers one complete concert. Until RCA sees fit to put it all in one place, there is *The Burbank Sessions, Vol. 1* (Audifon 62768), a two-LP, two-hour, thirty-eight-take set that is disguised as an official release from West Germany, but is in fact an American bootleg, dubbed directly from RCA master tapes. Working from memory, not a song list, Elvis goes back to Rufus Thomas' 1953 "Tiger Man," rolls through a few broken-off versions of Jimmy Reed's 1960 "Baby, What You Want Me to Do," playing with the tune until he dispenses with the words, presses down on his electric guitar, and hammers the rhythm into fury, charges through "One Night," "Lawdy, Miss Clawdy," "Blue Christmas," "Tryin' to Get to You," so many more. He attacks the tunes, struggles with them, backs away, roars forward, grabs hold, then shakes a number until he's taken every bit of it for himself. The music is full of humor, full of delight, full of blood—with Elvis's buddies shouting for another chorus or Elvis forcing one. Compared to this—very likely the very greatest rock 'n' roll ever recorded—the Million Dollar Quartet session is nothing. Even scattered, it makes up a body of work that is clearly the equal of the Sun sides and, in some ways, much superior: the feeling is more raw, more desperate, more alive. The Sun sides leave you satisfied; this leaves you both satisfied and nervous. As Elvis said—hoisting his mike stand like a harpoon, thrusting it out over the audience, and perhaps remembering a TV show of some twelve years before—"Moby Dick!"

Elvis TV Special (RCA 4088, RCA 3894; on video as *The '68 Comeback Special*, Music Media 462) reached #8 in 1969, the first top ten Presley LP in three years; "If I Can Dream," the single from the special (inspired by Martin Luther King's 1963 "I Have a Dream" speech, and by his 1968 assassination), reached #12. In May 1969 came *From Elvis in Memphis* (RCA 4155)—Elvis's first non-soundtrack, non-gospel, non-random, non-greatest hits album since *Elvis Is Back*—which reached #13. There were no weak spots. "Long Black Limousine" and Eddy Arnold's 1947 "I'll Hold You in My Heart (Till I Can Hold You in My Arms)" were powerful, mature performances, but best was "Any Day Now," a Burt Bacharach composition Elvis sang with an utterly controlled but naked passion—a naked piety, really—that cannot be heard in any of his other recordings.

"Suspicious Minds" (RCA 9764) was number one in the fall of 1969; it was Elvis's first chart-topper in seven years. Along with it came *From Memphis to Vegas/From Vegas to Memphis* (RCA 6020), a two-record set. One disc was made up of decent but unexciting studio material left over from the *From Elvis in Memphis* sessions (all of the released material from those dates was reissued in 1987 on the messily programmed, poorly remastered *The Memphis Record*, RCA 6221); the other was the first of many, many, many live albums—this one drawn from the first comeback shows at the International Hotel in Las Vegas—that in the '70s would serve the same function soundtrack albums had in the '60s: blind product. This was, though, a good live album; the seven-minute "Suspicious Minds" was astonishing.

THE APOTHEOSIS, 1970–77

His resurrection assured, Elvis settled into a public state of grace; his only sin, in Bob Dylan's words, was his lifelessness. Elvis played New York City for the first time (discounting '50s TV shows) in 1972; reviews were ecstatic (jaded rock critics went mad for El's version of "Bridge Over Troubled Water"), and

Elvis as Recorded at Madison Square Garden (RCA 4776) was in the stores a week after the concerts. Twenty songs, including "American Trilogy," were crammed onto the single LP, but clearly one had to be there. A good part of the magic must have come from the fans, and they took most of it home with them. Elvis reversed field later in the year with "Burning Love" (RCA 74-0769), an aching 45 that fought past records by Chuck Berry and Rick Nelson on its way to number one (on some charts; *Billboard* stopped it at #2). "The most exciting single Elvis has made since 'All Shook Up,'" Bob Christgau wrote in *Newsday*, adding: "Not only that, it's dirty. Who else could make 'It's coming closer, the flames are now licking my body' sound like an assignation with James Brown's back-up band?" Some said "Burning Love" reached the top only because of a brief revival of interest in the '50s, but they couldn't have been listening; this was a very rare kind of record, a natural hit, on the order of "I Heard It Through the Grapevine," "You're So Vain," or "Don't Be Cruel." Typically, RCA made it available on a budget LP called *Elvis Sings Burning Love and Hits from His Movies, Vol. 2*—though it has since appeared on countless reissues from Australia, West Germany, Japan, Thailand, and even the U.S.A.

His rocker's dues paid up again, the King floated on with numerous gruesome ballads ("Whadja expect," Christgau wrote at the end 1972, "'All the Young Dudes'?"), and in 1973 launched another live opus, *Aloha from Hawaii via Satellite* (RCA 6089, RCA 2642). This double album, issued to commemorate a planetwide TV special, featured a map of the world emblazoned with "WE LOVE ELVIS" in twenty-nine languages, if my count is accurate. There was one song for each tongue, more or less, though all were in English. *Aloha* was Elvis's first number one LP in nine years—the last, appropriately enough, had been *Roustabout*.

And they kept coming, album after album, the sloppy, mindless releases all too accurately reflecting the drugged and helpless off-stage life of the man himself. Occasionally the songs changed, but not often. Elvis gained and lost and gained weight; saw his wife leave him for a karate instructor; bought Cadillacs for, it seemed, anyone who would take one; and made the papers when, as began to happen regularly, he checked into a hospital for "rest." One was left to pore through the records for hidden gems—proof that, against all odds, the *truth* was still to be found—and it was, mostly in the form of old R&B hits. *Fool*, issued in 1973 (RCA 0293), contained a beautiful version of Ivory Joe Hunter's "I Will Be True" (the LP is no longer available, but this and a stunning 1966 "Beyond the Reef," which Elvis recorded solo, accompanying himself on piano, are on *Elvis Aron Presley*); 1974 brought a fast jump into the 1964 "Promised Land" (RCA 10074), Elvis's first successful cover of a Chuck Berry song, though the disc should have gone much higher than #14. It was followed by the bizarre *Having Fun with Elvis on Stage* (RCA 0818), which consisted of the King saying "Well . . . wellll . . . *welllll*" for thirty-seven minutes. In 1975 there was *Elvis Today* (RCA 1039), which offered a magnificent reading of Faye Adams's 1953 "Shake a Hand" and a priceless version of

Billy Swan's 1974 country hit "I Can Help" ("Have a laugh on me," Elvis changed the tune to say, "I can help"). In 1976, on *From Elvis Presley Boulevard, Memphis, Tennessee* (RCA 1506—the road ran past Graceland, which was to say that by this time Elvis was not leaving his house to record), there was an apocalyptic attack on Timi Yuro's 1961 "Hurt." In 1977, on *Moody Blue* (RCA 2428), Elvis sang Johnny Ace's "Pledging My Love," a song that had spelled death since 1955, when Ace shot himself while his version was climbing the charts. The release of Elvis's performance was no more fortuitous; it too was headed up the charts the day he died.

No matter how troubled, Elvis retained the power to be as exciting or as dull as he chose: that was always the rhythm of his career. In some ways, then, an album that appeared in late 1971, *Elvis Sings the Wonderful World of Christmas* (RCA 4579—out of print, but see *Reconsider Baby* or *Memories of Christmas*, RCA 4395), was the truest statement of all—for here, in the midst of ten painfully genteel Christmas songs, every one sung with sincerity and humility, one could find Elvis tomcatting his way through six blazing minutes of "Merry Christmas, Baby," a raunchy old Charles Brown blues. And that was what Elvis had to tell us: if his sin was his lifelessness, it was his sinfulness that brought him to life, even if something very much like a sense of sin finally did him in. Forty-five odd years from now, when RCA puts out its Double Golden Anniversary Hologram, that story will still be worth hearing.

ELVIS IN PRINT AND IN THE GRAVE

Elvis has inspired some of the very best rock writing, and much of the worst. While any number of "I Knew the King" books appeared following Elvis's death on August 16, 1977—and we will get to some of those—Jerry Hopkins' *Elvis* (New York: Simon and Schuster, 1971), supplemented by Hopkins' *Elvis: The Final Years* (New York: St. Martin's, 1980), remains the most useful biography. The book lacks any real point of view, it's wrong on Col. Parker, but it's neither sensationalist nor sycophantic, and I certainly couldn't have worked without it. Most helpful for detail, among many scholastic compendiums, discographies, concordances, logs, and other reference works is Fred L. Worth and Steve D. Tamerius's reliable and entertaining *All About Elvis* (New York: Bantam, 1981), an encyclopedia reissued and expanded as *Elvis: His Life from A to Z* (Chicago: Contemporary Books, 1988). Far more illuminating are these essays: Stanley Booth's 1968 "A Hound Dog, to the Manor Born" (in *The Complete Elvis*, ed. Martin Torgoff [N.Y.: Delilah/Putnam, 1982]), a moving, personal account of Elvis's emergence in Memphis in 1954 contrasted with his mid-'60s limbo; Jon Landau's "In Praise of Elvis Presley" (in Landau's *It's Too Late to Stop Now*, San Francisco: Straight Arrow, 1972), a report on a 1971 Boston concert (the piece was found among Elvis's effects after his death); Stu Werbin's "Elvis and the A-Bomb" (*Creem*, March 1972), a cosmic attempt to place Elvis in a cosmic context, written following the same concert Landau attended; Robert Christgau's "Elvis Presley: Aging Rock" (see Christgau's *Any Old Way You Choose It*, Baltimore: Penguin, 1973), an analysis based on Elvis's shows in Las Vegas in 1969 and his Madison Square Garden concerts in 1972; and Nik Cohn's chapter on Elvis in *Rock from the Beginning* (New York: Stein and Day, 1969), or the revised and updated version in (same book, new title) *Awopbopaloobop Alopbamboom* (London: Paladin, 1972—see also Cohn's *The Elvis Years*, a one-shot magazine published as *Circus Pinups #3* in 1975); Peter Guralnick's "Elvis Presley," in *The Rolling Stone Illustrated History of Rock & Roll*, ed. Jim Miller (New York: Rolling Stone Press/Random House, 1976 and 1981), and his "Elvis Presley and the American Dream" in Guralnick's *Lost Highway: Journeys & Arrivals of American Musicians* (New York: Harper & Row, 1989, originally published 1980). When Guralnick's forthcoming *Last Train to Memphis: The Rise of Elvis Presley* is published it should make other biographies redundant.

Elvis's death resulted in a frenzy of promotion and hucksterism, most of it licensed by Col. Parker himself—until all rights were taken over by Graceland Enterprises, Inc., sole heir Lisa Marie Presley's corporate parent, which by 1988 had so effectively worked the market that Elvis made the cover of *Forbes* magazine as the highest paid dead entertainer of the year. Most notable of the early official products was "Always Elvis," a wine advertised as "The wine Elvis would have drunk, if he drank wine"; most striking of the Graceland items was "Love Me Tender Chunks," a dog food not advertised as "The dog food Elvis would have eaten, if he'd been a dog," though fans filled in the slogan anyway. Below the counter, one could find "Elvis' Sweat," a glass vial-cum-greeting card produced by Maiden Jest, Inc. ("The IMPOSSIBLE has happened. Elvis *poured out* his soul for you, and NOW you can let his PERSPIRATION be an INSPIRATION").

Pressing plants ran night and day in 1977 to keep up with the demand for records; one optimistic collector asked $10,000 for an unidentified "original Elvis 78 on black plastic," though Elvis 78s were not made of plastic. Ads in British tabloids offered video cassettes of the autopsy performed on Elvis's corpse; a team of collectors tried to dig it up. In the tradition of James Dean, Elvis spoke frequently from the Beyond, usually through the magic of supermarket tabloids. Elvis impersonators roamed the land, the most interesting being "Orion," a masked singer record magnate Shelby Singleton, who at the time of Elvis's death owned the Sun catalogue, promoted as a prophet to make the blind see and the lame walk, the suggestion being that Elvis had staged his death (and also changed his name, face, and voice) in order to commune with his followers while escaping the pressures of fame. Scores of cripples and other unfortunates from across the South duly appeared at Orion's concerts, waiting patiently for the laying on of hands. Appalled, Seattle filmmaker John Myhre produced a six-minute movie, *He May Be Dead, But He's Still Elvis* (the phrase first appeared as graffiti on the walls surrounding Graceland)—in which,

Rolling Stone reported in 1979, "The King's decaying body is exhumed and brought back for one last concert tour (unfortunately, it keeps falling off its stool and collapsing onstage in a heap). The corpse is trotted out for record-store autographing sessions . . . Finally, slices of flesh are hacked off and sold in 'Piece o' Presley' packages." The notion of a King in hiding (a replay of similar legends about King Arthur, Frederick the Great, or Bonnie Prince Charlie) mushroomed into a national craze in 1988, when Elvis was sighted repeatedly in a supermarket in Kalamazoo, Michigan—a discovery pumped up by well-made photographs, taped telephone conversations (swiftly put on sale), a long-running series in *Doonesbury*, and a new single, the uncredited "Spelling on the Stone" (collected on the anonymous and hilariously bogus album of the same name, Curb/LS 10608). "There's a very large spiritual gap in this country, and it's being filled by charlatans, shysters and televisions," singer Don Henley said in 1989. "People are so hungry for a miracle, there've been more sightings of Jesus and Elvis than Bigfoot or the Loch Ness Monster."

Immediately after Elvis's death, dozens of tribute records were rushed onto the country market, including Misty's "Dead on Arrival," Leigh Grady's "Blue Christmas (Without Elvis)," and Billy Joe Burnette's "Welcome Home Elvis," which, sung as if it was in the voice of Jesse Garon Presley, Elvis's stillborn twin brother ("El, I been waitin' forty-two years . . . Not long ago, Mama joined me here . . . She's waitin' for ya, Elvis. Yeah, she's right over there. And soon our daddy will take our hand, and we'll be a happy family once again"), defied credence. Over the next decade there were far more punk songs about Elvis (as a stiff, Elvis was, in the aesthetics of punk, alive); by the end of the '80s, especially given the international commemoration ("celebration" is really the word) of the tenth anniversary of August 16, most of these tunes seemed to be about sin and redemption, excess and spiritual starvation. The whole discourse was perhaps caught in the beginning, with X's 1981 "Back 2 the Base" (on *Wild Gift*, Slash 107): a batteringly naturalistic account of a psychotic bus rider railing curses on the King ("Presley's been dead/The body means nothing/Man in the back says Presley sucked dicks/With a picture of Li'l Stevie over his head/I'm in the back with a hole in my throat"). Not only was it likely the best song about Elvis up to its time (Bill Parsons' 1958 "The All American Boy" was the only decent competition), it was, as Tom Carson wrote, "about how culture shapes lives—as indiscriminately as water shapes wood."

Millions upon millions of copies of bad books swiftly made their way into print—and, in most cases, just as swiftly out of it. (For a careful and frequently hilarious wrap-up of the first wave, see Robert K. Oermann and Al Cooley's review of *Elvis Presley: King of Kings*, and 37 other titles, in the *Journal of Country Music*, v. ix. n. 2, 1982; for the second wave, my review of *All Shook Up: Elvis Day by Day, 1954–1977*, and fourteen other artifacts, in the same publication, v. xi, n. 1, 1986). *Elvis: What Happened?* (New York: Ballantine, 1977), by former longtime Presley bodyguards Red West, Sonny West, and

Dave Hebler, with Steve Dunleavy as "As Told To," was the first of many scandal-bios, appearing only days before Elvis's multiple drug overdose; while in places quite obviously inaccurate and inflated, the book is worth reading. Less so are any number of memoirs by friends, distant relatives, in-laws, ex-wife, ex-wife's ex-lover, a nurse, a gatekeeper, and so on, though occultist Jess Stearns' *The Truth About Elvis* (New York: Jove, 1980)—heralded as "the book that Elvis planned to write," and written with Larry Geller, Elvis's hairdresser and "spiritual advisor"—deserves mention for its barely hedged thesis that the man we knew as Elvis Presley was in truth none other than . . . yes, the Son of God himself, back for another look. Most unsettling was Lucy de Barbin and Dary Maters' *Are You Lonesome Tonight? The Untold Story of Elvis Presley's One True Love—and the Child He Never Knew* (New York: Villard, 1987), in which de Barbin recounted every detail of the affair she shared with Presley—beginning in 1954, lasting until his death, producing two pregnancies and one child, who of course she never told Elvis about—an affair that, a reader had to conclude, began in 1954 in de Barbin's unconscious, which soon became her ego, and is her ego still. ("The way I see it," John Kordosh wrote in his *Creem* review of the book, "we're all Elvis's children. So where's my money?") As for Albert Goldman's *Elvis* (New York: McGraw-Hill, 1981), he did good work on Col. Parker; otherwise the bestseller, which, despite its countless errors, inventions, and racist smears, academics are still citing, was no more than a 598-page attempt to discredit Elvis, the culture that produced him, and the culture he helped create. "Like most country boys of his time," Goldman wrote of Presley, "he was uncircumcised . . . he saw his beauty disfigured by an ugly hillbilly pecker."

Out of all this, a few books of value appeared. Albert Wertheimer's *Elvis '56: In the Beginning* (New York: Collier, 1979) is a photo-journal by the only photographer (or, for that matter, reporter) ever given complete access to Elvis: it combines historic, kinetic images of Elvis in the studio, on tour, and behind the scenes with a serious, witty memoir (Wertheimer on Col. Parker: "He looked like a football referee from the Panama Canal Zone"). Just as indelible, but also indelibly subversive, is *Private Elvis* (Stuttgart: FEY, 1978), a production by Diego Cortez that combines a probing text by Duncan Smith with accidentally discovered photos by Rudolf Paulini: photos of Elvis consorting with whores, junkies, actresses, and strippers in a Munich nightclub in 1959. It's Elvis in montage, after the manner of Michael Lesy's *Wisconsin Death Trip*: a seamy, erotic smashup of American health with postwar European decay, and a version of the porn film Elvis's fans dreamed for twenty years.

Neal and Janice Gregory's *When Elvis Died* (Washington, D.C.: Communications Press, 1981) is a meticulously researched (even if they do say that Elvis's first appearance on "The Ed Sullivan Show" was seen by 82.6 percent of the American public—it is not certain that in 1956 82.6 percent of the American public knew Eisenhower was president) account of the press reaction to and panic over the great event: along with inside dope about why CBS decided not to lead with the story and how President Jimmy Carter's tribute was almost derailed (Oliver North and Richard Secord were not involved) come scores of memorable tales—the best of which I can't resist setting down. On the occasion of Elvis's death, the Gregorys report, a Mrs. Joel Hurstfield wrote to *The* [London] *Times*: "In 1956, the year when Elvis Presley's extraordinary talent burst upon the world, I started to teach in a large mixed comprehensive school in northwest London. I shall never forget the elderly mistress coming into the staff room one morning and saying sternly, 'I must speak to a boy called Elvis Presley because he has carved his name on every desk in the school.'"

Elvis: Images and Fancies (Jackson: University Press of Mississippi, 1979), ed. Jac L. Tharpe, is a collection of essays by academics and fans that reveals as much about Presley—as phenomenon, artist, and heartthrob—as any book I know. Charles Wolfe's "Presley and the Gospel Tradition" breaks new ground; Van K. Brock's "Images of Elvis, the South, and America" provides a needed analysis of Elvis's Pentecostal roots. Strongest of all is Linda Ray Pratt's "Elvis, or the Ironies of a Southern Identity" (reprinted in *The Complete Elvis*) which goes this book one better. I wrote, Pratt says, "that Elvis created a beautiful illusion, a fantasy that shut nothing out. The opposite was true. The fascination was the reality always showing through the illusion—the illusion of wealth and the psyche of poverty; the illusion of success and the pinch of ridicule; the illusion of invincibility and the tragedy of frailty; the illusion of complete control and the reality of inner chaos." Also rising above the heap were Elaine Dundy's *Elvis and Gladys* (New York: Macmillan, 1985), a sensitive study of ancestry and legacy with many coups of research, and Gary Panter's *Invasion of the Elvis Zombies* (New York: Raw, 1984), a three-part overlapping comic strip about Elvis's rise from the dead to wreak havoc, revenge, and have some fun. Two shorter pieces should be noted: Dave Marsh's "Elvis: The New Deal Origins of Rock 'n' Roll" (*Musician*, December 1982, first delivered as a talk in Memphis in August 1982), and Lester Bangs' "Notes for Review of Peter Guralnick's *Lost Highway*" (unpublished in Bangs' lifetime, but collected in his *Psychotic Reactions and Carburetor Dung*, ed. Greil Marcus, New York: Knopf, 1987). Bangs "begins slowly, mulling over rather humdrum notions about producer Sam Phillips's shamanhood," Mark Moses wrote. "But he quickly tires of one-step-after-another thinking, and lurches toward more scabrous observations like 'There was always something supernatural about him. Elvis was a force of nature. Other than that he was just a turd.' After he stews and steeps along these lines for a page or so, Bangs hits critical mass and launches into a fixated fantasy about eating the essence-of-Elvis-soaked drugs left in the King's corpse-belly. Reincarnating the departed Spirit, Bangs becomes the terminal Presley of *Elvis: What Happened?*, sweltering in an ennui imposed by Las Vegas but colored by Franz Kafka. Bangs/Elvis ponders whom to shoot out on a TV screen, decides singing and sex are not options anymore, and descends to a quivering moment of blankness and mystery: 'The point is that something I started doing to make people know I existed started rubbing out my existence, a little at a time, day by day. I could feel it going, seeping away, steady and calm . . . and nothin' comin' in to replace it. And I knew nothin' ever would.'"

As for fiction, the only novels of interest about Elvis were published before his death and remain almost completely unknown. Harlan Ellison's *Spider Kiss* (New York: Ace, 1983), originally issued in 1961 as *Rockabilly*, was the first, and it's still the best. At once a roman à clef, a trash rock novel, a prescient version of *Elvis: What Happened?*, and a clear look at the sources of American culture, it chronicles the rise and inevitable fall of a Southern flash; characters include a soul-searching flack (the narrator), a Col. Tom-style manager, and "Stag Preston," né Luther Sellers, a rockabilly hero who is not only a craven hype but a natural artist whose genius no evil, including his own, can ever quite snuff. Out of this material comes a story that makes sense, and an ending with some real tragedy in it.

Nik Cohn's *King Death* (New York: Harcourt Brace Jovanovich, 1975) is about the thanatology of pop: the tale of an English promoter (probably the same one who appears in the last verse of Bob Dylan's "Highway 61 Revisited") turning a professional killer, first glimpsed at work in Tupelo, into America's biggest star—*as* a killer. Almost all novelists who use pop as their subject exploit the repressed violence, twisted sexuality, and death wishes that seem to lie beneath the ecstasy of pop thrills; Cohn bypasses the usual fake apocalyptic ending (in which the star's big concert closes with an orgy of murder, mayhem, and, more often than not, cannibalism in the tradition of *The Golden Bough*) by making the underside of the story visible and present. Of course, that the killer—"King Death," as he's known to his fans—is from Tupelo is no accident. The book's dedication makes it clear that King Death is none other than the risen ghost of Jesse Garon Presley—in other words, a version of Elvis himself. Cohn doesn't mean the conceit as a joke, and it doesn't read like one; a lifelong fascination with the King, an attempt to understand, drives the book. (For more on the living Jesse Garon, see "Esau Smith: The Hairy and the Smooth," in Nick Tosches' *Unsung Heroes of Rock 'n' Roll*, New York: Scribner's, 1984, expanded edition Harmony Books, and London: Secker & Warburg, 1991.)

Though no Elvis novels of note have turned up since 1977 (the subject of the posthumous Elvis novel is typically the Elvis impersonator, as in William McCranor Henderson's serious but failed *Stark Raving Elvis*, New York: E. P. Dutton, 1984), the specter of the man has begun to make its way into fiction: as a motif, as a touchstone. A fictional character's reaction to the assassination of John F. Kennedy has long been used by novelists both to attach the character to the reader and to locate the character in American life; we can expect that a fictional character's attitude toward Elvis will be used in the same way in the future, but it's doubtful anyone will get more out of the device than William Price Fox did with *Dixiana Moon* (New York: Viking, 1981). Set following

Elvis's death, the story concerns a young New Yorker and an old-time Southern hustler who join forces to stage the ultimate revival: the Great Monzingo–Arlo Waters Jubilee Crusade and Famous Life of Christ Show, complete with snake-handling fundamentalists and Drano-drinking Pentecostals. One night, driving through the South, the New Yorker picks up an old Sun single on the radio. "Wonder what he was like," he says to his tent-show mentor. "He wasn't like anyone," says the would-have-been Col. Parker. "You start trying to compare Elvis to something and you can forget it . . . Bo, all you can do with a talent that big and that different is sort of point at it when you see it going by, and maybe listen for the ricochet."

The overwhelming, and continuing, response to Elvis's death—in the years since, Graceland reports, more people have visited the place than have visited the grave of JFK—suggests that people felt more than a sense of loss: it suggests they felt a sense of guilt, a theme I've tried to follow in *Dead Elvis: A Chronicle of a Cultural Obsession* (New York: Doubleday, 1991, and Harmondsworth: Penguin, 1992). The best of the obituaries that appeared caught this theme at the outset: Dave Marsh's "How Great Thou Art: Elvis in the Promised Land," in *Rolling Stone*'s superbly illustrated special issue (September 22, 1977—collected in Marsh's *Fortunate Son*, New York: Random House, 1985), and Lester Bangs' "How Long Will We Care?" in the *Village Voice* (August 29, 1977—collected as "Where Were You When Elvis Died?" in Bangs' *Psychotic Reactions and Carburetor Dung*). Bangs talked about the way Elvis, as private and distant a man as could be imagined, forged a generational solidarity in the '50s, and about the way that solidarity had broken apart in the '70s. He concluded with this paragraph, which may be Elvis's finest epitaph: "If love is truly going out of fashion forever, which I do not believe, then along with our nurtured indifference to each other will be an even more contemptuous indifference to each other's objects of reverence. I thought it was Iggy Stooge, you thought it was Joni Mitchell or whoever else seemed to speak for your own private, entirely circumscribed situation's many pains and few ecstasies. We will continue to fragment in this manner, because solipsism holds all the cards at present; it is a king whose domain engulfs even Elvis's. But I can guarantee you one thing: we will never agree on anything as we agreed on Elvis. So I won't bother saying goodbye to his corpse. I will say goodbye to you."

THE CARTER FAMILY, JIMMIE RODGERS & HANK WILLIAMS

The Carter Family (A. P., his wife Sarah, and his sister-in-law "Mother" Maybelle Addington) came from the Clinch Mountains in Virginia, near the Tennessee border. Ralph Peer of Victor recorded both the Carters and Jimmie Rodgers for the first time in August 1927 (see the anthology *The Bristol Sessions*, Country Music Foundation 011); they dominated country record sales and country radio for most of the next decade. Maybelle's guitar and autoharp playing has influenced almost every mainstream white guitarist since that time, and many black guitarists; the Carters' songs—traditional folk material, gospel, some blues, and 19th-century sentimental standards—have gone all over the world. Of many albums on the market, *The Famous Carter Family* (Harmony 11332) is still the best introduction, featuring "My Clinch Mountain Home," "Keep on the Sunny Side," "Can the Circle Be Unbroken," "Wildwood Flower," "Worried Man Blues," and the joyous "Gospel Ship." *The Original and Great Carter Family* (RCA/Camden 568—the same person who couldn't decide between "Gold" and "Golden" for Elvis's records must have titled this one) includes the mystical "Diamonds in the Rough," "Little Moses," and "Wabash Cannonball." Discs that do not say "The Original" usually indicate numbers cut after the Second World War by Maybelle and her daughters, without Sarah and A.P.; they bear little resemblance to the music made in the '20s and '30s. For more detail, see John Atkins' "The Carter Family" in *Stars of Country Music*, ed. Bill C. Malone and Judith McCulloh (Urbana: University of Illinois, 1975).

Jimmie Rodgers was born in Meridian, Mississippi, in 1897. He spent a good part of his youth on the railroad, listening to black minstrels and work gangs; when tuberculosis forced him to quit the rails in 1925, he turned to music. By the time he began to record in 1927 he had mastered a unique blues style: the "blue yodel" Howlin' Wolf said taught him how to howl. Rodgers' most striking album is *My Rough and Rowdy Ways* (RCA 2112), which collects "Blue Yodel No. 1 (T for Texas)," Rodgers' first real hit, "Blue Yodel No. 9" (backing by Louis Armstrong and Earl Hines), and "Long Tall Mama Blues." The fine *Never No Mo' Blues* (RCA 1232) includes "California Blues," Rodgers' ironic tribute to the dispossessed Okies and Arkies who sang his songs all the way to the coast. He died in 1933; the most complete biography is Nolan Porterfield's *Jimmie Rodgers: The Life and Times of America's Blue Yodeler* (Urbana: University of Illinois, 1979). The first "Jimmie Rodgers—Father of Country Music Festival" was held in Meridian in 1953, and featured a singing contest; Elvis, eighteen, hitchhiked 240 miles to compete.

Hank Williams was born in 1923; he left home to sing in 1937, and first recorded in 1946, almost precisely a generation after the first recordings by Rodgers and the Carters. He was the first country singer whose music reached every corner of the United States; in terms of music and impact, he might be called the white Ray Charles ("country Ray Charles" won't do; Charles was country himself). Dragged down by drinking, drugs, illness, and divorce, Williams' career was as chaotic as it was successful; by the end, he was banned from the Grand Ole Opry for his sins. He died on New Year's Day 1953, only twenty-nine years old, though the coroner refused to believe it; people still pay to see the death car, but they would do better to read Ralph J. Gleason's beautifully elegiac "Hank Williams, Roy Acuff, and Then God!" (in *The Rolling Stone Rock & Reader*, ed. Ben Fong-Torres, New York: Bantam, 1974), or Chet Flippo's disturbing *Your Cheatin' Heart* (New York: Doubleday/

Dolphin, 1985, originally published in 1981). *40 Greatest Hits* (Polydor 821 233–1) is the basic collection; most of Williams' work, undubbed and including much previously unreleased material, can be found on the Polydor *Hank Williams* series, eight double LPs programmed chronologically, supplemented by *The First Recordings* (Country Music Foundation 007) and *Just Me and My Guitar* (Country Music Foundation 006). Avoid the sets that present Hank Williams, Jr., singing along with tapes of his dead father; morbidity and necrophilia, as logical extensions of rural nostalgia, have always been part of country music, but this is too much.

CAMEOS: FROM CHARLIE RICH TO "LOUIE LOUIE"

Charlie Rich's "I Feel Like Going Home" was released in 1973 as the flipside of "The Most Beautiful Girl," and again in 1974 on *The Silver Fox* (Epic 33250). This harmless version had nothing to do with the performance I saw Rich dedicate to Richard Nixon; producer Billy Sherrill buried the vocal in choruses and horns, and smoothed away the broken melody and confusing chord changes that gave the music its power. Rich did record the tune as he meant it to be heard, on a rehearsal tape that for years his label denied even existed; Rich's piano was the only accompaniment, a strange wedding of Skip James' free hand and stately country gospel. The recording, perhaps the most distinctive of Rich's long career, finally saw the light of day on the 1981 anthology *Rockabilly Stars, Vol. 1* (Epic 37618).

    The most convincing of all white soul singers, Rich's 1957–62 work for Phillips International (a Sun subsidiary) can be found on *Original Hits and Midnight Demos* (Sun/Charly CDX10, UK, a two-record set), and on *Don't Put No Headstone on My Grave* (Zu-Zazz 2002, UK), which combines an unreleased 1962 session with hits remixed to omit overdubbed strings and choruses. Rich's more expressive mid-'60s recordings, cut with producer Jerry Kennedy in Nashville, are on *Fully Realized* (Mercury 7505), which combines the albums originally released as *The Many New Sides of Charlie Rich* (Smash 67070) and *The Best Years* (Smash 67078)—today, these long out-of-print LPs may be easier to find than the reissue. *The Best of Charlie Rich* (Epic 31933) contains music Rich cut for Epic before "Behind Closed Doors" made him a star in the early '70s: "Life's Little Ups and Downs," "Sittin' and Thinkin'," "A Woman Left Lonely," and the magnificent "Set Me Free" define how far a country singer whose spirit comes from the blues can go. Peter Guralnick's chronicle of Rich's career can be followed in "Lonely Weekends," in Guralnick's *Feel Like Going Home* (New York: Harper & Row, 1989, originally published 1971), an account of Rich's commercial failure, and in "Snapshots of Charlie Rich," in *Lost Highway*, an account of Rich's commercial success.

    Dolly Parton's 1969 "My Blue Ridge Mountain Boy" is best heard on *A Real Live Dolly Parton* (RCA 4387), an album (recorded at Sevier County High

School, Parton's alma mater) that also features "Bloody Bones," a ditty about orphans who burn down their orphanage; it can also be found on *My Blue Ridge Mountain Boy* (RCA 4188), or on *The Best of Dolly Parton* (RCA 4449), which isn't. The Allman Brothers' "Blue Sky" is on *Eat a Peach* (Capricorn 0102, 1972); their "Pony Boy" is on *Brothers and Sisters* (Capricorn 0111, 1973). William Moore's timeless 1928 celebration, "Old Country Rock," can be found on *Really! The Country Blues* (Origin Jazz Library 2).

As for the saga of "Louie Louie" (in 1988, in an interview with Bob Greene, Richard Berry finally confirmed—or, confronted with the age-old question for the first time, decided—that there was no comma in the song's title), by now it deserves a book, which Dave Marsh is working on. A joke in the late '60s, when bands like the Mothers of Invention would play it to make fun of the old-fashioned rock 'n' roll they had transcended, by the late '70s and in the '80s the tune was all pervasive, like a law of nature or an act of God. College radio stations put on "Louie Louie" marathons, competing with each other year by year to see which could find the most versions; the project reached its peak on KALX-FM in Berkeley, near the end of a twenty-four-hour no-repeat absurdity, when, because people were taping their own versions of the song as they listened to the broadcast, then bringing them down to the station, where they were immediately aired, it became clear that unless someone called a halt the show would never end. *The Best of Louie, Louie* (Rhino 605), with versions by Richard Berry, the Sandpipers, Black Flag, the Rice University Marching Band, Rockin' Robin Roberts (the Seattle singer who rescued the tune from oblivion in 1961), the Kingsmen, and others, augmented by *The Best of Louie Louie, Volume 2* (Rhino 70515), with renderings by the Soviet band Red Square and the Kinks, are only a hint of what has happened.

The records that tell the story I tell are "Riot in Cell Block #9," by the Robins (later the Coasters), lead vocal by Richard Berry, 1955 (originally on Spark; see *The Coasters—The Early Years*, Atco 371); "The Big Break," by Richard Berry, 1955 (originally on Flair; see *Richard Berry and the Dreamers*, United Superior 7798, though for some reason the spoken passages have been erased); "Louie Louie," by Richard Berry and the Pharaohs, 1956 (originally on Flip; see *The Best of Louie, Louie*, or *Richard Berry: "Louie, Louie"*, Earth Angel 901, Sweden); "Louie Louie" by the Kingsmen, 1963 (originally on Jerden; see *The Best of Louie, Louie*, or *The Best of the Kingsmen*, Scepter 18002); "Louie, Louie" by Paul Revere & the Raiders (originally on Sande—but wait a minute, does the band's name imply Paul Revere and the British invaders he supposedly warned against were working together?—see *Paul Revere & the Raiders' Greatest Hits*, Columbia 3164, or *The Best of Louie Louie, Volume 2*); and "Brother Louie," by Stories, 1973 (Kama Sutra 577).

The initial recording of the last tune was by the black and white U.K. band Hot Chocolate, 1973 (see *Greatest Hits*, Big Tree 76002); in their version, "Louie" was black and his girlfriend white, while with Stories it was the other way around: there is no bottom to this tale. And for those who must hear the *real* lyrics (which Richard Berry never wrote; neither musicologists nor anthropologists of urban folklore have ever figured out who did), Iggy and the Stooges sing every last one of them on *Metallic 'KO* (JEM/Skydog 82.854, France), cut at the band's last concert, in 1973, in a hail of beer cans and bottles.

SAM PHILLIPS, SUN RECORDS & ROCKABILLY MUSIC

Sam Phillips, for those who haven't guessed, is the secret hero of this book. I don't know if he was the right man in the right place at the right time, or much more than that, and I don't really care. The man's history is in the records he made. "This is like Paris at the turn of the century," said Memphian Jim Dickinson in 1982, trying to explain. "We saw a change in Memphis that affected the whole world."

"My greatest contribution," Phillips said in 1978, "was to open up an area of freedom within the artist himself, to help him express what *he* believed his message to be. Talking about egos—these people unfortunately did not *have* an ego. They had a desire—but at the same time to deal with a person that had dreamed, and dreamed, and dreamed, looked, heard, felt, to deal with them again under conditions where they were so afraid of being denied again—it took a pure instinctive quality on the part of any person that got the revealing aspects out of these people . . . I don't care if it was me or somebody else. Because I knew this—to curse these people or just to give the air of, 'Man, I'm better than you,' I'm wasting my time trying to record these people to get out of them what's truly in them. I *knew* this."*

Moonlighting from his jobs as a disc jockey and hotel big-band broadcast announcer, Phillips built a studio at 706 Union Avenue in Memphis—it was the town's first permanent recording facility—and in 1950 began recording local blues talent (along with speeches, weddings, and commercials), leasing the results to Chess in Chicago and Modern in Los Angeles. The Sun label was founded in 1952. Interesting releases pretty much ceased by about 1960; Phillips made his fortune less as a record man than as an early investor in the Holiday Inn chain.

After Phillips sold the label in 1968, a vast confusion of reissues began—hundreds of albums, on many labels, in many countries, collecting every hit and hundreds of unreleased masters; to unscramble solo LPs from anthologies, to judge every take six against its alternates, to measure sound and pressing

---

*From Peter Guralnick's *Lost Highway*. For more on Sun and related topics, see Margaret Mckee and Fred Chisenall's *Beale Black & Blue* (Baton Rouge: Louisiana State University, 1981); Nick Tosches' *Country: Living Legends and Dying Metaphors in America's Biggest Music* (New York: Scribner's, 1985, first published in 1977), a down-and-dirty account of America's lust for miscegenation as represented in its music; Colin Escott and Martin Hawkins's *Good Rockin' Tonight: Sun Records and the Birth of Rock 'n' Roll* (New York: St. Martin's Press, 1991), and their *Sun Records: The Discography* (Vollersode, W. Germany: Bear Family, 1987); for comment on Sun and the blues, see Robert Palmer's *Deep Blues* (New York: Viking, 1981).

quality, cover art, annotation, and photo research, and somehow make sense of it all would require a computer I don't have and a full-length book I'm not going to write. Only the briefest comments can be made here.

The nine-LP *Sun Records: The Blues Years, 1950–1956* (Sun/Charly Box 105, UK) is a great historical document, and also unfailingly listenable, hours of surprise, shock, and delight: it includes work by Howlin' Wolf, the Prisonaires, B. B. King, James Cotton, Pat Hare (the incredible "I'm Gonna Murder My Baby"), Junior Parker, Little Milton, "Hot Shot" Love, Billy "The Kid" Emerson, Rufus Thomas, Jackie Brenston (whose "Rocket 88," one of many "first" rock 'n' roll records, was a huge R&B hit in 1951), and much more. What you hear is not a production style, though there is that, but the invention and testing of a creative milieu. The ten-LP box *The Sun Country Years, 1950–1959* (Sun/Bear Family 5197, W. Germany) is of more academic interest; if the blues box is an epic, this is an everyday story. There is no hint of a change that could affect Memphis, let alone the rest of the world. The deep themes aren't refusal and desire, but acceptance and routine. There are gleaming anomalies: Howard Seratt's quiet folk-gospel, the rare sound of a man at peace with himself, and Cash King and the Miller Sisters' "Can't Find Time to Pray," a piece so delicate it almost hides its sting: "You must find time to die." Sam Phillips never released it, fearing it was too strong for the country market, and no doubt he was right. The set also includes cuts by Harmonica Frank, but it's racist programming, naming him "country" simply because he was white; he belongs in the blues box.

For Howlin' Wolf, see also *Ridin' in the Moonlight* (Ace 52), very early recordings from about 1950, featuring the explosive Willie Johnson on guitar and the pianist known as "Destruction"; *Moanin' in the Moonlight* (Chess 9183); *The Howlin' Wolf Masterworks, Vol. 1: The Bigfoot from Memphis* (Chess 6062, Japan), recordings from 1951 and '52; or *Memphis Days* (Bear Family CD 15460, W. Germany), which includes the chaotic "C.V. Wine Blues" (Wolf and his band had been hired to make a wine commercial, but they apparently drank up the samples first). *Delta Rhythm Kings* (Charly 30103, UK) collects Sun producer and talent scout Ike Turner's early powerhouse sessions, with Bonnie Turner's bizarre "Down in the Congo"; Harmonica Frank's work is on *The Great Original Recordings of Harmonica Frank* (Puritan 3003); for the Prisonaires, the doo-wop and gospel group Phillips recorded while they were still incarcerated, see *Five Beats Behind Bars* (Charly 30149, UK); for the electric, deep-soul recordings of Billy "The Kid" Emerson, see *Little Fine Healthy Thing* (Charly 30187, UK). And keep looking—though you may never stop.

With Elvis, Sun changed. Blues vanished almost completely; Phillips went for the main chance, which meant white boys who could sing country rock. Malcolm Yelvington—who looked like an accountant attending an office Halloween party in a cowboy costume, but who could sing country rock—was the first to record after Elvis; he's best heard on the anthology *Memphis Rocks the Country* (Redita 106, Holland), which contains "Drinkin' Wine Spo-Dee-O-Dee" and "Just Rollin' Along," or on the less shapely but easier to find Yelvington/Johnny Bernero LP, *Memphis Rockin' Country* (P-Vine 330, Japan).

When Elvis left Sun in the fall of 1955, dozens of new white singers were beginning to record in Texas, Nashville, Alabama, and other Southern centers; the rest were in Memphis, begging Sam Phillips for auditions. The best were Carl Perkins and Billy Lee Riley, who entered 706 Union Avenue in 1955, and Roy Orbison and Jerry Lee Lewis, who arrived in 1956.

Perkins made beautiful records for Sam Phillips—and nearly all of them, plus numerous surprising alternate takes, all superbly remastered, are on the three-LP *Carl Perkins—The Sun Years* (Sun/Charly Box 101, UK). There are "Blue Suede Shoes" and "Boppin' the Blues," and also his gentle recreation of the Platters' "Only You," the jailhouse rocker "Dixie Fried," the rough "That's Right," the stomping "Matchbox," and his celebration of race envy, "Put Your Cat Clothes On." Perkins cut many sides for many other labels in the '60s and after; he never really had another hit, or matched his first music. Some of the best of his later work is on *Carl Perkins* (Bopcat 207, Holland), which includes soulful early '60s material plus the fierce "Big Bad Blues," made in 1964 with the Nashville Teens. He tells his own story in Michael Lydon's *Rock Folk* (New York: Dial, 1971, Citadel Underground, 1991).

Billy Lee Riley cut "Trouble Bound" for the Memphis Fernwood label in 1955, playing all the instruments; he hit a dark, moody tone that only Presley surpassed. Phillips leased the disc and put it out on Sun (see the bootleg *Good Rocking Tonight*, Bopcat 100, Holland, or, if absolutely necessary, *Sun Sound Special—Billy Lee Riley*, Charly 30151, UK, otherwise awful). Riley recorded two unforgettably scorching sides: "Red Hot" and "Flying Saucers Rock 'n' Roll," the latter being one of the weirdest of early rock records—and early rock records were *weird* (see *The Legendary Sun Performers—Billy Lee Riley*, Charly 30131, UK). Riley drifted into session work and occasional releases under other names; he's still around, looking for that hit.

Roy Orbison and the Teenkings recorded "Ooby Dooby" b/w "Tryin' to Get to You" in early 1956 in Clovis, New Mexico, for the Je-Wel label; Phillips signed up Orbison and his band and had them cut a far stronger version of "Ooby Dooby," which hit #59 on the pop charts. The flipside, "Go Go Go," one of the most thrilling rockabilly records ever made, featured guitar work (by either Orbison or Johnny "Peanuts" Wilson) that formed Buddy Holly's hard rock style almost completely. These and other strong performances, including "Domino," which anticipated surf music, are on *Roy Orbison—The Sun Years* (Sun/Charly CDX4, UK), supplemented by *Problem Child* (Zu-Zazz 2006, UK). Orbison went to many memorable pseudo-operatic hits and occasional rockers in the '60s (best collected on *The All-Time Greatest Hits of Roy Orbison*, Monument 31484, which is out of print; for the time being, see the partially redundant *For the Lonely: A Roy Orbison Anthology, 1956—1965*, Rhino 71493); he experienced a startling revival after his 1963 "In Dreams," as mimed by

Dean Stockwell, was used as the centerpiece of David Lynch's corrosive 1986 film *Blue Velvet*. Orbison cut a new album, *Mystery Girl* (Virgin 91058), with contributions from Elvis Costello, Tom Petty, George Harrison, Bono of U2, and others; along with its hit single, "You Got It," it was a huge success—only weeks after Orbison died at fifty-two late in 1988. To the end, he wore a helmet of black hair, never moved on stage, and kept his dark glasses on. "I knew his voice was pure gold," Sam Phillips is reputed to have said. "I also knew that if anyone got a look at him he'd be dead inside of a week."

Jerry Lee Lewis started off playing Al Jolson songs at home, snuck into black-only dives with his cousin Jimmy Lee Swaggart, studied for the ministry at a Pentecostal academy, and turned to rock 'n' roll full time when he was expelled for sneaking too much boogie woogie into the hymns. He recorded far more extensively than any other Sun artist, remaining with the label until 1963: highlights ranged from the audition-session roadhouse stomp of "Deep Elem Blues" and "You Are My Sunshine" to international hits, from the insanely salacious "Big Legged Woman" to the 100 mph "Lovin' Up a Storm" through countless pure country renditions, novelty records, schmaltz, gospel, coon songs, and Stephen Foster. The best introduction, if you can find it, is *Rockin' Up a Storm* (Sun/Polydor 6641/162, UK); the monument is the extraordinary *Jerry Lee Lewis—The Sun Years* (Sun/Charly Box 102, UK), twelve LPs, 209 recordings, plus a treasure chest of banter, rant, obscenity, and philosophical disquisition. Unbelievably, the thing was incomplete: for the latest discoveries, see *Keep Your Hands Off It!* (Zu-Zazz 2003, UK), or for that matter *Classic Jerry Lee Lewis* (Bear Family 15420, W. Germany), 240 Sun performances collected on eight CDs.

After the scandal over his bigamous marriage to teenage cousin Myra, Lewis ultimately found his way to Nashville, producer Jerry Kennedy, and the Smash label; he promised that, in repentance, he would record only country music, abjuring the devil's music for ever more. He kept his promise on his singles, but broke it on his LPs, issuing *The Greatest Live Show on Earth* and a duet album with his sister Linda Gail that was even raunchier than his legend. The *Killer: 1963–1968* (Bear Family 15210, W. Germany), a ten-LP box, includes these and far more—notably, a riveting, album-length 1976 interview that in many ways says as much about the complexities of impulse, fame, and exile as Lewis's records. Other Bear Family boxes, each equally enormous, follow Lewis's story through the next years—the apogee of which, for me anyway, was "Drinkin' Wine Spo-Dee-O-Dee," a single taken from a session with U.K. rockers that cut a swath through everything else on the radio in 1973 (see *The Session*, Smash 8-203). New albums, and new wives, still appear erratically; Lewis's death has been announced any number of times in the last decade, but I have a hunch he will be the last to go. For the reasons why, see Nick Tosches' *Hellfire: The Jerry Lee Lewis Story* (New York: Delacorte/Dell, 1989, originally published in 1982), Lewis's life rendered in bedrock American prose, and Robert Palmer's *Jerry Lee Lewis Rocks!* (New York: Delilah, 1982), which combines excellent photos with a vivid, personal essay. Myra Lewis's *Great Balls of Fire: The Uncensored Story of Jerry Lee Lewis*, written with Murray Silver (New York: Quill, 1982), is hard to read; in 1989 it was made into the film *Great Balls of Fire!*, which featured a mugging star turn by Dennis Quaid, fabulous performance sequences, and a superb soundtrack by Lewis himself, who re-recorded his music as if decades were minutes (see *Great Balls of Fire!*, PolyGram 839 516).

Those were the titans of rockabilly. Other singers, deified by misty-eyed collectors, are far less impressive, save for the occasional glorious one-shot by the likes of Terry Clement and the Tune Tones ("Well, rich girl wears expensive perfume/Poor girl does the same," Clement screamed on "She's My Baby Doll": "My girl don't wear none at all/But you can smell her just the same"); certainly there are gems to ferret out, and some take the rockabilly style to places Sun never got to. There is Sonny Fisher's smoky sexual menace, authentically tough stuff from 1955 (see his *Texas Rockabilly*, Ace/Chiswick 10/14, UK); the Lonesome Drifter, whose authentically strange stuff can be found on the anthology *10 Years—Collector Records* (White Label 8816, Holland); thrillingly "pure" country rock (i.e., no drums) from Junior Thompson and Wayne McGinnis (see *Meteor: Hillbilly Bop, Memphis Style*, Meteor 5000, a good collection that includes Charlie Feathers' interesting "Tongue-Tied Jill"); and the blazing Willie Johnson-influenced guitar playing of Paul Burleson (fronted by the far less convincing vocals of Johnny Burnette) with the very early Memphis band the Rock 'n' Roll Trio (see *Tear It Up*, Solid Smoke 8001). But Warren Smith and Malcolm Yelvington had no real affinity for the black rhythms rockabilly took off from (though Smith, in his heart a modern Appalachian balladeer, can be heard for the quirky delight he was on *The Legendary Sun Performers—Warren Smith*, Charly 30132, UK, which includes the devastating "Red Cadillac and a Black Moustache," "Ubangi Stomp"—one of the only rockabilly records with the word "nigger" in it—"Black Jack David," and "So Long I'm Gone"). Charlie Feathers, despite his unforgettable "One Hand Loose," cut in 1956 for King (see the anthology *King-Federal Rockabillys*, King/Gusto 5016, or Feathers' *Jungle Fever*, Kay 5045, a collection of mostly '50s material), and his latter-day claim that he, *he* taught Elvis everything, was just a rather odd country singer. (After canonization by rockabilly followers, Feathers, who still performs in and around Memphis, released numerous third-rate true-believer LPs in the '70s——and then, rather shockingly, redeemed himself with "Gone and Left Me Blues" and "Rockin' with Red," spooky, sensuous late '70s performances that have no parallels in rockabilly, but that point to directions the music might have taken; see *Johnny Burnette's Rock and Roll Trio and Their Rockin' Friends from Memphis*, Rock-a-billy 1001.) But for every Hasil Adkins (a lunatic one-man band with a penchant for love songs about decapitation; see *Rock 'n Roll Tonight*, Dee-Jay Jamboree 2044, Sweden, or *Out to Hunch*, Norton ED-101, both of which contain his masterpiece, "Truly Ruly") there were dozens of

Carl Manns and Carl McVoys, not much more than fakes; Sonny Burgess, though wild-eyed enough, huffed and puffed more than he rocked (see *The Legendary Sun Performers—Sonny Burgess*, Charly 30136, UK). Outside of originals like Buddy Holly, (probably) Gene Vincent, (maybe) Eddie Cochran, and (for suburbia) Ricky Nelson, most rockabilly singers weren't even imitating blacks, let alone listening to the inner voice Sam Phillips wanted to hear: they were imitating Elvis. Fanatics call the likes of Alvis Wayne geniuses, but the aggression is full of doubt and the flash is almost always forced.

Rockabilly was a very special music. For all of its unchained energy and outrage, it demanded a fine balance between white impulses and black, between fantasies of freedom and the reality that produced those fantasies. The sound Sam Phillips got proves how well he understood this—but sometimes, working for that next hit, Phillips ran into mysteries in the music not even he could have expected.

In 1957, Phillips, Billy Lee Riley, and Jerry Lee Lewis were setting up to make "Great Balls of Fire," the follow-up to "Whole Lotta Shakin' Goin' On," Sun's biggest record. Suddenly, as one can hear on Lewis's *Sun Years* box, Jerry Lee objected. In 1949, as a kid in Ferriday, Louisiana, he had talked his way onto a bandstand for a chance to bang out "Drinkin' Wine Spo-Dee-O-Dee," but the road to Sun took him through the Southwest Bible College in Waxahachie, Texas; like all Sun rockabilly ravers, he was raised on the gospel. Sitting in Phillips' studio, reading over the lead sheet for "Great Balls of Fire," the meaning of the image must have hit him. "Great balls of fire": that was a Pentecostal image, that meant Judgment Day—and now Sam Phillips wanted Jerry Lee to turn that image into a smutty joke, to defile it. Jerry Lee rebelled.

JERRY LEE LEWIS: H-E-L-L!

SAM PHILLIPS: I don't believe it.

JLL: Great Godamighty, great balls of fire!

BILLY LEE RILEY: That's right.

SP: I don't believe it.

JLL: It says, WAKE, MAN! To the Joy of God! But when it comes to worldly music—that's rock 'n' roll—

BLR: Rock it out!

JLL: —or anything like that, you have done brought yourself into the world, and you're in the world, and you hadn't come on out of the world, *and you're still a sinner*.

You're a sinner—and when you be saved—*and borned again*—and *be made as a little child*—

And walk before God—

And be holy—

And brother, I mean that you got to be so pure! No sin shall enter there: *No sin!*

For it says, *No sin!* It doesn't say just a little bit, it says, NO SIN SHALL

ENTER THERE—brother, not one little bit! You've got to walk and *talk* with God to go to Heaven. You've got to be *so* good.

BLR: Hallelujah.

SP: All right. Now, look, Jerry. Religious conviction—doesn't mean anything—resembling extremism. [Phillips suddenly goes on the offensive.] *Do you mean to tell me* that you're gonna take the Bible, you're gonna take God's word, and you're gonna revolu*tionize* the whole universe? Now, listen! Jesus Christ was sent here by God Almighty. Did He convince, did He *save*, all the people in the world?

JLL: Naw, but He tried to!

SP: *He sure did.* NOW WAIT JUST A MINUTE! Jesus Christ—came into this world. He *tolerated* man. He didn't preach from one pulpit. He went around, and He *did good.*

JLL: That's right! He preached *everywhere*!

SP: Everywhere!

JLL: He preached on land!

SP: Everywhere! That's right! That's right!

JLL: He preached on the water!

SP: That's right, that's exactly right! Now—

JLL: And then He done everything! He *healed!*

SP: Now, now—here's, *here's the difference*—

JLL [speaking as if horns have sprouted on Phillips' head]: *Are you followin' those that heal?* Like Jesus Christ?

SP [confused]: Whatta you mean. I, I, what—

JLL [triumphant]: Well, it's happening every day!
The *blind* had eyes opened.
The *lame* were made to walk.

SP: *Jerry*—

JLL: The *crippled* were made to walk.

SP: All right now. Jesus Christ, in my opinion, is just as *real today*, as He was when He came into this world.

JLL: Right, right, you're so right you don't know what you're sayin'.

SP [back on the offensive]: Now then! I will say, *more so*—

BLR: Aw, let's *cut it.*

SP: Wait, wait, wait just a minute, we can't, we got to—now, look. Now, listen. I'm tellin' you outta my heart. I have studied the Bible, a little bit—

JLL: Well, I have too.

SP: I've studied it through and through and through and through and Jerry, Jerry, if you think, that you can't, can't do good, if you're a rock 'n' roll exponent—

JLL: *You can do good*, Mr. Phillips, don't get me wrong—

SP: Now, wait, wait—listen, when I say do good—

JLL: YOU CAN HAVE A KIND HEART!

SP [suddenly angry]: I don't *mean*, I don't *mean* just—

JLL: You can help people!

SP: YOU CAN SAVE SOULS!

JLL [appalled]: No. NO! No, no!

SP: Yes!

JLL: How can the *Devil* save souls? *What are you talkin' about?*

SP: Lissen, lissen—

JLL: I have the Devil in me! If I didn't I'd be a Christian!

SP: Well, you may *have* him—

JLL [fighting for his life]: JESUS! Heal this man! He cast the Devil out, the Devil says, Where can I go? He says, Can I go into this *swine?* He says, Yeah, go into him. Didn't he go into him?

SP: Jerry. The point I'm tryin' to make is—if you believe in what you're singin'—you got no alternative whatsoever—out of—LISTEN!—out of—

JLL: Mr. Phillips! I don't care, it ain't what you believe, it's [as if explaining to a child], *it's what's written in the Bible!*

SP: Well, wait a minute.

JLL: It's what is *there*, Mr. Phillips.

SP: No, no.

JLL: It's just what's there.

SP: No, by gosh, if it's not what you believe [and Phillips hits the clincher], *then how do you interpret the Bible!*

BLR: Man alive . . .

SP: Huh! How do you interpret the Bible if it's not what you believe!

JLL [confused]: Well, it's just *not* what you believe, you *just can't*—

BLR: Let's cut it, man . . .

And so they did; *Good Rocking Tonight*, the bootleg on which this conversation first appeared, follows it with a furious take of "Great Balls of Fire"—a take that, one might say, outsins the version Sam Phillips released to the public.

"Sam's crazy," Jerry Lee told John Grissim many years later. "Nutty as a fox squirrel. He's just like me, he ain't got no sense. Birds of a feather flock together. It took all of us to screw up the world. We've done it."

INDEX

"Acadian Driftwood," 197
Ace, Johnny, 48, 139, 147, 202, 248
Across 110th Street, 84–6
"Across the great Divide," 54
Acuff, Roy, 139, 239, 255
Adams, Faye, 247
Adkins, Hasil, 262
"Africa Talks to You 'The Asphalt
    Jungle'," 73
Agnew, Spiro, 118
Ain't But the One Way, 213
"Ain't Got No Home," 196
"Ain't No More Cane," 193
"Ain't That a Lot of Love," 197
"Ain't That Peculiar," 194
Akers, Garfield, 190
Ali, Muhammad, 68
Alk, Howard, 206
All About Elvis (Worth and Tamerius),
    248
"All Along the Watchtower," 34, 209
"All American Boy, The," 250
All Day Music, 223
*All God's Dangers: The Life of Nate
    Shaw*, 130
"All My Trials," 124
"All Shook Up," 18, 146, 148, 242, 247
*All Shook Up: Elvis Day by Day,
    1954–1977*, 250

All-Time Greatest Hits of Roy Orbison, 260
Allen, Rusty, 212
Allen, Steve, 169
Allman, Duane, 34
Allman Brothers, 146n, 162, 257
"Almost Grown," 203
Aloha (Dutch paper), 199
Aloha (LP), 247
Aloha from Elvis in Hawaii, 136n
Aloha from Hawaii via Satellite, 247
"America," 105
"American Bandstand," 219
American Son, 198
"American Trilogy," 124, 198, 247
Ames Brothers, 237
"Angel of the Morning," 242
Anthology (M. Gaye), 223
Anthology (Sly and the Family Stone),
    213
Anthology (Temptations), 222, 223
*Anthology of American Folk Music:
    Volume One: Ballads*, 208, 214, 219
    Volume Three: The Songs, 195–6
"Any Day," 34
"Any Day Now," 246
Any Old Way You Choose It (Christgau),
    249
"Anyway You Want Me," 168n, 242
"Appeal, The," 220

Archibald, 219

"Are You Lonesome To-night?," 235

Are You Lonesome Tonight? The Untold Story of Elvis Presley's One True Love—and the Child He Never Knew (de Barbin and Maters), 251

Armstrong, Louis, 130, 255

Arnold, Eddy, 246

Arnold, Kokomo, 149, 151, 238

Aronowitz, Al, 213

Arthur Crudup: Father of Rock and Roll, 237

"Arthur Godfrey's Talent Scouts," 240

Arthur or, The Decline and Fall of the British Empire, 112, 234

Association, 48

Atkins, Chet, 242

Atkins, John, 255

"Auld Lang Syne," 196

Autumn Records, 68, 211

Avalon, 230

Avedon, Richard, 90, 212

Awakenings, 230

Awopbopaloobop Alopbamboom (Cohn), 249

"Baby Don't Look Down," 226

Baby Don't You Do It (Don't Break My Heart)," 59, 194

"Baby Let Me Bang Your Box," 136n

"Baby, Let Me Follow You Down," 198

"Baby Let's Play House," 146, 157–8, 160, 161, 238

"Baby, What You Want Me to Do," 245

Bacharach, Burt, 246

"Back Door Man," 222

"Back in the U.S.A.," 20

Back on the Right Track, 213

"Back Stabbers," 80, 81, 87, 110, 223, 224

Back Stabbers, 223

"Back to Memphis," 194

"Back 2 the Base," 250

Baez, Joan, 193

Bagneris, Vernel, 217

Baker, Laverne, 233

"Ballad of a Thin Man," 92, 206, 207

"Ballad of Caryl Chessman, The," 203

Band, 4, 5, 39–64, 115, 138, 182, 187, 192–210, 226
    The Band, 46, 53–7, 60, 193, 196, 197, 199, 208
    before *Music from Big Pink*, 40–45, 201–8
    Cahoots, 46, 59–60, 195, 212
    with Dylan, 44, 45, 46n, 47, 64, 193, 196, 197, 198, 199, 204, 210

Moondog Matinee, 46–7, 62, 63, 196–7

Music from Big Pink, 40, 46–53, 57, 60, 192–3, 203, 208

Rock of Ages, 60, 61, 195–6

Stage Fright, 46, 58–9, 60, 61, 193–4, 198, 199

Bangs, Lester, 252–3, 254

"Barrister Pardon," 220

Basement Tapes, The, 193, 207–8

"Battle Hymn of the Republic, The," 124

"Be My Baby," 193

Be True to Your School, 233

Beach Boys, 48, 103, 212, 232–3

Beach Boys/Brian Wilson Rarities, 233

Beach Boys Party!, 233

Beale Black & Blue (Mckee and Chisnall), 258n

"Beale Street Remembered," 216

Beale Streeters, 202

Beatles, 40, 43, 44, 48, 69, 70, 72, 79, 97–8, 107, 111, 126, 160, 177, 233, 237n

Beau Brummels, 221

Beefheart, Captain, 191

"Beehive State, The," 227

Before the Flood, 209

"Behind Closed Doors," 154, 256

Bell, Thom, 87

Belle Album, The, 224

Benton Records, 183

Berigan, Bunny, 238

Bernero, Johnny, 237n, 260

Berry, Chuck, 20, 41, 67, 78, 115, 139, 144, 191, 194, 201, 203, 221, 240, 247

Berry, Richard, 155–6, 257, 258

"Bessie," 201

"Bessie Smith," 193

Best of Bobby "Blue" Bland, The, 202

Best of Bobby "Blue" Bland, Vol. 2, The, 202

Best of Charlie Rich, The, 256

Best of Dolly Parton, The, 257

Best of Elmore James, The, 189

Best of Jackie DeShannon, The, 227

Best of Jerry Butler, The, 222

Best of Junior Parker, The, 202

Best of Louie, Louie, The, 257

Best of Louie, Louie, Volume 2, The, 257

Best of Ronnie Hawkins, The, 203

Best of Ronnie Hawkins and the Hawks, The, 203

Best of Sun Rockabilly, Vol. 1, The, 183

Best of the Band, The, 197

Best of the Beach Boys, Vol. 2, 233

Best of the Fleetwoods, 226

Best of the Kingsmen, 257
Best of Wilson Pickett, Vol. 2, The, 221
Best Years, The, 256
"Beyond the Reef," 247
"Big Bad Blues," 260
"Big Bad Twist," 201n
"Big Boss Man," 125, 245
"Big Break, The," 156, 257
"Big Legged Woman," 143, 261
Big Sleep, The, 102, 232
Bigfoot from Memphis, The, 259
"Biggest Night of Her Life, The," 227
Bill Monroe's 16 Greatest Hits, 237
Billboard, 116, 147, 148, 181, 187, 211, 229, 238, 247
Binder, Steve, 125, 245
Biograph, 204, 205
Biography of a Phantom (McCormick), 185
Black, Bill, 141, 142, 149, 158, 237, 237n, 242
Black & Blues, 238
Black Culture and Black Consciousness (Levine), 216
Black Flag, 257
Black Ivory Productions, 225
"Black Jack David," 262
"Black Mare Blues," 191
Black Panther Party, 79, 92–3, 94n, 134n, 212
Blackwood Brothers, 139
Bland, Bobby "Blue," 19, 42, 43, 62, 157, 187, 196, 202
Blaze, 229
Blind Boy Grunt & the Hawks: The Basement Tapes, Volume One, 193
Blind Boy Grunt & the Hawks: The Basement Tapes, Volume Two, 193
Blonde on Blonde, 198, 204, 207, 208
"Bloody Bones," 257
Blowin' Your Mind, 72
Blue Angel, 100–101
"Blue Christmas," 126, 243, 246
"Blue Christmas (Without Elvis)," 250
Blues Classics, 183
Blue Hawaii, 170, 235, 244
"Blue Moon," 168, 238
"Blue Moon of Kentucky," 164–5, 237, 238
"Blue Sky," 162, 257
"Blue Suede Shoes," 53, 136, 240, 241, 260
Blue Velvet, 261
Blue Velvets, 34
"Blue Yodel No. 1," 255
"Blue Yodel No. 9," 255
"Bluebirds over the Mountain," 233
Blues Consolidated, 202

Blues for Mr Crump, 202
Blues in the Mississippi Night, 190, 219
Blues Line: A Collection of Lyrics from Leadbelly to Muddy Waters, The, 191
Blues That Made the Roosters Dance, 183
Bob Wills Anthology, The, 238
Bobby Marchan: Golden Classics, 222
BoDeans, 199
Boggs, Dock, 153
Bono, 261
"Boogaloosa Woman," 191
"Book of Love," 119
Booker T. & the MGs, 198
Boone, Pat, 226, 240
Booth, Stanley, 24, 139–40, 159, 191, 248
bootleg series, volumes 1–3, the, 186, 205, 208
"Boppin' the Blues," 260
Born Again, 119, 230–31
"Born to Lose," 109
"Bourgeois Blues," 222
Bowker, Gordon, 242
Bragg, Johnny, 237
"Brain Cloudy Blues," 149, 238
"Brave and Strong," 73
Brenston, Jackie, 259
"Bridge Over Troubled Water," 246
Brighter Side of Darkness, 87, 224
Bristol Sessions, 254
Brock, Van K., 252
Brooks, Harvey, 204
Broonzy, Big Bill, 139, 190, 205
"Brother Louie," 156, 257
Brothers and Sisters, 257
Brown, Charles, 248
Brown, James, 73, 213, 247
Brown, Rap, 68
Brown, Richard "Rabbit," 195–6
brown, Roy, 148, 202, 237, 239
Brown, Ruth, 217
Brown, Willie, 188
"Brown-Eyed Handsome Man," 221
Buchanan, Roy, 42
Buckingham, Lindsey, 230
Burbank Sessions, The, 245
Burgess, Sonny, 143, 263
Burleson, Paul, 262
"Burn On," 100, 113, 228
Burnette, Billy Joe, 250
Burnette, Johnny, 144
"Burning Love," 148, 247
Burton, James, 42
Buster, Prince, 220, 221
Butler, Jerry, 81n, 222
Butterfield, Paul, 197, 198
    Blues Band, 43, 204
Byrds, 207

"C. V. Wine Blues," 259
Caboots, 46, 59–60, 195, 197, 212
"Caledonia Mission," 46, 50
"California Blues," 255
"California Girls," 233
Call Me, 223
Calt, Stephen, 186
"Can the Circle Be Unbroken," 255
"Can *You* Please Crawl Out Your Window," 204
Canadian Squires, 44, 203
"Canned Heat Blues," 221
"Can't Find Time to Pray," 259
"Can't Help Falling in Love," 174, 235, 244
Capitol Records, 195
"Caravan," 198
Carl Perkins, 260
Carl Parkins — The Sun Years, 260
Carny, 198
"Caroline," 232
Carr, Leroy, 184
Carson, Tom, 250
Carter, A. P., 172, 254
Carter, Fred, Jr., 201
Carter, Jimmy, 197, 252
Carter, "Mother" Maybelle, 172, 254–5
Carter, Sarah, 254
Carter Family, 17, 130, 139, 171, 172, 173, 238, 254–6
"Carter Family, The," 255
Cash, Johnny, 66, 143, 144, 201n, 207, 239
Cash, W. J., 131–2, 133, 136, 150
Cashbox, 147
"Casual Love Affair," 236
Catskills, 207
Cavett, Dick, 1–3
"Cease to Exist," 233
"Celebrated Walking Blues, The," 188
"Celluloid Heroes," 234
Chandler, Raymond, 96–7, 102, 115, 192, 232, 233
"Change Is Gonna Come, A," 62
"Change Your Way," 230
Charles, Bobby, 197
Charles, Ray, 43, 109, 202, 242, 255
Charlie Patton: Founder of the Delta Blues 191
Charters, Sam, 190
Chase, Chevy, 230
Chess Box, The, 188, 221
Chess Records, 14, 189, 201n, 258
"Chest Fever," 46, 49, 50, 195, 196
Chi-Lites, 80, 81–2, 87, 223, 224
Chi-Lites' Greatest Hits, The, 223, 224
Chicago Blues: The Beginning, 189

Chicago/The Blues/Today!, 189
Chisenall, Fred, 258n
"Choice of Colors," 223
Christgau, Robert, 110, 209, 247, 249
"Christmas Time Again," 182
Chuck Berry's Golden Decade, Vol. I, 221
Cinderella, 237, 239
Circus Pinups, 249
Clapton, Eric, 27, 34–5, 187, 188, 189, 197
Clark, Dick, 219, 220
Clash, 221
Classic Jerry Lee Lewis, 261
Cleaver, Eldridge, 92, 93, 94, 94n, 224
Cleaver, Kathleen, 229
Cleopatra Jones, 82
Cline, Patsy, 17
Clinton, George, 213
"Cloud Nine," 222
Clovers, 203
"C'mon and Swim," 211
Coal Miner's Daughter, 198
Coasters, 48, 155–6, 195, 210, 212, 222, 257
Coasters — The Early Years, The, 212, 257
Cochran, Eddie, 144, 263
Cohen, Leonard, 101
Cohn, Nik, 122, 249, 253
"Coldest Day of My Life, The," 81, 224
Collins, Judy, 227
Color of Money, The, 198
Colson, Charles, 224
Columbia Records, 153, 183, 184, 186, 187, 188, 201n
"Come on in My Kitchen," 27, 33, 184
"Come Softly To Me," 226
Como, Perry, 157
Complete Buddy Holly, The, 238
Complete Elvis, The, 248, 252
Complete Robert Johnson: A Man and His Music, The, 184–5, 186–7
Complete Sun Sessions, The, 236, 238, 239
Compton, Richard, 232
Confidential, 74
Connery, Sean, 82
Consuls, 41n
Continentals, 210
Cooder, Ry, 185, 187
Cooke, Sam, 70
"Cool Drink of Water Blues," 202
Cooley, Al, 250
Cop Rock, 230
Coppock, Paul, 215
Coppola, Francis, 82
Cornelias Van Kujik, Andreas. *See* Parker, Col. Tom

Cortez, Diego, 251
Costello, Elvis, 118, 261
Cotton, James, 259
"Cottonfield Blues," 190
Country Blues Encores, 190
Country Blues—The First Generation, 196
"Country Boy," 226
Country: Living Legends and Dying Metaphors in America's Biggest Music (Tosches), 258n
Country Music, 145n
Crackers, 43–4, 207
Cramer, Floyd, 242
"Crawling Kingsnake," 221
Cream, 184, 188
Credibility Gap, 225
Creedence Clearwater Revival, 43, 211
Creem, 199, 248, 251
Crosby, Bing, 184, 226, 239
Crossroads (film), 185
"Crossroads," 25, 188
"Crossroads Blues," 21, 184
Crouse, Timothy, 212
Crudup, Arthur "Big Boy," 147, 155, 157, 197, 237
"Crying in the Chapel," 244
Cunningham, Buddy, 237
Curtis, King, 68, 195

Dalhart, Vernon, 229
Dance to the Music, 211
"Dance to the Music," 70, 211, 212
"Dancing in the Street," 222
Daniel, Peter, 229
"Daniel and the Sacred Harp," 59
Danko, Rick, 40–64, 194, 195, 198, 199, 208
    before The Band, 40–44, 201, 203, 206, 207, 208
    Music from Big Pink and, 46, 46n
Darin, Bobby, 228
Davies, Ray, 111–12, 233–4
Davis, Luther, 84
"Davy the Fat Boy," 100, 114, 227
Day, Doris, 90, 213
Day of the Locust, 102, 232
de Barbin, Lucy, 251
de Lyon, Sam, 216
Dead Elvis: A Chronicle of Cultural Obsession, 254
"Dead Man's Curve," 232
"Dead on Arrival," 250
Dean, Charles, and the Rondells, 183
"Death or Glory," 221
"Debutante Ball, The," 226
"Deck of Cards," 211

Deep Blues (Palmer), 185, 191, 258n
"Deep Elem Blues," 143, 261
Deep'n As It Come: The 1927 Mississippi Flood (Daniel), 229
Delta Blues, 184
Delta Blues—Vol. 1, 191
Delta Rhythm Kings, 259
Democratic Visas (Whitman), 177
DeShannon, Jackie, 226
"Desolation Row," 100
"Destruction," 259
Detroit 9000, 82
Devil Got My Woman, 191
"Devil Got My Woman," 184, 190
Diamond, Neil, 197
"Diamonds in the Rough," 255
Dickinson, Jim, 258
"Did He Call Today, Mama," 237
Diddley, Bo, 41, 43, 67, 193, 211
Dill, Danny, 192
Dion, 27
"Dirty, Dirty Feeling," 244
Dixiana Moon (Fox), 253–4
"Dixie," 124
"Dixie Flyer," 230–31
"Dixie Fred," 260
"Dizzy Miss Lizzy," 43
Dr. John, 197, 198, 219
Dr. Ross, 141
Doctorow, E. L., 230
Dogg, Swamp, 223
"Domino," 260
Domino, Fats, 41, 99, 143, 183, 203, 230, 231
Dominos, 240
Donahue, Tom, 68, 69, 211
"Done Somebody Wrong," 189
"Don't," 168n
"Don't Be Cruel," 146, 234, 240, 241, 247
"Don't Call Me Nigger, Whitey (Don't Call Me Whitey, Nigger)," 71
"Don't Do It," 196
"Don't Forbid Me," 240
Don't Look Back, 206
Don't Put No Headstone on My Grave, 256
"Don't Ya Tell Henry," 193
Doobie Brothers, 227
Dorsey, Thomas A., 235n
Down Home Music, 182n, 183
"Down in the Alley," 203
"Down in the Bottom," 202
"Down in the Congo," 259
Down on Stovall's Plantation, 188
Drifters, 81, 201, 210, 243, 244
Driggs, Frank, 186
"Drinkin' Wine Spo-Dee-O-Dee," 157, 260, 261, 263

Drop Down Mama, 189
Duke Records, 202
Duncan, Tommy, 149, 156
Dundy, Elaine, 252
Dunleavy, Steve, 251
Durden-Smith, Jo, 212
"Dust My Broom," 189
Dusty in Memphis, 231
Dylan, Bob, 13, 15, 34, 48, 68, 69, 75, 92, 100, 115, 116, 135, 153, 160, 175, 186, 197, 198, 199, 244, 246, 253
   The Band and, 44, 45, 46*n*, 47, 64, 192, 193, 196, 199, 204–10
   Blonde on Blonde, 198, 204, 207, 208
   John Wesley Harding, 21, 72, 208, 209
"Dynaflow," 189

Eagles, 228, 230, 233, 238
Early San Francisco, 211
"Earth Angel," 243
Earth, Wind & Fire, 214
Eat a Peach, 257
"Eat the Document," 206–7
Eckstine, Billy, 238
Edwards, Jonathan, 174
"Eek-a-Bo-Statik," 214
"Eight Days a Week," 98
Electric Spanking of War Babies, The, 213
Ellison, Harlan, 253
"Elmo James," 189
Elivs, 242
Elvis (Goldman), 251
Elvis (Hopkins), 248
Elvis—A Golden Celebration, 240, 241, 243
Elvis: A Legendary Performer, Vol. 1, 234–5
Elvis and Gladys (Dundy), 252
"Elvis and the A-Bomb," 248
Elvis Aron Presley, 241, 245, 247
Elvis as Recorded at Madison Square Garden, 247
Elvis' Christmas Album, 243
Elvis '56: In the Beginning, 240, 241, 251
Elvis for Everyone, 244
Elvis' Gold Records, Vol. 4, 244
Elvis' Golden Records, 242
Elvis' Golden Records, Vol. 3, 244
Elvis' Greatest Shit, 244–5
Elvis: His Life from A to Z (Worth and Tamerius), 248
Elvis: Images and Fancies, 252
Elvis is Back, 243, 244, 246
Elvis on Tour, 169*n*, 174
Elvis: One Night with You, 245

"Elvis, or the Ironies of a Southern Identity," 252
Elvis Presley, 238, 242
"Elvis Presley," 249
"Elvis Presley: Aging Rock," 249
"Elvis Presley and the American Dream," 249
Elvis Presley: King of Kings, 250
Elvis, Scotty and Bill: The First Year, 239
Elvis Sings Burning Love and Hits From His Movies, Vol. 2, 247
Elvis Sings the Wonderful World of Christmas, 248
Elvis: The Beginning Years, 239
Elvis: The Final Years (Hopkins), 248
Elvis: The Great Performances, 236
"Elvis: The New Deal Origins of Rock 'n' Roll," 252
Elvis Today, 247
"Elvis TV Special," 125–7, 245
Elvis TV Special, 245, 246
Elvis: What Happened? (West et al.), 250–51, 252–3
Elvis Years, The (Cohn), 249
Emerson, Billy "The Kid," 141, 239, 259
Emerson, Ralph Waldo, 121
"Endless Highway," 209
Epic Records, 212, 213, 256
Errico, Gregg, 211, 212
"Esau Smith: The Hairy and the Smooth," 253
Escott, Colin, 258*n*
Essential Elvis Presley, 243
Evans, Gil, 199
Evans, James, 200
"Even the Birds Were Blue," 191
"Evening with Sly Stone," 215
"Every Man a King," 228
"Everybody Is a Star," 71, 72, 76, 91, 94, 212
"Everybody Is a Star: The Travels of Sylvester Stewart" (Fong-Torres), 210
"Everyday People," 70, 90, 91, 211, 222
Evil, 201
Excello Records, 158
Exile on Main Street, 34, 80, 188

Face to Face, 234
"Fallen Angel," 199
"Fame and Fortune," 168*n*, 244
Family, The (Sanders), 233
"Family Affair," 73, 76–7, 212
"Family Again," 213
Famous Carter Family, The, 238, 255

Famous Isley Brothers Twisting and Shouting, The, 220
F&L records, 182
Farewell, My Lovely, 102, 232
"Farther Up the Road," 43, 202, 203
Fascination Records, 201*n*
Feathers, Charlie, 144, 238, 262
Feel Like Going Home (Guralnick), 191, 256
"Feel Like Going Home," 188
"Ferdinand the Imposter," 193, 226
Fernwood Records, 260
Fiedler, Leslie, 5, 89, 97
50,000,000 Elvis Fans Can't Be Wrong—Elvis' Gold Records, Vol. 2, 243
"Fingertips," 70
First Recordings, The, 256
Fisher, Eddie, 238
Fisher, Ella Scott, 214
Fisher, Sonny, 262
"Fishtail," 189
Fitzgerald, Ella, 236
Fitzgerald, F. Scott, 20, 23–4, 30
Five Beats Behind Bars, 259
Fleetwood Mac, 189
Fleetwoods, 226
"Flip, Flop and Fly," 240
Flippo, Chet, 255–6
Floyd, Harmonica Frank, 4–5, 11–18, 34, 47, 135, 146*n*, 177, 182–3, 184, 185, 259
  Sam Phillips and, 11–12, 17, 18, 182
"Flying Saucers Rock 'n' Roll," 260
Fogerty, John, 43
Foley, Red, 192, 235*n*, 239
Fong-Torres, Ben, 191–2, 199, 210, 212, 255
Fontana, D. J., 237*n*, 241, 242, 245
Fool, 247
"Fool," 168*n*
"(For God's Sake) Give More Power to the People," 81, 223
For the Lonely: A Roy Orbison Anthology, 1956–1965, 260
"For the Love of Money," 224
Forbes, 249
Ford, John, 110, 239
Fortunate Son (Marsh), 254
"Forty Days," 201
40 Greatest Hits, 256
Foster, Stephen, 261
"409," 233
Four Tops, 59, 87, 194, 224
"Four Until Late," 25
Fox, William Price, 253–4
"Framed," 222
Franciosa, Tony, 84–5, 86

Franklin, Aretha, 69
Franklin, Irma, 226
"Freddie's Dead," 80, 223
"Free Advice," 211
Freed, Alan, 196, 200, 201, 242
Freeman, Bobby, 211
Freewheelin, 13
Fresh, 90, 91, 92, 212–13, 224
"Friday Night," 226
Friedman, Tracy, 232
Frizzell, Lefty, 156, 192
"Froggy Went A-Courtin'," 208
From Elvis in Memphis, 127, 246
From Elvis Presley Boulevard, Memphis, Tennessee, 248
From Memphis to Vegas/From Vegas to Memphis, 246
Fully Realized, 256
Fulson, Lowell, 244
"Fun, Fun, Fun," 103
Fury Records, 200
Fusco, John, 185
"Future Blues," 188

Gabriel, Peter, 199
Gamble, Kenny, 86–7, 213
Garson, Marvin, 39
Gaye, Marvin, 48, 59, 80, 87, 194, 223, 224
"Genetic Method, The," 196
"Georgia on My Mind," 197
Georgia Tom and Friends, 1929/31, 235*n*
Georgia Tom Dorsey, 1928–1932: Come on Mama Do That Dance, 235*n*
"Get a Job," 70
"Get Up Jake," 47, 196
Get Yer Ya-Yas Out!, 188, 222
Get Your Ass in the Water and Swim Like Me!—Narrative Poetry from Black Oral Tradition, 221
"Get Your Rocks Off," 208
"Ghetto," 87
G.I. Blues, 166*n*, 235
Gibbons, Billy, 187
Gibbs, Georgia, 237
Gillett, Charlie, 159
"Gimme Shelter," 79
Girl Happy, 244
Gleason, Ralph J., 199, 206, 255
"Go Go Go," 260
"Go Go Liza Jane," 44, 203
"God Walks These Hills with Me," 192
Godard, Jean-Luc, 206
Godfather, The, 82, 102, 110
"God's Song (That's Why I Love Mankind)," 34, 100, 228

Goffin, Gerry, 226
"Goin' Away Walkin'," 14, 183
"Going Down Slow," 68, 202, 222
"Going to the River," 203
Golden Celebration, A, 245
"Golden Gridiron Boy," 226
Goldman, Albert, 244, 251
Goldmine, 232
Goldner, George, 200
"Gone and Left Me Blues," 262
"Gone Dead Train," 231
Good Old Boys, 116–18, 119, 228–9
Good Rockin' Blues, 237
"Good Rockin' Tonight," 146, 148,
    237
Good Rocking Tonight, 237, 239, 260,
    265
Good Rockin' Tonight: Sun Records and
    the Birth of Rock 'n' Roll, 258n
"Good Times," 214
Goodman, Benny, 238
"Gospel Ship," 255
Got My Own Bag of Tricks, 221
Graceland Enterprises, Inc., 249
Grady, Leigh, 250
Graham, Larry, 211, 212
"Grand Coulee Dam," 208
Gray, Glen, 238
Great Balls of Fire!, 262
Great Balls of Fire: The Uncensored Story
    of Jerry Lee Lewis (M. Lewis), 262
"Great Balls of Fire," 263–5
Great Gift Idea, A, 225
Great Lost Kinks Album, The, 234
"Great Medical Menagerist, The,"
    13–14, 182
Great Original Recordings of Harmonica
    Frank, The, 182, 259
"Great Pretender, The," 62
Great Society, 211
Great Twenty Eight, The, 221
Greatest Hits (Chi-Lites), 213–24
Greatest Hits (Fleetwoods), 226
Greatest Hits (Hot Chocolate), 257
Greatest Hits (Pickett), 222
Greatest Hits (Sly and the Family
    Stone), 212
Greatest Live Show on Earth, 261
Green, Al, 87, 223
Green, Peter, 189
Greenberg, Alan, 185
Greene, Bob, 257
Gregg, Bobby, 204
Gregory, Janice, 251–2
Gregory, Neal, 251–2
Grissim, John, 265
Grossman, Albert, 57
"Guitar Man," 125, 245

Gumbo, 219
"Guns of Brixton, The," 221
Gunter, Arthur, 158, 238
Gunter, Hardrock, 141
Guralnick, Peter, 185, 189, 191, 236,
    249, 256, 258n
Guthrie, Woody, 208

Haley, Bill, 201n
"Half a Man," 230
Hall, Tom T., 214
Hammond, John, Jr., 43, 203–4
Hampton, Lionel, 237
"Hank Williams, Roy Acuff, and Then
    God!," 255
Hank Williams (album series), 256
"Harbor Lights," 239
Harder They Come, The, 161
Hare, Pat, 259
Harmonica Frank, See Floyd,
    Harmonica Frank
Harmonica Frank Floyd, 183
Harper's Bizarre, 226
Harris, Wynonie, 148, 237
Harrison, George, 261
Harrison, Wilbert, 200, 220
Harvey, Steve, 232
"Have a Party," 203
"Have You Seen Her," 81, 224
Having Fun with Elvis on Stage, 247
Hawk, The, 203
Hawkins, Coleman, 218
Hawkins, Martin, 258n
Hawkins, Ronnie, 41–3, 197, 198,
    200–204
Hawks, 41–3, 58, 193, 196, 200–204,
    204–8
Hawks, Howard, 110
Hawthorne, Nathaniel, 103
"He Don't Love You," 203
He May Be Dead, But He's Still Elvis, 249
"Hear that Long Snake Moan," 191
Heard Ya Missed Me, Well I'm Back, 213
"Heartbreak Hotel," 234, 240, 245
"Heavenly Angel," 211
Hebler, Dave, 251
Hellfire: The Jerry Lee Lewis Story
    (Tosches), 261
"Hellhound on My Trail," 25, 35, 184,
    235
"Hellhound's Trail: Following Robert
    Johnson, The," 189
Helm, Levon, 13, 40–64, 193, 195,
    197, 198, 199, 200, 201, 203, 208,
    209, 240
    before The Band, 40–44, 199, 201,
    203, 207
    Music from Big Pink and, 49, 53

"Help Me with My Broken Heart," 210, 211
"Helter Skelter," 107
Henderson, Fletcher, 218
Henderson, William McCranor, 253
Hendrix, Jimi, 27, 68, 75, 78, 220, 242
Henley, Don, 230, 250
Henry, Clarence "Frogman," 13, 196
Heritage, 214
"Heroin," 104
"(He's) The Great Imposter," 226
"Hey Bo Diddley," 200
"Hey Boba Lu," 41–2, 201, 203
"Hey Good Lookin'," 132
Higgins, Joe, and the Honeydrippers, 237
High Energy, 213
High on You, 213
"High Y'All," 213
"Higher Ground," 224
Highway 61 Revisited, 204
"Highway 61 Revisited," 208, 209, 253
Hill, King Solomon, 231
Hillbilly Cat, The, 236
Hines, Earl, 255
His Hand in Mine, 244
Hit Man, 82
"Hold Your Head High," 227
Holiday, Billie, 225
Holly, Buddy, 13, 144, 151, 157, 238, 260, 263
"Hongry," 222
Honkies, 207
"Honky Tonkin'," 132
Hooker, John Lee, 221
Hopkins, Jerry, 149, 248
Horning, Ron, 199–200
Horstman, Dorothy, 192
Hot Chocolate, 257
"Hot Fun in the Summertime," 212
Hot Shot Love, 141, 259
"Hot Sun in the Summertime," 70
"Hound Dog," 18, 146, 150, 155, 158, 240, 242
"Hound Dog, to the Manor Born, A," 248
House, Son, 21, 23, 26, 28, 146n, 186, 190
"How Do You Think I Feel," 239
How Great Thou Art, 244
"How Great Thou Art," 174
"How Great Thou Art: Elvis in the Promised Land," 254
"How Long Will We Care?," 254
"How Many More Years," 42, 201
Howlin' Wolf, 202, 222
Howlin' Wolf Masterworks, Vol. 1, The, 259

Hudson, Garth, 40–64, 138, 194, 196, 197, 198, 199, 208, 209
  before The Band, 40–44, 201, 201n, 203, 205, 207
  Music from Big Pink and, 48, 49
Huey Lewis and the News, 199
Huff, Leon, 86–7
Hung Down Head, 244
Hunter, Ivory Joe, 238, 247
"Hurt," 248
Hurt, Mississippi John, 66–7, 214, 219
Hustler's Convention, 225–6
Hutchins, Paul, 201n
Hutchinson, Frank, 218–19
Hyland, Brian, 150n–51n

"I Ain't Got Nobody," 211
"I Asked for Water," 202
"I Believe I'll Dust My Broom," 184
"I Can Help," 248
"I Can See Clearly Now," 80, 223
I Can Tell, 203
"I Can't Turn You Loose," 211
"I Don't Believe You (She Acts Like We Never Have Met)," 205
"I Don't Care If the Sun Don't Shine," 163, 164, 237
"(I Don't Want To) Hang Up My Rock and Roll Shoes," 61, 195
"I Don't Want to Hear It Anymore," 231
"I Feel Like Going Home," 256
"I Feel So Bad," 244
"I Forgot to Remember to Forget," 163, 238
"I Get Around," 103, 233
"I Got a Woman," 242
"I Got You, Babe," 193
"I Guess I'll Be," 210
I Hear You Knocking, 243
"I Heard It Through the Grapevine," 48, 247
"I Just Learned How to Swim," 211
"I Love L.A.," 230, 231
"I Love to See You Smile," 231
"I Love You Because," 163–4, 234, 238
"I Pity the Fool," 187
"I Shall Be Free," 13
"I Shall Be Released," 46n 207, 208
"I Still Miss Someone," 207
"I Think It's Going to Rain Today," 227
"I Wanna Be Your Lover," 205
"I Want to Be a Single Girl Again," 193
"I Want to Play House with You," 238
"I Want to Take You Higher," 91, 212, 213
"I Want You," 205

"I Was the One," 168n, 240
"I Will Be true," 247
Ice-T., 221
"If I Can Dream," 168n, 245, 246
"If I Had Possession Over Judgment Day," 21, 183
"If You Want Me to Stay," 90, 212
Iggy and the Stooges, 258
"I'll Be Around," 87
"I'll Hold You in My Heart (Till I Can Hold You in My Arms)," 246
"I'll Never Let You Go (Little Darlin')," 164, 238
"I'll Never Stand in Your Way," 237, 237n
"I'll Take Care of You," 187
"I'll Take You There," 80, 223
"I'm Gonna Murder My Baby," 259
"I'm in Love Again," 231
"I'm Just a Fool," 210
"I'm Left, You're Right, She's Gone," 167–8, 238
"I'm Not Like Everybody Else," 111, 234
"I'm Not There (I'm Gone)," 208
"Images of Elvis, the South, and America," 252
Impressions, 223
"In Dreams," 260
"In Germany Before the War," 229
In My Life, 227
"In Praise of Elvis Presley," 248
Incredible and Unpredictable Sly and the Family Stone, The, 212
Ink Spots, 236, 237
"Inner City Blues," 80, 223
Innervisions, 225
Invasion of the Elvis Zombies (Panter), 252
Irving, John, 229
"Is It So Strange," 168n
"Is That All There Is," 232
Islands, 197
Isley Brothers, 220
Isley Brothers—The Complete UA Sessions, The, 220
It's Gonna Work Out Fine—The Best of the Sue Years, 220
"It's Money That I Love," 119, 230, 231
"It's Money That Matters," 231
"It's My Life, Baby," 202
"It's Now or Never," 244
"It's Only Make Believe," 41
It's Too Late to Stop Now (Landau), 248
"I've Been a Moonshiner," 186
"I've Been Loving You Too Long (To Stop Now)," 197
Ives, Charles, 227

Jackson, Bruce, 221
Jackson, George, 68, 74, 78, 79, 212
Jackson, Jonathan, 68
Jackson, 5, 71, 76
Jagger, Mick, 34, 67, 115, 160, 188
Jailhouse Rock, 243
"Jailhouse Rock," 159, 242, 245
Jailhouse Rock/Love in Las Vegas, 243
Jamerson, James, 194
James, Elmore, 188, 189
James, Harry, and His Royal Hawaiians, 239
James, Joni, 236
James, Skip, 21, 23, 26, 184, 190, 191, 266
"James Alley Blues," 195
Jan & Dean, 232
Jan & Dean Anthology Album, 232
Je-Wel Records, 260
Jefferson, Blind Lemon, 183, 229
Jefferson Airplane, 211
Jerry Lee Lewis Rocks! (Palmer), 261
Jerry Lee Lewis—The Sun Years, 261
Jessie, Young, 201
Jet, 213
"Jimmie Rodgers—Father of Country Music Festival," 255
Jimmie Rodgers: The Life and Times of America's Blue Yodeler (Porterfield), 255
"Jimmy Jazz," 221
John Mayall's Bluesbreakers Featuring Eric Clapton, 188
John Wesley Harding, 21, 72, 208, 209
"Johnny B. Goode," 139
Johnny Burnette's Rock and Roll Trio and Their Rockin' Friends from Memphis, 262
Johnny Shines, 189
Johnny Shines and Robert Lockwood: Dust My Broom, 189
Johnny Shines Band, The, 189
Johnson, Howard, 195
Johnson, Jack, 68
Johnson, Lonnie, 139, 183, 239
Johnson, Lyndon B., 14–16
Johnson, Robert, 4–5, 19–35, 47, 50, 68, 131, 171, 175, 183–90, 191, 197, 235
    death of, 20, 186
    influence of, 27–8, 34
    postwar blues and, 188–90
    rock 'n' roll and, 187–8
Johnson, Tommy, 21, 67, 190, 191, 202, 212
Johnson, Willie, 42, 201, 259, 262
"Joliet Blues," 189

"Jolly Coppers on Parade," 229
Jolson, Al, 261
Jones, Mickey, 204, 206
Jones, Rickie Lee, 230
Jones, Will "Pop," 200, 201
Jordanaires, 242
Journal of Country Music, 250
"Judge Dread," 220
"Judge Dread Dance," 220
*Judge Dread Featuring Buster
    Prince — Jamaica's Pride*, 220
Jungle Bush Beaters, 41n, 42
Jungle Fever, 262
Junior Parker, 202, 238
"Just Because," 163, 164, 238
"Just Like Tom Thumb's Blues," 205
Just Me and My Guitar, 256
"Just One Smile," 231
"Just Rollin' Along," 260

Kael, Pauline, 97, 193
"Kansas City," 200
Kapers, 41n
Kasper, Edward, 196
"Kassie Jones," 214
"Katie's Been Gone," 193
"Kaw-Liga," 131
Kaye, Sammy, 239
"K.C. Loving," 200
K-Doe, Ernie, 202
"Keep on the Sunny Side," 255
Keep Your Hands Off it!, 261
"Keeper of the Castle," 87, 224
Keisker, Marion, 147, 236
Kelly, Paul, 81n, 222
Kennedy, Jerry, 256, 261
Kennon, Larry, 182
Kenny, Bill, 237
Kenton, Stan, 143
Kermode, Frank, 88
Kiers, Roelof, 199
Kiersh, Edward, 214
Killer: 1963–1968, The, 261
King, B. B., 141, 259
King, Carole, 226
King, Cash, 259
King, Martin Luther, Jr., 78, 222, 225, 246
King Creole, 243
"King Creole," 159
King Death (Cohn), 253
King-Federal Rockabillys 262
"King Harvest (Has Surely Come),"
    55, 56, 57, 138
"King Kong Kitchie Kitchie
    Ki-Me-O," 208
King of Comedy, The, 198
King of the Delta Blues Singers, 235

King of the Delta Blues Singers, Vol. II,
    184
King Pin, 225
Kingsmen, 156, 257
Kink Kronikles, 234
Kinks, 111, 112, 213, 233–4
Kinks' Greatest Hits, 234
"Knockin' Lost John," 197
Knockin' on Dylan's Door, 199
Kokomo Arnold/Peetie Wheatstraw, 238
Kooper, Al, 48, 192, 204
Kordosh, John, 251

"Lady in Black, The," 192
Lady Sings the Blues, 82, 225
Laine, Frankie, 226
Lamb, Bob, 236
Lambert and Potter, 87
Land of Dreams, 230–31
Landau, Jon, 248–9
Langbroek, Hans, 236
Lanza, Mario, 139
Last Night's Dream, 189
Last Poets, 225
*Last Train to Memphis: The Rise of Elvis
    Presley* (Guralnick), 249
Last Waltz, The (film), 198
Last Waltz, The (album), 198, 199
Last Waltz concert, 197, 198
Latura, "Wild Bill," 216–17
La Vere, Steve, 182, 185, 186, 187
Law, Don, 26
"Lawdy, Miss Clawdy," 122, 219, 246
Lawrence, D. H., 91, 163
"Layla," 34–5
Leadbelly, 216
"Lead Me On," 19, 187
Leary, Timothy, 94n
"Leave Me Alone," 44, 203, 226
Led Zeppelin, 229
Lee, Curtis, 206
Lee, James, Jr., 216
Lee, James, Sr., 215
Lee, Peggy, 232
Lee, Samuel Stacker, 215–16
Leek, Edwin S., 236
*Legendary Sun Performers — Billy Lee
    Riley, The*, 260
*Legendary Sun Performers — Sonny
    Burgess, The*, 263
*Legendary Sun Performers — Warren
    Smith, The* 262
Leiber, Jerry, 155–6, 200, 212, 222,
    232, 243
Leimbacher, Ed, 242
Lennon, John, 43, 72
Leo, Malcolm, 240
Lesy, Michael, 251

"Let Him Run Wild," 233
Let It Bleed, 34, 187, 188, 222
"Let the Good Times Roll," 195
"Let's Burn Down the Cornfield," 228
"Let's Get It On," 224
"Let's Stay Together," 223
Let's Work Together, 220
Levine, Lawrence W., 216
Levon and the Hawks, 43–4, 53
Levon Helm, 98
Levon Helm and the RCO All-Stars, 198
Levy, Morris, 200
Lewis, Furry, 214, 216
Lewis, Jerry Lee, 11, 41, 61, 139, 141,
    143, 168–9, 182, 201, 203, 205,
    239–40, 260, 261–2, 263–4
Lewis, Linda Gail, 261
Lewis, Myra, 261, 262
Lewis, Smiley, 126, 243
Liberty Records, 226
Library of Congress, 188
Life, 211
Life and Times of Stagolee, The,
    217–18
"Life's Little Ups and Downs," 154,
    256
Lightnin' Rod, 225
"Like a Rolling Stone," 160, 206, 207
"Like a Rolling Stone, Again," 199
Lincoln, Abraham, 128, 129
"Lines in the Sand," 231
"Listen to the Lion," 153
Little Anthony, 210
"Little Birdie," 193
"Little Boy Blue," 184
Little Criminals, 116, 118, 229
Little Fine Healthy Thing, 239, 259
Little Junior's Blue Flames, 238
Little Milton, 259
"Little Moses," 255
"Little Red Rooster," 203
Little Richard, 1–3, 19, 34, 49, 58, 144,
    200, 240, 241
*Little Richard's Grooviest 17 Original
    Hits!*, 241
Little Sister, 213
"Little Sister," 244
"Little Wing," 75
"Livin' in a Dream," 197
Living Blues, 185
"Living for the City," 224
"Living Without You," 227
Lloyd Price's 16 Greatest Hits, 220
"Loan Me a Dime," 34
Lockwood, Robert Jr., 184, 188
"Lola," 112, 234
*Lola Versus Powerman and the
    Moneyground*, 112, 234

Lomax, Alan, 190–91
Lomax, John, 214
Lombardo, Guy, 239
London Calling, 221
London, Paul, and the Capers/Kapers,
    41*n*, 201*n*
"Lonely at the Top," 107, 228
Lonely Girl, 227
"Lonely Man, A," 81, 224
"Lonely Weekends," 256
Lonesome Drifter, 262
"Lonesome Suzie," 46
Long, Huey, 228, 229
Long, Shorty, 242
"Long Black Limousine," 146,
    161*n*–62*n*, 246
"Long Black Veil," 46, 192
"Long Distance Operator," 193
"Long Tall Mama Blues," 255
"Long Time Alone, A," 210, 211
Long Voyage Home, The, 239
Longet, Claudine, 226
"Look Out Cleveland," 56
"Look What You've Done for Me,"
    223
Lopez, Trini, 204
Los Lobos, 199
*Lost Highway: Journeys & Arrivals of
    American Musicians* (Guralnick),
    249, 256, 258*n*
"Louie Louie," 111, 156, 257–8
"Louisiana 1927," 228–9
Love in Vain (Greenberg), 185
"Love in Vain," 19, 33, 34, 184, 187,
    188
"Love Is Blind," 226
"Love Jones," 87, 224
"Love Me," 235, 241
"Love Me Like You Can," 200
Love Me Tender, 159, 234, 240,
    243
"Love Me Tender," 159, 234, 241
Love Story (Segal), 1, 2, 97
"Love Story," 227
"Love Train," 87, 223, 224
"Lovers by Night, Strangers by Day,"
    226
"Lovin' Up a Storm," 261
Loving You, 243
"Loving You," 159
"Loving You Is Sweeter Than Ever,"
    59, 194
"Lucinda," 228
"Lucky Old Sun, The," 109
Lydon, Michael, 260
Lydon, Susan, 114, 231
Lynch, David, 261
Lyons, Billy, 66, 215, 216

Ma Rainey's Black Bottom, 218
McCaskill, William, 215, 216
McCormick, Mack, 185, 186
McCulloh, Judith, 255
McDaniels, Gene, 226
MacDonald, Ross, 102, 232
McGhee, Brownie, 228
McGhee, Stick, 157
McGinnis, Wayne, 262
McIlwaine, Shields, 215–16
Mack, Lonnie, 42
Mckee, Margaret, 258n
McKee, Maria, 199
McPhatter, Clyde, 201
   and the Drifters, 240, 243
McVie, Christine, 230
McVoy, Carl, 263
Made in U.S.A., 233
"Maggie Campbell Blues," 190
Mailer, Norman, 15–16, 115
Malone, Bill C., 255
Malone, Mike, 217–18
"Mama Told Me Not to Come,"
   228
"Man Who Corrupted Hadleyburg,
   The," 61
Manfred Mann's Earth Band, 227
Manhattan Melodrama, 238
Mann, Manfred, 207
"Mannish Boy," 198
Mann, Carl, 263
Manson, Charles, 103, 233
Manuel, Richard, 40–64, 194, 197,
   202–3, 209
   before The Band, 40–44, 201, 204,
      205, 207, 208
   Moondog Matinee and, 62, 196
   Music from Big Pink and, 46, 48, 50,
      52, 53
   suicide of, 199, 200
Many New Sides of Charlie Rich, The,
   256
March, Little Peggy, 226
Marchan, Bobby, 68, 222
Marcus, Greil, 208, 235n, 250, 252
Marine, Gene, 92
Marsh, Dave, 91, 194, 220, 229, 252,
   254, 257
Martha and the Vandellas, 222
Martin, Dean, 139
Martin, Mary, 204
Martin, Steve, 230
Martini, Jerry, 211
"Mary Lou," 201
Masculin-Féminin, 206
"Matchbox," 260
Maters, Dary, 251
Mayall, John, 228

Maybe I'm Doing It Wrong, 232
"Maybe I'm Doing It Wrong," 228
Mayfield, Curtis, 80, 83, 83n, 223, 225
"Me and the Devil Blues," 22, 25–6,
   31, 33, 50, 184
Mello-Tones, 201n
Melody Maker, 185
Melville, Herman, 115, 123, 175
"Memo to My Son," 228
Memorial Album, 202
Memories of Christmas, 248
"Memphis," 193
Memphis and the Delta: The 1950s, 183
Memphis Days, 259
Memphis Down in Dixie (McIlwaine),
   215–16
Memphis Minnie, 229
Memphis *Press-Scimitar*, 148
Memphis Record, The, 246
Memphis Recording Service, 236
Memphis Rockin' Country, 237n, 260
Memphis Rocks the Country, 259–60
"Memphis to New Orleans," 183
"Merry Christmas, Baby," 248
Metallic 'KO 258
Meteor: Hillbilly Bop, Memphis Style,
   262
Mezzrow, Mezz, 157
Middle of Nowhere, The, 232
"Midnight Mover," 221
"Midnight Rambler," 222
"Midnight Train," 205
"Milk Cow Blues," 149, 238
"Milkcow Blues Boogie," 146, 146n,
   149–52, 159, 167, 238
Miller, Jim, 242, 249
Miller, Larry, 69
Miller, Perry, 24
Miller Sisters, 259
Million Dollar Quartet, 239, 246
"Milton Berle Show, The," 240
Mind of the South (Cash), 131–2
Mississippi Blues, 184
Mississippi Blues 1927–1940, The, 190
*Mississippi Blues: Transition, 1926–1937,
   The*, 190, 219
Mississippi Country Blues—Vol. 1 184
"Mississippi Flood, The," 229
Mississippi Sheiks, 183
"Mr. Blue," 226
Mr. Dynamo, 201
Misty, 250
Mitchell, Bobby, 69
Mitchell, Joni, 197
Mitchell, Willie, 87
"Mixed-Up Confusion," 13
"M'Lady," 91
Moanin' in the Moonlight, 201–2, 259

Modern, 258
Modern Screen, 134*n*
Mojo Man, 43, 203
Mojo Men, 211
Monarchs, 43
"Money Honey," 240
"Monkey Love," 182
Monotones, 48, 119
Monroe, Bill, 164, 237, 239
Monterey Pop Festival, 69
Moody Blue, 248
Moondog Matinee, 46–7, 62, 63, 196, 197
"Moondog Rock 'n' Roll Party," 196
Moore, Scotty, 149, 158, 165, 166, 237, 237*n*, 239, 242, 244, 245
   rockabilly records with Presley, 141, 142, 147, 237, 237*n*
Moore, William, 146*n*, 257
Morantz, Paul, 232
"More About John Henry," 214
Moreno, Rita, 1
"Morning Prayer," 191
Morrison, Van, 72, 153, 197, 198, 199
   and the Monarchs, 43
Moses, Mark, 252
"Most Beautiful Girl, The," 256
Mothers of Invention, 257
"Move It on Over," 132
"Moving Shadow of Richard Manuel, The," 199–200
Moynihan, Daniel Patrick, 87–8
"Muddy Water (A Mississippi Moan)," 229
Murray, Albert, 191
Muscle Shoals, 198
Music from Big Pink, 40, 46–53, 57, 60, 192–3, 208
Musician, 187, 252
"My Baby Is Gone," 168, 238
"My Baby Left me," 155, 237
"My Black Mama," 146*n*, 190
My Blue Ridge Mountain Boy, 257
"My Blue Ridge Mountain Boy," 256–7
"My Clinch Mountain Home," 255
"My Gal Is Red Hot," 41
"My Happiness," 236
"My Old Kentucky Home," 113–14, 228
My Rough and Rowdy Ways, 255
"My Way," 235
"My Yiddishe Mama," 136*n*
Myhre, John, 249
Myrrh Records, 224
Mystery Girl, 261
"Mystery Train," 159, 171–3, 196, 198, 238

Nash, Johnny, 80, 223
Nashville Teens, 260
Nation, 187
Natural, The, 230
Neill, Kenneth, 216
Nelson, Paul, 208
Nelson, Ricky, 42, 202–3, 247, 263
"Never Learn Not to Love," 233
Never No Mo' Blues, 255
New Frontier, 241
New Orleans Sessions, 219
"New Orleans Wins the War," 230–31
New West, 199
New York Times, The, 217
New York Times Magazine, The, 232
New Yorker, 89, 213
Newman, Alfred, 99, 227
Newman, Francisco, 66
Newman, Irving, 226
Newman, Lionel, 227
Newman, Randy, 4, 5, 13, 34, 96–119, 123, 224, 226–32, 233
   audience of, 98, 112–13, 116–19
   background of, 99, 226–7
   Born Again, 119, 230–31
   Good Old Boys, 116–18, 119, 228–9
   Land of Dreams 230–31
   Little Criminals, 116, 118, 229
   "Sail Away," 108–9, 111, 114, 224, 228
Newmark, Andy, 212
Newsday, 247
Newton, Huey, 92, 93, 94*n*
Nicol, Jimmy, 237*n*
Night Moves, 201
"Night They Drove Old Dixie Down, The," 55–6, 57, 193, 197, 198
"Night Train to Memphis," 239
Nighthawk Blues (Guralnick), 191
Nilsson, Harry, 231
Nilsson Sings Newman, 231
"992 Arguments," 87, 223
"19th Nervous Breakdown," 160
Nixon, Richard, 88, 89, 105, 118, 120*n*–21*n*, 154, 256
North Beach Records, 211
Northern Lights—Southern Cross, 197
"Notes for Review of Peter Guralnick's *Lost Highway*," 252
"(Now and Then There's) A Fool Such As I," 235
Nuggets, Vol. 7: Early San Francisco, 211
"Number One," 205

O'Bryant, Tilman, 218
"Obviously Fire Believers," 205

O'Connor, Sinéad, 199
"Odessa," 201
Oermann, Robert K., 250
"Oh Girl," 81, 224
O'Jays, 80, 81, 86–7, 110, 223, 224, 226
"Old Country Rock," 257
"Old Shep," 241
Oliver Paul, 191
Olympics, 210
"Omie Wise," 192
Omni-Americans: New Perspectives on Black Experience and American Culture, The (Murray), 191
"On Broadway," 81, 227
"On the Battlefield for My Lord," 210
"One Hand Loose," 262
One Million Dollar Quartet, The, 239–40
"One Night," 126, 127, 243, 246
"One Night of Sin," 126
"One of Us Must Know (Sooner or Later)," 204, 205
O'Neal, Ron, 84
"Only the Strong Survive," 81n, 222
"Only You," 260
"Ooby, Dooby, 260
"Orange Juice Blues (Blues for Breakfast)," 193
Orbison, Roy, 11, 143, 200, 260–61
Origin Jazz Library, 190
Original and Great Carter Family, The, 255
Original Hits and Midnight Demos 256
Original Meteor & Flair Sides, The, 189
Orioles, 237, 244
Otis, Johnny, 155, 157, 184
Out to Hunch, 262

Page, Patti, 237
Paget, Debra, 240
Palmer, Robert, 185, 191, 258n, 261
Panter, Gary, 252
"Pants," 230
"Papa Was a Rolling Stone," 80–81, 223
Paradise Hawaiian Style 244
"Paralyzed," 240
Parenthood, 231
Parker, Graham, 229
Parker, Junior, 42, 141, 171, 172, 173, 198, 202, 238, 239, 259
Parker, Col. Tom, 120n, 121, 125, 136n–7n, 145n, 157, 159, 236, 248, 249, 251, 254
Parks, Gordon, Jr., 83
Parks, Van Dyke, 227
Parliament-Funkadelic, 213
Parson, Bill, 250
Parton, Dolly, 137, 256–7

Patton, Charlie, 21, 191, 201
Paul Revere & the Raiders' Greatest Hits, 257
Paulini, Rudolf, 251
Paulman, Jimmy Ray "Luke", 42, 200, 201
Payne, Leon, 238
Payne, Uncle Silas, 11
Payne, Woody (pseud.), 187
"Peace in the Valley," 35, 235n, 243
Peer Ralph, 254
Penguins, 243
Penn, Irving, 195
Pennebaker, D. A., 206, 207
Performance, 231
Perkins, Carl, 11, 132, 133, 139, 141, 143, 144, 152, 201, 239, 240–41, 260
Peter, Paul & Mary, 207
Petty, Tom, 261
"Peyton Place," 226
Pharaohs, 257
Phillips, Sam, 13, 131, 157, 201, 202, 252, 258–61, 262, 263
    Harmonica Frank and, 11–12, 17, 18, 182
    Jerry Lee Lewis and, 263–5
    Elvis Presley and, 11, 18, 121, 141–2, 145–6, 147, 148, 156, 159, 160, 165, 166, 171, 172, 234, 236, 237, 239
    see also Sun Records
Phillips, Shawn, 105
Phillips International, 256
"Phonograph Blues," 23, 184
Photographing Children, 195
Piazza, Joey, 210
Pickett, Wilson, 67, 69, 82, 87, 221
Pied Pipers, 236
Pink Floyd, 199
Pinkston, Thomas, 215, 216
Planet Waves, 209
Plant, Robert, 187
Platters, 62, 260
"Play With Fire," 160
"Pledging My Love," 48, 248
"Poet," 74–5
"Political Science," 113, 228
Pomus, Doc, 201
"Pony Boy," 146n, 257
Poole, Charlie, 54
Pop Memories 1890–1954 (Whitburn), 181–2
Porterfield, Nolan, 255
"Positively Fourth Street," 204
"Possession Over Judgment Day," 185
Pratt, Linda Ray, 252

"Preaching Blues," 187
Precious Lord: New Recordings of the Great Gospel Songs of Thomas A. Dorsey, 235n
"Precious Lord," 235n
Presley, Elvis, 4, 5, 21, 43, 98, 116, 120–75, 177, 186, 198, 234–54
    after his death, 248–54
    ambition and talent of, 140, 141, 150, 158, 160, 162
    background of, 128–9, 137, 138–41, 150, 154
    the blues and, 132, 153, 154–5, 157, 172, 173
    country music of, 162–70
    from 1956 to 1959, 234–5, 238, 240–43
    from 1960 to 1967, 235, 243–5
    1968–1969 comeback, 125–7, 235, 245–6
    from 1970 to 1977, 246–8
    Sam Phillips and, 11, 18, 121, 141–2, 145–6, 147, 148, 156, 159, 160, 165, 166, 171, 172, 234, 235, 236, 237
    rockabilly and, 132, 141–3, 145–7, 155
    sense of differentness, 134–5
    with Sun Records, 121, 141–3, 145–6, 146n, 147–52, 155, 159, 160, 171–3, 174, 175, 234, 235–40
Presley, Gladys, 139–40, 158, 236
Presley, Jesse Garon, 250, 253
Presley, Lisa Marie, 249
Presley, Vernon, 137, 139–40
"Presley and the Gospel Tradition," 252
"Pretty Boy," 230
"Pretty Little Angel Eyes," 206
"Pretty Polly," 192
Price, Alan, 227
Price, Lloyd, 67, 68, 218, 219–20, 243
Primettes, 225
Prisonaires, 141, 237, 259
Private Elvis, 251
Problem Child, 260
"Promised Land," 247
Propes, Steve, 210
Psychotic Reactions and Carburetor Dung (Bangs), 252, 254
Pugh, John, 145n
"Put Your Cat Clothes On," 152, 260

Quaid, Dennis, 262
Quality label, 200
"Que Sera, Sera," 90, 91, 173, 213
Quicksilver Messenger Service, 211

Quinn, Anthony, 84, 85, 86
"Quinn the Eskimo (The Mighty Quinn)," 208

"Ra Ra Roo," 210
"Rag Mama Rag," 55, 56, 57, 195
"Rag Mop," 237
Raging Bull, 198
Ragtime (Doctorow), 230
Ragtime (film), 230
Rainey, Ma, 141, 218
"Ramblin'," 188
"Rambling on My Mind," 25, 184
Randolph, Boots, 244
"Randy Newman," 232
Randy Newman Creates Something New Under the Sun, 227
Randy Newman Live, 228, 229
Randy Newman Orchestra Plays Original Music from Peyton Place, The, 227
"Randy Newman – Out of Cole Porter, Hoagy Carmichael, Bob Dylan, Groucho Marx, Mark Twain, and Randy Newman," 232
Rare Rock-a-billy, Vol. 2, 183
"Rat, The," 210
Raymond, Alan, 240
Raymond, Susan, 240
Raymond Chandler Speaking (Chandler), 96, 232
RCA, 121, 143, 145n, 147, 150, 155, 159–60, 234, 235, 236, 237, 238, 239, 242, 243, 245, 247
"Ready Teddy," 169n, 241
"Real Gone Lover," 201n
Real Live Dolly Parton, A, 256–7
Really! The Country Blues, 146n, 190, 257
Reconsider Baby, 243, 244, 248
"Reconsider Baby," 146, 244
Record Research, 181–2
Recorded in San Francisco, 211
"Red Cadillac and a Black Moustache," 262
"Red Hot," 260
Redding, Otis, 69, 197
"Redneck," 223
Reed, Jerry, 245
Reed, Jimmy, 245
Reid, Vernon, 187
Remaining Titles, The, 191
Reporting: The Rolling Stone Style, 212
"Respect Yourself," 80, 223
"return of Staggerlee," 225
Revell, Don, 225
Revere, Paul and the Raiders, 156, 257
Rice University Marching Band, 257

Rich, Charlie, 141, 143, 153–4, 202, 256
Rich, Margaret Ann, 154
Richard Berry and the Dreamers, 257
Richard Berry: "Louie, Louie," 257
Rick Danko, 198
Ridin' in the Moonlight, 259
Right Stuff, The, 198
Riley, Billy Lee, 143, 260, 263
"Ring Tail Tom Cat Rag," 183
"Riot in Cell Block #9, 155–6, 212, 222, 257
"Rip It Up," 18
Ripley Cotton Choppers, 141
"Rising High Water Blues," 229
Rizzo, Frank, 79
Rizzo, Pat, 212
"Road Back from Dead Man's Curve, The," 232
Robbie Robertson, 199
"Robert Johnson" (Santoro), 187
Robert Johnson: King of the Delta Blues Singers, 184
Robert Johnson: The Complete Recordings, 186, 187, 188
Roberts, Rockin' Robin, 257
Robertson, Dominique, 64
Robertson, Robbie, 4, 40–64, 129–30, 187, 193, 194, 196–7, 198–9, 203, 207
   before The Band, 40–44, 62–3, 201–8
   The Band and, 54, 55, 56, 60
   Stage Fright and, 49, 193, 194
Robins, 155, 212, 256
Robinson, Bobby, 200
Robinson, Cynthia, 71, 91, 211
Robinson, Smokey, 75
Robots, 41*n*
"Rock!" 242
"Rock-a-Hula, Clarified," 199
"Rock a Little Baby," 182
"Rock and Roll Quarterly," 199
Rock and Roll Resurrection, 203
Rock Folk (Lydon), 260
Rock from the Beginning (Cohn), 249
Rock 'n Roll Tonight, 262
Rock 'n Roll Trio, 262
Rock of Ages, 60, 61, 195–6, 209
Rockabilly (Ellison), 253
Rockabilly Stars, Vol. 1, 256
"Rocket 88," 259
"Rockin' Chair," 56
"Rockin' Chair Daddy," 13, 18, 182
Rockin' Revols, 41*n*
Rockin' Ronald and the Rebels, 200
Rockin' Ronnie Hawkins, 200, 203
Rockin' Up a Storm, 261

"Rockin' with Red," 262
Rocking Chair, 202, 222
Rodgers, Jimmie, 17, 18, 130, 131, 139, 153, 156, 183, 184, 254, 255
Rogers, Kenny, 204
"Rollin' Stone," 188, 221
Rolling Stone, 112, 186, 192, 208, 232, 250, 254
Rolling Stone Illustrated History of Rock & Roll, 249
Rolling Stone Record Review, 199
Rolling Stone Rock & Roll Reader, The, 191, 199, 210, 255
Rolling Stones, 34, 43, 79–80, 115, 136, 146*n*, 160, 170, 184, 189, 207, 209, 233
   Exile on Main Street, 34, 80, 188
   Get Yer Ya-Yas Out! 188, 222
   Let It Bleed, 187, 188, 222
Ron Hawkins Quartet, 200
Ronnie Hawkins, 200–201, 203
Ronstadt, Linda, 228, 230
Roots of Robert Johnson, The, 184
"Rosie Lee," 201*n*
Ross, Diana, 82, 225
Ross, Shirley, 238
Roulette, 200
Roustabout, 134*n*, 244, 247
"Row Row Row Your Boat," 197
Rowan Brothers, 105
Roy Orbison — The Sun Years, 260
Royal Albert Hall Concert 1966, The, 206
Royales, "5", 202
rrracket time, 200
"Ruben Remus," 193
"Rudie Can't Fail," 221
Rulers, 221
"Rumor, The," 61, 193
Run-D.M.C., 221
"Run Red Run," 222
"Runnin' Away," 73
Rush, Merrilee, 242

Sackheim, Eric, 191
Sail Away, 228
"Sail Away," 108–9, 111, 114, 224, 228, 229, 231
Sail On, 189, 221
"St. James Infirmary," 187
Salvation, 228
Sam and Dave, 69
San Francisco Roots, 211
Sanders, Ed, 233
Sandpipers, 257
"Santa Claus Is Back in Town," 243
"Santa Fe," 208
Santoro, Gene, 187

Sgt. Pepper, 45, 69
"Satisfaction," 77, 115
"Save 'The Last Waltz' for Me,"
    199
"Saved," 62
Say Amen, Somebody, 235*n*
Scaggs, Boz, 34
Scanlon, Paul, 212
"Scat Swim," 211
Sherman, Tony, 187
Schoolly D, 221
"School's Out," 106
Scorsese, Martin, 198, 199
Seale, Bobby, 65–6, 92–3, 221
Searching for Robert Johnson, 185
Seattle, 242
"See You Later, Alligator," 197
"Seems Like a Freeze-Out," 205
Segal, Erich, 1–3
Seger, Bob, 201, 230
Self Portrait, 208
Seratt, Howard, 259
Session, The, 261
"Set Me Free," 256
Settles, Ron, 217
78 Quarterly, 186
"Sex Machine," 212
Sex Pistols, 214
Shadow Dancing in the USA, 191
Shag, 231
Shahn, Jonathan, 191
"Shake a Hand," 247
"Shampoo (the Whorehouse Special),"
    183
"Shanghai Rooster Breakdown," 183
"Shape I'm In, The," 51, 59, 194
"Share Your Love," 62, 196
Shaw, Greg, 182
"She Don't Understand Him Like I
    Do," 226
Shear, Barry, 84
Shelton Brothers, 238
Shep and the Limelights, 210
Sherrill, Billy, 256
"She's My Baby Doll," 262
"She's 19," 43, 203
"She's Your New Lover," 205
Shines, Johnny, 184, 188–9, 190, 191
Ship Ahoy, 224
Shirley and Lee, 195
"Shootout in Chinatown," 60
Short, Martin, 230
"Short People," 116, 118, 119, 229,
    230
Shuman, Mort, 201
"Sigmund Freud's Impersonation of
    Albert Einstein in America,"
    229–30

"Sign on the Cross," 208
Silhouettes, 70
Silva, Kathy, 213
Silver, Joan Micklin, 232
Silver, Murray, 262
Silver Fox, The, 256
Simon, John, 1–3
Simon, Paul, 230
Sinatra, Frank, 107
Singleton, Shelby, 249
"Sittin' and Thinkin'," 256
"Sittin' on Top of the World," 183
Sitting on Top of the World, 184
'68 Comeback, The, 246
*Skip James: King of the Delta Blues
    Singers*, 191
"Sky Is Crying, The," 189
"Sleep on the Porch," 210
Slick, Grace, 211
Slim, Memphis, 191
"Slippin' and Slidin'," 58
"Slipping into Darkness," 80, 223
Sly and the Family Stone, 69–95,
    210–14
    See also Stone, Sly
*Sly Stone — Recorded in San Francisco:
    1964–67*, 211
"Sly Stone: The Struggle for His
    Soul," 212
"Sly Stone's Heart of Darkness," 214
Small Talk, 213
Smash Records, 261
"Smiling Faces Somtimes (Tell Lies),"
    80, 223
Smith, Bessie, 225, 229
Smith, Duncan, 251
Smith, Harry, 196, 208, 214
Smith, Huey "Piano," 195
Smith, Warren, 143, 262
"Smokestack Lightning," 201–2
Smucker, Tom, 235*n*
"Snapshots of Charlie Rich," 256
"Snow," 226
"So Glad You're Mine," 147, 237
"So Long Dad," 227
"So Long I'm Gone," 262
Soledad Brother (Jackson), 74, 212
Solt, Andrew, 240
"Somebody to Love," 211
"Somebody's Waiting," 226
Something Else, 234
Something for Everybody, 160
Something Inside of Me, 189
"Something Is Happening," 207
Song Cycle, 227
Song of the South, The, 229
Sonny & Brownie, 228
"Sonny Boy," 193

Soul of Detroit, The, 225
Soulman, 214
Sound of Music, The, 97
Sound of the City, The (Gillett), 159
Sounder, 224, 225
South, Joe, 223
Southern Fried, 203
"Southern Love," 201
"Spanish Lace," 226
Specialty Sessions, The, 241
Spector, Phil, 159n, 206
"Spelling on the Stone," 250
Spencer, Jeremy, 189
Spencer, Ruth Albert, 199, 202
Spider Kiss (Ellison), 253
Spin, 214
Spinners, 87
Spinout, 244
"Spirit of Place," 163
"Spoonful," 202
Spoonful, 203
Springfield, Dusty, 231
Stabile, Dick, 238
"Stack-A-Lee I & II," 219
"Stack O'Lee Blues," 218, 219
"Stackalee," 218–19
Stage Fright, 46, 48–9, 60, 61, 192–3, 198
"Stage Show," 240
"Stagger Lee," 190, 219, 243
"Stagger Lee and Billy," 220
Staggerlee, 217
Staggerlee (Stack-a-lee, Stacker-Lee, Stagolee etc.), 65–8, 71, 73, 81, 82–6, 93, 94, 182, 214–22
Stand!, 74, 212
"Stand!," 72, 91, 212
Staple Singers, 80, 202, 223
Staples, Mavis, 198
Staples, Pop, 198
Stark Raving Elvis (Henderson), 253
Starks, Will, 216
Starr, Edwin, 223
Starr, Ringo, 199, 237n
Stars of Country Music, 255
"Stay," 70
"Stealing in the Name of the Lord," 222
Stearns, Jess, 251
Step It Up and Go, 183
"Steve Allen Show, The," 240
Stewart, Rod, 106, 153
Stewart Brothers, 210
Stewart Four, 210
Stockwell, Dean, 261
Stoller, Mike, 155–6, 200, 212, 222, 232, 243
Stone, Freddie, 211

Stone, Rosie, 90, 211
Stone, Sly, 4, 5, 34, 66–95, 116, 123, 173, 210–14, 222
  background of, 68–9, 210–11
  Fresh, 90, 91, 92, 212–13, 224
  Stand!, 74, 211–12
  There's a riot goin' on, 71–7, 78, 79, 80, 81, 86, 87, 88, 90, 91, 94, 95, 115, 212, 214
Stone, Vanetta, 213
"Stones I Throw (Will Free All Men), The," 44, 203
"Stones in My Passway," 23, 31–3, 184, 188
"Stop Breakin' Down Blues," 23, 184, 187, 188
"Stop What You Are Doing," 210
Stories, 156, 257
Storm, Billy, 226
"Story of a Rock and Roll Band, The," 230
Story of the Blues, The (Oliver), 191
Story of the Blues, The, 219
Strachwitz, Chris, 183
Stranded, 235n
"Stranger Blues," 189
"Strawberry Wine," 47
Strummer, Joe, 221
"Such a Night," 244
"Sugar Baby," 201n
Sullivan, Ed, 240
Sumlin, Hubert, 42, 202
Sun Country Years, 1950–1959, The, 183, 239, 259
Sun Records, 141, 143, 157, 200, 258–63
  Harmonica Frank on, 12, 13, 183
  Elvis Presley with, 121, 141–3, 145–6, 146n, 147–52, 155, 159, 160, 171–3, 174, 175, 234, 235–40, 259–60, 263
  see also Phillips, Sam
Sun Records: The Blue Years, 1950–1956, 238, 239, 259
Sun Records: The Discography, 258n
Sun Sound Special — Billy Lee Riley, 260
"Sunny Afternoon," 111, 234
Sunset Boulevard, 102
Superfly, 82–4, 223, 225
"Superfly," 80, 223
"Superman," 234
"Superstition," 80, 81, 223
"Surf City," 100, 103, 232
"Suspicious Minds," 127, 146, 168n, 246
"Suzanne" (Cohen), 101
"Suzanne" (Newman), 101, 103, 228
"Suzie Q," 42

Swan, Billy, 248
Swan Silvertones, 48
"Sweet Home Chicago," 184
"Sweet, Sweet Feeling (In this Place),"
  122

Taj Mahal, 188, 225
Taj Mahal, 188
"Take a Little Walk with Me," 184
"Take Her," 226
"Take Me Away," 227
Talking Book, 223
Tamerius, Steve D., 248
Taylor, James, 105
Taylor, Mick, 188
Tear it Up, 262
"Tears of Rage," 46, 46*n*, 50
Teenkings, 260
"Tell Me Mama," 184, 206
Temptations, 71, 76, 80, 80–1, 87, 194,
  222, 223
Ten Years — Collector Records, 183, 262
Ten Years Too Soon, 213
"Tennessee Saturday Night," 239
"Terraplane Blues," 23, 184, 189
Terry, Sonny, 228
Terry Clement and the Tune Tones,
  262
Texas Rockabilly, 262
"Thank you falettinme be mice elf
  Agin,' 70, 73, 74, 212
"Thank you for talkin' to me Africa,"
  34, 73, 74, 86
Tharpe, Jac L., 252
"That Lucky Old Sun," 109
"That's All Right (Mama)," 145*n*,
  146*n*, 147–8, 155, 165, 169*n*, 234,
  237
"That's Right," 260
"That's When Your Heartaches
  Begin," 236
"There Is Something on Your Mind,"
  68, 222
"(There'll Be) Peace in the Valley (For
  Me)," 235
There's a riot goin' on, 71–7, 78, 79, 80,
  81, 86, 87, 88, 90, 91, 94, 95, 115,
  212, 215, 223
"They Tell Me It's Summer," 226
"They're Red Hot," 184
"Things That I Used to Do, The," 219
"Third Man Theme," 62, 196
"Thirty Days," 201
This Is Elvis, 240, 241
"This Magic Moment," 210
This Price Is Right, 227
"This Time, You Gave Me a
  Mountain," 122

"This Wheel's on Fire," 46*n*
Thomas, Irma, 202, 226
Thomas, Pat, 215, 216
Thomas, Rufus "Bear Cat," 139, 141,
  245, 259
Thompson, Junior, 262
Thornton, Willie Mae, 155
Three Amigos, 230
Three Dog Night, 228
Thumper and the Trombones, 41*n*
"Tickle Me," 228
"Tiger Man," 245
Tikis, 211
Til, Sonny, 237
Times, The, 252
Tiny Tim, 193
"Tired of Being Alone," 223
To Kingdom Come, 194, 196
"To Kingdom Come," 46, 47, 49, 50
Tocqueville, Alexis de, 97, 170
"Tom Green's Farm," 189
Tommy, 112
*Tommy Johnson (1928–30): Complete
  Recordings in Chronological Order*,
  191, 221
"Tomorrow Is a Long Time," 244
"Tomorrow Night," 239
"Tongue-Tied Jill," 262
"Tonight's All Right for Love," 168*n*,
  235
"Too Much," 241
Too Wet to Plow, 190
Top Pop Albums 1955–1985 (Whitburn),
  181
Top Pop Singles 1955–1986 (Whitburn),
  181
Torgoff, Martin, 247
Tosches, Nick, 253, 258*n*, 261
Total Destruction of Your Mind, 223
Toussaint, Allen, 195, 217
"Train Whistle Boogie," 183
Transfusion, 203
"Traveling Riverside Blues," 25, 184
"Treat Me Nice," 242
Tribute to Woody Guthrie, A, 208
"Trouble," 245
"Trouble Bound," 260
Trouble in Paradise, 230
Trouble Man, 82
"Truly Ruly," 262
Truth About Elvis, The (Stearns), 251
"Tryin' to Get to You," 167, 235, 238,
  246, 260
Trying to Get to You, 238
Tubb, Ernest, 139, 156, 243
Turner, Bonnie, 259
Turner, Ike, 259
Turner, Ike and Tina, 220

Turner, Joe, 216, 240
"Tutti Frutti,' 3, 240
"Tweedlee Dee," 239
12 Songs, 227–8
"20th Century Man," 234
"Twilight," 197
Twitty, Conway, 41, 200
Two Steps from the Blues, 187, 202
Tyler, T. Texas, 211
Tyson, Cicely, 225

"Ubangi Stomp," 262
"Uh-Uh-Uh," 203
"Uncle Pen," 239
"Uncle Sam Needs You," 210
"Underneath the Harlem Moon," 101, 228
Undisputed Truth, 80, 223
"U.S. Male," 125, 245
Unsung Heroes of Rock 'n' Roll (Tosches), 253
"Up on Cripple Creek," 13, 55, 56–7, 193, 201, 209
U2, 199, 261

Valentino, Rudolph, 192
Vallee, Rudy, 239
Vee, Bobby, 150*n*–51*n*, 226
Vejtables, 211
Velvet Underground, 104
Ventura, Michael, 191
Village Voice, 185, 200, 254
Vincent, Gene, 41, 144, 263
"Vine Street," 227
Viscanes, 210
"Visions of Johanna," 205
Vocal Duets, 245
Vocalion Records, 21
Voices that Care, 231
von Sternberg, Josef, 95, 100

"Wabash Cannonball," 255
Wakely, Jimmy, 238
Walking Blues, 186
"Walking Blues," 21, 26, 184, 188
Wall: Live in Berlin, The, 199
"Wang-Dang-Doodle," 42, 202
War, 80, 223
"War," 223
Wardlow, Gayle, 186
Waring, Fred, and His Pennsylvanians, 218
Waronker, Lenny, 99
Washington Star, The, 217–18
"Waterloo Sunset," 112, 234
Waters, Muddy, 27, 43, 67, 147, 154, 188, 189, 191, 197, 198, 203, 221
Waters, Roger, 199

Watts, Charlie, 188
"Way Love Used to Be, The," 234
Wayne, Alvis, 263
"We Are the World," 231
"We Can Talk About It Now," 46, 51–3
"We Need Order," 87, 224
"We Shall Walk Through the Valley in Peace," 235*n*
"Wear My Ring Around Your Neck," 243
"Wedding in Cherokee County, A," 117
"Wedding Song," 209
"Weight, The," 46, 49–50, 51, 192, 196, 198
"Welcome Home Elvis," 250
Welding, Pete, 28
"Well Respected Man, A," 234
Welles, Orson, 111
Wenner, Jann, 244
Werbin, Stu, 120*n*, 248
"We're a Winner," 223
Wertheimer, Albert, 251
West, Nathanael, 102, 103, 232, 233
West, Red, 250
West, Sonny, 250
Westphal, Frank, and His Regal Novelty Orchestra, 218
"What About Us," 222
What's Going On, 223
What's That Sound?, 212
Wheat, Peter, and the Breadmen, 43
Wheels of Fire, 188
When Elvis Died (Gregory and Gregory), 251–2
"When I Grow Up to Be A Man," 233
"When I Paint My Masterpiece," 60
"When It Rains, It Really Pours," 239
"When the Levee Breaks," 229
"When the Sun Goes Down," 184
"When You Awake," 56, 59
"When You Walk in the Room," 185
"Where Were You When Elvis Died?" 254
"While the City Sleeps," 226
"Whispering Pines," 56
Whitburn, Joel, 181–2
White, Bukka, 24
"White Boy Lost in the Blues," 228
"White Christmas," 243
Whitman, Walt, 177, 210
Who, 112
"Who Do You Love," 43, 193, 198, 202, 203, 221
Who Killed George Jackson? (Durden-Smith), 212
"Whole Lotta Shakin' Goin' On," 169, 263

Whole New Thing, A, 211
Why Are We in Vietnam? (Mailer), 15–16
Wild Gift, 250
Wild Honey, 233
Wild in the Streets, 84
"Wildwood Flower," 255
Wilkin, Marijohn, 192
"Will the Circle Be Unbroken," 207–8
Williams, Hank, 17, 18, 48, 131, 132, 133, 137, 139, 156, 223, 255–6
Williams, Hank, Jr., 256
Williams, Larry, 41
Williams, Maurice, 70
Williams, Paul, 112
Williamson, Sonny Boy, 189, 190
Willis, Chuck, 61, 195, 244
Wills, Bob, 139, 149, 151
  and His Texas Playboys, 238
Wills, Johnnie Lee, 237
Wilson, Brian, 232
Wilson, Dennis, 233
Wilson, Jackie, 240
Wilson, Johnny "Peanuts," 260
Wilson, Tom, 184
Wilson, Woodrow, 128
Winfield, Paul, 225
Winner, Langdon, 243
Wire, 185
Wish Someone Would Care, 226
"Without You," 236, 237
Wolf, Howlin', 42–3, 59, 67, 99, 126, 141, 186, 191, 201–9, 222, 255, 259
Wolfe, Charles, 252
Womack, Bobby, 212, 213
"Woman Left Lonely, A," 256
Wonder, Stevie, 70, 80, 81, 87, 223, 224–5
Woodstock, 212
Woodstock Festival, 71, 212
Woodstock Times, 199

Word, Inc., 224
"World Is a Ghetto, The," 80
"Worried Man Blues," 171–2, 238, 255
Worth, Fred L., 248
"Wrong 'em Boyo," 221

X, 250

Yagman, Stephen, 217
Yardbirds, 189
Yazoo, 190, 191
"Yazoo Street Scandal," 193
"Yellow Man," 101–2, 210–11
"Yellow Moon," 228
Yelvington, Malcolm, 157, 237n, 259–60, 262
"You Are My Sunshine," 261
You Are What You Eat, 193
"You Can't Always Get What You Want," 77, 136, 160
"You Don't Know Me," 109
"You Got It," 261
"You Really Got Me," 213, 234
"You Say You Love Me," 193
You Won't Forget Me, 227
"You'll Be Mine," 202
Young, Neil, 75, 107
"Young and Beautiful," 243
Your Cheatin' Heart, 255–6
"You're a Heartbreaker," 146, 166–7, 237, 238
"(You're So Square) Baby I Don't Care," 18, 243
"You're So Vain," 247
"Yum Yum Yum," 210
Yuro, Timi, 248

Zimmerman: Ten of Swords, 1961–1966, 205, 206
Zinnerman, Ike, 185, 186